# MIND, REASON, AND BEING-IN-THE-WORLD

John McDowell and Hube[...] f world renown whose work has don[...] [...] [...]ds of analytic philosophy and phenomenology respectively. *Mind, Reason, and Being-in-the-World: The McDowell–Dreyfus Debate* opens with their debate over one of the most important and controversial subjects in philosophy: is human experience permeated with conceptual rationality, or does experience mark the limits of reason? Is all intelligibility rational, or is there a form of intelligibility at work in our skillful bodily rapport with the world that falls outside our intellectual capacities? McDowell and Dreyfus provide a fascinating insight into some fundamental differences between analytic philosophy and phenomenology as well as areas where they may have something in common.

Fifteen specially commissioned chapters by distinguished international contributors enrich the debate inaugurated by McDowell and Dreyfus, taking it in a number of different and important directions. Fundamental philosophical problems discussed include: the embodied mind, subjectivity and self-consciousness, intentionality, rationality, practical skills, human agency, and the history of philosophy from Kant to Heidegger. With the addition of these outstanding contributions, *Mind, Reason, and Being-in-the-World* should be considered essential reading for students and scholars of analytic philosophy and phenomenology.

**Contributors**: Lee Braver, Taylor Carman, Tim Crane, Hubert L. Dreyfus, Sebastian Gardner, John McDowell, Barbara Montero, Alva Noë, Robert B. Pippin, Joseph Rouse, Joseph K. Schear, Susanna Schellenberg, Charles Siewert, Charles Taylor, and Dan Zahavi.

**Joseph K. Schear** is Lecturer in Philosophy and Tutorial Fellow at Christ Church, University of Oxford.

# MIND, REASON, AND BEING-IN-THE-WORLD

The McDowell–Dreyfus Debate

*Edited by*
*Joseph K. Schear*

Routledge
Taylor & Francis Group
LONDON AND NEW YORK

This edition published 2013
by Routledge
2 Park Square, Milton Park, Abingdon, Oxon OX14 4RN

Simultaneously published in the USA and Canada
by Routledge
711 Third Avenue, New York, NY 10017, USA

*Routledge is an imprint of the Taylor & Francis Group, an informa business*

© 2013 Joseph K. Schear, selection and editorial matter; individual contributors, their contributions.

The right of the editor to be identified as the author of the editorial material, and of the authors for their individual chapters, has been asserted in accordance with sections 77 and 78 of the Copyright, Designs and Patents Act 1988.

All rights reserved. No part of this book may be reprinted or reproduced or utilised in any form or by any electronic, mechanical, or other means, now known or hereafter invented, including photocopying and recording, or in any information storage or retrieval system, without permission in writing from the publishers.

*British Library Cataloguing in Publication Data*
A catalogue record for this book is available from the British Library

*Library of Congress Cataloging in Publication Data*
Mind, reason, and being-in-the-world : the McDowell-Dreyfus debate / edited by Joseph K. Schear.
 p. cm.
Includes bibliographical references and index.
1. Perception (Philosophy) 2. McDowell, John Henry. 3. Dreyfus, Hubert L.
4. Analysis (Philosophy) 5. Phenomenology. I. Schear, Joseph K.
B828.45.M56 2012
121'.34—dc23
2012024840

ISBN: 978-0-415-48586-9 (hbk)
ISBN: 978-0-415-48587-6 (pbk)
ISBN: 978-0-203-07631-6 (ebk)

Typeset in Goudy
by Taylor & Francis Books

# CONTENTS

*Acknowledgments* vii
*Notes on contributors* viii

Introduction 1
JOSEPH K. SCHEAR

## PART I
## A battle of myths 13

1 The myth of the pervasiveness of the mental 15
  HUBERT L. DREYFUS

2 The myth of the mind as detached 41
  JOHN MCDOWELL

## PART II
## From Kant to existential phenomenology 59

3 Retrieving realism 61
  CHARLES TAYLOR

4 What is "conceptual activity"? 91
  ROBERT B. PIPPIN

5 Transcendental philosophy and the possibility of the given 110
  SEBASTIAN GARDNER

6 Never mind: thinking of subjectivity in the
  Dreyfus–McDowell debate 143
  LEE BRAVER

# CONTENTS

## PART III
## Intellectualism and understanding      163

7  Conceptualism and the scholastic fallacy      165
TAYLOR CARMAN

8  On overintellectualizing the intellect      178
ALVA NOË

9  Intellectualism, experience, and motor understanding      194
CHARLES SIEWERT

## PART IV
## Experience, concepts, and nonconceptual content      227

10  The given      229
TIM CRANE

11  What is conceptually articulated understanding?      250
JOSEPH ROUSE

12  A trilemma about mental content      272
SUSANNA SCHELLENBERG

## PART V
## Bodily skills, rationality, and self-consciousness      283

13  Are we essentially rational animals?      285
JOSEPH K. SCHEAR

14  A dancer reflects      303
BARBARA MONTERO

15  Mindedness, mindlessness, and first-person authority      320
DAN ZAHAVI

*Index*      344

# ACKNOWLEDGMENTS

First and foremost, I would like to thank Hubert L. Dreyfus and John McDowell for continuing the conversation. I would also like to thank the rest of the contributors for their contributions, their cooperation, and their patience. Tony Bruce at Routledge and Wayne Martin (as editor of *Inquiry*) first approached me about the idea of soliciting papers for a volume. I am exceedingly grateful to both for their wise advice along the way. I owe thanks to Robert B. Pippin, Mark Wrathall, and James Conant for their support of the project at various crucial points. Thanks are due to Adam Johnson at Routledge for his help. Elizabeth Cykowski provided timely and invaluable research assistance. Lastly, I thank Christ Church, Oxford for a grant to fund the research assistance and for providing an ideal setting to carry out this work.

# CONTRIBUTORS

**Lee Braver** is Department Chair and Associate Professor of Philosophy at Hiram College.

**Taylor Carman** is Professor of Philosophy at Barnard College, Columbia University.

**Tim Crane** is Knightbridge Professor of Philosophy at the University of Cambridge, and Fellow of Peterhouse.

**Hubert L. Dreyfus** is Professor of Philosophy at the University of California–Berkeley.

**Sebastian Gardner** is Professor of Philosophy at University College London.

**John McDowell** is Distinguished Professor of Philosophy at the University of Pittsburgh.

**Barbara Montero** is Associate Professor of Political Science, Economics, and Philosophy at the College of Staten Island, City University of New York.

**Alva Noë** is Professor of Philosophy at the University of California–Berkeley.

**Robert B. Pippin** is the Evelyn Stefansson Nef Distinguished Service Professor in the John U. Nef Committee on Social Thought, Department of Philosophy, and the College at the University of Chicago.

**Joseph Rouse** is Hedding Professor of Moral Science and Professor of Philosophy at Wesleyan University.

**Joseph K. Schear** is University Lecturer in Philosophy and Tutorial Fellow at Christ Church, University of Oxford.

**Susanna Schellenberg** is Associate Professor of Philosophy, Rutgers University.

CONTRIBUTORS

**Charles Siewert** is Professor of Philosophy at Rice University.

**Charles Taylor** is Professor Emeritus of Political Science and Philosophy at McGill University.

**Dan Zahavi** is Professor of Philosophy and Director of the Danish National Research Foundation's Center for Subjectivity Research, University of Copenhagen.

# INTRODUCTION

## Joseph K. Schear

No one in our day has done more than Hubert L. Dreyfus to make Anglophone philosophy less parochial. For some forty years, he has helped the rest of us understand what our European colleagues are up to, introduced us to them, and encouraged the study of their works.

Richard Rorty[1]

No book written in the past decade or so has generated more interest amongst professional philosophers than John McDowell's *Mind and World*.

Nicholas H. Smith[2]

### The background to the volume

Hubert L. Dreyfus took the occasion of his 2005 American Philosophical Association Presidential Address, "Overcoming the Myth of the Mental: How Philosophers Can Profit from the Phenomenology of Everyday Expertise," to attack John McDowell's position on mind and world. In McDowell's massively influential book, *Mind and World*, one of his primary targets, following Wilfred Sellars, is the "Myth of the Given."[3] The mythical idea of the given, McDowell contends, is the idea of an object being given to a subject to know without drawing on the rational capacities required to know the object.[4] In his Presidential Address, Dreyfus accuses McDowell of overreaching: in the urgency to avoid the Myth of the Given, McDowell falls prey to what Dreyfus dubs the "Myth of the Mental." The mythical idea of the mental, Dreyfus contends, is the idea that the "mind is everywhere the pure given is not," or alternatively, the claim that all intelligibility is pervaded by rational capacities.[5] And so began a debate between two of our most important and influential philosophers.

At the 2006 meeting of the American Philosophical Association in Washington, DC, Dreyfus and McDowell, along with John Haugeland, participated in a panel organized to thrash out what is at stake in the debate. McDowell clarified and defended his position against Dreyfus's charge ("What Myth?"), which was followed by a series of exchanges between them published collectively, in 2007, in the pages of *Inquiry*, under the editorship of Wayne Martin.[6] James Conant organized a workshop devoted to the exchanges in 2009 at the Wissenschaftskolleg zu Berlin, bringing together Dreyfus and McDowell, as well as a number of other philosophers (including several of the contributors to this volume), for three days of searching discussion. In the present volume, Dreyfus and McDowell have written essays especially for the volume, each summing up their respective positions. Thirteen previously unpublished essays, written by some of the many philosophers provoked by the debate, follow the opening two essays.

The central issue at stake between Dreyfus and McDowell is the extent to which conceptual rationality is involved in our skillful embodied rapport with the world. Examples of skills that figure in the exchange include opening doors, playing sports, and blitz chess, standing the appropriate distance from someone in conversation, chasing streetcars, and catching a frisbee, among others. McDowell urges that conceptual rationality is, as he puts it, "everywhere in our lives," including in our skillful embodied comportment.[7] Dreyfus, by contrast, seeks to identify and describe forms of "absorbed coping" that do not come within the scope of conceptual rationality. These skills, Dreyfus argues, open us to a world that solicits our bodily comportment, a world that is more basic than the objective reality to which we are open in McDowell's broadly epistemic conception of experience. We are not, Dreyfus urges, "full-time rational animals."[8]

Dreyfus's criticisms of McDowell are an effort to extend and elaborate his long-standing attack on various forms of intellectualism and rationalism in the theory of human intelligence. But this latest target has little interest in *artificial* reason: McDowell is not committed to any of the philosophical assumptions about the mind that Dreyfus famously identified as underlying the dogged optimism found in what John Haugeland called GOFAI (good old fashioned artificial intelligence).[9] A mark of the sophistication of this recent rationalist target, and surely the label in some sense fits, is that "rationalism," and indeed "intellectualism," are terms of criticism that McDowell himself is prone to deploy. For example, McDowell has long sought to protect Aristotle's teaching about virtue and practical wisdom from various excessively rationalistic and intellectualized deformations he believes it has suffered in the hands of other commentators. His effort to make this teaching safe is offered in the name (following David Wiggins) of a "careful and sensitive moral phenomenology."[10]

Along with Aristotle, the exegesis of figures such as Kant, Heidegger, Sartre, Merleau-Ponty, Gadamer, and Wittgenstein has figured in the debate between Dreyfus and McDowell. Anyone familiar with the work of Dreyfus and McDowell will not find this surprising. Both philosophers are exemplars of how to integrate historical exegesis with ambitious systematic philosophy (which is not to say that they do this in the same way). This is

INTRODUCTION

no small part of what makes their respective work so distinctive and exciting, and what has made their debate provoke so much interest across diverse spheres of the philosophical community. My aim in compiling this collection of essays has been to try and do justice to the broad scope of systematic and historical reflection the debate invites.

I have particularly sought to include contributions from philosophers who, like Dreyfus and McDowell, ignore the dreary and increasingly obsolete division between "analytic" philosophy and "continental" philosophy. (One way of ignoring the division, in the broad sense I mean, is to uncover ways in which current attempts at integration may be distorting; see chapter 5.) And while I could hardly have discouraged philosophers from keeping score, I did encourage the contributors to use the debate as a context to deepen and expand the discussion of the issues at stake. Topics in the philosophy of mind, metaphysics and epistemology, the philosophy of action, the theory of rationality, aesthetics, the theory of virtue, and philosophical methodology all come to life in the following chapters.

Among the many questions raised by the debate and explored in the contributions are the following: What is the place of reason in human life? Is all intelligibility *rational* intelligibility, or is there a form of intelligibility characteristic of our skilled bodily engagement with the world that falls outside the reach of reason? What is the relationship between bodily skills and intentional action? What are conceptual capacities? How do such capacities figure in bodily movement and perceptual experience? Does experience have nonconceptual content? Does embodied skilful comportment have nonconceptual content? How should we understand the distinctively human form of relation to the world while doing justice to our continuity with nonrational animals? What is the nature of the know-how at work in practical skills, and in what sense, if at all, is such know-how rational? Is reflection essential to, or rather an enemy of, expert performance? Does virtuous action require having a reason for one's action? What does the charge of "intellectualism" amount to, and who ultimately is more guilty of it, McDowell or Dreyfus? Does the first-person authority characteristic of conscious experience require rationality and language? What is the role of phenomenological reflection in addressing these questions? What is the relationship between phenomenological methods in philosophy and transcendental philosophy? Is the tradition of existential phenomenology (Heidegger, Sartre, Merleau-Ponty) an extension, or rather a decisive critique, of Kant's project in the *Critique of Pure Reason*? What does Kant mean by "apperception," and by "synthesis"? What does Heidegger mean by "being-in-the-world," and by "thinking"? What does Sartre mean by the "prereflective *cogito*"? What does Merleau-Ponty mean by "motor intentionality"?

Anyone interested in these and related questions will discover much of interest in the rich set of chapters that follows. The volume is particularly valuable for those interested in the increasing influence of the phenomenological tradition on contemporary philosophy, and correlatively, the increasing influence of contemporary debates on our reception of the phenomenological tradition.

Of course, no single volume devoted to an exchange as fertile as that between Dreyfus and McDowell can possibly do justice to all the relevant topics and themes worth investigating. Historical lacunae in this volume include an independent discussion of Aristotle on virtue and practical wisdom, on the one hand, and a focused interpretation of Sartre's theory of self-consciousness, on the other. Systematic lacunae include an in-depth discussion, raised by McDowell's debt to Anscombe, of practical self-knowledge in action, on the one hand, and a thorough investigation, raised by Dreyfus's contribution, of social norms and their role in our relation to the world, on the other. The volume, I hope, will help provoke readers to take up these and no doubt other avenues of approach to the McDowell–Dreyfus dispute in future work.

## The structure and content of the book

The volume is divided into five parts. Part I, "A battle of myths," contains the new essays by Dreyfus and McDowell. Dreyfus (chapter 1) redubs his charge against McDowell "The Myth of the Pervasiveness of the Mental." The original label "The Myth of the Mental" had the misleading implication that the mental as such is a myth, which Dreyfus of course does not endorse. Dreyfus sums up the basic contours of his case against McDowell's thesis that conceptual capacities must be always and everywhere operative in human experience. Presenting a number of putative counterexamples to McDowell's thesis, while drawing on select passages in the work of the existential phenomenologists Heidegger, Sartre, and Merleau-Ponty, Dreyfus aims to identify and describe the "nonconceptual world of absorbed coping." Dreyfus puts on display forms of absorbed embodied activity in which the "mind/world distance" he deems characteristic of conceptual rationality is not in play. McDowell begins his account of the relation of mind and world, as Dreyfus puts it, "too late."

Dreyfus then moves to his argument for the nonconceptuality of social norms at work in our everyday relating to others. Styles of normative comportment, examples of which include distance standing in conversation and living out gender roles, are charged with meaning – e.g. the meaning of intimacy in one's culture, or the meaning of what it is to be masculine or feminine. However, Dreyfus notes that participants in these practices need not be, and generally are not, able to cite such meanings as reasons for their comportment. Indeed, agents are typically not even aware of these meanings, yet the meanings are nonetheless at work in their comportment. If this

## INTRODUCTION

absorbed coping is not rational engagement, yet it is more than a kind of instinctual behavior, what is it? Dreyfus's aim in the paper is to call our attention to a distinctively human way of being-in-the-world that falls outside what Dreyfus sees as the limited space of options that controls McDowell's thinking.

In defense of his claim that rational mindedness pervades our lives, McDowell replies that Dreyfus's allegation itself rests on a myth, "The Myth of the Mind as Detached" (chapter 2). According to this myth, mindedness implies the presence of a detached self. But McDowell rejects this implication, and so does not accept the conception of rational mindedness to which Dreyfus objects. McDowell stresses, furthermore, that part of his point in claiming that rational mindedness is pervasive in our lives is to insist that mindedness does not always involve detachment.

McDowell agrees with Dreyfus that any adequate conception of our active life in the world must accommodate absorbed coping and acting in flow; he seeks to make room for these phenomena within his picture by focusing especially on Dreyfus's case of the chess master absorbed in lightning chess. McDowell urges that the chess master's absorption does not prevent him from knowing what he is up to, and that, moreover, if the chess master really is a master, he will be able to give rational explanations of his moves as intelligible responses to the forces on the board. So understood, the chess master's expert play is a case of "cultivated rationality" in operation. This is precisely the "actualization" of conceptual capacities in experience and action that McDowell is keen to highlight. As for normative social comportment such as appropriate distance standing in conversation, McDowell is prepared to grant that such comportment is not pervaded by rational mindedness. However, he insists that the exercises of such socialized dispositions, as modes of responsiveness to cultural norms, are not exercises of genuine agency in his sense. So distance standing, McDowell submits, does not threaten his basic thesis about the pervasively rational nature of intentional agency – the case is "no more relevant ... than is, say, the distinctively human character of the things a Xhosa speaker does with her tongue and palate in sounding those click consonants."[11]

Part II, "From Kant to existential phenomenology," contains the more historical and exegetical contributions, though in each chapter the readings are informed by, and in the service of, systematic philosophical aims.

Charles Taylor (chapter 3), whose pioneering work in post-Kantian philosophy and the philosophy of mind is everywhere in the background of the exchanges between Dreyfus and McDowell, offers a characteristically wide-ranging historical narrative. Taylor traces the slow overcoming of what he calls the modern "mediational" picture of our relation to the world. After identifying the diverse and powerful sources that have made the mediational picture attractive, Taylor sketches an alternative picture of our being in "contact" with the world, strands of which are present in the work of Kant, Hegel, Heidegger, Wittgenstein, and Merleau-Ponty. Taylor reads the exchange between McDowell and Dreyfus as a testament to the progress contemporary philosophy has made in this "retrieval of realism."

Robert B. Pippin (chapter 4) explores what he deems the key historical connection of the exchange, namely Kant's claim that experience is apperceptive. Pippin is of course keen to defend the claim; the precise interpretation of it has been a rich source of contention between Pippin and McDowell in recent exchanges. In his chapter, Pippin takes Dreyfus's denial of the claim as an invitation to spell out in a fresh way what precisely the Kantian thought comes to. After sketching an interpretation of Kant's conception of the categorial unity of experience, Pippin proceeds to uncover the Aristotelian inheritance at work in Sellars's Kantian account of the conceptual form of intuitional content. Pippin develops these resources to propose a distinctively sensory actualization of conceptual powers that, avoiding intellectualism about experience, nevertheless provides for a distinction between a nonrational animal's immersion in its environment and our self-correcting reason-responsive openness to a world. Pippin concludes his essay with some suggestive Hegelian considerations about the "mediated immediacy" of reason in human life.

In his bold historical survey, "Transcendental philosophy and the possibility of the given," Sebastian Gardner (chapter 5) argues that transcendental philosophy is devoted to the preempirical explanation of the very possibility of a subject's being presented with an object ("the given"). This explanatory project extends beyond its original setting in Kant's theory of synthesis, Fichte's theory of object-positing, and Hegel's idealist metaphysics of reason, Gardner contends, for it was adopted by the main practitioners of the phenomenological tradition, including Heidegger and Merleau-Ponty. Both McDowell and Dreyfus, on Gardner's reading, ultimately back away from the true explanatory obligations of transcendental philosophy – McDowell by setting his sights narrowly on the justifiability of beliefs, and Dreyfus by settling for a merely descriptive approach to "the mind." Gardner diagnoses the dispute between them as rooted in their respective ways of refusing, or at least scaling down, the aspirations of transcendental philosophy. Concluding his essay with some suggestive remarks about the possible tension between McDowell's transcendentalism and his (Wittgensteinian) therapeutic approach to philosophy, Gardner also casts suspicion on making the unification of post-analytic philosophy and post-Kantian continental philosophy a regulative ideal.

Lee Braver (chapter 6) surveys the history of Dreyfus's influential pursuit of the idea that "mindedness is the enemy of embodied coping," before challenging its Heideggerian provenance. Braver claims that Heidegger

## INTRODUCTION

himself considered mindless coping the enemy of a lucid awareness of being. Braver proceeds to draw on Heidegger's late work (as well as Wittgenstein's late work) to offer a phenomenology of thinking: Braver urges that the absorbed character Dreyfus stresses as characteristic of embodied skills is also characteristic of abstract thinking and deliberation.

Part III, "Intellectualism and understanding," contains contributions which mount one form or another of the charge of intellectualism. The central positive theme of these essays is the sense in which understanding, either intellectual or "motor," does or does not enter into experience. In each piece, the systematic argument is partly moved by readings of figures in the tradition of phenomenology.

Taylor Carman (chapter 7) charges McDowell with committing the "scholastic fallacy," namely the illicit projection of the structure and content of reflection into unreflective experience. This is a standing temptation for reflection, especially for the philosopher, whose business after all is to reflect, hence the difficulty of phenomenology. However, Carman urges that by careful attention to the skillful social intelligence at work in the art of conversation, we can resist succumbing to the scholastic fallacy. Carman exploits the example to distinguish the baby from the bathwater of Dreyfus's critique of McDowell. The baby lies in the distinction between the kind of content involved in the "engaged" attitude and, by contrast, the detachable and abstractable contents suitable to rational inference, deliberation, and decision.

Dreyfus charges McDowell, in effect, with an overintellectualizing of experience and activity: Alva Noë (chapter 8) claims that this charge rests on, as his title announces, an "overintellectualizing of the intellect." With this diagnosis, that Dreyfus mistakenly thinks the only legitimate exercise of the understanding is deliberative judgment or contemplation, Noë joins forces with McDowell's contribution. Noë proceeds to develop the idea of a nonjudgmental use of concepts in experience, understood as ways of achieving access to the world. (This allows Noë to reply to some recent criticism of his own views by his colleague John Campbell.) Noë proposes furthermore that we take the involvement of understanding and criticism in aesthetic experience as a paradigm for the sense in which understanding informs perceptual experience more generally. Doing so, Noë concludes, promises insight into the nature of phenomenology.

In his "Intellectualism, experience, and motor understanding," Charles Siewert (chapter 9) grants McDowell's claim that our nature as self-conscious reasoners pervasively shapes our perceptual experience. However, Siewert rejects McDowell's claim that every aspect of experience is (as McDowell puts it) "present in a form in which it is suitable to constitute the content of conceptual capacities." Siewert argues that there are nonfocal variations in appearance that structure visual experience of objects, which are sufficient for intentionality, but are not "conceptually ready." Siewert proceeds to develop the argument by appropriating Merleau-Ponty's account of the motor understanding at work in experiencing objects. The essay culminates with a sympathetic and detailed interpretation (and revised translation) of the passage in Merleau-Ponty's *Phenomenology of Perception*, mocked by McDowell, that loomed so large in the *Inquiry* exchanges between Dreyfus and McDowell.[12]

Part IV, "Experience, concepts, and nonconceptual content," contains contributions about the nature of conceptual capacities and the problem of the content of experience. Each chapter, prompted by the McDowell–Dreyfus exchange, offers a new intervention in the debate, inaugurated by Gareth Evans, about whether the content of perceptual experience is conceptual or nonconceptual.

C. I. Lewis's view of the "given" in his 1929 book *The Mind and World Order* was one of Wilfred Sellars's targets in his 1956 attack on the "Myth of the Given" – an attack that has of course been central to McDowell's project. In his essay "The Given," Tim Crane (chapter 10) seeks to revive a nonmythical conception of the given, moved by the question: What precisely is given or conveyed to the subject in experience? After surveying various options for specifying the content of expreience in propositionalist terms (Russellian, Fregean, and the Lewis/Stalnaker view), Crane distinguishes the phenomenological conception of the content of experience from a semantic one. Drawing on Frege's conception of "ideas" and Husserl's account of "real content," Crane offers a new case for his long-standing commitment to the nonconceptual (phenomenological) content of experience.

Joseph Rouse (chapter 11) distinguishes a descriptive account of concepts from a normative account of concepts. He claims that Dreyfus's criticisms of McDowell's claim that conceptual understanding is pervasive in perception rest on attributing to McDowell a descriptive account. However, McDowell, as well as John Haugeland, adopts a normative approach, which Rouse claims is ultimately orthogonal to Dreyfus's concerns. Rouse proceeds to propose a "merger" between McDowell and Dreyfus. Building on Dreyfus's phenomenology of absorbed coping, Rouse sketches a theory of discursive practice according to which conceptual understanding itself is a form of practical–perceptual coping with the environment.

Susanna Schellenberg (chapter 12) sheds light on the debate between Dreyfus and McDowell about the role and nature of concepts in perceptual experience, by considering the following trilemma:

(C1) Nonrational animals and humans can be in mental states with the same kind of content when they are perceptually related to the very same environment.
(C2) Nonrational animals do not possess concepts.
(C3) Content is constituted by modes of presentations and is, thus, conceptually structured.

INTRODUCTION

She discusses reasons for accepting and rejecting each of the three claims. By developing a substantive notion of modes of presentation as constituting nonconceptual content, she argues that the trilemma is best resolved by giving up (C3). In doing so, she discusses the nature of mental content and its relation to bodily skills and conceptual capacities as well as the notions of conceptual and nonconceptual content.

Part V, "Bodily skills, rationality, and self-consciousness," contains essays devoted to exploring the relationship between bodily skills and our capacity for self-conscious rationality and reflection, as well as the question of whether self-consciousness requires rationality.

In "Are we essentially rational animals?," my contribution to the volume (chapter 13), I claim, first, that the McDowell–Dreyfus exchange, to the extent that it is a real dispute, is about this question. I then distinguish two of Dreyfus's arguments against McDowell – the argument from critical distance, on the one hand, and the phenomenological argument from the "merging" structure of embodied skillful comportment, on the other. The first argument, I suggest, misfires. The second, by contrast, promises to meet its target; the question of its persuasiveness turns on whether Dreyfus's phenomenology of "merging" is faithful. I close by considering a separate argument for our essentially rational way of being, sympathetic to McDowell, that calls attention to our power to ask the question of what, or who, we are. This argument, I urge, supports only a weak reading of our essentially rational character with which Dreyfus, and certainly Heidegger, need not disagree. This raises an open and pressing an exegetical question about Heidegger and the problem of reason, with which I conclude.

In her "A dancer reflects," Barbara Montero (chapter 14), a professional ballet dancer turned philosopher, attacks what she calls the principle of automaticity in the theory of expertise. This principle has long been endorsed by Dreyfus, among other philosophers and psychologists. The principle states, roughly, that expert action does not involve thought or cognition (e.g. self-reflection, planning, predicting, deliberating). In addition to some neurological data that might seem to support the principle, Montero considers the widely held "maxim of cognitive interference," that thinking about what you are doing while doing it interferes with performing. Montero argues that the psychological evidence available does not decisively support the principle. She proceeds to offer some first-personal observations on how thinking and deliberate consideration are essential to the expert performance of, say, the White Swan *pas de deux*.

Dan Zahavi (chapter 15) seeks to reject an assumption about mindedness that he deems McDowell and Dreyfus both share, namely that the first-personal character of conscious experience involves conceptuality, rationality, and language. Dreyfus, according to Zahavi, assumes this to reject the idea that self-consciousness is operative at the level of absorbed coping. But if, drawing on Sartre and Heidegger, we can recognize a more basic form of self-acquaintance prior to and independent of rational self-consciousness, we can see that absorbed coping, so far as it is conscious, indeed involves a sense of self. Recognizing this primitive reflexivity, Zahavi further contends, puts a serious burden of proof on McDowell, whose conception of mature adult subjectivity renders the transition from nonlinguistic infant self-awareness to conceptual self-awareness a "miracle."

## Notes

1 Foreword to Wrathall and Malpas (eds), *Heidegger, Authenticity, and Modernity*.
2 Introduction to Smith (ed.), *Reading McDowell*.
3 The book is composed of lectures first delivered as the John Locke lectures in Oxford in Trinity Term, 1991.
4 See Lectures I–III of McDowell, *Mind and World*. For a more recent statement by McDowell, on which my formulation draws, see his "Avoiding the Myth of the Given," in Lindgaard (ed.), *John McDowell: Experience, Norm, and Nature*.
5 Dreyfus, "Overcoming the Myth of the Mental," p. 52.
6 McDowell, "What Myth?"; Dreyfus, "Return of the Myth of the Mental"; McDowell, "Response to Dreyfus"; Dreyfus, "Response to McDowell." While the statements of their respective positions in this volume are self-contained and reliable summaries, readers interested in every twist and turn are encouraged to consult the *Inquiry* exchanges.
7 McDowell, "What Myth?," p. 343.
8 Dreyfus, "Return of the Myth of the Mental," p. 354.
9 See part II of Dreyfus's well-known and now victorious *What Computers Can't Do*.
10 See, for example, McDowell's classic essay, "Virtue and Reason," reprinted in his *Mind, Value, and Reality*, as well as his more recent paper, "Deliberation and Moral Development in Aristotle's Ethics," reprinted as chapter 3 in his collection, *The Engaged Intellect*.
11 McDowell, "The myth of the mind as detached," this volume, p. 55.
12 The passage in the standard translation, as it figured in the exchanges, reads: "In perception we do not think the object and we do not think ourselves thinking it, we are given over to the object and merge into this body which is better informed than we are about the world, and about the motives we have and the means at our disposal." Merleau-Ponty, *Phenomenology of Perception*, p. 277.

## Bibliography

Dreyfus, H., "Overcoming the Myth of the Mental: How Philosophers Can Profit from the Phenomenology of Everyday Expertise," *Proceedings and Addresses of the American Philosophical Association* 79 (2005): 47–65.
——, "Response to McDowell," *Inquiry* 50, no. 4 (2007): 371–77.
——, "The Return of the Myth of the Mental," *Inquiry* 50, no. 4 (2007): 352–65.
——*What Computers Can't Do: A Critique of Artificial Reason*, Cambridge, MA: MIT Press, 1972.
Lindgaard, J. (ed.), *John McDowell: Experience, Norm, and Nature*, Oxford: Blackwell, 2008.

McDowell, J., *The Engaged Intellect: Philosophical Essays*, Cambridge, MA: Harvard University Press, 2009.
——, *Mind and World*, Cambridge, MA: Harvard University Press, 1994.
——, *Mind, Value, and Reality*, Cambridge, MA: Harvard University Press, 1998.
——, "Response to Dreyfus," *Inquiry* 50, no. 4 (2007): 366–70.
——, "What Myth?," *Inquiry* 50, no. 4 (2007): 338–51.
Merleau-Ponty, M., *Phenomenology of Perception*, trans. C. Smith, London: Routledge, 1958.
Smith, N. H. (ed.) *Reading McDowell: On Mind and World*, London: Routledge, 2002.
Wrathall, M. and Malpas, J. (eds), *Heidegger, Authenticity, and Modernity: Essays in Honor of Hubert L. Dreyfus*, vol. 1, Cambridge, MA: MIT Press, 2000.

# Part I

# A BATTLE OF MYTHS

# Part 1

# A BATTLE OF MYTHS

# 1

# THE MYTH OF THE PERVASIVENESS OF THE MENTAL

*Hubert L. Dreyfus*

### John McDowell's general conceptualist thesis

In *Mind and World* John McDowell sounds like he is channeling Heidegger when he speaks of "our unproblematic openness to the world"[1] and how "we find ourselves always already engaged with the world."[2] His view is also seemingly similar to Merleau-Ponty's when he notes that: "[a]n experiencing and acting subject is ... herself embodied ... "[3] Moreover, like these existential phenomenologists, McDowell makes the bold claim that "this is a framework for reflection that really stands a chance of making traditional philosophy obsolete."[4]

But, unlike the existential phenomenologists, McDowell speaks of this embodied engagement in the world as pervaded by *conceptuality*. And he goes on to argue in a Kantian vein that perception and action must be conceptual – in effect, that intuitions require concepts so as not to be blind and that conceptual capacities must be operative in a bodily movement for it to count as an action. As he puts it, according to Kant:

> [E]xperiences are actualizations of our sentient nature in which conceptual capacities are inextricably implicated. The parallel is this: intentional bodily capacities are actualizations of our active nature in which conceptual capacities are inextricably implicated.[5]

McDowell's thesis here is what I've called the Myth of the Mental. The Myth is not the claim that conceptual activity is required for *some* types of perceiving and acting. That claim is obviously true. Our practices open a world in which, among other things, perceptions can serve to justify judgments about an independent reality and actions can be judged as to whether they correspond to the requirements of the current situation. But

McDowell holds that for such a normative relation of mind and world to be possible perception and action must be *pervaded* by conceptuality.

He comments:

> Dreyfus dismisses the thesis that mind is pervasive in a distinctively human life as a myth, on the ground that the thesis cannot be combined with a proper phenomenology of embodied coping skills and proper placement of embodied coping skills in an account of our orientation towards the world. But I have been arguing that this is wrong. Acknowledging the pervasiveness of mind in a distinctively human life is consistent with appreciating those phenomenological insights.[6]

McDowell notes that "[t]he world is embraceable in thought" and goes on to claim that "that constitutes a background without which the special way in which experience takes hold of the world would not be intelligible."[7] But it isn't obvious that there is only *one* way experience takes hold of the world so that *all* forms of human experience must be embraceable in *thought*.

Existential phenomenologists such as Martin Heidegger and Maurice Merleau-Ponty point out that access to an *independent thinkable* world requires as its background a *familiar graspable* world that, so long as we are absorbed in it, is operative as a field of forces, but which vanishes when we try to think it.

In contrast, McDowell concludes:

> To avoid making it unintelligible how the deliverances of sensibility can stand in grounding relations to paradigmatic exercises of the understanding such as judgments and beliefs ... we must insist that the understanding is already inextricably implicated in the deliverances of sensibility themselves.[8]
>
> To understand *empirical content in general*, we need to see it in its dynamic place in a self-critical activity, the activity by which we aim to comprehend the world as it impinges on our senses.[9]

McDowell adds:

> I use the word "transcendental," in what I hope is sufficiently close to a Kantian way, to characterize this sort of concern with the very possibility of thought's being directed at the objective world.[10]

The Myth of the Mental is just this transcendental claim that, in order for the mind to relate to the world at all, *every* way we relate to the world must be pervaded by self-critical conceptuality.

## The nonconceptual world of absorbed coping

Merleau-Ponty describes a perspicuous example of the world of total absorption – a world pervaded not by critical conceptuality but by lines of force:

> For the player in action the soccer field is not an "object." It is pervaded by lines of force ... and is articulated into sectors (for example, the "openings" between the adversaries), which *call for a certain mode of action. The field itself is not given;* ... the player *becomes one with it (fait corps avec lui).* ... At this moment consciousness is nothing but the dialectic of milieu and action. Each maneuver undertaken by [i.e. called forth from] the player modifies the character of the field and establishes new lines of force in which the action in turn unfolds and is accomplished, again altering the phenomenal field.[11]

Note that the field of forces is not *given* to the soccer player. He has no distance from it. Rather he *becomes one with it*, "fait corps avec lui."

Merleau-Ponty's description of the soccer player's unmediated relation to the soccer "field" may seem an extreme case. Heidegger, however, describes our everyday activity as a similar sort of absorption in a familiar field of relevant affordances[12] directly soliciting our responses. He says:

> [W]hat is first of all "given" is the "for writing," the "for going in and out," ... "for sitting." That is, writing, going-in-and-out, sitting, and the like are that wherein we *a priori* move. What we know when we "know our way around."[13]

McDowell, like the existential phenomenologists, avoids the Cartesian Myth of the Given as an indubitable foundation for knowledge, but he still accepts the Cartesian separation between the world and the perceivers and agents to whom the world is given. He claims that human agents are *"embodied"* and *"involved,"* indeed, even *"immersed"* in the world, but, for McDowell, as minds we are always nonetheless *distanced* in the sense that we are never *merged* with the world. We always stand over against it bringing our subjective perspective to bear on an independent objective reality. As McDowell puts it: "[A] concept [is] what ensures that thoughts ... have the necessary distance from what would determine them to be true."[14] For there to be knowledge, the propositional structures in the mind must correspond to the propositionally structured facts in the world. According to McDowell, all forms of involvement manifest this mind/world distance, and so must be mediated by conceptuality.

Existential phenomenologists contend, on the contrary, that the world we are drawn into when we are absorbed in coping does not stand over against us as a set of facts that can be captured in propositions but rather is *directly lived* by the absorbed coper as a shifting field of attractions and repulsions. Being drawn and responding to the draw are interdefined in one unitary phenomenon. In Heidegger's terms, "Dasein [human being] ... is nothing but ... concerned absorption in the world."[15] Heidegger's talk of "that wherein we *a priori* move" points to this *always already* "operative" absorption.

Heidegger calls the mode of awareness in which absorbed coping takes account of things without our *apprehending* them in *thought*, "circumspection."[16] He describes coming into the classroom as an example of this everyday "unthought" in which our skilled dispositions mesh with the field of familiar affordances:

> The view in which the equipmental contexture stands at first, completely unobtrusive and unthought, is the view ... of our practical everyday orientation. "Unthought" means that it is not thematically apprehended for deliberate thinking about things; instead, in circumspection, we find our bearings in regard to them. ... When we enter here through the door, we do not apprehend the seats, and the same holds for the doorknob.[17]

To be true to the phenomenon we should add that when we are ready to leave a familiar room we not only do not need to *think that* the door affords going out. We need not even respond to the door *as* affording going out. Indeed, we needn't apprehend the door at all. From the perspective of the skilled coper absorbed in the solicitation of a familiar affordance, the affording object, as Heidegger puts it, "withdraws."[18] We need not even be aware of the solicitations to go out *as* solicitations. Thanks to our background familiarity, when it is appropriate to leave, we are simply drawn to go out. In general, the absorbed coper is directly drawn by each solicitation in an appropriate way: the chairs draw him to sit on them, the floorboards to walk on them, the walls may draw him to hang pictures on them, the windows to open them, and the door may draw him to go out.

It might seem an argument for the pervasiveness of conceptuality that we often have to use concepts to find our way about in an unfamiliar situation. But, as in an unfamiliar city, we have to start to find our way by using concepts, but our situation gradually comes to make sense to us in a nonconceptual way as we learn our way around in it. Once our situation becomes familiar our skilled dispositions respond directly to the solicitations of the relevant affordances. Indeed, once a skill is acquired, concepts used in learning the skill need play no further role. It is not even necessary that to learn a practice one needs to have been aware of the relevant concepts. Our ability to act normally is usually picked up by imitating authorities without concepts playing any conscious role.

One could, of course, introduce a still weaker understanding of conceptuality to justify the claim that concepts are pervasive. One could hold that any sort of absorbed coping, no matter how learned, would count as conceptual as long as it had become *second nature*; that is, as long as it was a natural propensity that has been taken over and shaped by a culture. That is, one could call everyday background coping practices conceptual even if no conceptual awareness were involved in acquiring and practicing them. In any case, since such practices normally are unthought, even if we choose to declare our trained normative background practices conceptual, they clearly cannot play the role concepts normally play in grounding judgments and beliefs, i.e. in "adjusting thinking to experience."[19]

It seems that, when a transcendental requirement runs up against phenomenological counterexamples, saving the pervasiveness claim requires weakening that claim until what remains of it need have nothing to do with the job – in this case justifying judgments – for which it was allegedly required.

But, although conceptuality is not pervasive, in that it does not characterize everyday absorbed background coping, there is, according to Heidegger, still a place for the conceptual. In *Being and Time* Heidegger describes a case of hammering where the hammer does not withdraw, but where the hammer shows up *as* too heavy. Heidegger's focus on what he calls the unready-to-hand brings his account of action into proximity to McDowell's. In the face of a disturbance, a distance opens up between the coper and what he is acting on which is bridged by a situation-specific concept. The coper can make the judgment that the hammer is too heavy.

Thus, like McDowell, Heidegger is interested in what makes the relation of mind and world possible. But he primarily wants to describe what makes the concepts necessary for relating mind and world themselves possible. To bring out how our nonconceptual background understanding is the basis of concepts, Heidegger describes the badly placed chalkboard he is writing on as he lectures.[20]

To begin with, like McDowell, Heidegger notes, and then sets aside, traditional desituated conceptuality:

> As an example of a simple assertion we shall take the statement "The board is black." [But] we can sense straightaway that this statement is, as it were, ready-made for logic and the study of grammar.[21]

So he takes instead as his paradigm an assertion made by an involved coper:

> "The board is badly positioned," [he says] is simpler in the sense of something spoken naturally and spontaneously. ... [22]

Then Heidegger begins to lay out an account of the experience of what, in *Being and Time*, he calls the unready-to-hand:

> The position is bad *for those* who are sitting at the other side of the lecture room or bad ... *for the one who* is writing and has to go over to the board each time rather than having it more favorably situated behind him. Accordingly, the position is not a determinacy of the board itself, such as its black color, ... but a determinacy that is merely relative to us who are here in this very situation. This determinate quality of the board – its bad position – is therefore not a so-called objective property, but is relative to the subject.[23]

But this account, which would presumably fit into McDowell's world of facts and judgments about them, is still too traditional for Heidegger. As if objecting to McDowell's view, Heidegger continues:

> [But] the board is not – as this rash interpretation concluded – badly positioned in relation to us who are factically to be found here, rather the board is badly positioned in this lecture room. [If] we think of the room not as tiered, but as a dance hall, then the board would be sitting quite favorably in the corner, out of the way. ... [24]

And Heidegger then introduces the skilled familiarity in which we live – a familiarity that, in order to function, must remain in the background:

> It is out of the manifestness of the lecture room that we experience the bad position of the board in the first place. Precisely this manifestness of the lecture room within which the board is badly positioned is what does not explicitly appear at all in the assertion. We do not first attain the manifestness of the lecture room via the assertion "The board is badly positioned," rather this manifestness is the *condition of the possibility* of the board in general being something we can make judgments about.[25]

The manifestness of the lecture room as a meaningful mini-world is the cumulative skill we have built up through our attending and giving lectures over the years. It is this know-how that orients us in the lecture room and enables us to deal with the things in it. In Heidegger's example, the manifestness of the lecture room is the condition of the possibility of making propositional judgments about the position of the blackboard. The ongoing background coping makes possible the judgment that the blackboard is badly placed. And Heidegger goes on to point out that this background familiarity is holistic and nonpropositional:

> What is decisive in this interpretation of assertion is that we do not make a judgment in relation to an isolated object, but in this judgment we speak out of this whole that we have already experienced and are familiar with, and which we call the lecture room.[26]

The familiar forces we are absorbed in when we make the judgment that the blackboard is badly placed is not made up of propositional structures to which we can affix bits of language.

Heidegger stresses the nonconceptuality of this holistic background know-how he calls understanding:

> [P]recisely in order to experience *what* and *how* beings in each case *are* in themselves as the beings that they *are*, we must – although not conceptually – already understand something like the what-being and that-being of beings.[27]

The background condition of the possibility of making judgments that such and such is the case, then, must be already pervasively operative. In that, McDowell and Heidegger would agree. But they differ as to what these a priori conditions consist in and what they reveal. For McDowell making judgments requires operative concepts that correspond to a propositionally structured totality of facts. For Heidegger what is required are nonconceptual coping skills that disclose a space in which things can then be encountered as what and how they are. In disclosing a holistic background by orienting ourselves in it we are not subjects striving to get it right about an independent objective reality, but rather we are absorbed into a field of forces drawing us to keep up our ongoing coping like a pilot staying on the beam. Since there is no mind/world distance in such activity, there is no need for conceptual content to mediate a mind/world relation.

We must therefore distinguish two opposed, but hopefully supplementary, accounts of our relation to reality (Box 1.1).

Existential phenomenologists like Heidegger and Merleau-Ponty describe as basic how, in our everyday absorbed coping, we merge with the familiar world of attractions and repulsions; transcendental thinkers like McDowell, in contrast, take as basic how in our perceiving, thinking, and acting we take up a distanced relation to an independent reality.

According to the existential phenomenologists, the transcendental account is not wrong but it is secondary. The phenomenologists claim that the absorption into the field of attractions and repulsions they have brought to light is a primordial nonconceptual mode of coping *on the basis of which* the conceptual world makes sense. As Heidegger puts it:

Dasein exists in the manner of *being-in-the-world*, and this basic determination of its existence is the *presupposition for being able to apprehend anything at all*.

And he adds: "By hyphenating the term being-in-the-world we mean to indicate that this structure is a unitary one."[28]

But since McDowell passes over the world of nonconceptual absorbed coping, he is committed to the transcendental claim that to do the job of relating mind and world (without hyphens) conceptuality must be pervasive and always operative. Since conceptuality makes possible the mind's getting it right about an independent reality, it is a universal and necessary condition of the possibility of perception and action.

### Box 1.1 The worlds of distance and absorption

Merleau-Ponty and McDowell agree that we are open directly to the world. But there are two meanings of "world" and two correlated kinds of openness. In general, McDowell thinks of the world in largely descriptive terms, and our openness to it as distanced taking it in; Merleau-Ponty, by contrast, thinks of the world in proto-normative terms, and our openness to it as abandonment to our absorption in it.

| McDowell | Merleau-Ponty |
|---|---|
| *World* ||
| Totality of facts, including affordances | A web of attractions and repulsions |
| Facts about what one ought to do that give one reasons to act and that serve as justifications of one's actions | |
| Propositional structures | Solicitations to act (not propositional structures) |
| *Characteristics of openness to the world* ||
| Entertaining propositions that such and such is the case | Drawn to act in such and such a way |
| Formal "I do" | Loss of self-consciousness in the flow |
| *Capacity to step back* and criticize any particular proposition about what is the case and any reasons for one's actions | Being always already absorbed in proto-normative forces of attraction and repulsion |
| *Level of skill* ||
| *Competent* – Self-conscious reflection and deliberation | *Master* – Flow and mastery, undermined by reflection and deliberation |

The moral of the blackboard example is that McDowell begins his description of the relation of mind and world too late. That human beings are open to a world of facts presupposes a nonpropositional, nonintentional, ongoing background activity that discloses our familiar world without the mediation of conceptual content. Only on the basis of this pervasive activity can human beings relate to things and equipment.

McDowell's account of the *necessity* of conceptuality to make possible our mind-to-world relation seems to me convincing. My objection to his view is that he assumes that his account of our concept-based, minded, rational relation to the totality of facts is the whole story as to how we, in general, relate to the world. I don't question McDowell's transcendental "*must*," but I do question his *überhaupt*.

My questions to McDowell therefore are: (1) What supports the claim that conceptuality *must pervade all* aspects of our relation to reality? (2) What does it mean for a conceptual capacity to be operative? And (3) How could our conceptual capacity be *always* operative? Since concepts devoted to getting it right about a distanced reality decouple us from the world of normative forces, it would seem that concepts must precisely *not* be always operative.

## The nonconceptuality of social norms

In our everyday relating to others we find a similar nonconceptual phenomenon. We are always already absorbed in a nonconceptual background understanding of our shared social world. So, for example, we are directly drawn to the appropriate distance to stand from these people, in this light, in this elevator, with this background noise, and so forth. We are not aware of what we are doing, nor were our parents, who passed this complex skill on to us, aware that they had it. Still, as long as we stay absorbed this skill opens us to being drawn to cope with ever-new situations. If we step back and try to position ourselves appropriately, however, we will no longer find ourselves drawn to a specific appropriate distance, and so we will quite likely end up positioning ourselves inappropriately.[29]

McDowell's calls our normative social background comportment "second nature." As he puts it: "Our nature is largely second nature, and our second nature is the way it is not just because of the potentialities we were born with, but also because of our upbringing, our *Bildung*."[30] But McDowell does not go on to tell us just how, thanks to *Bildung*, our instinctual first nature becomes socialized into second nature. Rather than broadening his account to include all forms of socialized comportment, McDowell follows Sellars in restricting second nature to rational behavior, which in turn depends on mastering a language. He tells us:

> Sellars glosses the space of reasons as the logical space "of justifying and being able to justify what one says." ... Acquiring command of a language, which is coming to inhabit the logical space of reasons, is acquiring a second nature.[31]

McDowell thus limits second nature to the result of *Bildung* and limits *Bildung* to a development of our conceptual capacities. He notes:

> Molding ethical character, which includes imposing a specific shape on the practical intellect, is a particular case of a general phenomenon: initiation into conceptual capacities, which include responsiveness to other rational demands besides those of ethics.[32]

But there is a lot more "shaping" going on when we are being socialized than molding us into language-speaking rational animals. Besides acquiring practices like distance standing by imitation, prelinguistic infants pick up unawares styles of normative comportment such as gender roles and ethnic stereotypes. In general, the cultural practices picked up by prelinguistic children pervade all the ways they encounter things and people.

A striking example of the early development of preconceptual/prelinguistic background practices can be seen in a description of the contrast in child-rearing practices in the 1970s in the United States and Japan:

> A Japanese baby seems passive. ... He lies quietly ... while his mother, in her care, does [a great deal of] lulling, carrying, and rocking of her baby. She seems to try to soothe and quiet the child, and to communicate with him physically rather than verbally. On the other hand, the American infant is more active ... and exploring of his environment, and his mother, in her care, does more looking at and chatting to her baby. She seems to stimulate the baby to activity and vocal response.
>
> It is as if the American mother wanted to have a vocal, active baby, and the Japanese mother wanted to have a quiet, contented baby. In terms of styles of caretaking of the mothers in the two cultures, they get what they apparently want. ... A great deal of cultural learning has taken place by three to four months of age ... babies have learned by this time to be Japanese and American babies.[33]

Pierre Bourdieu offers an excellent description of just how this unnoticed, pervasive, prelinguistic, embodying of one's culture works to open a space of meaning that is neither merely culturally formed first nature[34] nor in the space of rational second nature. Bourdieu writes:

> The essential part of the *modus operandi* which defines practical mastery is transmitted in practice ... without attaining the level of

discourse. The child imitates not "models" but other people's actions. Body *hexis* speaks *directly* to the motor function, in the form of a pattern of postures ... *charged with a host of social meanings.*[35]

Bourdieu is denying that human socialization is the imposing of cultural demands on a preexistent meaningless instinctual nature.[36] For Bourdieu, influenced by Heidegger and Merleau-Ponty, the mistake is thinking of instincts as in the realm of first nature and of culture as imposing a form on them. That would be the social version of the Cartesian understanding of tools as the result of adding function predicates to bare things – a view still put forward by Husserl (and John Searle)[37] and rejected by Heidegger in *Being and Time*. Where socialization is concerned, there is no ground floor of bare individual instincts or bare objects on which culture meanings are imposed one by one, but, rather, human beings are *from the start* absorbed into a holistic web of interconnected meanings that they pick up directly by imitation. As Heidegger puts it, being-in-the-world is always already being-with.[38]

That this social imitation is not merely the result of animal training but picks up a style that opens a meaningful world can be see if we return to the case of Japanese and American babies. The quiet, contented Japanese baby is directly attuned by the mother to a culture that values social integration, that takes tradition seriously, that strives for consensus, and that sees a delicate china teacup as the paradigm of what it is to be an object. By contrast, the vocal, active American baby has from the start been attuned to a cultural style of aggressive individuals who value progress and cultivate the ability to interact with others by means of compromise. The paradigm object in such a culture is likely to be something like a styrofoam cup: convenient, readily available, and easily disposed of.

We could call our absorbed, holistic, pervasive socialization second nature, but speaking of second nature is misleading if it suggests that a basic first nature of meaningless instinctual isolable dispositions is first of all given and is then shaped into a socialized second nature. This would be a throwback to a social version of the Myth of the Given. It suggests a version of the ground floor/superstructure view that McDowell rightly wants to reject.

Rather, when absorbed in coping we are directly drawn to meaningful social comportment like standing an appropriate distance from our fellows. This activity manifests the meaning of intimacy in our culture. Likewise we are directly drawn to act in a way that is recognized and responded to as masculine or feminine, and, indeed, we are drawn to deal in a culturally appropriate way with everything that is. Such a pervasive and always operative *ontological* "second nature" opens a *space of meaning* that governs all forms of cultural coping.

This holistic space of meaning cannot be understood as the result of the imposition of a form on a matter that is *given* by nature nor can it be understood as the result of doing what is required by reason. Indeed, unlike responding to psychological impulses or to rational demands, absorption in the space of meaning is *sui generis*.

McDowell, however, seems obliged to understand all human activity as either in the space of shaped natural reactions, or in the space of reasons. With only these two "spaces" at his disposal for making sense of human comportment, McDowell would seem to be obliged to classify our socialized, prelinguistic, preconceptual background practices as a kind of instinctual first nature, while treating our conceptual/linguistic practices as exhausting second nature.

But why would one let oneself be led to make the counterintuitive move of relegating our nonconceptual, nonlinguistic yet meaningful comportment to instinct rather than introducing a third space, namely that of meaningful normative forces? The only reason would seem to be that if we take seriously in our ontology the space of nonconceptual, nonlinguistic normative forces it stands out as a striking counterexample to the claim that *all* distinctively human activity is pervaded by conceptuality. Indeed, in order to save the thesis of the pervasiveness of the conceptual, a vast amount of distinctively human comportment from distance standing, to gender roles, to cultural styles would have to be declared second nature and so have to be understood as culturally formed instinct.

Even if one chooses to think of social coping in terms of second nature, there seem to be two different conflicting accounts of second nature involved here. There is the second nature that results from the way any human beings are always already absorbed in coping in the style of some specific culture, and there is the second nature described by Sellars and McDowell – a specific set of dispositions to think logically that the Athenians presumably instilled in their infants, who passed them on to us.

That *some* customs or other are necessary cannot be doubted, but the sense of second nature that makes critical reflection an obligation might well itself need to be criticized. Rather than take for granted that critical rationality is the defining feature of human beings, we should ask: What is rationality? Is it required? Should it be? Does it permeate all our activity? How does it relate to mastery? If critical distance undermines expertise, we had better not view rationality as a pervasive obligation. Heidegger's proposal, as we have already noted, is that what is essential to being human is not critical rationality but being drawn directly to take up a stand on what it means to be.

In sum, although both Heidegger and McDowell recognize the importance of social background practices, McDowell and the existential phenomenologists give a radically different account of their nature and role. For McDowell such practices are a second nature that requires our conforming to rational demands – so the more pervasive and operative our second nature is the more the world is available for rational criticism. The existential phenomenologists, on the contrary, highlight how our comportment and thought is governed by our unthinking absorption in an unthinkable background field of forces. And they conclude that the more we are absorbed in this pervasive and always operative space of meaning, the less it is available to thought.

One might contend, however, that while background coping is largely unthought, it is not unthinkable. There are in fact two types of unthought: ontic and ontological. Heidegger is giving an ontic account in his description of entering his classroom without noticing the door or the doorknob – what he calls unthematized encountering. But I can notice the door and list its properties. Likewise, making explicit our background assumptions and practices is the job of consciousness-raising groups that try, for example, to list the features of what it is to be feminine or masculine in our culture. But we have to remember that, although it is sometimes necessary to make explicit and confront conflicting or repressive background practices and to deal with resistant doorknobs, such reflection would normally get in the way of expert ongoing everyday coping.

That thematizing usually undermines expert practice suggests that thinking transforms the perceptual and social field. A field of forces only exists when there is no distance between the absorbed coper and the field. Once one brings the background to the foreground and distances it from the thinker it is radically transformed. We have seen that a soccer field shows up entirely differently to a skilled player absorbed in the game than it does to an observer no matter how skilled. Sociologists can work out the rules governing distance standing, but such facts fail to capture the absorbed practice. Likewise, we can make explicit many facts about Japanese social practices, but they only make sense on the basis of an unthinkable background style available only to those absorbed in it. Thus the perceptual/social field is in principle unthinkable. In so far as I'm absorbed in the field of forces I can't think them, and in so far as I distance myself in order to think them they vanish.

Once it is treated as a set of facts, the perceptual/social field can no longer function as a space of meaning. Rather, to make the world intelligible the space of meaning must remain the holistic background in which we live. It seems that McDowell has no place in his ontology for this holistic, pervasive, prelinguistic, preconceptual background in which we are always already absorbed.

## The restricted role of the mind in absorbed coping

We have seen that in fully absorbed coping, mind and world cannot be separated. Rather, at ground level, we are directly merged into a field of attractive and repulsive forces. Thus, there is no place in the phenomenon of fully absorbed coping for intentional content mediating between mind and world. Now we must add that there is also no place for an "I." But we will also need to describe where mental content and the thinking subject make their appearance.

Sartre makes a convincing case that an ego that does the coping is not part of the content of the experience of the absorbed coper. He notes:

> When I run after a streetcar, when I look at the time, when I am absorbed in contemplating a portrait, there is no *I*. ... I am then plunged into the world of objects ... it is they which present themselves ... with attractive and repellant qualities – but *me*, I have disappeared.[39]

Indeed, in total absorption, sometimes called flow, one is so fully absorbed in one's activity that one is not even marginally thinking about what one is doing. Merleau-Ponty writes similarly of a master orator:

> The orator does not think before speaking, nor even while speaking; his speech is his thought. The end of the speech or text will be *the lifting of a spell*. It is at this stage that thoughts on the speech or text will be able to arise.[40]

It seems that masters in all domains can perform at their best only when they go into this sort of nonthinking spell.

Everyday background coping is like flow in that there need be no ego involved. We engage in such background flow when crossing a familiar busy street while having a conversation. The familiar background coping can support a foreground coping in which the "I do" is operative. In Heidegger's example, when walking into the classroom he copes with the door, benches, and doorknob without being aware of them, while at the same time presumably focusing on what he will say in his lecture. When lecturing, however, if everything is going well, he may be fully in flow. In such fully absorbed coping the background coping goes all the way up to engulf the foreground, so to speak, and then the lecturer will be, as Merleau-Ponty says, as if under a spell.

McDowell, however, holds that an "I" must at least always be capable of accompanying the experience of acting. He says:

> Self-awareness in action is practical, not theoretical. It is a matter of an "I do" rather than an "I think." ... Conceiving action in terms of the "I do" is a way of registering *the essentially first-person character of the realization of practical rational capacities that acting is*.[41]

That is, just as Kant argues that the "I think" *must be able* to accompany my thoughts even in cases when it does not actually accompany them, so McDowell seems to hold that, given the first-person nature of action, an "I do" *must be able* to accompany my experience of acting even in those cases when, in fact, it is not part of the contents of my consciousness. It follows that even when Dasein is coping in a way that is fully absorbed so that no "I do" *actually* accompanies its activity, practical action as such is so structured that a monitoring "I do" always *could* accompany its activity.

But the claim that *all* action involves the capacity to be accompanied by an "I do" does not fit the phenomenon of absorbed coping. When Dasein is totally merged with the world there is no place for *content*, neither experiential nor propositional – there is nothing that is in any sense inner. That is, when the coper is in flow, there is not only no "I do" in the *contents* of his or her experience but, unlike the "I think" that could always come to accompany one's experience, there is no way an "I do" could be introduced into the absorbed activity of the coper in flow without abolishing that activity by creating a distance between agent and world.

But McDowell adds an important qualification:

> The presence of the "I do" in a philosophical account of action marks the *distinctive form* of a kind of phenomenon, like the presence of the "I think," as at least able to accompany representations, in Kant's account of empirical consciousness.[42]

It seems that McDowell in inserting an always possible "I do" into his account of action is not making a psychological nor a phenomenological claim, but defining the form of an action. An action is something someone does. That is its essential first-person character. Since all action is *a realization of a practical rational capacity*, it *must in principle* involve an ego that does the acting and is aware of doing it. So in this formal sense the ego must be *pervasive* and always *operative* in *all* human action. But it would be a pun to think that *realizing* a practical capacity in my coping requires that I *realize* what I am doing.

So what is the argument that the ego as "the *form* of a kind of phenomenon" requires that an ego *actually* pervade and be operative in one's activity? What justifies the move from a formal claim, to a pervasiveness claim? An *actual* "I do" does, indeed, accompany deliberate actions, but the "I do" that is supposedly the *form of all action* and therefore *pervasive and always operative* seems to be a ghostly shadow of the mental which has no place for the phenomenon of flow.[43]

In our earlier exchange, I questioned McDowell's claim that conceptuality (conceptual content, mindedness, and rationality) is always pervasive and operative, because it seemed to me that the idea of an always operative capacity did not make sense. Now, however, thanks to our discussion, I see that the idea of an always operative pervasive capacity not only makes sense; it illuminates a basic notion in *Being and Time*. Heidegger has his own understanding of the self as pervasive and always operative but it does not require even marginal self-awareness.

Heidegger defines Dasein as a being whose being is an issue for it. That means that Dasein is a case of a way of life[44] and that a way of life is pervaded by a certain style. Heidegger calls the fact that each person's life is pervaded by a certain style or stand on its own being, "mineness."[45] According to Heidegger, even though there need be no "I" in my experience of coping, my activity, as opposed to that of nonhuman animals, is pervaded by "mineness."[46] For example, when I respond to my chair by sitting in it, it is not just my chair that solicits sitting. Rather, it is my chair at the table where my computer is with my books scattered around it. My coping skills are also taking account of the time (a time for work), the ambient lighting (sufficient for work), and the whole room (nothing wrong that would disturb work). My world is thus pervaded by the style of hard work. Only what enters my world, either by helping me work or by getting in the way of my work, counts for me. That is, the chair draws me to sit in a setting that is already organized according to my way of life – an organization that makes all the relations make sense and the solicitations draw me on.[47] Nothing solicits human beings independent of a context organized by their individual style of life. Heidegger sums up Dasein's constitutive background mineness with the claim that "*Dasein is its world existingly.*"[48]

Heidegger sees Dasein's mineness as pervasive, but at the same time denies a pervasive ego because he sees that the way a lifestyle organizes one's world doesn't require an agent doing the organizing. A Dasein can be fully absorbed in being a soccer mom, a devoted teacher, a victim of discrimination, or a workaholic without *thinking* of its way of life under some such a description, indeed, without being aware that it has a way of life at all. (Happily, having a way of life doesn't require having a life plan, since such a plan would only get in the way of one's fluidly adaptive coping.)

But how can activity be guided without a self's representation of its goal? The answer is that in familiar situations there need be no representation of conditions of satisfaction; rather, the absorbed coper behaves like a pilot following a landing beacon. For the pilot there need be no representation of a goal. When things are going well, the beacon is silent. However, when the plane deviates from the optimal path a beeper sounds. The pilot can then remain in flow and directly respond to the signal by "automatically" correcting his course, or he may sense a tension that draws him to correct his course. Only when things are not developing normally and no alternative perspective directly draws the coper to replace the current one, does the coper have to represent a goal and deliberate as to how to reach it. Only then the ego enters consciousness, and at the same time, mastery is lost.

## THE MYTH OF THE PERVASIVENESS OF THE MENTAL

It would seem that one way to support the claim that absorbed coping nonetheless always requires an ego is to claim that coping behavior must always be composed of subsidiary movements and that these must be inaugurated and organized by an ego's representation of a goal. Thus every action has as its condition of satisfaction that "I" attain a specific goal. On this view even distance standing must, for example, be a subsidiary movement in an attempt to stand the right distance from someone so as to have a conversation. But distance standing need not be a subsidiary activity organized by a goal. Not when, for example, people, with no goal in mind, distribute themselves in an appropriate way in an elevator. In any case, it is not plausible to claim that one's general tendency to continue coping has conditions of satisfaction, although it may have conditions of improvement. That is, as we saw in the case of the landing beacon, one can sense a tension when coping is not going smoothly without having a representation of what it would be for our coping activity to succeed. The experience of coping going well or badly is a kind of normativity that does not require an ego's representation of conditions of satisfaction.

But, if the absorbed coper in flow is not monitoring his performance, how can he keep track of whether or not things are going as expected? What alerts the absorbed coper in flow to an unexpected change in the situation that requires attention? It cannot be that an "I" has all along been monitoring the coper's activity. As we have seen, for an expert to remain in flow and so perform at his best, he must let himself be merged into the field of forces and all monitoring must stop.

The phenomenon seems to be that when coping runs into some sort of resistance or breakdown that blocks it – when the current solicitations don't lead to follow-up solicitations as they normally do – the coper suddenly finds himself paying attention. It's as if the absence of tension (like the silence of the landing beacon) gives way to an overall background sense that things are not going well (the beep). Then at some moment that background tension gives rise to an ego that focuses on the specific problem. In Heidegger's example in *Being and Time*, when hammering becomes difficult, the hammer no longer withdraws into the background but its heaviness becomes a foreground issue for the coper who, in turn, presumably no longer experiences his absorbed coping as pervaded by mineness, but experiences himself as a thinking, acting, self-aware subject distinct from its world. Of course, all this is very sketchy and needs to be spelled out in detail (in Box 1.2).

The bottom line is that philosophers should not deny the possibility of mind-free practical activity by claiming that we always have to bring together mind and world by means of the pervasive conceptual operations of a self-aware self. But, in return, existential phenomenologists need to spell out in much greater detail how conceptuality arises on the basis of being-in-the-world.

## Box 1.2 Three ways of being-in-the-world

*1. Subject-Object intentionality.*

**Example**: The hammer weighs five pounds.
**Heidegger terminology**: Presence-at-hand (*Vorhandenheit*)

| *Mindedness* | *Conceptuality* | *Rationality* |
|---|---|---|
| Subject<br>I do<br>Goals<br>Representations | Free distance<br>Conceptual content<br>Conditions of satisfaction | Able to answer what are you doing<br>and why are you doing it questions |

*2. Coping with the unfamiliar.*

**Example**: The hammer is too heavy.
**Heidegger terminology**: Unreadiness-to-hand (*Un-zuhandenheit*); Primordial intentionality

| *Prereflective cogito* | *Situational significance* | *Disturbance* |
|---|---|---|
| Prereflective monitoring | Situational aspects<br><br>Motor intentional content | Coaching<br>Improving<br>Inspecting |

*3. Absorption in the flow.*

**Example**: Hammer withdraws.
**Heidegger terminology**: Familiarity, Readiness-to-hand (*Zuhandenheit*)

| *Mineness* | *Significance* | *Motivation* |
|---|---|---|
| Being its world existingly | Circumspection<br><br>Attractions and repulsions<br>Conditions of improvement | Direct responsiveness to attractions and repulsions<br>Drawn toward lowering tension and improving grip<br><br>Unable to answer what and why questions |

## The trivialization of rationality

McDowell asserts that "conceptual rationality is everywhere in our lives."[49] He tells us:

> [T]he power of spontaneity comprises a network of conceptual capacities linked by putatively rational connections, with the connections essentially subject to critical reflection.[50]

And he spells this out as follows:

> [E]xperience has its content by virtue of the drawing into operation ... capacities that are genuinely elements in a faculty of spontaneity. The very same capacities must also be able to be exercised in *judgments*, and that requires them to be *rationally* linked into a *whole system of concepts and conceptions* within which their possessor engages in a *continuing activity* of adjusting her *thinking* to experience.[51]

According to McDowell, one must always be capable of acting for a reason one is aware of *as* a reason, and one must be able to appeal to such a reason to justify one's action. However, one could object that the *competent* coper must, indeed, act on the basis of reasons and rules that adjust his thinking and acting to experience, but the master is precisely unable to appeal to a reason to justify his actions. Masters agree that mastery is achieved only when the master ceases to base his actions on reasons and instead is absorbed into a field of attractive and repulsive forces that directly draw him to cope. No distanced relation to the situation can access what draws the master to make his masterful moves. A neutral observer or a merely competent player could know all the demonstrative facts about a chess position and its context and still have no idea what move to make.

To evaluate McDowell's claim concerning the pervasiveness of reason, it helps to contrast it with Sartre's description of his direct reaction to Peter. Sartre says:

> I pity Peter, and I go to his assistance. For my consciousness only one thing exists at that moment: Peter-having-to-be-helped. This quality of "having-to-be-helped" lies in Peter. It acts on me like a force.[52]

McDowell, in contrast, would hold that, for Sartre's response to Peter to be rational, the *thought* of Peter *as* needing help must have served Sartre as the *reason* for his action. As McDowell puts it:

> [T]*hat* the situation *requires* a certain sort of behavior is ... [the kind person's] reason for behaving in that way, on each of the relevant occasions. *So it must be something of which, on each of the relevant occasions, he is aware.*[53]

But it does not follow that in order to act kindly the kind person must be *aware* of the situation *as* a situation calling for kindness. Having dealt, successfully and unsuccessfully with thousands of previous situations involving kindness, the helpful person has tuned his dispositions to respond directly to the whole situation. Thus, as Sartre sees, the kind person will be directly drawn to help *Peter-in-need*. Such openness to a force isn't thinkable. It is only on the basis of a retrospective illusion created by reflection that the situation will seem to all involved to have been one that required kindness.

McDowell's account looks plausible because, by speaking of what is "required," it confounds two perspectives. For a *detached observer* the situation looks like one that "requires a certain sort of behavior" and he acts *for that reason*. For the *absorbed coper*, however, there need be nothing but a force emanating from Peter directly drawing forth a kind action. The thought that the kind person must be aware of, and act on the basis of, a reason, namely that Peter needs help, covers up this important distinction. McDowell is entitled to claim that the virtuous agent has the capacity to take a distanced stance and in such a case to take the requirements of the situation as reasons for acting as he does. However, McDowell is not entitled to his claim that such a capacity for rational action *pervades all practical activity even absorbed coping* and must always be *operative*.

Moreover, in evaluating the pervasiveness claim it is important to bear in mind that taking a critical distance undermines absorption and so degrades mastery. In the case of kindness, the reflective response would most likely be delayed and general rather than instantaneous and specific. This observation may seem to be a boringly familiar refrain, but I want to stress that, if critical distance just amounted to making one's implicit reasons for acting explicit rather than engaging in an entirely different form of activity, we should not expect any kind of degradation in performance when the performer acts for reasons.

In the course of discussing whether the virtuous person needs to be able to classify his virtuous activity *as* virtuous, McDowell seems to assume an implausible account of the role of reasons in the virtuous person's actions. He says:

> [I]t is enough if [the kind person] thinks of what he does, when – as we put it – he shows himself to be kind, under some such description as "the thing to do."[54]

But, if McDowell is suggesting that the kind person needs some minimal *reason* to account for his kind action, the trouble is that thinking of the action as "the thing to do" is *more than enough*. That the virtuous person requires a reason to act is the equivalent of what Bernard Williams in another context calls one thought too many.[55]

In blitz chess, at a second a move, the absorbed master does not have time to make a move because he thinks that it is the thing to do. Likewise, the kind person absorbed in the blitz of human interaction does not normally act in a kindly way because he *thinks* the person before him needs help. After much experience, the chess master is directly drawn by the forces on the board to make a masterful move, and, in the same way, the kind person, as Sartre sees, is directly drawn to act by the force of the needy person's apparent need. In neither case does the master make his move *for a reason*.

To sum up: In all domains, masters learn primarily not from *analyzing* their successes and failures but from the *results* of hundreds of thousands of actions.[56] And what they learn are not critically justifiable *concepts* but sensitivity to subtler and subtler *similarities and differences of perceptual patterns*. Thus, learning changes, not the master's *mind*, but his *world*.

If he could say anything at all about his reason for making a particular move, the master could only respond to the demand for a reason by saying "I made the move because I was drawn to make it." Thus the master's reason for acting looks superficially similar to that of the woman in McDowell's example who, after spontaneously catching a Frisbee, responds to a request for her motivation for her action with McDowell's suggested reply – "No particular reason. I just felt like it."[57] The woman's inability to provide a rational *motivation* and the master's inability to provide a rational *explanation* of why a certain move worked are examples of the limitation of rationality. In both cases rationality is not pervasive.

But perhaps to justify his move the master might follow McDowell's use of demonstrative concepts and, while performing a kind act or making a winning move, explain his action by saying, "in *this* situation always do *this*."[58] But has he thus justified his action? Has he given a reason? Has he laid himself open to criticism? It seems he has only given a reason in the trivial sense, that leaves no room for rational critique. Surely such a reply to a request for a reason is not an exercise of spontaneity as McDowell defines it. It is not "an active undertaking in which a subject takes rational control of the shape of her thinking."[59] The master's and the woman's direct responses do not contribute to adjusting their *thinking* to experience; rather they demonstrate the limits of a supposedly pervasive rationality that can only be saved by trivializing it.

One might try to save the claim that human beings always operate in the space of reasons by claiming that the chess master's and the Frisbee catcher's inability to give reasons is the null case and therefore still in the space of reasons. This would be a plausible response but for the fact that the phenomenology of mastery suggests that nonrational absorbed coping is not a privative form of reason giving but a positive phenomenon.

To see the phenomenon at issue here we need to distinguish between the genuine null case – the lack of a reason where there should be one – and the positive absence of a reason – an absence that leaves room for the forces of attraction and repulsion. An example of the genuine null case would be a recognition by the Frisbee player of her inability to do something she ought to be able to do, namely give an account of her action. So for her the null case would be experienced as facing a legitimate demand that she is nonetheless unable to meet. An example of a positive absence of a reason would be, for example, the case of the grandmaster who would not find his lack of a reason for his move disturbing. Rather, the absence of a reason leaves the master open to the forces in the perceptual field.

## Conclusion

If I understand him rightly, McDowell accepts the transcendental argument that the conditions of the possibility of the mind relating its content to the world requires conceptual capacities, and these capacities *must be always and everywhere operative* in human experience. Phenomenologists, on the contrary, contend that this argument is based on the phenomenologically unjustified assumption that we are basically minds distanced from the world, so that the mind has to be related to the world by mental activity, whereas, when one is fully absorbed in coping the mind/world dichotomy disappears. The assumption that there is an essential distance between mind and world that must be bridged by concepts, thoughts, and reasons is what I have been calling the Myth of the Pervasiveness of the Mental.

## Notes

1 McDowell, *Mind and World*, p. 155.
2 Ibid., p. 34.
3 Ibid., p. 111.
4 Ibid.
5 Ibid., pp. 89–90.
6 McDowell, "What Myth?," pp. 338–51, p. 346.
7 Ibid., p. 33.
8 McDowell, *Mind and World*, p. 46. There is an intriguing formal similarity here between the Myth of the Given and the Myth of the Mental. Both "the Given" and "Conceptuality" are introduced to make it intelligible how "the deliverances of sensibility can stand in grounding relations to paradigmatic exercises of the understanding such as judgments and beliefs." "The Given," however, turns out to be a myth since an indubitable, self-sufficient Given is impossible and, in any case, unnecessary to make intelligible how knowledge is grounded. If, as the existential phenomenologists claim, conceptuality is not self-sufficient and pervasive and so cannot by itself make the relation of sensibility and world intelligible, and if, as in the case of "the Given," this is not a problem since the grounding of judgments the conceptualist seeks is not necessary for understanding how the embodied coper is at grips with the world, one could view "the Mental" as likewise a myth.
9 Ibid., p. 34 (my italics).
10 McDowell, *Engaged Intellect*, p. 243.

11 Merleau-Ponty, *Structure of Behavior*, pp. 168–69 (my italics and brackets). In his passing reference to consciousness here Merleau-Ponty is suggesting a minimalist, nonmental gloss on what consciousness is. All consciousness means in this minimum sense is being drawn to act. We shall see that one does not have to be aware that one is being so drawn. Consciousness is simply our direct responsiveness to a shifting field of forces.
12 "Affordance" is a term introduced by J. J. Gibson to describe objective features of the world in terms of their meaning to the creatures that use them. Thus a hole *affords* hiding to a rabbit but not an elephant. To us floors afford walking on, apples afford eating, etc. (See Gibson, *Ecological Approach to Visual Perception*, pp. 127–43.) The Gestaltists were unhappy with the term "affordance." They were interested not in our perception of objective features of the world but in how such features are related to the needs and desires of perceivers. So they introduced the term *solicitations*. For Gibson an apple *affords* eating, i.e. is edible, whether anyone is hungry or not, but the Gestaltists add that only when one is hungry does an apple *solicit* eating, i.e. look delicious. So one can think of solicitations as relevant affordances.
13 Heidegger, lectures of 1925–26, published as *Logik: Die Frage nach der Wahrheit*, p. 144 (my translation). The scare quotes around "given" are to be taken seriously. They do the same job of denying the separation of mind and world as does Merleau-Ponty's denial of the given in his soccer description.
14 McDowell, *Mind and World*, p. 57. McDowell's saying that our most basic experience of the world is "distanced" in this sense is compatible with his speaking in another context of our being "whole-heartedly engaged in the relevant parts of the 'whirl of organism'" and of "our immersion in our familiar forms of life" (McDowell, *Mind, Value and Reality*, p. 63).
15 Heidegger, *History of the Concept of Time*, p. 197.
16 Heidegger, *Being and Time*, p. 107.
17 Heidegger, *Basic Problems of Phenomenology*, p. 163.
18 Heidegger, *Being and Time*, p. 99.
19 McDowell, *Mind and World*, p. 47.
20 To avoid misunderstanding at this crucial point, it is important to bear in mind that what I have been calling skillful coping, Heidegger calls "understanding." He says:

> In ordinary language, we ... say "He understands how to handle men," "He knows how to talk." Understanding here means "knowing how" [*können*], "being capable of."
>
> (Heidegger, *History of the Concept of Time*, p. 298)

21 Heidegger, *Fundamental Concepts of Metaphysics*, p. 343.
22 Ibid.
23 Ibid., p. 344.
24 Ibid.
25 Ibid., p. 345.
26 Ibid., p. 347.
27 Ibid., p. 357.
28 Ibid., p. 164.
29 Similarly, we do not normally notice, let alone think about, our gestures while speaking. We are not even aware that we are gesturing, let alone why we are making the particular movements we are led to make. If one tries to gesture appropriately while giving a speech, one ends up looking as wooden as Al Gore during his presidential campaign.

30 McDowell, *Mind and World*, p. 87.
31 McDowell, "Experiencing the World," in *Engaged Intellect*, p. 247.
32 Ibid., p. 84.
33 W. Caudill and H. Weinstein, "Maternal Care and Infant Behavior in Japan and in America," in Lavatelli and Stendler (eds), *Readings in Child Behavior and Development*, p. 78.
34 In a discussion at a conference at the Wissenschaftskolleg zu Berlin (May 2009) McDowell characterized distance standing as a "culturally formed instinct." I'm grateful to the Wissenschaftskolleg for having organized the conference at which this discussion took place.
35 Bourdieu, *Outline of a Theory of Practice*, p. 87.
36 That is, indeed, the way toilet training works for nonhuman animals and human babies alike, so it cannot be the specific sort of human socialization we are seeking to describe.
37 Searle, *Construction of Social Reality*, p. 23.
38 Heidegger, *Being and Time*, pp. 149, 163.
39 Sartre, *Transcendence of the Ego*, pp. 48–49.
40 Merleau-Ponty, *Phenomenology of Perception*, p. 209 (my italics).
41 McDowell, "Response to Dreyfus," pp. 366–67.
42 Ibid.
43 It may be that there is a mode of mindless absorption so total that the coper doesn't realize anything. This phenomenon of *unconscious* coping is recognized as the way to maximum performance in sports. In a description of the training of Olympic swimmers Chuck Warner tells us that:

> In the ... pyramid of qualities of a champion, ... the individual's ability to turn off the conscious mind and allow the subconscious "automatic pilot" to take over sits at the top.
> (Warner, *Four Champions, One Gold Medal*, p. 96)

An Olympic swimmer on autopilot is in a way like a sleepwalker, but he is a master swimmer swimming at his best. His highly trained body is responding in a refined way to the familiar currents drawing him through the water.
44 I owe this way of thinking of Dasein's mineness to John Haugeland. See Haugeland, "Heidegger on Being a Person."
45 Heidegger, *Being and Time*, p. 67.
46 According to Heidegger, animals exhibit an absorbed way of coping that is similar to ours but importantly different in three respects.

  (1) Human beings live in a world in which affordances matter to us and draw us to act not merely on the basis of our needs and previous experience, as they do animals, but on the basis of our nonconceptual background sense of how to live.
  (2) Animals are "captivated" by their environment. When animals are being drawn by one solicitation they are insensitive to all others (except for a preprogrammed set of always-relevant affordances such as predators and prey). Thus, given a particular situation, animals have a *fixed horizon* of potentially relevant *solicitations*. Human beings, however, are open to a background of potentially relevant whole *situations*, each of which opens a changing horizon of potentially relevant solicitations.
  (3) When a familiar situation does not evolve in a familiar way, our absorption can suddenly end, and be replaced by *reflection*. Animals facing a breakdown are simply stunned and then captivated by a new solicitation.

47 Thanks to Charles Spinosa for this example.
48 Heidegger, *Being and Time*, p. 364.
49 McDowell, "What Myth?," p. 349.
50 McDowell, *Mind and World*, p. 124.
51 Ibid., pp. 46–47 (my italics).
52 Sartre, *Transcendence of the Ego*, p. 56.
53 McDowell, *Mind, Value and Reality*, p. 51 (my italics).
54 Ibid., p. 51.
55 Williams, "Persons, Character, Morality," in *Moral Luck*, p. 18.
56 The same phenomenon can be seen in sports. David Foster Wallace points it out in commenting on Roger Federer:

> For promising junior players, refining the kinesthetic sense is the main goal of the extreme daily practice regimens we often hear about. The training here is both muscular and neurological. Hitting thousands of strokes, day after day, develops the ability to do by "feel" what cannot be done by regular conscious thought. Repetitive practice like this often looks tedious or even cruel to an outsider, but the outsider can't feel what's going on inside the player – tiny adjustments, over and over, and a sense of each change's effects that gets more and more acute even as it recedes from normal consciousness.
> (D. F. Wallace, "Federer as Religious Experience," *New York Times*, August 20, 2006)

57 McDowell, "Response to Dreyfus," p. 369.
58 Not to say, "In this *type* of situation always do this *type* of thing," since that only pushes off the question, as to how to account for the similarity.
59 McDowell, *Mind and World*, p. 60.

# Bibliography

Bourdieu, P., *Outline of a Theory of Practice*, Cambridge: Cambridge University Press, 1977.

Gibson, J. J., *The Ecological Approach to Visual Perception*, Hillsdale, NJ: Laurence Erlbaum Assoc., 1986.

Haugeland, J., "Heidegger on Being a Person," *Noûs* 16 (1982): 15–26.

Heidegger, M., *Basic Problems of Phenomenology*, trans. A. Hofstadter, Bloomington: Indiana University Press, 1982.

——, *Being and Time*, trans. J. Macquarrie and E. Robinson, New York: Harper & Row, 1962.

——, *The Fundamental Concepts of Metaphysics: World, Finitude, Solitude*, trans. W. McNeill and N. Walker, Bloomington: Indiana University Press, 1995.

——, *The History of the Concept of Time*, trans. T. Kisiel, Bloomington: Indiana University Press, 1985.

——, *Logik: Die Frage nach der Wahrheit*, Gesamtausgabe, vol. 21, Frankfurt am Main: Vittorio Klostermann, 1976.

Lavatelli, C. S. and Stendler, F. (eds), *Readings in Child Behavior and Development*, New York: Harcourt Brace, 1972.

McDowell, J., *The Engaged Intellect: Philosophical Essays*, Cambridge, MA: Harvard University Press, 2009.

——, *Mind and World*, Cambridge, MA: Harvard University Press, 1994.
——, *Mind, Value and Reality*, Cambridge, MA: Harvard University Press, 2001.
——, "Response to Dreyfus," *Inquiry* 50, no. 4 (2007): 366–67.
——, "What Myth?" *Inquiry* 50, no. 4 (2007): 338–51.
Merleau-Ponty, M., *Phenomenology of Perception*, trans. C. Smith, London: Routledge & Kegan Paul, 2002.
——, *The Structure of Behavior*, 2nd edn, trans. A. L. Fisher, Boston, MA: Beacon Press, 1966.
Sartre, J.-P., *The Transcendence of the Ego*, trans. F. Williams and R. Kirkpatrick, New York: The Noonday Press, 1957.
Searle, J. R., *The Construction of Social Reality*, New York: Free Press, 1995.
Warner, C., *Four Champions, One Gold Medal*, Phoenix, AZ: Sports Publications International, 1999.
Williams, B., *Moral Luck*, Cambridge: Cambridge University Press, 1981.

# 2

# THE MYTH OF THE MIND AS DETACHED

## John McDowell

### 1

I have urged that rational mindedness pervades the lives of the rational animals we are, informing in particular our perceptual experience and our exercises of agency.

Hubert Dreyfus thinks that is a myth, the Myth of the Pervasiveness of the Mental. But his objections are at cross-purposes to my thesis. In interpreting me, Dreyfus brings to bear a conception of mindedness that is not mine.

Dreyfus assumes, and thinks I accept, that if mindedness informs an experience, the subject has a detached contemplative relation to the world she experiences, and that if mindedness informs an action, the agent has a detached monitoring relation to what she is doing. But this assumption that mindedness implies detachment does not fit what I mean when I say that mindedness is pervasive. I agree with Dreyfus that if the claim is understood like that it should be dismissed as mythical. We should not pretend to find a detached self in all our experiencing and acting.

Dreyfus's interpretation of the pervasiveness thesis reflects his accepting what is, by my lights, the real myth in this area, the Myth of Mind as Detached. I think we should discard the idea that mindedness implies the presence of a detached self. That leaves the pervasiveness thesis invulnerable to Dreyfus's objections.

### 2

I first made the claim of pervasiveness in its application to perceptual experience. I claimed that as enjoyed by rational animals, experience is an actualization of conceptual capacities.[1]

The point of this was that it enables us to credit the experience of rational subjects with the epistemological significance it intuitively has, while avoiding the risk that, in taking experience to be capable of figuring in the warrant for perceptual beliefs, we fall into the Myth of the Given.

The epistemological significance of the experience of rational subjects is that when our experiencing is perceiving, as it can be, features of the environment are perceptually present to us in a way that provides us with opportunities for knowledge, of a kind that is special to rational knowers: knowledge that is, to echo Wilfrid Sellars, a standing in the space of reasons.[2]

In taking experiences to put their subjects in a position to have knowledge of the kind that is a standing in the space of reasons, we risk falling into the Myth of the Given. But we can avoid the risk if we hold that in the experiencing itself, capacities that belong to their subject's rationality are in play: capacities that their possessor could exercise (perhaps only after equipping herself with ways of deploying their content in discursive activity; this is a complication that I shall come back to) in deciding what reason requires her to think about this or that. That is what it means for capacities to be conceptual in the relevant sense: they are capacities whose content is of a form that fits it to figure in discursive activity.

The idea is not that our experiential knowledge is always the result of determining what reason requires us to think about some question. Normally when experience provides us with knowledge that such and such is the case, we simply find ourselves in possession of the knowledge; we do not get into that position by wondering whether such and such is the case and judging that it is. When I say that the knowledge experience yields to rational subjects is of a kind that is special to rational subjects, I mean that in such knowledge, capacities of the sort that *can* figure in that kind of intellectual activity are in play, not that a subject who has such knowledge on the basis of experience is in that position as a result of actually engaging in that kind of intellectual activity.[3]

And my claim is that for experience to make knowledge of that kind available, capacities of the relevant sort must be operative in the experiencing itself. We should not suppose conceptual capacities come into play, in connection with empirical knowledge, only downstream from experience – only when someone decides what to think on the basis of experience, with experience conceived as something she enjoys anyway, independently of any involvement of conceptual capacities.

Now Dreyfus thinks the very idea of conceptual capacities, as I exploit it in this claim, brings into my picture of experience a detached self, standing over against and contemplatively oriented towards an independent reality. But this has no basis in the way the idea of conceptual capacities figures in my picture.

If my picture had subjects of experience constantly wondering whether to think that this or that is the case and resolving such questions by making judgments, it might be right to suppose that for me an experiencing subject is always self-consciously contemplating a reality she stands over against, so as to decide what to think about it. But that is not my picture. As I said, we normally just find ourselves knowing things that experience gives us to know.

A perceptual experience typically affords multiple opportunities for knowing that things are a certain way. The subject of an experience typically does not even attend to many of the ways it puts her in a position to know things to be, let alone consider in each case whether to judge that things are that way. Indeed, with many of those opportunities for knowledge, the subject is not even able to address the question whether to judge that things are the way in question. For that, she would need to acquire something that, in the sort of case I have in mind, she does not already have: means for making explicit – out loud or in the extended sense in which the idea of making things explicit applies to judging – the relevant ways her experience discloses things as being.

Experience discloses the ways things are, whether or not its subject has the means to make those aspects of its content explicit in judgments or assertions. And in either case, having it disclosed to one in experience that things are a certain way is already an actualization of capacities that are conceptual in the relevant sense. That things are a certain way can be there for a subject to know, in her experience, whether or not she has resources for explicitly judging (or saying) that they are that way; and to avoid the Myth of the Given we have to suppose its being there for her to know draws on capacities that belong to her faculty for knowledge of that distinctive kind, capacities that belong to her rationality. Making the content in question explicit – even if the subject first has to acquire means to do that – does not make the content newly conceptual in any sense that is relevant to my claim. It was conceptual already.[4]

If a rational subject does not yet have means to make explicit some way her experience reveals things to be, it is always possible for her to equip herself with such means. In *Mind and World* I illustrate this with color experience. Of course no subject is ready in advance with expressions for all the shades of color she might see. But while one is enjoying a visual experience in which something is presented as having a certain shade of color, determinate to the extent made possible by the acuity of one's power to discriminate colors, one can exploit the visual presence to one of a sample of the shade in order to introduce an expression for the way the thing is presented as being, thus: " ... has *that* shade of color."

If what can be expressed by such a phrase were restricted to the occasion of the experience in which the sample that gives the demonstrative its reference is visually present to the subject, that might threaten our right to suppose the phrase expresses a concept. For the phrase to express a concept, there would need to be a certain generality in its significance. The threat here is that in "That thing has *that* shade" there is only a fraudulent appearance of expressing a way objects can be, so that one could significantly say that the object in question is that way. I respond to this threat as follows:

> We can ensure that what we have in view is genuinely recognizable as a conceptual capacity if we insist that the very same capacity to embrace a colour in mind can in principle persist beyond the duration of the experience itself. In the presence of the original sample, "that shade" can give expression to a concept of a shade; what ensures that it is a concept – what ensures that thoughts that exploit it have the necessary distance from what would determine them to be true – is that the associated capacity can persist into the future, if only for a short time, and that, having persisted, it can be used also in thoughts about what is by then the past, if only the recent past.[5]

Now Dreyfus cobbles together words from this passage to construct a purported quotation. He represents me as saying this: "[A] concept [is] what ensures that thoughts ... have the necessary distance from what would determine them to be true."[6] And he adduces this as evidence that according to me we are always distanced from the world of our experience. (I think this is the only textual basis he offers for finding that view in what I have said about the experience of rational subjects.)

But the purported quotation distorts the grammar of what I wrote, and what I wrote does not say what Dreyfus represents it as saying.[7] It should not seem contentious that a conceptual capacity would need to be able to be exercised in thought; as I have insisted, that does not imply that such capacities can be actualized only in discursive activity. And it should not seem contentious that what determines the content of a thought must be distinct from what would determine it as true. Otherwise we would have only that fraudulent appearance, the threat that my remarks are aimed at averting. This uncontroversial difference between what determines the content of a thought and what would determine it to be true is the only distance I speak of here. There is no implication that there must always be a distance between a *subject* – even a subject who is thinking – and the world; there is much less an implication that whenever a conceptual capacity is actualized, even in the unreflective way in which, on my account, conceptual capacities are actualized in perceptual experience itself, the actualization is mental activity on the part of a subject with a distanced contemplative orientation towards the world she experiences.

Dreyfus here tries to provide evidence for attributing to me the idea that a subject of experience is always detached from the world, but the attempt misfires. His interpretation of me reflects his assuming that I accept the Myth of Mind as Detached. But when I claim that mindedness is pervasive

# THE MYTH OF THE MIND AS DETACHED

in our lives, it is part of my point that mindedness does not always involve detachment. As I said, his objections are at cross-purposes to my claim.

## 3

Something similar happens in Dreyfus's treatment of the pervasiveness thesis as it applies to acting.

Here what he saddles me with is a picture in which a rational agent is always at least marginally monitoring what she is doing, standing ready to intervene with full-blown monitoring if need be. As Dreyfus insists, this picture has no room for "total absorption" in activity, a mode of activity in which "one is not even marginally thinking about what one is doing."[8] That is what he calls "flow." Merleau-Ponty's soccer player and the chess master playing lightning chess exemplify acting in flow.

And here again, the picture Dreyfus attributes to me is not mine. I agree with him that it would be disastrous for an account of agency if it had no room for acting in flow. Here as in the case of experience, his interpretation of my picture of acting is shaped by his importing the assumption that mindedness necessarily brings detachment with it. As I have been insisting, it is part of my point that we should reject that assumption. My picture can perfectly well accommodate acting in flow.

In a previous move in this conversation, in the course of urging that we should reject the Myth of Mind as Detached, I wrote:

> This supposed connection of rationality with detachment is particularly damaging in the case of action. The involvement of rationality in human action, in my picture, is not a result of adding an "I think" to representations of one's actions. That would fit a detached, contemplative [I might have said "monitoring"] stance towards one's actions, but that is not my picture. Self-awareness in action is practical, not theoretical. It is a matter of an "I do" rather than an "I think." And the "I do" is not a representation added to representations, as Kant's "I think" is. Conceiving action in terms of the "I do" is a way of registering the essentially first-person character of the realization of practical rational capacities that acting is. The presence of the "I do" in a philosophical account of action marks the distinctive *form* of a kind of phenomenon, like the presence of the "I think," as at least able to accompany representations, in Kant's account of empirical consciousness.[9]

What Dreyfus makes of this is that according to me "an 'I' must at least always be capable of accompanying the experience of acting."[10] But I spoke, not of an *experience* of acting, but of acting itself. And I spoke of the "I do," not as *accompanying* acting, let alone as merely capable of accompanying it, but as characterizing its form. My claim was that the "I do" characterizes the form of actions as such, whether reflectively engaged in or not, as the possibility of accompaniment by the "I think" characterizes the form of the representations of self-conscious subjects, even representations that, in Kant's account of empirical consciousness, do not involve explicit thinking.

Let me try to spell out the idea in terms of one of Dreyfus's examples of acting in flow, the chess master absorbed in lightning chess.

The chess master's absorption does not prevent him from knowing what he is doing in an instance of the self-knowledge that characterizes an agent.[11] It is true, and for some purposes it would be important to stress, that if one compels him to *say* what he thus knows, in response to the question "What are you doing?," one will break the flow. If he has only a second for the next move, he does not have time to respond to a request for an expression of his self-knowledge in making his present move. But he has that self-knowledge, even if it goes unexpressed and even if he does not explicitly think its content – as he does not, unless the flow is broken. At the price of breaking the flow, he can say straight off, without any need for reflection or investigation, what he is doing – certainly at the level of, for instance, "I am moving this bishop," and perhaps also at levels that bring in a wider intentional context, as in "I am threatening my opponent's queen." I have granted that if he *does* say such things, he is no longer acting in flow. But if he says such things, he gives expression to knowledge he already had when he was acting in flow. The self-knowledge that such sayings express does not come into being only when it is expressed. And, as the form of the sayings brings out, what is known in a bit of knowledge of this kind is an instance of the "I do."

## 4

The Myth of Mind as Detached also shapes, to its disadvantage, Dreyfus's understanding of acting for reasons. It leads him to think, and to think I think, that someone can be acting for a reason only if her action issues from distanced critical reflection on the situation in which she is acting.

As Dreyfus insists, that is not how it is with the chess master playing lightning chess, or with an ideal exemplar of the virtue of kindness. He writes:

> [T]he chess master is directly drawn by the forces on the board to make a masterful move, and, in the same way, the kind person, as Sartre sees, is directly drawn to act by the force of the needy person's apparent need. In neither case does the master make his move *for a reason*.[12]

I agree (of course) that the actions of the lightning chess player and the ideally kind person do not issue from a distanced critical relation to the situations in which they act. But on a much better conception of what it is to act for reasons, which becomes available to us when we discard the Myth of Mind as Detached, both of them *do* act for reasons. The chess master's being drawn to make his move by the forces on the board is his cultivated rationality at work. And the kind person's being drawn to respond to the other person's need for help is his cultivated rationality at work. Dreyfus assumes that acting for reasons, acting in a way that is rationality in operation, is restricted to cases in which an agent deliberates about what to do and acts in the light of the result. But that assumption is not mine, and I think it should be rejected.

The distinctive self-knowledge of an agent is not only knowledge of *what* she is doing, but also knowledge of *why* she is doing it, on an interpretation on which one answers the "Why?" question by giving a reason for which one is acting.[13] And this self-knowledge is present when agents are acting in flow, no less than when action issues from a distanced rational relation to the situation. As with the "What?" question, if we compel an agent who is acting in flow to answer the "Why?" question, that will break the flow. But here again, that does not matter. What matters is that the agent can answer the "Why?" question straight off, without any need for reflection or investigation. As with the "What?" question, such an answer gives expression to something she already knew when she was acting in flow, in an instance of the self-knowledge that characterizes an agent.

Consider again the chess master absorbed in lightning chess. Dreyfus says, "the [chess] master could only respond to the demand for a reason by saying 'I made the move because I was drawn to make it.'"[14] And he suggests that in saying this, the chess master would be confessing an inability to give a rational explanation of his move, and that this shows that rationality is not pervasive.

But on an understanding of what it is to act for reasons that is not shaped by the Myth of Mind as Detached, things look very different. As I said, the chess master's responding to the forces on the board is his rationality at work. If he explains his move as a response to the forces on the board, as Dreyfus of course accepts that he can, he is giving a rational explanation of it.

Moreover, if he really is a master, it must be within his powers to be more specific. We can expect him to be able to say such things as this: "It's a good move, because it threatens my opponent's queen." As before, we cannot compel him to talk about his move without breaking the flow. But as before, that does not matter. He will be saying things he already knew while he was acting in flow.

And suppose someone queries whether his move is a good one, perhaps suggesting that it leaves him vulnerable to a counter that strengthens his opponent's position. If he really is a master, he will be able to engage with this, perhaps saying something on these lines: "That isn't a good counter; if he makes that move, I can get into a strong position with this riposte: ... " That would be to continue a conversation of which one possible terminus would be his saying something like this: "I see that my move wasn't as good, in the light of the forces on the board, as it struck me as being."

Of course the chess master will need to break the flow in order to engage in this kind of conversation, and in this analysis of possible continuations of the game it is no longer plausible that he is merely giving expression to things he already knew when he was acting in flow. But the fact that the conversation breaks the flow is still irrelevant. As I have insisted, he is giving expression to something he already knew if he explains his move as a response to the forces on the board, and that is to give a rational explanation of it; his response to the forces on the board is a rational response. And the knowledge of why he is making his move, which he can express by citing the forces on the board, cannot be insulated from the ability he has, chess master that he is, to consider how cogent a justification the forces on the board provide for his move – the ability that would be on display in the sort of conversation I have envisaged. This brings out how right it is to insist, as I have, that his being drawn by the forces on the board, even in lightning chess, is his rationality in operation. The cultivated rationality that would be manifested in a conversation about possible continuations of the game is also operative in his being drawn to make his move by the forces on the board, in a mode of play in which there is no time for analysis. On a sane conception of what acting for a reason is, a conception we bring within our reach by discarding the Myth of Mind as Detached, the master *is* acting for a reason when he makes his move in response to the forces on the board.

Even when absorbed in lightning chess, the master has the self-understanding that characterizes a rational agent. He knows what he is up to; he knows what he is doing and why.

In our previous exchange, I offered, as a simple example of how rationality pervades the action of rational agents, a case in which a person catches a Frisbee on the spur of the moment. Catching a Frisbee is something a dog can do, and of course a dog's exercising its ability to do that is not informed by rationality. But when a rational animal, a human adult, catches a Frisbee she is exercising a capacity that belongs to her rationality; she is realizing a concept of a thing to do. Even if she does not have the concept of a Frisbee, there is a concept that she is realizing, perhaps the concept of catching *this*. (I was imagining a situation in which what is in fact a Frisbee is flying towards the person as she walks across a park.) I wrote:

> The point of saying that the rational agent, unlike the dog, is realizing a concept in doing what she does is that her doing, under a

specification that captures the content of the practical concept that she is realizing, comes within the scope of her practical rationality – even if only in that, if asked why she caught the Frisbee, she would answer "No particular reason; I just felt like it."[15]

Now Dreyfus assimilates the chess master acting in flow to my Frisbee catcher. He suggests that both are unable to give a reason for what they do, and he speculates that I might try to save the pervasiveness claim by claiming that this supposedly shared inability to give reasons is the null case, and so still in the space of reasons. But the appearance of a similarity between these cases is just another reflection of how the Myth of Mind as Detached distorts Dreyfus's conception of acting for reasons, and consequently skews his understanding of my position.

The case of the Frisbee catcher is indeed a limiting case of practical rationality at work, a limiting case of the knowledge of what one is up to – knowledge of what one is doing and why – that characterizes a rational agent. The Frisbee catcher acknowledges that the question "Why?" is appropriately directed at her in respect of her catching the Frisbee (or, in the variant, catching *that*), and that is to say she acknowledges that in doing that she is acting intentionally. As I put it, in doing that she is realizing a concept of a thing to do. Her acknowledgment that the question is appropriate is implicit in her giving what we might describe as a null answer to it (like "None" in response to the question "How much money do you have in your pocket?") – as opposed to responding in a way that constitutes a rejection of the question, for instance, by saying "Oh, I didn't know I was doing that."

The chess master is quite different. He has a nonlimiting case of knowledge of what he is up to. As I have explained, once we discard the idea that rational self-knowledge can be had only from a detached standpoint, we can recognize that he is making his moves in self-consciously rational response to the forces on the board. That his move is his response to the forces on the board is a nonnull answer to the "Why?" question.

It is only in cases of casual or, as we might say, aimless action, like catching a Frisbee on the spur of the moment, that the response to a request for one's reason for acting can be the null response, "No particular reason."[16] The Frisbee catcher's null response is not at all like the chess master's response to the request for his reason, that the forces on the board drew him to make his move. Even at the level of an unspecific citing of the forces on the board, the chess master's response to the request for his reason is not a null response.

There is no trivialization here. One does not trivialize the idea of a pervasive rationality if one acknowledges the possibility of limiting cases, such as the case of the casual Frisbee catcher. Acting in flow, as exemplified by the chess master playing lightning chess, is *not* a limiting case of rationality in operation.

Dreyfus says that the chess master's and the Frisbee catcher's responses to requests for their reasons for doing what they do "do not contribute to adjusting their *thinking* to experience."[17] And he seems to think this constitutes a ground for denying that "spontaneity as McDowell defines it" is operative in their responding as they do.[18] I find it mysterious how this can have struck him as telling against my picture.

What he would need to argue in order to reject the pervasiveness thesis is that conceptual capacities are not operative in the chess master's or the Frisbee catcher's *acting* as they do. (Surely it is obvious that conceptual capacities are operative in their meaningful responses to requests for their reasons.) Of course it is true that these agents are not adjusting their thinking to experience, either in responding as they do to requests for their reasons – the topic Dreyfus oddly focuses on – or in acting as they do, the topic that, as far as I can see, he ought to be focusing on. But that does nothing to show that conceptual capacities are not in play in their exercises of agency, which is what Dreyfus would need to show in order to take issue with the pervasiveness thesis as applied to acting. In my treatment of *experience* (not acting), I exploit the idea that adjusting one's thinking to experience is an exercise of the faculty that conceptual capacities belong to; that is a way of bringing out why the faculty is appropriately described as a faculty of spontaneity. But that is not to give a definition of spontaneity, as Dreyfus implies. And I do not claim that capacities that belong to the faculty, appropriately so described, are operative only when one is adjusting one's thinking to experience. That is not my picture of the actualization of conceptual capacities in experience, where the idea of adjusting our thinking to experience does have a role. And the idea of adjusting our thinking to experience has no role in my picture of the realization of conceptual capacities in intentional action.

## 5

As I noted, null responses to the "Why?" question – "No particular reason" and the like – need to be distinguished from rejections of the question, notably "I didn't know I was doing that." If someone is doing something that she does not know she is doing, as can of course happen, her doing *that* falls outside the scope of the pervasiveness thesis as it applies to acting.

This is how it is, typically, with movements that are explicable in terms of our being drawn to stand at the culturally appropriate distance from conversation partners, fellow occupants of elevators, and so forth. As Dreyfus himself says, we are not aware of what we are doing in the movements that place us at the appropriate distance from relevant others. Suppose someone asks: "Why did you take a step back at that point in the conversation?" The response "Oh, did I? I wasn't aware of doing that" – if it is truthful – shows that the backward step was not an exercise of agency in the sense that involves the agent's knowing what she is doing and why. It is not a counterinstance to the pervasiveness thesis, but falls outside its scope.

In trying to make trouble for me over this kind of feature of our social comportment, Dreyfus mischaracterizes my use of the idea of second nature. He says: "McDowell follows Sellars in restricting second nature to rational behavior."[19] But so far as I know, Sellars does not exploit the idea of second nature. I do, but I do not restrict it to operations of rationality, though I appeal to it only in that context. The concept of second nature applies to any responsive propensities that are not inborn or provided for by ordinary biological maturation but acquired through, for instance, training. Obedience to commands is second nature to a trained dog, and of course it does not involve rationality. As I said, it is true that I appeal to second nature only in connection with rationality; that is because it is only in connection with rationality that we face the supposed problem I try to disarm by appealing to second nature. If we recognize that the capacity to respond to reasons is second nature to those who have it, we are immunized against any tendency to suppose that we must explicate responsiveness to reasons in restrictively naturalistic terms, on pain of being forced to conceive it as unnatural or supernatural.[20] But to say that responsiveness to reasons is second nature to those who have it is not to imply that nothing else is second nature to them. In fact it seems obvious that the dispositions that are operative in distance standing are second nature to those who have them. This leaves untouched the point that the movements that manifest those dispositions are outside the scope of the pervasiveness thesis.

Of course these dispositions are culturally formed. That does nothing to bring their manifestations within the scope of the pervasiveness thesis. The pervasiveness thesis as it applies to action is that our rationality informs our exercises of agency. There is no implication that nothing else besides our rationality has any role in determining anything that we can truly be said to do. It is no problem for the pervasiveness thesis that in some movements we make (for instance, in a conversation), we are responsive – without being aware of it, as Dreyfus himself says – to culturally instituted norms of distance standing. The pervasiveness thesis does not imply that informedness by rationality reaches to every aspect of everything we do. Rationality need not inform the steps backward and the like that reflect our responsiveness to the norms of distance standing, any more than it need inform, for instance, its being with the right hand that most human beings, other things being equal, will reach for something they have occasion to pick up. In one and not the other of these cases we have responsiveness to a cultural norm, but that makes no difference to the fact that neither is a counterinstance to the pervasiveness thesis properly understood.

## 6

Up to this point I have considered the two major areas of application for the pervasiveness thesis, experience and agency, separately so far as possible. (Dreyfus sometimes conflates my treatments of them, as in the remark I considered at the end of §4, p. 50.) But it would be wrong to think these two areas of application for the thesis are simply separate. A subject of experience is an agent who has to act in the world she experiences. A practically disinterested orientation towards reality is a rare and special phenomenon in human life.

Here too the Myth of Mind as Detached distorts Dreyfus's understanding of my view. If I accepted the Myth, it would be true that I "[pass] over the world of ... absorbed coping," as he says I do.[21] And in that case there might seem to be some go in the idea that for me the world as a subject's experience discloses it to her is devoid of intrinsic practical significance, capable of impinging on her practical rationality only in that the facts that constitute such a world can figure in deliberation about what she should do, guided or controlled by independent motivational states. But I do not accept the Myth, and I agree with Dreyfus and Merleau-Ponty that the world of the absorbed coper – in fact the world of agents in general, whether they are acting reflectively or not – is richly populated with solicitations to act.

Dreyfus knows at least some of my writing about virtue. But he seems to have considered that work of mine only with a view to reading into it the idea – which, as I have pointed out, is not mine – that the cultivated rationality of virtuous agents is limited to actions that issue from explicit deliberation about what to do. He seems not to have noticed that part of my agenda in that area of my work is precisely to attack a conception according to which the world in which one acts is normatively inert. I did not use the term "solicitations," but it would have been appropriate in setting out the picture I was trying to give. In my picture, actions that manifest virtue are responses to *requirements* to act that agents confront in the situations they act in, so that if one fails to act as virtue requires, without being prevented, that reveals at least partial blindness to facts about the world.

In our previous exchange I protested against Dreyfus's saddling me with a conception of the world as normatively inert.[22] But, resolutely reading into my picture the assumption that rationality necessarily involves detachment, Dreyfus ignores my protest, and goes on saying things like this: "In general, McDowell thinks of the world in largely descriptive terms" (see Box 1.1) – this in supposed contrast with Merleau-Ponty, who thinks of the world of the absorbed agent as "a web of attractions and repulsions."[23] Let me say again:

> Openness to the world is enjoyed by subjects who are essentially agents. What they are open to is not restricted to objects of disinterested contemplation.[24]

Dreyfus persists in attributing to me a picture that contradicts this, but that is because even in the face of my denials he goes on reading my thinking in terms of the Myth of Mind as Detached. As I have been insisting, the idea that rational mindedness always involves detachment is his assumption, not mine.

Dreyfus asks: "How could our conceptual capacity be *always* operative?"[25] And he goes on: "Since concepts devoted to getting it right about a distanced reality decouple us from the world of normative forces, it would seem that concepts must precisely *not* be always operative."[26]

But this presupposes something I deny: that our conceptual capacities are, just as such and in all their actualizations, distanced. A *capacity* to step back from situations and consider whether features of them constitute reasons for thinking or acting in this or that way is a central element in what it is to have conceptual capacities at all. But that is not to say that the capacity for distance is actualized whenever conceptual capacities are in play. Exactly not: the capacity for distance is *not* actualized in unreflective perceptual experience or in unreflective intentional agency, but conceptual capacities are operative in both.

Actualizing the capacity for distance would indeed undermine absorbed coping; it would, as Dreyfus puts it, decouple us from the world of normative forces to which the absorbed coper directly responds. Chuck Knoblauch exemplifies this. He lost his skill of throwing efficiently to first base, because he actualized the capacity for distance that is an element in having conceptual capacities at all, in respect of the concept of throwing to first base, which he was formerly able to realize unreflectively. His trouble came when he started thinking about the mechanics of throwing to first base, and thereby distanced himself from the situational requirements to which a skilled second baseman responds unreflectively.

But that leaves untouched my claim that when Knoblauch still had his skill and exercised it, he was exercising a conceptual capacity, in the sense that is relevant to my pervasiveness thesis. He was realizing a concept of a thing to do. He knew what he was doing – throwing to first base – and why – to get the runner out. Dreyfus's idea that conceptual capacities must not be operative in skilled action is just a reflection of the Myth of Mind as Detached, with its implication, which I deny, that just any actualization of conceptual capacities distances the subject from the world.[27]

## 7

I would not dream of disputing that there is an important difference between absorbed coping, on the one hand, and, on the other, acting in response to deliberation about what to do, or reflectively adjusting one's thinking to experience. I can even acknowledge that there is a sense in which the capacity for absorbed coping is a foundation for the capacity to deliberate about what to think or what to do. (I shall come back to this.)

My claim is that capacities that are conceptual, capacities that belong to their possessor's rationality, are operative not only in reflective thought and action but also at the ground-floor level at which there is absorbed coping and acting in flow. I have been unable to get Dreyfus to engage with this claim. As he interprets me, it cannot be the ground-floor level that I am talking about. He thinks I "pass over" the ground-floor level. Evidently he thinks the very meaning of terms like "conceptual" and "belonging to their possessor's rationality" establishes that capacities that those terms apply to can be in play only in detached intellectual activity. But that is not how I use such terms.

The issue here is not about the proper use of "conceptual" or "rational." Of course Dreyfus is free to use those expressions as he pleases. But so long as he goes on assuming that I share with him a use that restricts operations of conceptual capacities (capacities that belong to rationality) to their exercise in detached intellectual activity, so that the very meaning of the expressions establishes that such capacities cannot be operative at the ground-floor level, he is simply not engaging with my picture. For a substantive objection to my picture, Dreyfus would need to confront the idea of a repertoire of capacities that are in play not only in explicit deliberation about what to think or what to do but also in the absorbed coping that occupies the ground floor. But he proceeds as if it were common ground that actualizations of capacities that belong to rationality always involve detachment, and the result is that the idea he would need to confront never comes into view for him.

In the early stages of this conversation, Dreyfus characterized the level he claimed I could not accommodate in terms of bodily skills we share with "animals." (As if we were not animals.) This gave me no trouble; of course there are things both we and nonrational animals can do, for instance, unreflectively avoiding obstacles in making our way around, but that is consistent with holding that in our case doing such things is our rationality in operation, as it cannot be in the case of nonrational animals.

Dreyfus now seems to have dropped that way of posing his objection to me. He does not suggest that a human agent in flow approximates to the condition of a nonrational animal absorbed in its activity. On the contrary, he acknowledges that even at the ground-floor level human activity is distinctively human.[28] And that is well accommodated by the idea of a repertoire of capacities that are in play not only at upper levels but also on the ground floor. Human beings are rational animals. What could be more natural than to hold that capacities that belong to what differentiates human beings from other animals, their rationality, are operative in activity that is essentially human, including activity at the ground-floor level?

The norms of distance standing are culturally instituted, and perhaps as such distinctively human. But as I argued, distance standing does not come within the scope of the pervasiveness thesis; it is not a ground-floor phenomenon in the relevant sense. The pervasiveness thesis, put in the terms I am working with here, is that the differentia of rational animals informs their experience, in so far as their experience puts them in a position to know things, and informs their intentional acting. The distinctively human character of distance standing is no more relevant to the pervasiveness thesis than is, say, the distinctively human character of the things a Xhosa speaker does with her tongue and palate in sounding those click consonants.

I said I would come back to my acknowledgment of a sense in which the ground-floor level is a foundation for higher levels. There could not be a subject whose every cognitive and practical move included discursive activity; discursive activity figures only in lives that also include absorbed coping. But the dependence goes in the other direction also. Unreflectively absorbed experiencing and acting characterize the lives of rational animals only because they are engaged in by subjects that also reflect about what to think and what to do.

This is particularly striking in the case of experience. As I said in §2, much of what experience gives to a rational subject to know is not within her powers of deciding what to think, without a further step of equipping herself with means to make the relevant content explicit in judgment. But the capacities that are actualized in those aspects of an experience are already conceptual in the relevant sense; the content an experience has by virtue of its being those capacities that are actualized in it is already content of a kind that fits it to be annexed to ways of making things explicit. And such content cannot figure in a subject's life unless it is a life that includes judging. Similarly, unreflective action can instantiate the "I do" only because it is engaged in by a subject who on other occasions explicitly decides what to do.

Dreyfus finds a Cartesian flavor in my picture; he says I accept "the Cartesian separation between the world and the perceivers and agents to whom the world is given."[29] But this just reflects his reading me through the lens of the Myth of Mind as Detached.

What does have a Cartesian character is the assumption whose grip on Dreyfus's thinking prevents him from hearing the pervasiveness thesis as I mean it: the assumption that rational mindedness is always detached, so that it must be absent from the absorbed coping that occupies the ground floor. If there were the connection Dreyfus assumes between rationality and detachment, rationality could only be externally related to the characteristic phenomena of animal life as they figure in the lives of human beings; in particular, it could only be externally related to our sensory awareness and our moving of our limbs. That would mean that the only role for a rational subject in human life would be that of a detached I that deliberates about what to think and do, responding to contents externally provided for it by sensory awareness, and initiating and supervising bodily movements from a position outside them. And that is a markedly Cartesian picture of how rationality relates to the animal phenomena that figure in the lives of human beings.

We definitively avoid this echo of Cartesian thinking if we hold that the rational capacities that can be deliberatively exercised with explicit self-consciousness are operative also at the ground-floor level. The subject of unreflective experience is the I of the "I think," and the agent of absorbed activity is the I of the "I do." When the "I think" accompanies a representation or the "I do" becomes explicit, that does not bring rationality newly into the picture, as an external adjunct to sensory awareness and movements of limbs. Our rational mindedness is *in* our sensory awareness and intentional bodily movements, whether or not they are explicitly self-conscious.

I will end by repeating what I said at the end of my previous contribution to this conversation:

> If we let our conception of mindedness be controlled by the thought that mindedness is operative even in our unreflective perceiving and acting, we can regain an integrated conception of ourselves as animals, and – what comes with that – beings whose life is pervasively bodily, but of a distinctively rational kind.[30]

## Notes

Thanks to Hubert Dreyfus for starting and continuing this conversation, to James Conant for organizing the workshop on the nature of practical intelligence held at the Wissenschaftskolleg zu Berlin in May 2009, to the Wissenschaftskolleg for its hospitality, and to the other participants in the workshop for their contributions.

1 In McDowell, *Mind and World*. In that work I reserved the term "experience" for something enjoyed exclusively by rational subjects, and thus needed a different way of talking for the sensory awareness of their environment had by non-rational animals. Here I am attributing a special form of experience to rational subjects. The divergence between these two ways of putting things is only terminological.

2 See §36 of Sellars, "Empiricism and the Philosophy of Mind." The point is not that the word "know" applies only to the kind of knowledge that is a standing in the space of reasons. There need be no implication that nonrational animals can be said to know things only by a kind of courtesy. But their knowledge is not of the kind that is characteristic of rational animals, and that is the kind that our experience makes available to us.

3 Dreyfus is not always careful about this, for instance, when, in purporting to describe my view, he moves freely between talk of conceptuality and talk of

conceptual *activity*. The involvement of conceptual capacities in experience, on my account, is exactly not a matter of activity on the part of the subject.
4 See "What Myth?," pp. 347–48; and, for a bit more elaboration, "Avoiding the Myth of the Given."
5 *Mind and World*, p. 57.
6 Dreyfus, this volume, p. 17.
7 The clause "what ensures that thoughts ... have the necessary distance ... " is in apposition to, and elaborates the significance of, the clause "what ensures that it is a concept." My sentence gives two specifications of what is ensured by the capacity's persisting beyond the occasion of the experience. It does not purport to say what a concept is.
8 Dreyfus, this volume, p. 28.
9 "Response to Dreyfus,", p. 367.
10 Dreyfus, this volume, p. 28.
11 This kind of self-knowledge is a central theme in Anscombe, *Intention*.
12 Dreyfus, this volume, p. 35.
13 Again, the relevance of this "Why?" question to the topic of intentional action is a central theme of Anscombe's *Intention*. Anscombe does not identify the relevant sense of the question in terms of its being a request for a reason. It is that, but she wants to use the question as a way into understanding a battery of concepts including that of a reason for acting, and given that purpose it would be question-begging to exploit the idea of a reason in specifying the relevant sense of the question. See *Intention*, p. 10. My purposes here do not require this self-denial.
14 Dreyfus, this volume, p. 35.
15 McDowell, "Response to Dreyfus," p. 369.
16 See Anscombe, *Intention*, pp. 26–28. In such cases, there is nothing wrong with the null response. Contrast Dreyfus's suggestion that the null response constitutes an admission of inability to do something one ought to be able to do.
17 Dreyfus, this volume, p. 35.
18 Ibid.
19 Ibid., p. 23.
20 Dreyfus seems not to have understood my appeal to second nature. He says: "McDowell ... seems obliged to understand all human activity as either in the space of shaped natural reactions, or in the space of reasons" (Dreyfus, this volume, p. 26). But the point of my appeal to second nature is that activity in the space of reasons *is* in the space of shaped natural reactions; that is how I disarm the idea that we must accept a restrictive naturalism if we are to avoid conceiving responsiveness to reasons as unnatural or supernatural. I think this confusion underlies Dreyfus's objection to my remark that the dispositions operative in distance standing constitute a culturally formed instinct.
21 Dreyfus, this volume, p. 22. Dreyfus says "nonconceptual absorbed coping," but that is just a reflection of his assuming that the agent of any coping that was a realization of conceptual capacities would have to be detached and so could not be absorbed – the assumption that I am protesting against.
22 See McDowell, "Response to Dreyfus," p. 369.
23 Dreyfus, "Return of the Myth of the Mental," p. 357.
24 McDowell, "Response to Dreyfus," p. 369.
25 Dreyfus, this volume, p. 23.
26 Ibid.
27 See my discussion of Dreyfus's attempt to make trouble for me with the Knoblauch case in "Response to Dreyfus," pp. 367–68.

28 Dreyfus accepted something on these lines in the discussion at the Berlin meeting.
29 Dreyfus, this volume, p. 17.
30 "Response to Dreyfus," p. 370.

## Bibliography

Anscombe, G. E. M., *Intention*, 2nd edn, Cambridge, MA: Harvard University Press, 2000.

Dreyfus, H., "The Return of the Myth of the Mental," *Inquiry* 50, no. 4 (2007): 352–65.

McDowell, J., "Avoiding the Myth of the Given," in *Having the World in View: Essays on Kant, Hegel, and Sellars*, Cambridge, MA: Harvard University Press, 2009, pp. 256–72.

——, *Mind and World*, Cambridge, MA: Harvard University Press, 1994; 2nd edn, 1996.

——, "Response to Dreyfus," *Inquiry* 50, no. 4 (2007): 366–70.

——, "What Myth?" *Inquiry* 50, no. 4 (2007): 338–51.

Sellars, W., "Empiricism and the Philosophy of Mind," in *Science, Perception, and Reality*, London: Routledge & Kegan Paul, 1963.

# Part II

# FROM KANT TO EXISTENTIAL PHENOMENOLOGY

# 3

# RETRIEVING REALISM

## Charles Taylor

### 1

"Ein *Bild* hielt uns gefangen." So speaks Wittgenstein in §115 of the *Philosophical Investigations*.[1] What he is referring to is the powerful picture of mind-in-world which inhabits and underlies what we could call the modern epistemological tradition, which begins with Descartes. The point he wants to convey with the use of the word *"Bild"* is that there is something here different and deeper than a theory. It is a largely unreflected background understanding which provides the context for, and thus influences all our theorizing in this area. The claim could be interpreted as saying that the mainline epistemological thinking which descends from Descartes has been contained within, hence shaped by this not fully explicit picture – that this has been a kind of captivity, because it has prevented us from seeing what is wrong with this whole line of thought. At certain points, we are unable to think "outside the box," because the picture seems so obvious, so commonsensical, so unchallengeable.[2]

To identify the picture would be to grasp a big mistake, something like a framework mistake, which distorts our understanding, and at the same time prevents us from seeing this distortion for what it is.

I think Wittgenstein was right about this. There is a big mistake operating in our culture, a kind of operative (mis)understanding of what it is to know, which has had dire effects on both theory and practice in a host of domains. To sum it up in a pithy formula, we might say that we (mis)understand knowledge as "mediational." In its original form, this emerged in the idea that we grasp external reality through internal representations. Descartes in one of his letters declared himself "assuré que je ne puis avoir aucune connaissance de ce qui est hors de moi, que par l'entremise des idées que j'ai eu en moi."[3] This sentence makes sense against a certain topology of mind and world. The reality I want to know is outside the mind; my knowledge of it is within. This knowledge consists in states of mind which purport to represent accurately what is out there. When they do correctly and reliably represent this reality, then there is knowledge. I have knowledge of things only through (*par l'entremise de*) these inner states, which we can call "ideas."

I want to call this picture "mediational," because of the force of the claim which emerges in the crucial phrase "only through." In knowledge I have a kind of contact with outer reality, but I get this only through some inner states. One crucial aspect of the picture which is being taken as given here, and is thus on the road to being hardened into an unchallengeable context, is the inner/outer structure. The reality we seek to grasp is outside, the states whereby we seek to grasp it are inside. The mediating elements here are "ideas," inner representations; and so the picture in this variant could be called "representational." But this, as we shall see, is not the only variant. This particular version has been challenged, but what has often escaped attention is the deeper topology which gives the unnoticed context for both the original version and the challenges.

This last point is the hardest one to make convincing. In all sorts of ways, Descartes passes in contemporary philosophy for a much-refuted thinker. His way of making the inner–outer distinction was via a radical differentiation between physical and mental substances, and this dualism has very few defenders today. Moreover, the mediating element, the idea, this particulate content of the mind, available to introspection, seems dubious, and worse, irrelevant to most contemporary accounts of knowledge. And one could go on in the litany of rejections.

And yet, something essential remains. Take the "linguistic turn." For many philosophers today, if we wanted to give the contents of the mind, we should have recourse not to little images in the mind, but rather to something like sentences held true by an agent, or more colloquially the person's beliefs. This shift is important, but it keeps the mediational structure intact. The mediating element is no longer something psychic, but rather "linguistic." This allows it in a way to be "outside," in the sense of the Cartesian distinction, because sentences circulate in public space, between speakers. But in another way, in that the sentence's being held true is a fact about individual speakers, and their (often unvoiced) thoughts, we recreate the same basic pattern: the reality is out there, the holdings true are in minds; we have knowledge when these beliefs (sentences held true) reliably correspond to the reality; we have knowledge through the beliefs. (Knowledge is "justified, true belief.")

Then take the materialist turn. We deny Cartesian dualism, by denying one of its terms. There is no "mental substance," everything is matter, and thinking itself arises out of matter. This is the kind of position which Quine espoused, for instance. And yet Quine recreated a similar structure in the new metaphysical context. Our knowledge comes to us through "surface irritations," the points in our receptors where the various stimuli from the environment impinge. It is these which are the basis of our knowledge. Alternatively, he sometimes takes the immediate description of what is impinging, observation sentences, as basic, and he sees the edifice of science as built under the requirement that shows how (most of) these hold. In either variant, there is a mediational, or "only through," structure here. The proof of the indeterminacy of translation, of the uncertainty of reference, of the plurality of scientific accounts, comes from considerations that the choice between different ontological or scientific postulates will always remain not fully determined by these basic starting points.

"Inner" is being given a materialist sense here, in this "naturalized epistemology." Our knowledge of the external world comes in "through" the receptors, and so they define the boundary only in a "scientific," and not a "metaphysical," way. Similarly, we see the Cartesian structure repeated in various conjectures about a brain in a vat, which might be fooled into thinking that it was really in an embodied agent in a world, as long as a fiendish scientist was giving it the right input. Just as the old epistemology worried that as long as the contents of our minds remain the same, some evil demon might be controlling the input so that the world could change without our being any the wiser, so contemporaries reedit a structurally similar nightmare around the brain. This has become the material replacement of the mind, supposedly because it is what causally underlies thinking. The mediational structure, and the mediating interface of inputs (now controlled by the fiendish scientist), and hence a parallel "only through" claim, all survive the "materialist" transposition.

If one asks the proponent of the brain-in-the-vat hypothesis why he focuses on the brain, he will reply something to the effect that thinking "supervenes on" the brain. But how does he know this? How do we know that you don't need more than the brain, maybe the brain and nervous system, or maybe even the whole organism, or (more likely) the whole organism in its environment, in order to get what we understand as perception and thinking? The answer is that no one knows. The brain-in-the-vat hypothesis only looks plausible because of the force of the mediational structure, our captivity in the picture implicit in modern epistemology, which requires something to play the role of "inside."

Let's take another transposition, the critical turn. I mean the shift inaugurated by Kant. Here the basic relation is no longer the picture-like internal representation and outer reality. Rather what Kant calls "representation" (*Vorstellung*) often seems to be the same as outer (empirical) reality. But these representations can only arise where the stuff of intuition – which comes in another sense from "outside," in that it is something we receive, as we are "affected" (*affiziert*) by things – is shaped by the categories which are the products of our minds. The "only through" claim here takes a rather different form. It is only through the shaping of the categories that our intuitions furnish objects for us, that there is experience and knowledge. Without the concepts which we provide, intuition would be "blind." "Inner," "outer," and "only through" all take on new meanings (indeed, in the case of the first two, more than one meaning) in Kant's work. But the basic structure survives. That the continuity here is a significant and fateful one will emerge later in the discussion.

We can already see that the underlying picture of epistemology still holds a lot more captives than the critics of Cartesian dualism, or mentalism, or "foundationalism" usually realize. Indeed, it holds many of these very critics in its thrall. We shall see later that even many who declare themselves "postmoderns" have not escaped the prison. I hope this will become evident later in the argument. But for the moment we should just bear in mind that various forms of skepticism about the powers of the mind and the reach of science have not been absent from the tradition. It was born in an argument against skepticism (Descartes); and it has had its famous skeptical turns (Hume, not to speak of Quine's ontological relativity). Why this had to be so will be discussed later. For the moment, I must be content with the hints at a deep continuity which I have offered in the preceding paragraphs.

## 2

The connection between skepticism and modern epistemology is plain at the very beginning, in the work of Descartes. He uses skepticism, we might say, not to further a skeptic's agenda, but to establish his own topology of self, mind, and world. The reader is bludgeoned in the first *Meditation* with the full barrage of skeptical argument. The point is not, as with the ancients, or more recently Montaigne, to get us to realize how little we know. On the contrary, the argument will end with the most daring and far-reaching claims to certainty. The strategic point of these opening arguments is to force us to distinguish between inner and outer, between the reality of bodily things, and that of the contents of the mind. When we realize how vulnerable our supposedly reliable knowledge of external reality is to skeptical arguments, and then later come to see that what we cannot doubt is the content of our own "ideas," we will be cured forever of that muddled elision of bodily and mental, which arises from the substantial union of body and mind, but which is the major source of obscure and confused thought.

This major difference of strategic goal is what marks Descartes off from his sources for Meditation I, the ancient thinkers of the Pyrrhonian tradition. Descartes' assimilation of their arguments has led us to forget how different was their enterprise, even though some near contemporaries, like Montaigne, were still in continuity with ancient thought, and even though, one might add, there was a partial recovery of this older way of thinking with Hume.

The point of ancient skepticism was to show us how little we really could claim to know. For every type of claim to knowledge, a counterclaim could be made to seem plausible. Do we think we can be sure of the existence of physical objects around us? Well, how about the stick which looks bent in water? and so on. In all these cases, reflection shows us that the issue is ultimately undecidable. "*Isostheneia*" reigns, that is, both sides are equally weak. So you can't have real knowledge.

What was the point of showing this? Our goal in life is serenity, a state of "*ataraxia*" or untroubledness. But to achieve this, we have to give up on unattainable goals, like sure science. But don't we need some knowledge of things to go about living our lives? This was the criticism which seems to have occurred frequently to nonphilosophers in the ancient world, if we judge by the stories of philosophers who bumped into walls, or fell into wells. The skeptics' answer was that we have all that we need in the way things look to us. If we follow these appearances, we will usually fare well. We don't need to seek on top of this some scientific certainty that the appearances track "reality."

Not only do we not need this, and not only will it needlessly agitate us to try vainly to seek it, but Sextus Empiricus argues that such knowledge, were we to have it, would only disturb our serenity. His claim is that any belief that something is by nature good or bad leads to perturbation, making us want it when we don't have it, and fear losing it when we do have it. Of course, you can be cold or thirsty, but you make things worse by opining that what you suffer is evil by nature.[4]

What these arguments do for you is that they bring about a kind of conversion, whereby from an anxious seeker after truth, you become capable of suspending judgment, and then living without scientific certainty, "*adoxasts*."

The "appearances" here being appealed to can easily be identified with Descartes' "ideas." But this is a mistake, as Burnyeat argues.[5] This is because "appearances" don't make up an ontologically defined class, over against realities. They are more like: the way things look to us at some moment, rather than a particular kind of mental content. Indeed, there is no need to place this way-things-look in the mind at all. The stick looking bent in water could be equally seen as a feature of sticks-in-water. Or else the appearance can be the way we feel as ensouled bodies, e.g. cold, hot, in pain, etc. *Phainomena*, *phantasiai*, don't always mean sensibles (*aisthêta*). For they cover e.g. the *phantasia* that not all *phantasiai* are true, or the conclusion of the skeptics' argument that everything is relative.[6]

The distinction applies to the supposed epistemic status of how things look, whether they ever deserve the more honorific condition of real knowledge. It doesn't establish *phantasiai* as a particular kind of entity. But this is exactly what Descartes sets out to do. It is crucial to his argument to establish "ideas" as a particular kind of inner, mental entity, which are marked out from the external ones in that they are in certain respects immune to skeptical argument. It is an important stage in Descartes' argument to show that one can have certain knowledge about appearances. That is why the ontological indeterminacy of the ancient *phantasia* has to be cleared up. My feeling cold or hot or in pain has to be ontologically segmented into an external, physical condition of low or high temperature, or tissue damage, on one hand, and some inner, purely mental impression on the other. Descartes replaces the traditional ancient topology of the soul, which is tripartite: *aesthêsis*, *phantasia*, *nous* (sensation, imagination, intellect, *entendement*) with the new single chamber in which everything appears together. Rorty describes this as the "notion of a single inner space in which bodily and perceptual sensations, ... mathematical truths, moral rules, the idea of God, moods of depression, and all the rest of what we now call 'mental' were objects of quasi-observation."[7]

This corresponds to the new generic term: *cogitare*, *penser*, which subsumes the full range of psychic states beneath it: "Qu'est-ce qu'une chose qui pense? C'est-à-dire une chose qui doute, qui conçoit, qui affirme, qui nie, qui veut, qui ne veut pas, qui imagine aussi, et qui sent."[8] The senses and imagination are now distinguished in that they are the source of some of these *cogitationes* and not others, and realizing this shows us how to treat them, and what confidence we should repose in them. But there is only one locus where all appear.

By the same token this single locus is radically distinct from the body, where the ancient loci were distinguished by their greater or lesser degree of interpenetration with our bodily existence. A new, and radical dualism has been established, which I want to call in the further stages of my argument the "dualist sorting."

Why is this important for Descartes's strategy? Because, by carving out ideas as a particular kind of thing, one whose *esse* is *percipi*, that is, whose basic mode of existence is to appear to us "inwardly," we isolate a kind of entity about which we can be certain. We stop the rot of skepticism, the endless retreat before the fact of *isostheneia*, we arrive at a firm footing: at least this is indubitable. And the point of that is to provide a foundation for returning to reconquer some of the territory seemingly ceded in Meditation I. Descartes, like General MacArthur, finds his safe haven, his Australia, from which his vow to return can be fulfilled. For via the *cogito*, and then the proof of the existence of God, we move from the undeniable fact of our having certain ideas, to certainty in a scientifically established order of external things. Skepticism turns out to undercut itself, once it is used to establish the new dualism between inner and outer, and hence the new terrain of the inner, whose contents are (supposedly) immune to skeptical argument. Nothing further from the ancient (or Montaignian) agenda could be conceived.

This is one of the motivations for the invention of the new kind of entity, the "idea." But this was also overdetermined. It came to be not only because of the role it was destined to play in a foundationalist enterprise, but also under the influence of the mechanization of the world picture which was coming about through the work of Galileo and other agents of the scientific revolution. Perception, considered as a process in material nature, could best be conceived as the impression created in the mind by surrounding reality. As Locke later put it, ideas "are produced in us ... by the operation of insensible particles on the senses."[9] From this point of view, the idea is the first effect that this process of impinging makes on the mind, prior to any combinations or connections which the mind itself sets up. It is what the mind receives purely passively, the "impression" made on it, to use the expression later introduced by Hume. Again, in Locke's terms: "In this part the understanding is merely passive; and whether or not it will have these beginnings, and as it were materials of knowledge, is not in its own power."[10]

Mechanistic explanation provided a place for this entity, the passive impression. This was how it was defined in the causal account. But the strategic account, in terms of the foundationalist enterprise, also needed an entity of this kind. It defined the point where the project of foundationalist reconstruction of knowledge could start. On the strategic account the basic idea (later called by Locke the "simple idea") was the content that could not itself be construed as the product of interpretation or inference by the mind. For if so, one would have to dig down further to what was interpreted or inferred from in order to get solid foundations. On the causal account, this same idea was seen as purely passively received, a bare impression. The given prior to interpretation, and the passively received come together as two sides of the same entity, two ways of describing its basic nature. Causal passivity and freedom from interpretation are taken as two descriptions of the same condition. This is the basis of what was later called the Myth of the (purely) Given, and of all the confusions between the "space of causes" and the "space of reasons" which this involved. It also amounts to a reification of thinking.[11]

3

This dualist theory of representation, of knowledge as the inner depiction of outer reality, which we see crystallizing in the seventeenth century with Descartes and Locke, is the origin of what I'm calling the tradition of mediational epistemology. I'm arguing that there is an important tradition here, whose members are bound together by a certain picture (*Bild*) of mind in world, even though they are in vigorous disagreement with each other on many issues, and even though contemporary members see themselves as totally liberated from the thrall of Cartesianism.

What then is this picture? Otherwise put, what are the elements of continuity, which straddle all the differences, even those which seem to contemporaries so vital? I want to identity four, interwoven strands. In certain cases, one or other of these may be broken, but the continuity is maintained by the rest.

(1) The first is the "only through" structure, the one which justifies the title "mediational": our knowledge of, or access to, the world "outside" us, beyond the boundaries of the mind/organism, comes about only through some features in the mind/organism. These can be seen as representations or depictions, either ideas, or beliefs, or sentences held true. Or they can be seen, following the critical tradition, as categorial forms, ways we have of conceptually structuring the input, of making sense of it for ourselves. Often these two combine, in the notion that our depictions of outer reality are inescapably structured by the categories which either emerge from our nature, or have developed over time. In either case, the epistemic relation to the surrounding world only exists in and through these forms and/or depictions.

(2) It is a normal implication of this mediational picture that the content of our knowledge can be analyzed into clearly defined, explicit elements. It consists of "ideas" which we have assembled, in the Cartesian–Lockean variant. Or it consists of beliefs, or sentences held true, in a common contemporary variant. The model here is the explicit, the formulated. Ideally, one could imagine making an inventory of what we know. Even though this would be impossible to complete, in one sense, because the possible entailments of what we believe are potentially endless, nevertheless we would always be dealing with explicit entailments of explicit elements.

(3) In seeking to justify our beliefs, we can never go beyond/below these explicit, formulated elements, and in particular those, if any, which have the status of immediate givens.

(4) The fourth strand is what I called above the dualist sorting, the distinction mental/physical. What continues here is the conceptual opposition, not the actual belief in a dualism. Many contemporaries scornfully reject the idea of souls or immaterial substances of any kind. The whole furniture of heaven and earth ultimately can be explained as matter. But in this they are operating within the same conceptual grid. First, that which they claim to be the universal basis of all phenomena is exactly the "physical" as it emerges out of the Cartesian revolution, that is, the material world no longer seen as the expression or manifestation of meaning or "Ideas," devoid of inner teleology, the realm of purely efficient causation. So the move to materialism accepts the sorting, but claims that only one term is really instantiated. But, second, the "mental" has to remain a category for them, in that materialism is more a program than a theory; they have still to show that thinking, feeling, knowledge, action – all the phenomena in the range of mind or intelligence – can be explained in

purely material terms. But to explain something you first have to pick it out; and they in fact pick it out in the basic terms of the dualist sorting, the "mental" as the realm of inner appearance, where to be is to be experienced. Hence the focus on sensation and raw feels and "qualia" in the whole reductive enterprise, which aims to convince us that in the end, these "are" only brain states.

The dualist sorting: that there are bodily, extended things; and then there are things which are not these, and so "mental," nonextended, perfectly nonphysical; this comes with mechanization of the world picture. We now have mental/physical as an obvious distinction. But also the problem of relating them; the "mind–body" problem. This is a very modern conception. We would have had trouble explaining this way of conceiving things to Plato, or Aristotle.

But even we, if we reflect a little, can see that this way of carving things up is not necessarily "obvious." Take "physical" desire; as against other, "higher," less physical desires. We can still make sense of this distinction, even though we may also want to reject the implicit hierarchy in the name of some humanist moral stance, affirming the value of sensual life. And then we can look backward, to the older topology of sense, imagination, intellect – *aisthesis, phantasia, nous* – which I mentioned above. This is quite different from the modern idea of the "mind" as a single "space," which we referred to above in connection with Descartes.

Herbert Feigl defined the distinction in these terms: the "mental" was defined by the "phenomenal," something we have direct access to by "acquaintance." "Acquaintance as such" means "the direct experience itself, as lived through, enjoyed, or suffered."[12]

The idea here is to take something which is only available from the first-person (singular) perspective; and consider it as a separate entity. So you don't have one entity, say, my life as it is unfolding, which is seen from different perspectives. But alongside the externally observable reality, we postulate something whose *esse* is *percipi*, to borrow the expression from Berkeley. This is explained in terms of inner/outer structure, although the rationalizations of the inner reality are different. We can think of them as just "appearance" for modern materialism. But for Descartes and the first version of epistemology, we have here immaterial substance. That's why it's not available from outside.

The older, premodern ontologies didn't carve things up this way. What we think of as mind and body interpenetrate. For Plato and Aristotle, for instance, the things around us are shaped by Ideas, or Forms. Their models were partly living things, and partly artifacts. Purpose was everywhere. But this was also true of the implicit ontologies of everyday life in premodern times, where people lived in what we can call, building on Weber's expression, an enchanted world. There one found things, for instance, which had causal powers which were defined in meaning terms – like love potions. These were not conceived like a modern aphrodisiac, which may make you desire but doesn't determine the ultimate human meaning of this desire. They were really love potions. King Marke forgives Tristan and Isolde because he sees that their transgression came about in the grip of this magic power.

Or think of a relic which cures; this is not like medicine, which works on specific maladies. Here you are cured of whatever ails you. Or take melancholy, which was black bile. The idea was that mood and substance were one. "Modern" beliefs don't have this structure. We do know chemicals whose ingestion can induce depression. The depression is an effect, due to the way the drug impacts on our body chemistry. We don't see the meaning as consubstantial to the drug itself.

We can think of the drug's effect as an invasion, something you can fight against. You may even get a sense of relief when you learn that you feel bad because of some chemical, because then it hasn't really touched you. You are not gloomy for some good reason. You can disengage from the mood. But in the old days, when you heard that you had black bile, then you knew you were in the grips of the real thing.[13]

Modern post-Cartesian dualism is not like Platonic dualism. Because for Plato, the lower is expressive of the higher. So we disengage from the lower by loving the higher through it. This is the movement of Eros, as described in the *Symposium*. But Descartes disengages from the bodily through objectifying it, seeing it as just dead, unexpressive stuff.

In fact, we can say that the founding move of the modern dualist sorting, and of the mechanization of the world picture, was this Cartesian kind of disengagement, which disinvests the world of objects around us of any meaning, be it the ordinary everyday meanings that things have for us as embodied agents – being available or out of reach, pressing on us or open, attractive or repulsive, inviting or forbidden – or be it the intrinsic purposes defined by Ideas. Descartes wanted not only, following Galileo, to deny the older teleological view of nature, but strove for a more thoroughgoing objectification of the material, one which would include our own lived bodies as well. We had to step from the ordinary, embodied perspective, in which the felt heat was seen as in the object, and the pain as in the tooth, and grasp the process in the way an outside observer can, where certain experiences in the mind are caused by certain conditions in the physical world, say, the kinetic energy of molecules in the object, or the decay in the tooth.

That this is this step which generates clarity and distinctness in this domain of sensations and secondary properties is made evident by Descartes on a number of occasions. In one place, he says that "les idées que j'ay du froid & de la chaleur sont si peu claires & si peu distinctes," while in another, he says: "nous connoissons clairement et distinctement la douleur, la couleur & les autres sentimens, lors que nous les considerons simplement comme ... des pensées"; in yet another, he speaks of "ces sentimens ou perceptions des sens n'ayant esté mises en moy que pour signifier à mon esprit quelles choses sont convenables ou nuisibles au composé dont il est partie, & jusques là estant assez claires & et assez distinctes." In other words, grasped from outside, as body-to-mind causal connections with a survival function, these obscure experiences become clear.[14]

It is this dualist sorting, and the underlying disengagement from the embodied stance, which has been consecrated in the tradition as the proper "scientific" stance to things human. This is just as much, if not more, in evidence in the materialist ambition to explain all action and thinking in terms of matter disinvested of meaning, as it was in the original dualist perspective of Descartes and Locke.[15] And it is reflected as well in the impoverished category of the "mental" as inner appearance, whether or not it is ultimately to be shown "identical" to brain states.

This is the point behind the claim often made by critics of this mediational tradition, that modern reductive theories of the mind are essentially still "Cartesian," an accusation which seems wildly misplaced and unfair to the protagonists of this reductivism. We can take the vogue in recent decades for accounts of thinking which were based on the idea that the brain operates in some respects like a digital computer. These were very popular for a number of decades, and have not really been fully replaced in the imagination of many thinkers in cognitive science.

The computer model exhibits all four of the continuing strands of the mediational tradition outlined above. (1) It speaks of the mind as receiving "inputs" from the environment, and producing "outputs." (2) Computations proceed on the basis of bits of clearly defined information, which get processed. The brain computes explicit bits of information. (3) The brain as a computer is a purely "syntactic engine," its computations get their "reference" to the world through these "inputs." And (4) the account proceeds on the materialist basis that these mental operations are to be explained by the physical operations of the underlying engine, the brain. Mechanism and formalism – that is, being driven by formal procedures – which Descartes distributed between his two substances, body and mind, are now reunited in the body. But this is no mere external synthesis. Thinking by explicit formal rules consorts with mechanism, because both exclude the kind of not totally transparent intuitions that humans have as embodied, social, and cultural agents: knowing whether I can jump this ditch, whether you are mad with me, that the atmosphere at the party has suddenly become tense.

Indeed, this connection underlays one of Turing's key intuitions, that a purely formal system must be operable by a machine, because then you know that none of these nontransparent intuitions are, unknown and unbidden, filling in the gaps in the reasoning. As Marvin Minsky put it: "If the procedure can be carried out by some very simple machine, so that there can be no question of or need for 'innovation' or 'intelligence,' then we can be sure that the specification is complete, and that we have an 'effective procedure.'"[16] This is what John Haugeland speaks of as the "automation principle: wherever the legal moves of a formal system are fully determined by algorithms, then that system can be automated."[17]

## 4

Now I'm sure that many readers will not see the continuing force of these four strands – the "only through" structure (1), the explicitness of content (2), which one can't get beyond/below (3), and the dualist sorting (4) – as at all surprising, let along worrying. Are not these the inevitable conclusions of common sense informed by modern science? What else can we think about these matters?

I, in my turn, am not surprised or perturbed by this reaction. What else do you expect when we're dealing with one of these deeply embedded pictures in Wittgenstein's sense, which "hold us captive" just because they seem so obvious, so unchallengeable, so without alternative?

But we shouldn't leave things here, at a standoff, in which each side is unruffled by the claims of the others. And I would certainly like to take us beyond this point, and to make it convincing that there is a picture, and an inadequate one, which has dominated thinking for too long. I can't accomplish this here. But perhaps at this point, it would help to loosen up some too-firm intuitions to point out that there are and have been alternatives to the picture defined by (1)–(4).

What is involved in an alternative? If the four elements define a mediational theory, an alternative view would have to be called a "contact theory." Where a mediation theory seeks knowledge as arising through some mediational element, so that we have contact with the real in knowledge only through some intermediary, depiction or category, contact theories give an account of knowledge as our attaining unmediated contact with the reality known.

This sounds like what used to be called "naive realism," pronounced in a condescending tone of voice; for of course, it appears terribly unsophisticated and prereflective to those who are into the mediational picture. But some rather sophisticated views in our philosophical tradition were contact theories. For instance, Plato's account of real knowledge, as against shadowy and evanescent opinion, in the *Republic*, turns on what reality one is in contact with, the really real and unchanging, or the ever-changing flux. He invokes the image of the eye of the soul, which is either turned towards the dark side of the universe, focused only on the ever-moving and temporary copies, or swivels around to the side where light illuminates the eternal Ideas.[18] Here there is no hint of a mediating element, nothing separates us from reality. Real knowledge is a kind of unmediated contact.

Of course, we might protest that all this is metaphor, not real "theory." But then we might look at Aristotle, and the view of knowledge he presents in the *de Anima*. Here he says that actualized knowledge (*epistemê*) is one with the object.[19] The idea seems to be that just as the real object is what it is because it is shaped by the Form (*eidos*) appropriate to its kind, so the intellect (*nous*) in its own very different way can come to be shaped by different *eidê*. In correct knowledge of an object, the nous comes to be shaped by the same *eidos* as forms the object. There is no question here of a copy or a depiction; there is one and only one *eidos* of any kind. When I see this animal and know it as a sheep, mind and object are one because they come together in being formed by the same *eidos*.[20] That is why it is *actualized* knowledge which is one with its object. If I can introduce an image here to make the underlying idea intuitively stronger, we can think of the Form as a kind of rhythm giving shape to both objects and intellects. Where there is knowledge, the selfsame rhythm joins both mind and thing. They become one in this single movement. There is unmediated contact.

So I broke down and had recourse to metaphor after all. This may say something about philosophical theorizing, rather than about my lack of theoretical capacity. But at least I hope to have shown that contact theories have been propounded in our philosophical tradition, and that they are not necessarily irremediably weird. But in the case of these two famous ancients, the understanding of contact very much depends on their ontology – depends, in fact, on the theory of Forms, the idea that the reality around us is what it is in virtue of being shaped by Ideas. But once we have been through the Galilean revolution, and the mechanization of the world picture, even if we don't extend this to human thought and action, this older cosmically embedded teleology can no longer appear plausible to us.

And so what in fact has emerged in modern philosophy is a new kind of contact theory, not dependent on the old teleology. This type of theory reached a high degree of self-clarity and articulation during the early twentieth century. Prominent among its framers were, for instance, Heidegger, Merleau-Ponty, and Wittgenstein. A basic move which gives rise to this theory is a reembedding of thought and knowledge in the bodily and social-cultural contexts in which it takes place. The attempt is to articulate the framework or context within which our explicit depictions of reality make sense, and to show how this is inseparable from our activity as the kind of embodied, social, and cultural beings we are. The contact here is not achieved on the level of Ideas, but is rather something primordial, something we never escape. It is the contact of living, active beings, whose life form involves acting in and on a world which also acts on them. These beings are at grips with a world and each other; this original contact provides the sense-making context for all their knowledge constructions, which, however, based on mediating depictions, rely for their meaning on this primordial and indissoluble involvement in the surrounding reality.

Indeed, it might perhaps be better to designate these theories with a stronger term than "contact"; we might speak of them as "immersion theories."

5

I'd like to make a second preliminary point, in lieu of engaging in the hard work of refutation. I want to lay out here a contrast in the logics of mediational and contact theories. Because a failure to appreciate these differences has led to a great deal of cross-purposes, of uncomprehending talking past each other.

For contact theories, truth is self-authenticating. When you're there, you know you're there. But for the mediational variety, this can never be. A common approach here is to take knowledge to be justified, true belief. First there is belief, that is, what I'm inclined to say about some matter. To rise to the level of knowledge, this has first, to be true, say, to correspond to the way things are; then there have to be good grounds for holding the belief. The definition of good grounds focuses us on the search for marks or criteria.

There are two important features of justification here, which mark the difference with contact theories. One is that I am supposed to be able to account for my confidence that this belief is true in terms of a finite number of features which I can separate out, isolate, and take as criteria.

Now in many contexts in life, it doesn't seem intuitively obvious that this requirement is appropriate. I'm certain that we're now in 2001, that I'm in the Laurentians, that I'm trying to write some lectures on epistemology, and so on. If you ask me why I'm so sure, I can only splutter, I don't know what to say. Perhaps better put, I don't know where to start. There are too many things to say here. But this doesn't get to the heart of what seems queer. It's not just that there are a heap of independently identifiable signs. It's much more that there are considerations of a quite different order. These things belong to the background which is being taken as firm as we go about examining/questioning other things.

Wittgenstein, in *On Certainty*, mentions the kind of issue which would arise if someone asked whether the world hasn't started only five minutes ago.[21] There it is, as we experience it, with all that we take as signs of earlier ages, including our memory beliefs, and fossils in the rocks, but it nevertheless all came into being just a few minutes ago. When someone raises this somewhat far-fetched supposition, and we reject it, does this mean that we have always had a belief that the world stretches back into the mists of time? Have we been proceeding on the "assumption" that the world goes way back? This doesn't seem right. Rather we should say that a world stretching back indefinitely operated as a kind of framework or context which made sense of a great many questions we asked and explicit enquiries we engaged in, such as the dating of these fossils, estimating the age of these mountains, explaining certain features of the landscape by the hypothesis that there was once a sea here, and the like. This framework wasn't an assumption, or a belief; it was just taken, unquestioned, as the framework. Indeed, it never occurred to us that we could question it in this way, until this strange suggestion was made.

Does this mean that we weren't careful enough; we hadn't got down to the real rock-bottom reasons for our beliefs? So that we should reconstruct our knowledge, now with the additional premise that the world didn't start just five minutes ago? But Wittgenstein's point is that this kind of foundational ambition is vain. We are always and inevitably thinking within such taken-as-there frameworks. Otherwise put, the number of things which an eccentric, philosophical mind could raise questions about is indefinite, endless. We would never get to the bottom. In the nature of things, some or other such framework will always be there, making sense of what we do. Frameworks shift, when we learn to problematize certain things, but as a class they are inescapable. In particular, where and when we are form part of the framework of our lives, in relation to which we go about the things we're doing, including the things we question and argue about.

By contrast, the mediational approach seems to want to take each belief as though it were there on its own, standing alone, frameworkless. That is why it makes sense to think of justification purely in terms of criteria. Why do this? Because it seems right, prudent. Because we have been wrong, the framework has often turned out to be unreliable, to have error built into it. For instance, the original macro-time framework of our civilization was contained within the Bible story, understood not "literally," because this issue didn't arise in its present form until modern times, but understood in the way similar legends have usually been understood. The story gives us the train of important events since the beginning. Then later, in the eighteenth century and after, there arose the sense of the "dark abyss of time." Within this later framework, the hypothesis of a recent genesis replete with signs of longer existence arises as a "literalist" response, intended to reassert biblical authority.

So there have been corrections; and where they have been made, we usually have good reasons for them. So what's wrong with saying that we always need reasons, even when we're unaware that we are believing certain things without proper reasons? Doesn't accepting the framework uncritically amount to a kind of dogmatism, a claim that we could never be wrong? Well no, because there are scenarios of error and correction, as we just saw with our time framework. And there are other more banal, recognized predicaments: we have been conned, drugged, manipulated. Various error stories can be proposed to challenge our position. If a supposition of this kind is raised, we might have to check things out, in relation to this story. But the response of the contact theorist is that this (exceptional) case would also have to be handled in the context of our general grasp on our world.

The point is that unless we can make sense of a foundationalist justification which goes right down to unchallengeable elements, uninterpreted impressions, or "simple ideas," we will always be thinking within frameworks which are vulnerable to potential challenges and revisions. Our confidence in these at any one time reflects our sense that by operating within them we are in contact with reality. This confidence may (we can say, almost certainly will) turn out to be misplaced in some as yet unpredictable respects. But never totally, because we will only be able to cope with these errors within an amended framework. Within the frameworks, we of course cope with issues by giving reasons, invoking criteria. We frame representations about which we ask whether they really apply. We treat our beliefs, theories, as over against reality, to be related to it. But all this goes on within a larger context of presumed contact with reality. The presumption can be erroneous, but never totally. That is the aspect which contact theories grasp, and mediational accounts lose from view.

In virtue of our framework, certain suppositions will appear frivolous, even absurd, like the "five minutes ago" story above. Perhaps we're wrong here, perhaps the far-out innovators are on to something? This can happen; but it certainly isn't always so. Think of the strained, obsessively suspicious arguments of contemporary Holocaust deniers.

The second feature differentiating the understandings of justification concerns how we inhabit time. Our general sense of things, where/when we are, what we're about, is path dependent. I know I'm here, in the Laurentians, because I've come here. Our grasp of things is not only couched in a timeless or an instantaneous present. We also have perfect-tensed understandings. We are here, because we have made our way here; "we are come," as older use has it.

The grasp on things of temporal beings is not couched in a series of present-tensed claims, that things are thus and so, for which some of the criterial signs are memories, which purport to be of past events, we might say aorist events. In Benveniste's famous discussion, the French perfect (*le passé composé*) relates the events described to the speaker's situation, whereas the aorist (*le passé simple*) leaves this relation indeterminate.[22] The point I am making here is that there are certain aspects of our grasp on reality which can only properly be couched in perfect-tensed statements. Like knowing you're here.

This is part of what underlies the self-authenticating nature of the truth on the contact view. You know because you're there. This is inseparable from having come there. We have what we could call a transitional grasp on reality. We'll get to this later, in connection with the modes of argument available when we confront different outlooks. But let's take the banal case of dreaming. We wake up, and it is this which assures us that we are really there, in contact with reality. A similar point was made by Plato in relation to the dialectic. You know you're there – in contact with the really real – because you've climbed there out of error.

The convincing power of the skeptical argument connected with dreaming, as we see in Descartes's Meditation I, comes from its placing us within the dream. At that moment, we can be, indeed, usually are, fooled. But in our perfect-tensed awareness of having awakened, there is no further question.

But what about the supposition that life itself is dreamlike? *La vida es sueño*, as Calderòn would have it? Perhaps this is so, but only in relation to a deeper awakening; and we can only know this is so in that awakening.

The mediational construal of the dream predicament, as with Descartes, sees my situation as my having been confronted with a convincing appearance, which now seems unreal. But the perfect-tensed awareness is clear that this was not convincing; things were wandering all over the place. Dreams are notoriously wayward and fantastic once one tries to describe them on waking. Only my critical distance from this was zero, or very small. The same is true of many hallucinations.

These two points belong together. That our particulate awarenesses, our grasp on particular things, are embedded in a more general framework, which gives them their sense. This take is holistic: you can't break it down into a heap of particulate grasps. And – what is the same thing from another side – it is inescapable: all particulate grasps suppose it, lean on it. Second, this holistic take has temporal depth. This is the point explored by Heidegger with the notion of *Zeitlichkeit*.

The central issue between the two views concerns the framework. Of course, contact theorists agree that certain questions can be treated by invoking criteria, the ones raised within the framework. But not all can be. Mediational theories tend to make this treatment everywhere applicable. At the heart of the mediational theory is an invocation of good method, and its universal applicability. It assumes the stance of an enquiring mind, distrustful of easy illusions. Or it adopts a forensic style, like a good trial lawyer. Don't just accept the overall picture you're being offered; break things down. What did you really see, Mr Jones? Please tell us exactly. No inferences, please.

This stance got much plausibility from the awareness, inseparable from the Galilean revolution, of the unreliability of the common sense, "natural" take on things. The sun does indeed seem to "go down"; the cart seems to stop as soon as you leave off pushing it. But we know that things happen very differently.

The refusal of any limits to this good forensic method is foundationalism. That's what Descartes and Locke offer us. You start from the purely given, and then build up by responsible inferences. This classical epistemology in fact ontologized good method. The right way to deal with puzzles and build a trustworthy body of knowledge is to break the issue down into subquestions, identify the chains of inference, dig down to an inference-free starting point, and then build by a reliable procedure. Once this comes to seem the all-purpose nostrum for thinking, then one has an overwhelming motivation to believe that that is how the mind actually works in taking in the world. Because if not, one has to draw the devastating conclusion that the only reliable method is inapplicable in the most important context of all: where we build our knowledge of the world. So epistemology dictates ontology. Foundationalism defines how the mind in fact functions. Only it can do it sloppily, without attention, following external authority; or it can do it carefully, self-critically, self-responsibly.

We can see how cross-purposes can easily arise. For the imagination nourished out of this mediational tradition, it seems that we can normally give reasons for our beliefs, find criteria which show them to be right. Where this is not the case, it is because we have got to rock bottom, to the purely given, prior to all interpretation. This purely given is the "incorrigible"; we can doubt it, but we can't improve on it, amend it, or check it. So when contact theorists talk of things we know because we're there, things we grasp without identifiable criteria, it naturally appears as though they're talking about matters which are "incorrigible." But this, as we saw above, is not the case. Frameworks can be challenged, and amended. But something subject to amendment, which is nevertheless known without criteria, doesn't make sense on a foundationalist understanding; and so we often end up talking past each other. The irony is that this carefully constructed foundationalist theory ended up producing another, unreflective "*Bild*," a new "common sense," which needs to be challenged.

## 6

Some of the motivation for the mediational theory was implicit in the previous paragraphs. It reflects a stance of critical awareness, unwilling simply to take things on authority, or to accept the first-off, easiest, most convenient interpretation. It calls for a self-responsible verification in reason of the beliefs that are too often taken over unthinkingly. But this is not only an epistemic stance; it is part of a broader ideal, that of freedom and personal responsibility, which determines a way of being in the world in general, and not just a way of practicing science.

And indeed, we are aware that this ethic of personal responsibility has been a key component of Western modernity. It is central to the Reformed spiritualities, on both the Protestant and the Catholic side, and then it takes on secularized forms, and comes to expression in the ideals of reason and autonomy, and the political norms of self-government. In fact, "critical" has become a key word of approbation, as a self-description it counts as an endorsement of one's stance.

At a deeper level, the stance of disengagement has also benefited from a powerful ethical charge. It is strongly valued insofar as it is seen as inseparable from freedom, responsibility, and self-transparency, which we gain by reflection on our own thinking. But the objectification of the world which it achieves is also the condition of a certain control over it. As long as we see ourselves in a cosmos which manifests certain moral and spiritual meanings, our attitudes are or ought to be determined by the significances which are inherent in things. But once we come to see the world as mechanism, a domain of effective causation, but without inherent purpose, then we are free to treat it as a neutral field where our main concern is how to effect our own purposes. Instrumental reason becomes the only appropriate category, and knowledge can be seen as the basis of power.

At a deeper level again, disengagement is not only a source of power, it is also the instrument of disenchantment. The world ceases to be the locus of spirits and magic forces. One of the age-old primordial sources of fear and awe in human life, which so easily can be renewed in the infancy of each one of us, is negated and dried up. There is a sense of invulnerability, opposed to the immemorial sense of being at the mercy of spirits and forces; but there is also the intuition that this invulnerability was hard won. It required effort, and also courage, to face down the primordial fears, and abandon the sense of comfort in our niche that a meaningful cosmos offers. And this generates a feeling of pride.

Modern disengaged agency continuously generates a discourse of self-congratulation, lauding the courage and effort that produced the free, critical agent. Typical is Ernest Jones's depiction of Freud as a hero of modernity in succession to Copernicus and Darwin. Each one of these was willing to abandon the self-flattering and comforting picture of a meaningful world in which we had pride of place, be it the world at the center of the cosmos, humans as quite different from animals, or the human mind as riding high beyond bodily feeling, in order to face the discomforting, even anguishing truth.

So a lot more is going for mediational epistemology, beyond its supposed efficacy in producing valid and reliable beliefs. Powerful ideals, and a sense of dignity attach to this way of being, and these help to make it seem unchallengeable and devoid of a worthy alternative. But in order to understand the attempts to deconstruct the mediational view, we should also note that the disengaged stance has generated forceful reactions which have been gathering strength since the Romantic period. The sense has grown that this stance cuts us off from the world, from nature, from society, even from our own emotional nature. We are divided beings needing to be healed. The objective instrumental stance towards nature makes communion with it, or a sense of inclusion in it impossible. Self-responsibility pushes us back to the first-person singular, makes us give primacy to the monological over the dialogical.

All of these complaints, right or wrong, have helped feed the challenge to the mediational view. The battle between the two construals, mediational and contact, is far from being a bloodless debate over scientific method. It is deeply involved in the contrary ethical and metaphysical passions of the modern age.

## 7

Of course, to be convinced that the mediational view is a "picture" in Wittgenstein's sense, and a distorting one, one has to follow the arguments which have "deconstructed" it. I can't enter into these here, but I will conclude this chapter with some general remarks.

In fact, the battle in our culture within which the deconstruction takes place is at least 200 years old, and the process of refutation, and the emergence of the new, modern contact view has also been in process for some time. Now there are two basic axes of refutation. I said above that the erroneous picture understands knowledge as the (correct) inner representation of outer reality. (1) One line of refutation consists in showing that our grasp of the world cannot be entirely representational; that is, it certainly involves representations, but these are not the whole story, not even the crucial part of the story. (2) But according to the dominant picture, derived originally from Descartes, this inner picture is in the individual mind. Knowledge, properly understood, not only consists of representations, but is also lodged primarily within individual minds. These individual minds may exchange knowledge; there may be some form of social pooling, as with libraries, encyclopediae, Internet sites, but this shared knowledge is ultimately a compound of the knowings of individuals. Building valid knowledge out of the original input is primarily a monological process. A second line of refutation targets this monological thesis. Its aim is to show that our grasp of the world is first of all shared, and then only secondarily imparted to each one of us, as we are inducted into the language and culture of our society. Of course, we can then make additions and modifications as individuals, but these affect what is originally a common store which each of us receives from outside.

Refutation on line (1) goes after the primacy of representation; the attack on line (2) targets *individual* representation, the primacy of the monological.

Many of the prominent figures in the deconstruction of the mediational view have operated on both axes. Hegel, Wittgenstein, and Heidegger come to mind. But much important argumentation has concentrated on axis (1).

In a sense, the earliest move on this axis goes back to Kant, even though in crucial ways he still remained within the mediational view. Hegel represents another crucial stage; but it wasn't until the first half of the twentieth century that the alternative approach reaches a full articulation.

There are many strands to this refutation/deconstruction, as one might expect. One attacks the "Myth of the Given," the idea that our knowledge is grounded in the reception of preinterpreted data. This seems to make experience problematic. We reason, argue, make inferences, and arrive at an understanding of the world. But our framework understanding, which most of these theories try to retain, is that we also learn from the world; we take things in, come to know things, on the basis of which we reason. It was this dual source of our knowledge which mediational epistemologies were meant to capture in their basic structure: receptivity produces the basic elements of input, and then reasoning processes these into science.

But the very boundary set up by the mediational element seemed to make it hard to conceive how these two sources could work together. What seemed like obvious solutions just enhanced another set of problems, those connected with skepticism and nonrealism. These solutions would amount to the idea that receptivity is to be understood in purely causal terms, that it just delivers certain results which we can't get behind; and reason then does what it can to make sense of these.

But beyond this, the very idea of a boundary can be made to seem highly problematic. Critical reasoning is something we do, an activity, in the realm of spontaneity and freedom. But, as far as knowledge of the world is concerned, it is meant to be responsive to the way things are. Spontaneity has to be merged somehow with receptivity. But it is hard to see how this can be, if we conceive of spontaneity as a kind of limitless freedom, which at the point of contact has to hit a world under adamantine, post-Galilean "laws of nature." The schizophrenic nature of boundary events, inexplicably partaking of both nature and freedom, is an inevitable consequence of this way of seeing things.

And so the very idea of a boundary event, between a realm of causes and a realm of reasons, begins to seem contradictory. This event would have to be in a sense amphibious, belonging to both. Yet are their natures not contradictory: on the one hand, an object, or a factual state of affairs, the causal upshot in our receptors of outside stimulation; on the other, certain *claims* – to the effect that so and so – which could figure as reasons to adopt some broader view or other? This is the consideration which has led some philosophers to denounce the Myth of the purely Given, the brute, uninterpreted fact.[23]

The problem has been to account for experience, for how we take in information from the world. In a sense we have to receive this information; we are the passive party. In another, we have to know how to "grasp" it; we are active. How do these two combine?

This has been the notorious problem of the tradition of modern philosophy which has been defined by the modern epistemology. In certain well-known classical writers, the absence of any plausible theory of experience was patent. Leibniz in the end denied it altogether, and saw a picture of the world as present in its entirety within the monad. Hume seemed to go to the other extreme, and allow that all our knowledge comes to us through experience – hence the vaunted title "empiricist"; but this was at the cost of denying the active dimension altogether; so that the deliverances of experience were unconnected bits of information, and what seems to ordinary people as the undeniable connections were denounced as projections of the mind. Even the self disappears in this caricatural passivism.

Kant notoriously tried to unite both Hume and Leibniz. At least he saw the problem, of how to combine spontaneity and receptivity. But he was still too caught up in the mediationalist structure to propound a believable solution.[24]

## 8

But the most influential strand in the twentieth century was what I will call the "metacritical" one.[25] The idea of a metacritique here is, as the name suggests, to enquire into the basis of first-order critical theory. This claims to reflect on the conditions of our everyday or scientific knowledge claims, and to upset the ordinary precritical view we have of them. The metacritique reflects in turn on the conditions of our making this kind of critique. But the search for conditions takes place in a different dimension, as yet unexplored by the founders of the mediational tradition – though not by Kant: this is what makes him the hinge figure. The attempt is to explore the context which has to be taken as given if we are to make sense of the critical enterprise, and beyond this of our experience of the world as such. Just what is the understanding of mind-in-world which would make sense of the suppositions of mediational theory? And is this consistent with the understanding which makes sense of experience as we actually live it?

I've already been engaged in an answer to the first question in this chapter, as I tried to articulate the Cartesian view of mind-in-world, and to show the importance of the dualist sorting, for instance. Now even the answer to this first question can be very unsettling for the mediational approach. Since this was developed in the first instance with foundationalist intent, the aim being to find a solid basis for knowledge by digging down to the purely given which we can't see behind, to be told that the enterprise depends on adopting a particular view of mind-in-world, to which there are after all alternatives, is utterly devastating. For if the argument can only proceed by our taking on board one among other possible interpretations of mind-in-world, then the claim to have reached the foundation is voided – unless this interpretation can in turn be solidly grounded.

This argumentative move, where one puts foundationalism in contradiction with itself, is made to good effect by Hegel in the Introduction to *The Phenomenology of Spirit*.[26] What this shows is what I wanted to claim above, that foundationalism can only proceed if one is in the grips of a *"Bild"* in Wittgenstein's sense, an unreflected embedding in one construal which is felt to be the only possible one, hence beyond all question.

But even in this Introduction, Hegel is concerned with more than this pragmatic refutation. He wants to go on to explore the second question: What are the conditions which make sense of our experience of the world? He sees these as being defined in a series of negative moves whereby in each case we show the inadequacy of an earlier construal and amend it accordingly. The path towards an adequate construal is therefore defined as a dialectical movement, and the notion "experience" itself is given a richer sense, designating these moments of critical transition.

Now paradoxically, what Hegel is drawing on here to criticize Kant is what I would designate as the foundational move in this search for the sense-making conditions of experience; and this was the one made by Kant himself in the Transcendental Deduction. He inaugurates the line of argument that has been continued by the major "deconstructors" of the disengaged picture. This line undermines the picture by bringing out the background we need for the operations described in the picture to make sense, whereby it becomes clear that this background can't fit within the limits that the disengaged view prescribes. Once understood against its background, the account shows itself to be untenable.

Kant is not really the pioneer in this kind of argument, if we mean by this that he intended to refute the disengaged view as such. Because he unfortunately didn't. But he did manage to upset one of its crucial features, at least in an earlier variant. The arguments of the Transcendental Deduction can be seen in a number of different lights. But one way to take them is as a final laying to rest of a certain atomism of the input which had been espoused by empiricism. As this came to Kant through Hume, it seemed to be suggesting that the original level of knowledge of reality (whatever that turned out to be) came in particulate bits, individual "impressions." This level of information could be isolated from a later stage in which these bits were connected together, e.g. in beliefs about cause–effect relations. We find ourselves forming such beliefs, but we can, by taking a stance of reflexive scrutiny (which we saw above is fundamental to the modern epistemology), separate the basic level from these too hasty conclusions we leap to. This analysis allegedly reveals, for instance, that nothing in the phenomenal field corresponds to the necessary connection we too easily interpolate between "cause" and "effect."[27]

Kant undercuts this whole way of thinking by showing that it supposes, for each particulate impression, that it is being taken as a bit of potential information. It purports to be about something. The primitive distinction recognized by empiricists between impressions of sensation and those of reflection amount to an acknowledgment of this. The buzzing in my head is discriminated from the noise I hear from the neighboring woods, in that the first is a component in how I feel, and the second seems to tell me something about what's happening out there. So even a particulate "sensation," really to be sensation (in the empiricist sense, that is, as opposed to reflection), has to have this dimension of "aboutness." This will later be called "intentionality," but Kant speaks of the necessary relation to an object of knowledge. "Wir finden aber, daß unser Gedanke von der Beziehung aller Erkenntnis auf ihren Gegenstand etwas von Notwendigkeit bei sich führe. ... "[28]

With this point secured, Kant argues that this relationship to an object would be impossible if we really were to take the impression as an utterly isolated content, without any link to others. To see it as about something is to place it somewhere, at the minimum out in the world, as against in me, to give it a location in a world which, while it is in many respects indeterminate and unknown for me, cannot be wholly so. The unity of this world is presupposed by anything which could present itself as a particulate bit of *information*, and so whatever we mean by such a particulate bit, it couldn't be utterly without relation to all others. The background condition for this favorite supposition of empiricist philosophy, the simple impression, forbids us from giving it the radical sense which Hume seemed to propose for it. To attempt to violate this background condition is to fall into incoherence. Really, to succeed in breaking all links between individual impressions would be to lose all sense of awareness of anything. "Diese Wahrnehmungen würden aber alsdann auch zu keiner Erfahrung gehören, folglich ohne Objekt und nichts als ein blindes Spiel der Vorstellungen, d.i. weniger als ein Traum sein."[29]

The Transcendental Deduction, and related arguments in the *Critique of Pure Reason*, can be seen as a turning point in modern philosophy. With hindsight, we can see this as the first attempt to articulate the background that the modern disengaged picture itself requires for the operations it described to be intelligible, and to use this articulation to undermine the picture. Once one goes through this transition, the whole philosophical landscape changes, because the issue of background understanding is out in the open. A crucial feature of the reified views which arise from ontologizing the canonical procedures of modern epistemology is that they make this issue invisible. The conditions of intelligibility are built into the elements and processes of the mind as internal properties. The isolated impression *is* intelligible information on its own, just as the house is red or the table is square. It has all the particulate, separable existence of an external object. Locke treats simple ideas as analogous to the materials we use for building.[30] This outlook forgets that for something to be intelligibly X is for it to *count as* intelligibly X, and that there are always contextual conditions for anything to count as something.

In its original Kantian form, this revolution sweeps away the atomism of modern epistemology. In this respect, he is followed by all those who have come after. In a sense the very move which dereifies our account of the knowing agent has an inherently holistic bent. What was formerly built into the elements is now attributed to the background which they all share.

Heidegger and Wittgenstein follow this pioneering Kantian form of argument. In *Sein und Zeit*, Heidegger argues that things are disclosed first as part of a world, that is, as the correlates of concernful involvement, and within a totality of such involvements. This undercuts certain basic features of the disengaged picture. First, following Kant, the atomism of input is denied by the notion of a totality of involvements. But it also undercuts another basic feature of the classical picture, that the primary input is neutral, and is only, at a later stage, attributed some meaning by the agent. This idea is negated by the basic thesis that things are first disclosed in a world as ready-to-hand (*zuhanden*). To think of this character as something we project on to things which are first perceived neutrally is to make a fundamental mistake.[31]

Heidegger's discussion in *Sein und Zeit* is sometimes taken by unsympathetic readers to be an interesting description of everyday existence which has no relevance to the philosophical issues of ontology he claims to be discussing. So we usually treat things as tools or obstacles, in their relevance to our activities, what does this show about the priority of neutral information? Of course, we aren't *aware* of things most of the time as neutral objects, but this doesn't show that the disengaged account isn't right. Our ordinary everyday consciousness must itself be seen as a construct. We mustn't make the pre-Galilean mistake of thinking that things are as they appear, even in matters of the mind. So runs a common complaint by supporters of the disengaged view against "phenomenology."

But Heidegger's intention is plainly other than just reminding us of what it's like to live in the world at an everyday level. The purport of the argument is the same as Kant's and could be invoked like his as an answer to the challenge I have just given voice to. The aim is to show that grasping things as neutral objects is one of our possibilities only against the background of a way of being in the world in which things are disclosed as ready-to-hand. Grasping things neutrally requires modifying our stance to them which primitively has to be one of involvement. Heidegger is arguing like Kant that the comportment to things described in the disengaged view requires for its intelligibility to be situated within an enframing and continuing stance to the world which is antithetical to it, hence that this comportment couldn't be original and fundamental. The very condition of its possibility forbids us from giving this neutralizing stance the paradigmatic and basic place in our lives that the disengaged picture supposes.

This argument about the conditions of possibility, the conditions of intelligibly realizing the stance, is carried in Heidegger's use of the term *ursprünglich*. It doesn't just mean: prior in time, but something stronger. Our *ursprünglich* stance comes before but also as a condition of what follows and modifies it. It is also carried in his repeated use of the phrase *zunächst und zumeist*. Once again this sounds deceptively weak. It is applied to a way of being that is not just there earlier and more frequently, but also provides the background for what is not it.

Wittgenstein's line of argument in the *Philosophical Investigations* is even more obviously parallel with Kant's. In a sense, he does for an atomism of meaning what Kant did for an atomism of information input. His target is a theory of language and meaning, which, although he finds its paradigm statement in Augustine, was also espoused and developed by thinkers of the disengaged view. The atomism of meaning consisted in the view that a word was given meaning by being linked to an object in a relation of "naming" or "signifying." There is not only a parallel here to the atomism of input of post-Cartesian epistemology, but the two were interwoven in the classical statements of this theory of the mind. Locke argues that a word gets its meaning not by signifying the object directly, but rather the idea in the mind which represents this object.[32] This amendment to the Augustinian theory is what opens the way to the supposition that each person might speak a different language, since different inner ideas might correspond in each person's mind to some public object which is being named. A quite private language, in which words mean things for me that no one else can know, now seems a distinct possibility, a skeptical threat not to be easily conjured away. It is against this "modernized" form of the theory that Wittgenstein's array of arguments is largely deployed.

The atomism of meaning turns out to be untenable for exactly the same reason as Kant demonstrated for the atomism of input. Its proponents suppose that a word can be given meaning in some ceremony of naming, or that its meaning can be imparted by pointing to the object it names. A good part of Wittgenstein's argument in the *Investigations* consists in showing that the condition of this kind of "ostensive definition" working is that the learner understand a great deal about the workings of language, and the place of this particular word in it. The "grammar" of the relevant part of the language is presupposed, because this "zeigt den Posten an, an den das neue Wort gestellt wird."[33] Naming something seems like a primitive, self-sufficient operation, but when one takes it as such, "so vergißt man, daß schon viel in der Sprache vorbereitet sein muß, damit das bloße Benennen einen Sinn hat."[34]

Wittgenstein talks explicitly here in this last remark about the conditions of intelligibility. The idea that the meaning of a word just consists in its relation to the object it names, a conception which is by its nature atomistic, comes to grief on the realization that each such relation draws on a background understanding and doesn't make sense without it. But this understanding concerns not individual words, but the language games in which they figure, and eventually the whole form of life in which these games have sense. The Augustinian theory does come close to modeling bits of our understanding of language. But when we see the conditions of intelligibility of these bits, we are forced to abandon it as a model for language understanding in general. The theory was born of a reifying move. It built this background understanding into the individual relations word–thing and made them self-sufficient. The liberating step comes when one sees that they need a background, and can explore this in all its richness and variety.

The theory supposes this whole background understanding, which we only acquire when we learn language, as already built into the first word–thing relation we learn. This is the kind of position we're in when we learn a *second* language. We already know what it is for a word to have a place in the whole, and usually have a sense of what the place is of the word they're now trying to teach us. The error is to read this condition back into the acquisition of our original language. "Und nun können wir ... sagen: Augustinus beschreibe das Lernen der menschlichen Sprache so, als käme das Kind in ein fremdes Land und verstehe die Sprache des Landes nicht; das heißt: so als habe es bereits eine Sprache, nur nicht diese."[35]

## 9

The discussion which has developed out of the work of these authors has reached unparalleled articulation and sophistication as we enter the twenty-first century. The interesting debate between John McDowell and Hubert Dreyfus, and the way in which their differences have been clarified and refined, is an index of the progress we have made in recent decades.

## Notes

1 The actual text of §115 reads: "Ein *Bild* hielt uns gefangen. Und heraus konnten wir nicht, denn es lag in unsrer Sprache, und sie schien es uns unerbittlich zu wiederholen." In my discussion, I argue more that the picture is anchored in our whole way of thinking, our way of objectifying the world, and thus our way of life, and therefore also in our language.
2 Wittgenstein actually says in this section that the grammar of our language endlessly repeats the picture to us, and that's why it is so hard to escape. I think this sense of what is implicit in grammar actually depends on something more complex in our background understanding of mind, agency, and world.
3 Letter to Gibieuf of 19 January 1642; English in *Descartes: Philosophical Letters*, p. 123.
4 Groarke, *Greek Skepticism*, p. 134.
5 I have drawn on Miles Burnyeat's discussion here; see "Can the Skeptic Live with His Skepticism?" and "Idealism and Greek Philosophy," in Vesey (ed.), *Idealism, Past and Present*.

6 Burnyeat, "Can the Skeptic Live with His Skepticism?," p. 121.
7 Rorty, *Philosophy and the Mirror of Nature*, p. 50.
8 Descartes, *Méditations* II, in *Oeuvres de Descartes*, IX-1, 22.
9 Locke, *An Essay concerning Human Understanding*, 2.8.13 (bk. 2, ch. 8, §13). In 4.2.11, Locke speaks of "globules."
10 Ibid., 2.1.25. See also 2.30.3, where Locke says that the mind is "wholly passive in respect of its simple ideas"; and 2.2.2, where he says that it is not in our power to create or to destroy a simple idea.
11 This is most clearly evident in Locke, who pushes the metaphor of construction out of building materials to the utmost in his account of the operations of the mind. Ideas are "materials," and man's "power, however managed by art and skill, reaches no farther than to compound and divide the materials that are made to his hand" (2.2.2). And after speaking of the formation of complex ideas out of simple ones, Locke says: "This shows man's power, and its ways of operation, to be much the same in the material and intellectual world. For the materials in both being such as he has no power over, either to make or to destroy, all that man can do is either to unite them together, or to set them by one another, or wholly separate them" (2.12.1).
12 Feigl, *"Mental" and the "Physical,"* p. 37.
13 I have discussed this point at further length in *Sources of the Self*, ch. 11.
14 Quotations respectively from *Méditations* III, IX-1, 34; *Principles of Philosophy*, I.68, IX-2, 56; *Méditations* VI, in *Oeuvres de Descartes*, IX-1, 66. See also Alan Gewirth's discussion in his "Clearness and Distinctness in Descartes," in Doney (ed.), *Descartes*, p. 260n33.
15 The aim of "scientific naturalism," as Jennifer Hornsby describes it, is to account for the actions, feelings, intentions, etc. of persons from the "objective, third-personal perspective" that natural scientists adopt. The underlying belief is that everything which is real must be intelligible from that perspective. Hornsby's argument is that many of the phenomena of personal life just disappear when we adopt this perspective. Against this pervasive current in modern thought, she proposes a "naive" naturalism, which recognizes the difference between human and inanimate. See Hornsby, *Simple Mindedness*, pp. 4–5. I am very much in agreement with this position, even appreciating the irony of the title she gives to a thesis which is immensely more sophisticated than the knee-jerk scientism she opposes.
16 See Minsky, *Computation*, p. 105.
17 See Haugeland, *Artificial Intelligence*, p. 82.
18 Plato, *Republic*, 518c–d; Plato speaks here of a "conversion," a "turning around" (*periagôgê*).
19 "to d' auto estin hê kat' energeian epistêmê tô pragmati," *de Anima*, bk. III, 430a20; and again at 431a1.
20 Later Aristotle says that "knowledge is the knowable and sensation is the sensible." This doesn't mean that the sensible and cognitive faculties are identical with the object as a material entity; "for the stone doesn't exist in the soul, but only the form of a stone" (431b22, 432a1). It is in the *eidos* that the mind and object come together.
21 Wittgenstein starts an issue of this kind in *On Certainty*, §84, and it then recurs periodically throughout the work.
22 Benveniste, *Problèmes de Linguistique Générale*.
23 See McDowell, *Mind and World*, Lecture 1.
24 I have drawn on the extremely insightful work of Sam Todes, whose doctoral dissertation has been published as *Body and World*.

25 I take my cue here from a work by Hamann, *The Metacritique of Pure Reason*, commenting on Kant.
26 Hegel points out that the main epistemological tradition he is attacking supposes one or other picture of the mind-in-the-world: either the mind can grasp reality through certain instruments; or reality comes to it through a "medium."
27 Hume, *An Enquiry concerning Human Understanding*, ch. 7.
28 Kant, *Kritik der reinen Vernunft*, A104, p. 104.
29 Ibid., A112.
30 Locke, *An Essay concerning Human Understanding*, 2.2.2.
31 "Die Seinsart dieses Seienden ist die Zuhandenheit. Sie darf jedoch nicht als blosser Auffassungscharakter verstanden werden, als würden dem zunächst begegnenden 'Seienden' solche 'Aspekte' aufgeredet, als würde ein zunächst an sich vorhandener Weltstoff in dieser Weise 'subjektiv gefärbt.'" Heidegger, *Sein und Zeit*, p. 71.
32 Locke, *An Essay concerning Human Understanding*, 3.2.2.
33 Wittgenstein, *Philosophical Investigations*, I §257.
34 Ibid.
35 Ibid., I §32.

# Bibliography

Benveniste, É., *Problèmes de linguistique générale*, Paris: Gallimard, 1966.
Descartes, R., *Descartes: Philosophical Letters*, trans. A. Kenny, Oxford: University Press, 1970.
——, *Méditations métaphysiques*, Paris: Presses Universitaires de France, 1956.
——, *Oeuvres de Descartes*, ed. C. Adam and P. Tannery, Paris: Vrin, 1973–76.
——, *The Principles of Philosophy*, in *The Philosophical Writings of Descartes*, vol. I, trans. J. Cottingham, R. Stoothoff, and D. Murdoch, Cambridge: Cambridge University Press, 1985.
Doney, W. (ed.) *Descartes: A Collection of Critical Essays*, Garden City, NY: Doubleday, 1967.
Feigl, H., *The "Mental" and the "Physical,"* Minneapolis: University of Minnesota Press, 1967.
Groarke, L., *Greek Skepticism*, McGill-Queen's University Press, 1990.
Haugeland, J., *Artificial Intelligence: The Very Idea*, Cambridge, MA: Bradford/MIT Press, 1985.
Hegel, G. W. F., *Die Phänomenologie des Geistes*, Hamburg: Meiner, 1988.
Heidegger, M., *Sein und Zeit*, Tübingen: Niemeyer, 1967.
Hornsby, J., *Simple Mindedness: In Defense of Naive Naturalism in the Philosophy of Mind*, Cambridge, MA: Harvard University Press, 1997.
Hume, D., *An Enquiry concerning Human Understanding*, ed. P. Millican, Oxford: Oxford University Press, 2007.
Kant, I., *Kritik der reinen Vernunft*, vol. 4 of *Kant's gesammelte Schriften*, ed. Ko?niglich preußischen Akademie der Wissenschaften, Berlin: Walter de Gruyter, 1903.
Locke, J., *An Essay concerning Human Understanding*, ed. P. H. Nidditch, Oxford: Clarendon Press, 1975.
McDowell, J., *Mind and World*, Cambridge, MA: Harvard University Press, 1994.
Minsky, M., *Computation: Finite and Infinite Machines*, Englewood Cliffs, NJ: Prentice Hall, 1967.

Rorty, R., *Philosophy and the Mirror of Nature*, Princeton, NJ: University Press, 2009.
Taylor, C., *Sources of the Self*, Cambridge, MA: Harvard University Press, 1989.
Todes, S., *Body and World*, Cambridge, MA: MIT Press, 2001.
Vesey, G. (ed.), *Idealism, Past and Present*, Cambridge: Cambridge University Press, 1982.
Wittgenstein, L., *Philosophical Investigations*, trans. G. E. M. Anscombe, Oxford: Blackwell, 2001.

# 4

# WHAT IS "CONCEPTUAL ACTIVITY"?

*Robert B. Pippin*

## 1

One of the most discussed and disputed claims in John McDowell's *Mind and World* is the claim that we should not think that in experience, conceptual capacities are "exercised on non-conceptual deliverances of sensibility."[1] Rather, "conceptual capacities are already operative in the deliverances of sensibility themselves."[2] Such capacities are said to be operative, but not in the same way they are operative when the faculty of assertoric judgment is explicitly exercised. This position preserves the passivity and receptivity necessary for McDowell to defend a picture of our thought as constrained by the world. ("The constraints come from outside thinking, but not from outside what is thinkable."[3]) And it maintains his Sellarsian criticism of the "Myth of the Given," such that when we trace justification back we do not reach something that, because nonconceptual, could not play any role in such justification. The fact that the deliverances of sensibility are conceptually shaped (I will take this to mean "have a conceptual form") ensures that sensibility can indeed play such a justificatory role in perceptual beliefs.

Opponents of this view come in all sorts of philosophical shapes and sizes. A major party, perhaps the dominant one, wants to defend a contrary view about nonconceptual sensory content and, often, a naturalistic view of perception in which the relation between receptivity and perceptual content is not one of justification but of some sort of causal "triggering."[4] Others have various axes to grind (such as superfine points of Kant interpretation) but many express puzzlement over the unusual dimension of the claim that while conceptual capacities are operative in sensory uptake, "we" are not, where "we" means full subjects of the spontaneity of judgment.[5]

Hubert Dreyfus's recent criticism of McDowell in "Overcoming the Myth of the Mental: How Philosophers Can Profit from the Phenomenology of Everyday Expertise" intervenes in these debates in a novel way.

Dreyfus criticizes what he takes to be McDowell's view that all aspects of any conscious intelligibility must be conceptually structured, but he does not do so in the name of nonconceptual sensory content triggering perceptual states. Rather he defends a form of intelligibility that he locates in the phenomenological tradition and the possibility of which bypasses the conceptual–nonconceptual account of the sensory. Sensory content as such is not the issue at all for Dreyfus. For there is not only a mode of experience which cannot be said to be conceptually structured or "permeated" with conceptuality, and which cannot be said to direct or guide sensory attentiveness "from without," but one which Dreyfus and this tradition understand to be *basic*, primary, that only abstraction from which could yield, secondarily, conceptually articulated claims. This modality is "everyday expertise" like expertise in chess, carpentry, athletic activity, and the like. Dreyfus then produces several examples of "skillful coping" to make clear the fact that the coping subject is not only not following rules or attentive to the justification of her claims; it would also be a mistake to say that such rule-following has become implicit, but still operative.[6] Once suitably trained or coached, there is no sort of reliance on rules. They have "withdrawn" altogether.

Now it seems straightaway still quite important to be able to explain how such expert coping can be *contentful* on this account. It would of course have to be determinately contentful in some sense: someone hammering a nail in the extended activity of constructing a house must be said to be all *about constructing*, not performing exactly the same bodily movement but being about practicing hammering, or giving a demonstration for an apprentice or providing an example for a philosophy class. In this approach it is not to be conceptually contentful, but it has what Dreyfus, following Merleau-Ponty, calls "motivational content."[7] This is instead something like a dispositionally differentiated responsiveness to various situations, but one not guided by norms, concepts, principles, rules, and the like. (I think Dreyfus assumes that such "guidance" must be what a claim for conceptual mediation must involve. As we shall see, this is a complex point to assume and can be dangerously misleading.) Suitably disposed, one is just drawn into the specific, determinate activity motivated by some situation or other. (These situations are, following Gibson, called "affordances," as in: "Food affords eating, doors afford going in and out," etc.[8] And so responding best to such affordances actually involves not noticing them as such, but "rather, as Heidegger says, they 'withdraw' and we must simply 'press into' them."[9] This is so much so, the activity is so unreflective, that Dreyfus can even formulate it by saying that there is "*no* content" in such engaged coping. The explanation of the possibility of such content will prove to be a decisive issue in what follows. I want to claim that the only way to explain such differences in content is by appealing to different determinate forms of mindedness in each of the possibilities and that *that* difference ultimately has to involve different modalities [forms] of conceptually informed mindedness. But this of course is just the point at issue and, as we shall see, everything depends on the precise description of that modality.)

The first exchange between Dreyfus and McDowell is largely taken up with a clarification about what the claim for the conceptual character of experience amounts to, what the issue in dispute actually is. For McDowell the central claim means that for human animals experience and agency are "permeated with," responsive everywhere to, rationality. This, though, does not mean, as Dreyfus had first assumed, that experience is everywhere subsumed "under content determinately expressible in abstraction from any situation."[10] As an exchange about Aristotle and the practically wise man, the *phronimos*, makes clear, McDowell is not committed (has never been committed, anywhere in his writings) to any such "situation-independent" notion of rational normativity, much less any claim that successful coping must be the result of explicit or even implicit rule-following, with rules understood as some sort of generality. The *phronimos* displays practical rationality even though he does not decide what to do by appeal to universal reasons or to the ideal of what a practically wise man would do. The rationality in question is "in" action, not "behind" action.[11] There is no way to formalize or render situation independent the wise man's judgmental finesse. This in/behind formulation is another important distinction, to which we shall return.

Once that issue is cleared away, each of the interlocutors is left in the last exchange facing a difficult question. McDowell presses Dreyfus on the differences that must exist between *human* openness to affordances and what Gadamer calls "merely inhabiting an environment," the mere responsiveness typical of animals.[12] Our openness is genuine openness, McDowell argues, not just differential responsiveness, and "once affordances are figuring for a subject as features of the world, they are no longer just inputs to a natural motivational makeup; they are available to a subject's rationality."[13] Although there are aspects of our responsiveness to such affordances that can be described in a way that corresponds exactly with animal responsiveness, that is no reason for saying, McDowell rightly (by my lights) insists, that *our* capacity is exhausted by such a similarity. For ours is also genuinely world disclosive, and this not only means that such openness is such that any aspect of it can become the subject of rational deliberation. *Being* so oriented comes with Kantian conditions. Here is McDowell on those conditions:

> [a]ny aspect of [a world-disclosing experience's] content hangs together with other aspects in a unity of the sort Kant identifies as categorical. And Kant connects the categorical unity that provides for world-disclosingness with the transcendental unity of apperception. Experiences in which the world is disclosed are

apperceptive. Perception discloses the world only to a subject capable of the "I think" that expresses apperception.[14]

This is, I think, the key historical connection in all the exchanges and the one I want to pursue; Kant's claim that the "I think" must be able to accompany all my representations, or the pervasiveness of apperceptive consciousness if consciousness is to have an object at all, whether perceptual content as such or motivational content, in Dreyfus's sense. The anti-Humean or antiassociationist claim is that all my experiences *can* be mine, can belong to an identical subject of its experiences, and so satisfy the minimum condition of experience – avoiding disjointed and disconnected experiences – only if they are all, as Kant says, "brought" to the unity of apperception, only in so far as in, say, perceiving over time, objects or events are held in view in a way. The question is what this could mean, if one is to avoid the "intellectualism" that both McDowell and Dreyfus say they want no part of. Read straightforwardly, it can certainly sound like Kant is introducing a great deal of active mental machinery as a condition of contentfulness and so, even if not burdened with what Dreyfus has called representationalism or computationalism, still embracing what he has called intellectualism. At any rate, it is this "supreme condition" that Dreyfus, Heidegger, and Merleau-Ponty are all denying, and I think that McDowell is right that without this element a self-oriented "openness" cannot be distinguished from merely inhabiting and being directed by an environment. What I want to suggest is that understanding Kant on the apperceptive nature of consciousness will help with the issues brought out in this exchange.

Indeed we do not need the contrast with animal sentience to make this point. We can distinguish in our own experience between genuinely *bodily* copings that are not "open to a world" (that is, *rationally* responsive) and those that are, and we need some marker to distinguish them. One can say that "my body knows" how to perspire at just the rate to keep my body temperature constant, and trying to work out reflectively and retrospectively what would have been the right rate would be as pointless as trying to figure out how many times I should breathe a minute or how I might regulate my digestion. Distinguishing between "my body knows how to do it" in the engaged-coping examples and *this* sense of "my body knows how to do it" without some version of appropriate and attentive (apperceptive) mindedness looks to be quite difficult.[15] And if we don't concede the distinction, then McDowell is right about a formulation of the point by Merleau-Ponty: that we would be stuck saying something as awkward and implausible as

> [i]n perception we do not think the object and we do not think ourselves thinking it, we are given over to the object and *we merge into this body* which is better informed than we are about the world.[16]

The counterclaim would be that Merleau-Ponty has got the first part right (we do not think the object and we do not think ourselves thinking it) but goes far too far in thinking this means we should say that we "merge with our body."

I call this an unresolved aspect of Dreyfus's position because when he tries to respond to this request for a differentiation between openness to a world and being captivated (*benommen*) by an environment (beyond the secondary fact that humans can reflect on their coping, train up, monitor explicitly, etc.), he introduces Heideggerian locutions that seem to me either to concede the point or circumlocuitously avoid it. Human beings are said to be "free to open themselves to being bound."[17] But as soon as one has conceded just this element of subjectivity, whatever it is, that humans can be said to open *themselves* in any way, or to orient *themselves* rather than just *become* oriented (as if guided by a radio beacon, as Dreyfus once says) then McDowell's apperceptive point has been conceded (again, with the caveat that everything comes down to formulating this apperceptive condition properly). This is an even more pressing question if we recall an important point that Sean Kelly makes, quoted in Dreyfus's first lecture.

> [I]t is part of my visual experience that my body is drawn to move, or, at any rate, that the context should change, in a certain way. These are inherently normative, rather than descriptive features of visual experience. They don't represent in some objective, determinate fashion the way the world is, they say something about how the world ought to be for me to see it better.[18]

If affordances solicit me to act in this way, then we have a picture already "fraught with ought" in Sellars's famous phrase and McDowell has all he needs to make his point (or at least to have an entering wedge). If my body is drawn to move in a way sensitive to genuinely normative proprieties, and we are to distinguish this from the perspiring case, then I am so sensitive, and that must mean minded in a way that actively tracks the salient, relevant features and actively screens out the irrelevant. All of that cannot be said simply to "happen." (One indication that this is so: in my engaged coping I can be careless, sloppy, lazy, or careful and extremely attentive. This is an indication of how an engagement is sustained and that is an indication of a structurally complex level of mindedness, not unmindedness.)[19] Once we have agreed (as I hope to show in a moment) that the self-consciousness involved in this constant attentiveness to and assessment of "how well it is going" does not involve any parallel, intentional, object-directed self-monitoring, we are in no danger of assuming two levels or types of attentive awareness and are very close to the root problem in Kant: the nature of the apperception claim.[20] Dreyfus's descriptions of his favorite example, the grandmaster playing speed chess, often disguise this issue by emphasizing the issue of speed, as if that alone establishes that we "have no time to think; we just respond." But this is a deceptive picture of a grandmaster, as if playing on dumb instinct. Every grandmaster instantly recognizes what sort of opening he faces among the twenty possible ones (often even named as such), if he is playing black, what any possible opening invites if he is playing white, and they know a great deal about what is opened up or closed down by various, again usually named, responses. And such situations occur frequently throughout the game. He is not playing mindlessly, but is able to play fast because he is so elaborately minded, and that mindedness is in play in a way very different than when he is writing a chess manual. (More on that below.)

On the other hand, we are left on McDowell's side with the claim that there is and must be a form of conceptual mindedness in unreflective coping that is not merely implicit normative attentiveness (as if all that were important in Dreyfus's distinctly human coping would be the implicit ability to step back and reflect). In unreflective coping, McDowell notes, nothing like that capacity is relevant to the issue even though it is present, yet "even so the capacities operative in one's perceiving or acting are conceptual, and their operations are conceptual."[21] But also there is "nothing discursively explicit in these goings-on."[22] Whatever these conceptual operations are, while they are the exercise of conceptual capacities that can be fully engaged in explicit discursive activity, they are not so engaged in the conceptual shapings of sensibility. Dreyfus, it seems to me, has the right to ask, if such conceptual shaping is not discursive, not merely implicit, and certainly not the application of situation-independent universal rules, what then *is* conceptual activity of this sort and what does it mean to say it is unbounded?[23]

Earlier I made what must have sounded like the improbable suggestion that something about all this could be learned by examining more closely what I called the historical source of the controversy, which I take to be Kant's twin, related claims (actually they are the same claim) about the inseparability of concept and intuition in experience, and the pervasively apperceptive character of all human experience (any possibly contentful experience, whether explicitly intentional or "motivationally" contentful). And there is just as much to learn from the legacy of these claims in the classical German Idealist tradition. I want now to try to make good on that suggestion.

## 2

Consider first Kant's canonical formulation of the apperceptive condition.

> The transcendental unity of apperception forms out of all possible appearances, which can stand alongside one another in experience, a connection of these representations according to laws. For this

unity of consciousness would be impossible if the mind in knowledge of the manifold could not become conscious of the identity of function whereby it synthetically combines it in one knowledge.[24]

This is the claim that Kant sometimes summarizes by saying, "It must be possible for the 'I think' to accompany all my representations,"[25] and we might think (as Henry Allison does) that this claim for the "necessity of a possibility" of itself would not have to imply anything about actual mental operations. It just concerns a possibility. However, this possibility must also tell us something about the character of the unity that Kant counts as what it is for representations to have content. Kant held that what distinguishes an object in our experience from the mere subjective play of representations is rule-governed unity. His famous definition of an object is just "that in the concept of which a manifold is united."[26] Furthermore, Kant also says that

> This thoroughgoing identity of apperception of a manifold which is given in intuition contains a synthesis of representations, and is possible *only through the consciousness of this synthesis.*[27]

And he remarks that:

> That relation [of different representations to the identity of the subject] comes about, not simply through accompanying each representation with consciousness, but *only in so far as I conjoin one representation with another and am conscious of the synthesis of them.* Only in so far, therefore, as I can unite a manifold of given representations in one consciousness, is it possible for me to represent the identity of the consciousness in these representations.[28]

It is, to say the least, highly improbable that by saying "I am uniting representations in one consciousness," Kant meant that in all experience I am actually always undertaking a grand, intentional project of representation–unification. I suggest with McDowell that we understand him to be saying that everywhere our attentiveness to the world and others is and has to be reason responsive (or normatively attuned, one might put it). This means that the unity constitutive of possible objective purport is in a sense always putative or challengeable one might say. It is by our being always potentially reason responsive that experience can be said to be normatively directed and unified,[29] such that experience comes to have the determinate shape it does: an experience of a subject identical in all its experiences.[30] As Kant says, if cinnabar were sometimes red, sometimes not, sometimes heavy, sometimes not, our experience could not have objective purport. If *we* could not discriminate between a subjective succession of representations of an objectively, simultaneously existing object, and a subjective succession of representations of an objectively, successively occurring event, if we could not count recurring representations as representations of the same object, or not, and so forth (distinctions *we have to make*, that cannot be "read off" from any sensible deliverance, or simply "delivered," even if we do not have to make it "as such"), then we would have no basis for the kind of attentiveness and discrimination by virtue of which an experience of a single subject through time would be possible. But as we shall see, everything comes down to how we understand the difference between such a synthesis as a "perceptual taking" in this sense, and as a judgmental taking, and therewith what an apperceptive awareness of such a synthesis amounts to.

### 3

I want now to take up some suggestions from Wilfrid Sellars about this issue and follow through its implications in some of his articles. The first and most important suggestion comes from §33 of *Science and Metaphysics*, where, in support of the claim that "it would be a radical mistake to construe mental acts as actions," he writes of our perceptual takings that "It is nonsense to speak of taking something to be the case 'on purpose.' Taking is an act in the Aristotelian sense of 'actuality' rather than in the specialized practical sense that refers to conduct."[31] (By "perceptual takings," as in taking there to be a book on the table, I understand Sellars to be referring to perceiving [in the sense, he says, of "noticing"] a book on the table, not taking it that what I am seeing on the table is a book; he is not talking about "judgmental taking.")

What we want to understand (in order to disabuse ourselves of any worry about intellectualism or "overintellectualizing" perceptual experience) is how considering perceptual takings as "actualities" might help in such disabusing. However, these remarks are part of a larger Sellarsian picture built up of the notions of form and content, as well as actuality and potentiality, and we need a few more elements of that picture before we can appreciate the force of this claim about "conceptual actualization." We need especially to take on board, here without defense, and only for the sake of understanding this one issue, a controversial aspect of Sellars's Kant interpretation.[32] What we have been referring to as the "content of experience" is for Sellars a manifold of empirical intuitions, once we realize that such empirical intuitions are conceptually informed, that they have, as I am trying to say here, a conceptual form.

Here is a passage from Sellars's essay "Some Remarks on Kant's Theory of Experience," explaining his famous denial that the concept/intuition distinction in Kant is congruent with the conceptual/nonconceptual distinction.

Actually, the pattern of Kant's thought stands out far more clearly if we interpret him as clear about the difference between *general* conceptual representations (sortal and attributive), on the one hand, and, on the other, *intuition* as a special class of *nongeneral* conceptual representations, but to add to this interpretation the idea that he was *not* clear about the difference between intuitions in this sense and sensations. "Intuitive" representations would consist of those conceptual representations of individuals (roughly, individual concepts) which have the form illustrated by

this-line

as contrasted with

the line I drew yesterday

which is an individual concept having the form of a definite description.[33]

So it is the notion of conceptual activity relevant to these "this-such," intuitional representations – to the content of experience as the experience of discriminated particular objects and events – that we want to understand.

And we note right away that by understanding the way such conceivings are in play as "actualizations," Sellars does not mean that we should think that some sort of mental activity is merely triggered into operation, or let us say, occurs nonapperceptively. He says that the "evoking" by a red object in sunlight of "this is red" from a person who knows the language to which this sentence belongs is "no *mere* conditioned response."[34] This is just as true of the evokings of intuitional representations because, in the same way:

To know the language of perception is to be in a position to let one's thoughts be guided by the world in a way that contrasts with free association, with day-dreaming, and, more interestingly, with the coherent imaginings of the storyteller.[35]

This "letting be guided" is thus somehow neither a causal notion of evocation (causally wrung out of us) nor a judgment in the sense of a "decision" of sorts about what is before me. (I do not think that Sellars means us to understand these distinct conceptual uses [individuating, not sortal or attributive uses], these "this-cube intuitional representations" as incompletely discursive, as something like free-floating subject terms, poised for completion by some predicate, as what McDowell calls "fragmentary discursive content."[36] They amount to logically distinct representations [what in Kant would be the individual use of concepts, since there are no individual concepts for Kant], and they don't need to be articulated in this linguistic form to have that distinct logical form. More on this later.)

However, it is quite important to Sellars and to Kant that such representings be distinctly intuitional, so there is a great deal more to the story lying behind Sellars's understanding of the "this" in "this such." For example,

> Kant seems to have taken it for granted that the intuitive representings must be absolutely determinate [in a precise where and when – RP] and that to represent an absolutely determinate cube, for example, is to "draw it in thought" (A102, B138, B162). This difficult doctrine requires that the logical powers of the concept *cube* involve not only the inferential powers characteristic of its role as the predicate of full-fledged judgment, but also the powers involved in "constructing" or "drawing" determinate "this-cube" representings in accordance with a rule, and knowing what one is doing.[37]

This raises quite an involved and complicated question. Kant assumes constantly that the form of sensibility is distinct from the form of the understanding. This does not mean that intuitions are nonconceptual. But it must mean that the actualization of our conceptual powers in "the immediate presence" of a particular is *a different sort of actualization* than in the actualization of the understanding in forming representations among concepts, and this has to be explained by appeal to the actualization of what Kant considers another sort of power, a formal intuition involved in the actualization of any empirical intuition.

At any rate, it is in this sense that Sellars can formulate his own version of Kant's "same-function" claim.

> In receptivity we do the same sort of thing we do in the "spontaneity" of imagination, but we do it as receptive to guidance by objects we come to represent.[38]

The "same thing" is conceiving, but "in receptivity" is a dialectical notion we need more of the picture to understand.

We need this above all. Sellars then warns against a temptation (a temptation I think at play in many of the accusations about "overintellectualizing").

> The temptation is to think of the "content" of an act as an entity that is "contained" by it. But if the "form" of a judging is the structure by virtue of which it is possessed of certain *generic* logical or epistemic powers, surely the content must be the character by virtue of which the act has *specific* modes of these generic logical or epistemic powers.[39]

So it is not the case that we should think of the subject–predicate logical form or the substance–property categorical form or any general form as "empty" containers or something analogous to empty shapes or molds which are either "filled" by sense impressions of, say, the "Tom-is-tall" sort when we encounter the tall Tom, or which are sufficiently stimulated to "stamp" sensory impressions with the Tom-is-tall form. "Tom is tall" *is* just the specific way *the S is P form* is actual, manifests in actuality the discriminatory power that having *the S is P form* enables. It is "enmattered" just by being this specific mode of actualization of the capacity, not by being some stuff that is shaped. (So I think we should discard phrases like "conceptually shaped deliverances of sensibility.") And an empirical intuition, a perception of a particular, a perception of a particular-with-attribute, or the determination of a specific temporal relation between events, are the ways any such generic powers are, differentially, specifically actualized in sensible creatures like us.

And we can already note that none of this is guilty of cognitivism or intellectualism or, maybe the term should be "explicitism." One's seeing the tall Tom approaching involves the actualization just described without one thinking or judging "There is that tall Tom" or "Tom is tall" or any application of concepts to sensory material. Just as the *phronimos*'s practical rationality is *in* the way he attends to, ignores, selects, and dwells on (or not) aspects of the events and possibilities before him, the power of seeing *is* for us a conceptual power. That does not mean it is not a "truly sensual seeing" power but *rather* a "conceptual" or judgmental power. Because it is a conceptual power (apperceptive in the nondyadic, non-self-monitoring sense discussed previously) it can always, as we see, also be "attuned" to or "open" to, say, it actually not being Tom I see. We see the tall Tom in a way always open to cues that it is not Tom because in perceptually taking it to be Tom, I am apperceptively aware of it being such a taking. Not aware of Tom and aware of the taking, but aware of Tom in that way, in that adverbial sense. That is the way we *see*; it is not a seeing also "monitored" by a self-conscious I.

This is also relevant to how the way animals have representations is different from ours. Theirs are intentional in their way, but they do not have the status of "cognitions," as McDowell puts it. A dog might see a human figure far away (upwind, let us say) and seeing an unknown person, begin barking, only later to start wagging her tail as the known person it really is comes into view. *But the dog did not correct herself.* Here we do want to say that a perceptual cue prompted a response (one we can even call a rational response), and then a different perceptual cue (with more detail of visual features in view) prompted a different behavioral response. (I've never noticed my dog Molly become embarrassed that she made such a mistake – which she often makes – since she has no way of knowing that she made a mistake. That is not how she sees; she sees one set of cues then she sees another. This would be one way of saying she has no unity of apperception.)

And here we might as well take fully on board the form–matter, potentiality–actuality language Sellars is suggesting, and so the kind of hylomorphism most interesting: soul–body hylomorphism. In the standard analogy (from Book II of Aristotle's *De Anima*), if the eye were body (matter), *seeing*, the power of sight, would be its soul (form), the distinct way of the being-at-work or first actuality of its body. (There is thus no true separability [even if distinguishability]; a "dead" eye is not an eye anymore, except homonymously.)

So in a human sensibly receptive creature, subject to sensory impressions, specific conceptual intuitings (this-suches) would be the distinctive actuality, the distinctive being-at-work of such a capacity in creatures like us. The temptation to think that for creatures like us, we must distinguish the sensory manifold from the form which informs it, is the great temptation to be avoided, Sellars is insisting. The power of the eye's sight is not a power "added" to a material eye, as if there could be an eye identical in all respects to a normal eye, but which cannot see, and which is then "infused" with the seeing power. The seeing power *is* the distinct being at work of that body.

Analogously: when Kant famously says that "intuitions without concepts are blind," he does not mean that we are first subject to blind intuitions which can be said to become "informing" and "guiding" intuitions "after" concepts are applied to them. There are no blind intuitions, waiting to be conceptualized. Kant means to be rejecting the idea of nonconceptual content, not specifying its initial blindness. Blind intuitions are no more determinate intuitions than dead eyes are eyes. It is thus also a mistake to ask a question like "how do sensations guide or constrain the application of concepts," the same mistake as asking "How do we compare our judgments about states of affairs or our experiences of states of affairs with the states of affairs"? Experience is not guided by sensations; it *is* sensory awareness and can only be sensory awareness, a way of being on to particular objects and events, if it has the power of discrimination, a conceiving power, actualized sensorily. Likewise, the contents of experience are states of affairs. Any reluctance to judge on the basis of such experience comes from what else we experience not from any comparison.[40]

This Sellarsian picture gives us a somewhat clearer way to state the difference between what we earlier called perceptual and judgmental taking. Consider this formulation by "early" McDowell (prior to essays like "Avoiding the Myth of the Given").

> An ostensible seeing that there is a red cube in front of one would be an actualization of the same conceptual capacities that would be exercised in judging that there is a red cube in front of one, with

the same togetherness. [McDowell will give up "the same togetherness."] This captures the fact that such an ostensible seeing would "contain" a claim whose content would be the same as that of the corresponding judgment. [He gives this up too.]

As actualizations of conceptual capacities with the appropriate togetherness, the judgment and the ostensible seeing would be alike. *They would differ only in the way the conceptual capacities are actualized.* [This is what seems to me exactly right, and not to require what now follows.] In the judgment, there would be a free, responsible exercise of the conceptual capacities; in the ostensible seeing, they would be involuntarily drawn into operation under ostensible *necessitation* from an ostensibly seen object.[41]

These formulations, as McDowell realizes, might lead one to think that ostensible seeings are so necessitated that when we correct what we wrongly took to be what we saw, we are just *otherwise necessitated*. I have tried to say why this is not so. Ostensible seeings are just that, *ostensible* as such, apperceived and so always *subject* to correction, not alternate necessitation. And it suggests that cognitive claims are simply up to us, as if we *could* irresponsibly judge there to be an elephant in the seminar when there is not one.

I say "as McDowell realizes," because the problem with the formulation he uses is certainly not lost on him. In "Conceptual Capacities in Perception," he says:

> Moreover, coming to believe something on the basis of experience is not in general happily conceived as deciding what to think. ... it would be absurd to talk of deciding what to think, as if one exercised an option. One does not choose to accept that things are the way one's experience plainly reveals that they are.[42]

But if we take seriously the distinction between actualization and activity for both instances, then perhaps we do not need the involuntary/voluntary distinction. The conceptual capacities that are brought into play, actualized, in a perceptual experience (that is, properly understood, in empirical intuitions of the world) amount to the kind of actualization called for in the seamless and generally unproblematic perceptual experience of the world. But those capacities (the same capacities) can be brought into play in another way, at another register, when, in that experience, the actualization of an order of reflectiveness and assertoric claim-making is called for, which, while always available, is mostly not called for. This actualization is called for whenever something discordant in our perceptual experience occurs (we perceive at a later time aspects of the world inconsistent with what we took ourselves to be perceiving earlier, say, or when a question is posed: "Did you really see the cube?") The *modes of actualization* are different, not the *relation to the will*.

There is no question that describing such a perceptual or sensory actualization requires more than philosophy's usual share of metaphors. Several very useful ones, for example, are given by Peter Strawson, in his piece "Imagination and Perception." I appeal to him because he raises a number of points familiar in the phenomenological tradition, but also makes clear the connection with the conceptual-activity issue. In discussing the role of imagination in experience (often the vehicle of the sensory actualization of our conceptual capacities), Strawson notes the necessity for some role for the thought of (or apperception of) other actual or possible perceptions in our coming to take a present perception as a perception of a distinct object. In describing this "peculiarly intimate relation"[43] of such imagined perceptions to a present perception, he notes that he is not claiming that an actual occurrence of the memory or imagination of such perceptions is a dated event, and he falls back to saying, "Still, in a way, we can say in such a case that the past perceptions are alive in the present perception."[44] Or "It seems, then, not too much to say that the actual occurrent perception of an enduring object as an object of a certain kind, or as a particular object of that kind, is, as it were, soaked with or animated by, or infused with – the metaphors are *à choix* – the thought of other past or possible perceptions of the same object."[45] He goes on to talk about Wittgenstein on aspectual seeing and uses similar images as when Wittgenstein talks of the "echo of the thought in sight." Or when visual experience can be said to be suddenly "irradiated by a concept" as opposed to cases where it is "more or less steadily soaked with the concept."[46]

The point of all these metaphors, of course, is to find as many ways as possible to suggest some modality of conceptual activity other than assertoric judging or acts of conceptual sorting ("this is an A, this is a B, etc."), or deliberate rule-following. We can claim that we cannot be successfully onto objects without the actualization of a sortal discriminatory power, even while insisting that the actualization of that power in the sensory presence of the object is quite different from its actualization in judgmental sorting. We thus have on the one hand a way to address all the concerns noted in the "engaged-coping" version of this engagement: an inadequate account of experiential content, an inadequate differentiation from animal absorption, a conflation of bodily responsiveness with sensory attentiveness, and so forth. On the other hand, we can account for all these by pointing to our conceptual mindedness (concepts as *sensible forms*) all without saying that the contrary position McDowell wants to defend consists in construing seeing as a kind of judging or rule-following or concept application.

Finally, this is even clearer in practical contexts, especially in consideration of something like practical apperception, the self-relation by virtue of which what I am doing is this deed of mine, not that, and not something happening to me or that I suffer. The full claim, which would require a lengthy separate discussion, is that my intention (conceptually mediated mindedness in this context) should be said to be "in" the action, not "before" or "behind" it, in much the same way McDowell discussed rationality for the *phronimos*.[47] In initiating and then sustaining an action I obviously know what I am doing and have some sense of why, and so can be said to be going about my task "knowingly" without that having to mean that, as the deed unfolds, I keep checking to see if my intention is being fulfilled, or if the action still fits the act description under which I became committed to the intention, or if I still regarded it as justified. I can clearly be said to be attentive to all this without being attentive *to* the intention and act description and evaluation "*as such.*"

Likewise what gets attended to in practice as salient, of ethical significance; what goes "properly" *unnoticed* in a division of labor in a well-functioning egalitarian society (race, gender, etc.); what occurrence raises a question, demands attention, what does not; who is taken to be of relevance to the moral community, who is not; and so forth – can all be imagined to be of great, attended to, but unreflected weight in our practical world, some so deeply unreflective and strongly held that it is hard to imagine ever questioning them. We have all of this "in mind." And yet it is highly implausible that such historically and culturally quite variant shared forms of practice could be said to have any immediate, direct presence in our experience "on their own," as if pressing on our attention in themselves or "from the outside," or as if affordances *just* draw us in *on their own*. (They wouldn't afford anything if we weren't so minded.) A highly complex conceptual or normative interpretive framework is at work and is available for reflection, without it being the case that such a being at work is a matter of some explicit "reflective endorsement," or the result of an articulated moral evaluation somehow "going on" as a mental event and so a distinct component of such normative attentiveness.

The lesson from all of this is Hegelian, as of course McDowell realizes. Here is a typical Hegelian formulation of the thesis I have been defending. It is from his *Encyclopedia Logic* and repeats in a different way the "inseparability claim." As if responding to Dreyfus *avant la lettre*, after commenting on the kind of knowledge possessed by practiced experts like mathematicians, Hegel says,

> The facility that we attain in any sort of knowledge, art, or technical expertness, consists in having the particular knowledge or kind of action present to our mind in any case that occurs, *even, we may say, immediate in our very limbs*, in an outgoing activity. In all these instances, immediacy of knowledge is so far from excluding

mediation, that the two things are linked together – immediate knowledge being actually the product and result of mediated knowledge.[48]

## Notes

1. McDowell, *Mind and World*, p. 39.
2. Ibid.
3. Ibid., p. 28.
4. An example of such a position and such a reading of Kant: Hanna, *Kant and the Foundations of Analytic Philosophy*. For a concentrated presentation of his core view, see his "Kant and Nonconceptual Content."
5. I used to be one these puzzled critics. See "Leaving Nature Behind" and "Postscript," in *Persistence of Subjectivity*, and "McDowell's Germans." I no longer believe that this is the core problem but I want here mostly to try to state the correct formulation of the claim about "actualization" and briefly explore what issues that opens up onto.
6. This is where, I think, things start to go wrong. Everything depends on what one means by "implicit." There are two different senses at issue and they need to be distinguished. One involves the implicit possibility that one can shift from an unreflective engagement to an explicit, reflective deliberation. The other holds that quite a complex, conceptually articulated engagement can become implicit, *unattended to as such*, but nevertheless *responsible* for those aspects in our engagement with the world without which there could not be determinate content to experience. The latter sense is, I want to claim, what is appealed to by Kant and especially by Hegel. Focusing on the first sense creates a bit of a red herring in the exchange.
7. Dreyfus, "Overcoming the Myth of the Mental," p. 58.
8. Ibid., p. 56.
9. Ibid.
10. McDowell, "What Myth?," p. 339.
11. Ibid., p. 351.
12. Ibid., p. 346ff.
13. Ibid. One should add: they are in themselves or as such available because they *are* actualizations of a rational capacity. McDowell's claim is meant to exclude the possibility that things can be as Dreyfus says they are, and this availability is then "tacked on," as it is put in Matthew Boyle's valuable paper, "Additive Theories of Rationality: A Critique."
14. Ibid.
15. Dreyfus's use of Todes's example of balance could go either way (see Dreyfus, "Response to McDowell," p. 375). In one sense balance is strictly an inner-ear response mechanism; on the other hand, it can be overridden in some cases, can be made available for a directed response for the sake of some risk or extra caution.
16. Merleau-Ponty, *Phenomenology of Perception*, p. 277; my emphasis. See McDowell on "too many person-like things in the picture," "Response to Dreyfus," p. 369.
17. Dreyfus, "Return of the Myth of the Mental," p. 355.
18. Quoted by Dreyfus in "Overcoming the Myth of the Mental," p. 57. The passage is from Kelly's paper, "Seeing Things in Merleau-Ponty," and the most interesting example at issue concerns how the eye seems to "know" just what to do to maximize accuracy of color perception. It is clear that Kelly wants to

distinguish this from the perspiration cases by saying that in the vision case, we can intervene, override, begin to reflect, etc., and the dispute concerns whether this potentiality must show that this must make a difference in the sort and level of mindedness in the activity, or not. Kelly argues "not," and wants to say that in such relfectiveness we are not rendering a capacity's realization explicit but transforming and even in one sense falsifying the original capacity/experience.

19 For various reasons too complicated to get into here, Dreyfus wants to deny this by saying that only engaged copings that are truly "in the flow" and self-forgetful count as the phenomena he wants. Anything less than that full absorption and we've got someone directing their activities in some way and so they have been "knocked out of the flow."

20 I don't see how it helps at all to say that "the brain, which is comparing current performance with how things went in the past, sends an alarm signal that something is going wrong" (Dreyfus, "Response to McDowell," p. 374). That is just the insertion of yet another excess "person-like" thing in the picture. When "the brain" detects something going wrong, what happens; does it then tell me?

21 McDowell, "Response to Dreyfus," p. 366.

22 Ibid.

23 There are other suggestive formulations in McDowell's work; one is that what it means for sensibility to be able to make things available for cognition is that it "draws on" our conceptual powers, but only that ("Avoiding the Myth of the Given," in *Having the World in View*, p. 257). Others are that the higher cognitive capacities "are in play" or are "operative," that there is an "actualization" of capacities that are conceptual. (In one sense if we count what Dreyfus calls "attentiveness" as what McDowell wants to call "mindedness," there is not much difference between them, as Dreyfus suggests a bit in his last word in the exchange.).

24 Kant, *Critique of Pure Reason*, A108.

25 Ibid., B131.

26 Ibid., B137.

27 Ibid., B133; my emphasis.

28 Ibid.; my emphasis.

29 I realize that this kind of formulation ("directed") is exactly what some critics (like Tyler Burge) are worried about, but that all depends on what we take such self-direction to entail. I see no reason why one has to be wedded to an "intellectualist" interpretation either in this case in general or in the case of one "leading" a life. One has no choice about the latter and it rarely involves the formulation and attention to a "life plan."

30 Again, this would be in the way a life has to be led, rather than merely endured or subsists.

31 Sellars, *Science and Metaphysics*, p. 74.

32 It is not controversial for me. See *Hegel's Idealism*, ch. 2.

33 Sellars, "Some Remarks on Kant's Theory of Experience," p. 636.

34 Ibid., p. 637.

35 Ibid.

36 McDowell, "Avoiding the Myth of the Given," p. 272. That would be the case if Sellars had written something like "this cube. ... " But his dash is important.

37 Sellars, "Some Remarks on Kant's Theory of Experience," p. 643.

38 Ibid., p. 637.

39 Ibid., p. 639.

40 Compare Hegel's formulation. In the *Encyclopedia Philosophy of Spirit*, in trying to distinguish sensory receptivity as the mere modification of sensibility from intuition he says,

> [i]ntuition on the other hand is consciousness filled with the certainty of reason, whose object is rationally determined and consequently not an individual torn asunder into its various aspects but a totality, a unified fullness of determinations.
>
> (*Hegel's Philosophy of Mind*, §449)

41 McDowell, "Logical Form of an Intuition," p. 458; my emphasis.
42 McDowell, "Conceptual Capacities in Perception," in *Having the World in View*, p. 139.
43 Strawson, "Imagination and Perception," p. 58.
44 Ibid.
45 Ibid., p. 59.
46 Ibid., p. 64.
47 I argue for this in chapter 6 of *Hegel's Practical Philosophy*.
48 Hegel, *Hegel's Logic*, §66; my emphasis.

## Bibliography

Boyle, M., "Additive Theories of Rationality: A Critique," *European Journal of Philosophy* (forthcoming).

Dreyfus, H., "Overcoming the Myth of the Mental: How Philosophers Can Profit from the Phenomenology of Everyday Expertise," Presidential Address, *Proceedings and Addresses of the American Philosophical Association* 79, no. 2 (2005): 47–65.

——, "Response to McDowell," *Inquiry* 50, no. 4 (2007): 371–77.

——, "Return of the Myth of the Mental," *Inquiry* 50, no. 4 (2007): 352–65.

Hanna, R., *Kant and the Foundations of Analytic Philosophy*, Oxford: Oxford University Press, 2004.

——, "Kant and Nonconceptual Content," *European Journal of Philosophy* 13 (2005): 247–90.

Hegel, G. W. F., *Hegel's Logic: Being Part One of the Encyclopedia of the Philosophical Sciences*, trans. W. Wallace, Oxford: Oxford University Press, 1975.

——, *Hegel's Philosophy of Mind: Being Part Three of the Encyclopaedia of the Philosophical Sciences*, trans. W. Wallace and A. V. Miller, Oxford: Clarendon Press, 1971.

Kant, I., *Critique of Pure Reason*, trans. P. Guyer and A. W. Wood, Cambridge: Cambridge University Press, 1998.

Kelly, S. D., "Seeing Things in Merleau-Ponty," in C. Tarman (ed.), *The Cambridge Companion to Merleau-Ponty*, Cambridge: Cambridge University Press, 2005, pp. 74–110.

McDowell, J., *Having the World in View: Essays on Kant, Hegel and Sellars*, Cambridge, MA: Harvard University Press, 2009.

——, "The Logical Form of an Intuition," *Journal of Philosophy* 95, no. 9 (1998): 451–70.

——, *Mind and World*, Cambridge, MA: Harvard University Press, 1996.

——, "Response to Dreyfus," *Inquiry* 50, no. 4 (2007): 366–70.

——, "What Myth?" *Inquiry* 50, no. 4 (2007): 338–51.

Merleau-Ponty, M., *Phenomenology of Perception*, London: Routledge & Kegan Paul, 1962.
Pippin, R., *Hegel's Idealism: The Satisfactions of Self-Consciousness*, Cambridge: Cambridge University Press, 1989.
———, *Hegel's Practical Philosophy*, Cambridge: Cambridge University Press, 2009.
———, "McDowell's Germans," *European Journal of Philosophy* 15, no. 3 (2007): 411–34.
———, *The Persistence of Subjectivity: On the Kantian Aftermath*, Cambridge: Cambridge University Press, 2005.
Sellars, W., *Science and Metaphysics*, London: Routledge & Kegan Paul, 1968.
———, "Some Remarks on Kant's Theory of Experience," *Journal of Philosophy* 64, no. 20 (1967): 633–47.
Strawson, P. F., "Imagination and Perception," in *Freedom and Resentment and Other Essays*, Abingdon, Oxon: Routledge, 2008, pp. 50–72.

# 5

# TRANSCENDENTAL PHILOSOPHY AND THE POSSIBILITY OF THE GIVEN

*Sebastian Gardner*

In his Presidential Address to the American Philosophical Association, Dreyfus introduces his thesis concerning "nonconceptual embodied coping" (henceforth NCEC) in the context of cognitive science.[1] NCEC comprises the claim that "embodied beings like us take as input energy from the physical universe and process it in such a way as to open them to a world ... without their *minds* needing to impose a meaning on a meaningless Given, nor their *brains* converting the stimulus input into reflex responses."[2] Dreyfus defends NCEC as an alternative to the cognitivism of Minsky *et al.*, claiming that it receives support from the existence of the frame problem and other difficulties which cognitivism encounters in modeling the competences manifested in the performance of everyday tasks in terms of computationally realized symbolic representations. NCEC is supported independently and directly, Dreyfus argues, by Walter Freeman's work in the neurosciences, and by empirical studies and direct examination of the phenomena associated with the exercise of basic skills and the acquisition of expertise. Dreyfus describes these last considerations as "phenomenological" and claims NCEC as a thesis found also in Merleau-Ponty and Heidegger.

This makes clear the nature of the philosophical context to which Dreyfus's claim belongs: NCEC is a thesis concerning the nature of the mental content adduced in psychological explanation, held to be supported by empirical considerations and compatible with neurological explanation, the proper measure of which in its competition with other accounts of mental content is provided by the criteria standardly employed in adjudicating a posteriori-grounded theories of the mind.

In this regard, how does McDowell's thesis that conceptuality is ubiquitous in mental content (CC) compare? As Dreyfus notes, quoting from *Mind and World*, McDowell's "basic point" has a different orientation: CC derives from consideration of what is required for the *justification* of perception-based belief.[3] McDowell's contribution to the *Inquiry* debate consists in exploring ways in which CC, as a thesis formulated originally in the context of epistemology and argued in *Mind and World* to be required for the possibility of knowledge as such, allows itself to be extended into the sorts of domains which occupy Dreyfus, McDowell's aim being to show that the sphere defined by justification is not too narrow to encompass the data which Dreyfus cites as evidence for NCEC.

Reciprocally, Dreyfus accepts that McDowell's question of justification needs to be addressed, but he regards it as simply one consideration among others to be thrown into the mix: saying how justification is possible, according to Dreyfus, is equivalent to explaining "how conceptual content arises from nonconceptual content,"[4] and a beginning is made on this task, Dreyfus suggests, in Samuel Todes's *Body and World*, while more help can be found in *Being and Time*. Dreyfus concedes that phenomenologists "lack a detailed and convincing account of how rationality and language grow out of nonconceptual and nonlinguistic coping,"[5] but regards this as merely work for the future: he sees no difficulty in principle with the task of working out the "step-by-step genesis of the conceptual categories that structure the space of reasons."[6]

Despite their different starting points, Dreyfus and McDowell understand themselves to be arguing about the same topic, namely the extent to which content is conceptual, and accordingly regard their respective theses NCEC and CC as contradictories. Now it is no mystery that a thesis originating in epistemological reflection should come into contact with a thesis in the philosophy of mind: if solutions to epistemological problems involve claims regarding the nature of the mind and its contents, then these claims may be expected to agree with conclusions about the mind arrived at through reflection on the nature of psychological explanation, on the reasonable assumption that the mind must be one and the same thing in both contexts. From a slightly different angle, however, the configuration of the debate is puzzling. McDowell's CC is a thesis of Kantian lineage, and Kant's philosophy is transcendental, and in Kant's terms it is a mistake to allow the relevance of a posteriori theorizing about the mind into transcendental questions. Similarly, the historical figures of key importance for Dreyfus, and who are also to some extent important for McDowell – Heidegger and Merleau-Ponty – belong firmly to the post-Kantian tradition and (in the relevant writings) describe their claims and concerns as transcendental. To be sure, Merleau-Ponty makes use of empirical psychology in a way that Heidegger does not, and neither is a neo-Kantian of any stripe, but it would be absurd to suggest that *Phenomenology of Perception*, let alone *Being and Time*, is simply a work in the philosophy of mind as that subdiscipline's agenda is conceived by contemporary analytic philosophers.

So the question stands: How does it come about that in the *Inquiry* debate certain claims which apparently belong to the context of transcendental philosophy are treated as being on the same level as empirically grounded theories of the mind? It may be answered that neither Dreyfus nor McDowell employs Kant's distinction of empirical and transcendental standpoints and that this is due not to any oversight but to their considered rejection of it. Be that as it may, there is all the same something to be clarified: at the very least, it would be helpful to have a clearer picture of how Dreyfus and McDowell, in view of their repudiation of Kant's separation of spheres in favor of forms of nonreductive naturalism, stand in relation to the historical figures who cast long shadows over their writings and whose philosophical authority they, to some degree, draw upon. This is particularly important, I would add, in light of Dreyfus's programmatic remark that the "time is ripe to follow McDowell and others in putting aside the outmoded opposition between analytic and continental philosophy."[7]

The question of what the concept of the transcendental amounts to and its historical vicissitudes is obviously much too large for the present occasion. However, a full answer to that question is unnecessary for my purposes, which require only that I make plausible the notion that there is a type of philosophical concern abiding from Kant to Merleau-Ponty which is staked on upholding the segregation of transcendental from empirical issues and disjoined from the project of philosophy of mind. To this end I will focus on the topic, central to Dreyfus's and McDowell's concerns, of the given. What follows in the next section is a selective review of certain key moments in the treatment of the given in the history of transcendental philosophy. In the section following ("Dreyfus, McDowell, and transcendentalism"), I will explain the bearing of my historical account on Dreyfus and McDowell.

## Transcendental theories of the given: a very brief history

### I

The *locus classicus* of transcendental philosophy's rejection of the Given is of course Kant's "Transcendental Deduction of the Pure Concepts of the Understanding." This section of the *Critique* is extraordinarily dense and its interpretation a matter of disagreement. One well-known view, articulated famously by P. F. Strawson, maintains that a sharp line can and should be drawn between the sound epistemological argument contained (at least incipiently) in the Deduction, and the package of "transcendental psychology" with which Kant (unfortunately) conjoins it. On Strawson's account, the latter, which involves a story of multiple faculties engaged in atemporal acts of synthesis, is tethered to Kant's incoherent metaphysics of transcendental idealism, and merely obscures the austere epistemological argument at the core of the Deduction, which after careful reconstruction will be seen to comprise a convincing refutation of Humean skepticism, fulfilling the Deduction's aim of validating empirical knowledge.[8]

Let it be granted for the moment that an austere analytical argument, directed at the justification of empirical belief, can be extracted from the Deduction. Does it follow that the synthesis story is otiose? In light of the Deduction's extremely high concentration of themes and multilayered structure, and of Kant's own remarks concerning its purposes,[9] it is reasonable to hypothesize that the presence of elements in the Deduction which do not contribute directly to the anti-Humean aim of empirical justification is due to its having other targets and ambitions, distinct from, albeit connected with, the aim of showing that rational grounds can be supplied for commonsense beliefs about empirical reality. The notion I wish to explore is accordingly that the synthesis story is intended to explain how it is possible, in a specific sense which will need to be clarified, for empirical objects to be given to us, and that it is attached to a philosophical method the employment of which cannot be recast in the form of an austere Strawsonian transcendental argument.[10]

One sense of "the given" is that of a purely sensory item, bare acquaintance with which suffices for noninferentially justified judgment of the item. Call this, following Sellars and McDowell, the Given. Certainly Kant rejects this, for reasons which run in close parallel with those of McDowell. A different sense of the given, which survives rejection of the Given, is that in which it is a noncontingent part of ordinary natural consciousness that the deliverances of perceptual experience are immediately intelligible and its objects immediately, unproblematically judgable. The existence of the given in this lower-case sense is of course not merely accepted but stressed by Dreyfus and McDowell.[11] The Myth of the Given can then be taken to reflect a genuine, underlying, prephilosophical datum: what makes Givenness mythic is just the supposition that this datum is adequately *explained* by a theory of items' presence to consciousness as due to their sheer impact on a merely receptive subject.

With the acknowledgment of the reality of the given, but the rejection of the Given, what philosophical tasks are set, or problems posed? From here we might go directly to McDowell's claim that CC captures what needs to be supposed in order for our cognitive and other rational modes of being-in-the-world to be made sense of, and to Dreyfus's counterclaim that the given demands NCEC. Instead, I want to indicate a different path, which leads us to discover a purpose for Kant's theory of synthesis. To bring this into focus, it will help to refer to Fichte.

Fichte offers the following characterization of the given, in terms which avoid the Myth: among the immediate inner and outer determinations of consciousness are, he says, some which are found to be "accompanied by a feeling of necessity."[12] That any particular determination, or representation, is accompanied by a "feeling of necessity" is contingent, but it is no contingency that we are in general subject to such determinations. Another name for this fact, Fichte says, is simply "experience," *Erfahrung*: "the system of experience is nothing but thinking accompanied by a feeling of necessity."[13] Fichte identifies the primary, if not total, task of philosophy with the explanation of experience: the "object" of philosophy is the *Erklärungsgrund der Erfahrung*. Fichte accepts that, in advance of our actually producing an adequate explanation, it may be doubted that the question is answerable, but not that there *is* a question to be answered. Implied in the acceptance of *Erfahrung* as as the explanandum of transcendental enquiry, Fichte continues, is our acceptance of grounds which "must necessarily lie *outside of all experience*": it "follows from the mere thought of a basis or reason that it must lie outside of what it grounds or explains,"[14] hence it "would be contradictory" to suppose that "the explanatory ground of experience" belongs to experience itself or comprises a "portion of experience."[15] The datum of givenness or fact of *Erfahrung* can be regarded as requiring transcendental explanation, then, only if the subject has not already been conceived as a worldly empirical item in causal communion with other empirical items, since once that conception is accepted, the possibility of *Erfahrung* has been presupposed, and the only questions which then remain to be considered concern which particular empirical items induce which particular representations, and by means of what mechanism they do so. Fichte identifies the preempirical standpoint presupposed by transcendental enquiry with pure I-consciousness. An alternative way of formulating the relevant "premundane" standpoint, closer to Kant's, is to say that philosophical reflection on the given must take as its starting point what Mark Sacks helpfully calls a "minimally conceived domain of presentation," incorporating no more than the distinction between a content presented, and the recognition thereof.[16]

I want to suggest that from this starting point, paths of reflection leading to Kant's theory of synthesis may be plotted. Before describing these, it will be best to remind ourselves of two important objections to Kant's theory, advanced by F. H. Jacobi and G. E. Schulze (among others) in the early days of Kant reception and reiterated many times subsequently.

The core elements of Kant's theory are (1) the conception of synthesis as *unifying activity* of the subject's, and (2) the notion of *bestowal of conceptual form* on sensible material. To the first it is objected that, even if logical absurdity does not result from hypothesizing a nontemporal subject intentionally crafting experience behind the scenes, the hypothesis in any case contradicts the Critical aim of an immanent metaphysics of experience. The obvious objection to the second is that it too results in frustration of Kant's higher purposes, since if bestowal of conceptual form consists in its material imposition on intrasubjective sensory items, then "empirically real" objects reduce to configurations of sense-data, and "objectivity" to relations between them, collapsing transcendental idealism into Berkeley's empirical idealism.

Clearly, if the theory of synthesis is to amount to anything more than an outline for a possible subpersonal empirical theory of cognition, then the implications alleged must be avoided: synthesis must not be understood as an act description referring to a mental doing on a par with say "remembering" or "attending," nor, more fundamentally, as any sort of operation performed on a mental object. The latter would, in fact, reduce Kant's idealism to a form of transcendental realism in which the direction of migration[17] of properties has merely been reversed, yielding a story of the transposition of form from the subject's faculty of representation to its mental object. What ought, however, to be understood by transcendental idealism – if it really does, as Kant claims, break at the deepest level with all previous conceptions of cognition – is a position which allows us to *avoid* having to think of form as needing to move or be transported from one locale to another. The theory of synthesis should close the subject/object divide, not by telling a story of migration, but by building the agreement of the object's form with the subject's mode of cognition into the original situation of a subject's being presented with an object.

Everything turns, accordingly, on finding a way of construing the theory of synthesis which steers clear of the imagery of a process of modification of preexistent, materially real items. One way in which this may be done is by treating the theory as articulating essential structural features of the domain of presentation.

To conceive a domain of presentation is in the first instance to picture a space with a certain asymmetrical shape, in which a pole of necessary unity, that of the subject-presented-to, contrasts with a pole of necessary multiplicity or heterogeneity, that of the objects comprising the "presented domain," in Sacks's terminology. Since objects presented within the domain must come together in such a way that a single unified field is constituted, the rudimentary idea of a domain of presentation incorporates not only the opposition of a One to a Many, but also a resolution of this opposition in favor of the One, a *conversion* or transposition of the manifold into a unity. Also involved, as a simple consequence of the domain's being so to speak looked *into* rather than looked *at* from – in McDowell's phrase, sideways on – is the fact of our own location at one end of this structure, constituting the pole of the One rather than that of the Many; with this is correlated the *directionality* of perspective within a domain of presentation, the fact that the object is *for* the subject and the subject orientated *towards* the object, not vice versa. Joining up these several points, we arrive at the idea that the process or function in virtue of which the manifold of a domain achieves unity consists in operations performed by the subject.

Supporting this identification is the consideration that the conditions of possibility of the given which we are attempting to lay out cannot be external to the domain of presentation itself: if the domain were insulated from the conditions which, according to our theory, make it possible, then the theory would imply that the domain of presentation is not intelligible to itself, or at least, it would fail to show that and how it is intelligible to itself; a strictly external theory would not serve the internalist end, which is set when we take the domain of presentation as our starting point. The subject of presentation must stand, then, in some precomprehending relation to the structures described in the theory, and since this cannot of course consist in its being presented with those structures as objects, the appropriate inference is that the structures are realized for the subject in the form of operations which it performs. The subject accordingly relates to the structures as, in Henry Allison's instrumental-cum-teleological characterization, objectivating "vehicles" of cognition.[18]

The introduction of activity into the theory of the given is motivated in addition by the second core element of the theory of synthesis. To the extent that the domain constitutes a field of items which the subject can potentially single out in thought, a specific mode of givenness on the part of objects is presupposed. In order for an object to figure *in* my domain of presentation, as opposed to merely being accessible *by way* of it, the object must be directly and immediately thinkable.[19] The coextensiveness of what-is-presented with what-is-immediately-thinkable requires in turn that certain conditions are met.

First: If being presented with an object, and thinking that object, were opposed as instances of pure passivity and pure activity respectively, then the relation between *figuring in the domain* and *being thinkable* would be a contingent, external relation in need of mediation, and incompatible with the object's immediate thinkability. This is avoided if the activity explicit in the thought of objects is regarded as subtending the domain itself, that is, as implicated in the simple fact of an item's inclusion within it: if the domain shares its ground with whatever sponsors acts of thought, then it is intelligible that it should comprise a space across which thought can extend itself.

Second: If objects are to be immediately thinkable, then they must present themselves not as mere *candidates* or *occasions* for concept application, but as already having some determinate character. This determining of consciousness is part of what Fichte means by a "feeling of necessity." In order for some object to be immediately thinkable, the application of a (basic, identifying) concept to the object must not proceed "externally," by way of another, prior act of thought, rather the object must be *presented as incorporating* the conceptual character it is or can be thought to have. If we then ask how such a state of affairs is possible – How can there be an internal relation between a concept and an object-as-presented? – the answer suggests itself, again, that the object owes its conceptual subsumability to the same active operation as is responsible for its simply figuring in the domain of presentation.

These two conditions explain why the domain of presentation is not split down the middle, why it does not find itself divided between active concept deployment and passive object reception: if nothing separates thinking *that O is F* and thinking *O itself* – if these can occur in the same breath – then it is intelligible that empirical belief should ensue from perceptual experience in such a way that the latter is grasped as grounding the former with nothing intervening.

Finally: If subjective operations are invoked in order to account for, on the one hand, the unity of the domain of presentation, and on the other, the immediate intelligibility of presented objects, then it is a short and reasonable step to identify the two processes, i.e. to suppose that unification and conceptualization comprise one and the same operation. With which we arrive at the core of Kant's theory of synthesis.

All too obviously, these remarks do not suffice to validate the specifics of the theory of synthesis found in Kant, nor even do they show that synthesis must employ a priori concepts. My present purpose, however, is more limited. All I wish to have made, at least, roughly intelligible and partly plausible is the supposition that Kant's theory of synthesis attempts to address the complex explanandum which the given presents, through a form of explanation which is concerned with neither conceptual nor causal relations, and which instead attempts to exhibit the structures which constitute the perspective of a domain of presentation. These structures are conditions of possibility, and yet, since they do not bear directly on the rationality or justifiability of our beliefs, they differ from the necessary conditions established by Strawsonian transcendental arguments.

The relevant distinction between these two versions or conceptions of conditions of possibility is drawn very clearly by Paul Guyer, who repudiates the non-Strawsonian sense of condition of possibility which he finds endorsed by Allison. Correctly understood, Guyer argues, Kant's arguments yield only "an epistemological model of the confirmation of beliefs," "the basic framework for the *justification* of beliefs": Kantian conditions of possibility are "principles which would have to be appealed to in the justification of empirical claims to knowledge," "conditions for verifying or confirming empirical judgements."[20] Allison's conception of a condition which is not psychological and yet not equivalent to a justification, Guyer considers there to be no room for.

The theory of synthesis attempts to occupy the space between psychology and justification which Guyer excludes. Whether it has a chance of success depends on its avoiding the objections cited earlier, and on there being some philosophical need to which it answers. On the first count, my earlier comments show that the theory of synthesis need not be regarded as assuming an existentially independent item as input, on which causal action is subsequently exercised, and so does not tell a story of "imposition." As regards the second issue, that of philosophical need, consider how

McDowell formulates CC: "if an experience is world-disclosing, which implies that it is categorially unified, *all* its content is present in a *form* in which ... it is suitable to constitute contents of conceptual capacities."[21] "All that would be needed for a bit of it to come to constitute the content of a conceptual capacity," McDowell continues, is that it "be focused on and made to be the meaning of a linguistic expression." While Kant might agree with McDowell that being focused on and linguistically articulated are all that "being a content of a conceptual capacity" requires *once* categorially unified content has *been given*, the point of the theory of synthesis is to explain how any such content *can be given* in the first instance: the theory of synthesis is Kant's shot at locating Fichte's *Erklärungsgrund der Erfahrung*, and it is in those terms that it needs to be assessed.

Whether a theory such as Kant's theory of synthesis counts as "epistemological" depends, therefore, on how broadly we understand the project of epistemology. If epistemology is defined, following Strawson and Guyer, in terms of responding to the threat of skepticism and/or determining the rational grounds of belief and warrantedness of our knowledge claims – an exclusively "juridical" conception of epistemology, as it may be called – then the theory of synthesis does not belong to it. But if epistemology encompasses also what might be called the *metaphysics* of cognition – an account of what cognition *is* and of its subjective grounds, in respects which go beyond their juridical properties – then the theory of synthesis forms part of it.[22]

## II

One structural feature of the minimally conceived domain of presentation is its presupposition, as we have seen, of a distinction of subject and object more fundamental than the distinction drawn by Kant between inner and outer sense – since even in the case where an object presented is inner, its distinction from the subject to whom it is presented must be articulated. Fichte's transformation of Kant's theory of synthesis into the *Wissenschaftslehre*'s theory of object-positing may be regarded as deriving from this point. Fichte's claim is that something can *be given* if and only if I as it were give it to myself, i.e. *posit* the object *in opposition to* myself; only in this way, Fichte argues, can the primordial subject/object distinction be explicated. This thesis presupposes Fichte's independent account of the priority and intrinsic intelligibility of the self-relation, and it is motivated by (among other things) the inadequacy of what Fichte perceives as the only possible alternative, evidenced by K. L. Reinhold's attempt at a reconstruction of Kant's account of the given, which for that reason merits brief discussion.[23]

One important ground of dissatisfaction with Kant's account of the given in the early reception of his philosophy focused on Kant's attempt to establish rational communication within the given between its intellectual and sensible components. Salomon Maimon, arguing that this aim of Kant's Deduction remained unrealized and so that Hume had not been refuted, inferred from Kant's failure the need to retrieve Leibniz's conception of sensibility as defectively articulated intellection, and to reconceive cognition as involving at the final limit *elimination* of the given: "what is required for completeness in the thought of an object is that nothing in it should be given and everything thought."[24]

As the objections of Maimon and others accumulated, defenders of Kant's theoretical philosophy proposed ways to repair its perceived weaknesses, and on Reinhold's account, its defense demanded above all that it be equipped with an indubitable and universally accessible foundation. To this end Reinhold assigned absolute priority within the Kantian system to the concept of "*Vorstellung*," by which he understood not representation in the sense of an item within a mind, but the total *structure* of representation inclusive of the distinction of the representing subject and the object represented.[25] The reality of this structure, Reinhold argued, is assured apodictically by each and every "fact of consciousness," since *Vorstellung* is simply the genus to which the various species of such facts – thought, sensation, etc. – belong. By enclosing all the elements of cognition within an overarching unity, Reinhold supposed that misconceptions concerning the nature of our cognitive powers, responsible in turn for false (skeptical and dogmatic) views of the scope of our cognition, could be disposed of.[26]

While agreeing that Reinhold's strategy is of the kind needed, Fichte argued that Reinhold omits, crucially, the *ground* of the distinction of subject and object which defines the structure.[27] That distinction cannot be supposed to simply "exist" or "occur" within the sphere of representation, in the way that a line may be drawn on a map, or a fissure appear in a natural object – it must be registered by the subject for whom it obtains, and its being registered cannot comprise a distinct state of affairs from its obtaining, since it can obtain only in so far as it is registered by the subject. One cannot, therefore, *start* with the sphere that Reinhold calls *Vorstellung*; rather, priority must be assigned to the "I," which must be regarded as *producing* that sphere, i.e. as *making* the subject/object distinction in the dual sense of both *cognizing* it and making it *exist*. In a way that goes beyond Kant – who treats the subject as producing the unity of the object but not the articulated sphere of representation itself – Fichte proposes the "I" as the ground which, though "present in consciousness,"[28] lies "outside of all experience" and provides its fundamental condition of possibility. Fichte, like Reinhold, can agree therefore with Maimon that the possibility of the given would be unaccountable if the heterogeneity of sensibility and understanding were allowed to remain an ultimate and irreducible condition of cognition, but since Fichte's theory of the I's object-positing promises a transcendental explanation of the existence of sensibility, Maimon's objection is overtaken.[29]

If the *Wissenschaftslehre* succeeds, then it will have been shown that *Erfahrung* constitutes bona fide, skeptic-proof cognition, and Maimon's neo-Leibnizian elimination of the given will be undermined. The two aims, the juridical-epistemological and the metaphysically grounding, which in Kant's Deduction allow themselves to be separated, are therefore united in the *Wissenschaftslehre*: while Kant's theory of synthesis pursues an aim which stands to one side of the task of refuting skepticism, Fichte's theory of object-positing is intended to achieve both the explanatory purpose of Kant's theory of synthesis, and a juridical, antiskeptical purpose.

Fichte's objection to Reinhold can be understood from an additional angle, one which is especially helpful for present purposes. Reinhold's avowed methodology, no less than Fichte's, is that of reflection on the minimal domain of presentation: the foundation of his post-Kantian philosophy of elements, Reinhold explains, is the power of representation *as such*,[30] not the power of representation conceived as a power *of the mind*, and his concern is exclusively with the "inner conditions" for representation, these being those which "must occur within representation itself."[31]

Since Reinhold followed the correct method, why did he go astray? On Fichte's account, the reason is that Reinhold – driven by the thought that Critical philosophy requires an indubitable foundation, and in the grip of the assumption that indubitability is uniquely a property of *facts* – theorized the domain of presentation as if it could be treated as *itself* a fact, i.e. made an object for, or content of, itself, and thus could view itself sideways on. Reinhold attempted to construct a model which would validate itself, as required for the refutation of skepticism and by the Kantian constraint of internal intelligibility, but misconstrued this reflexivity as if it were an empirical matter, with the result that his account of the given fails to explain how the distinction essential to the existence of a domain of presentation comes to be articulated. As Schulze pointed out, Reinhold's project led him to attempt to determine *Vorstellung* as a thing in itself.[32] By contrast, Fichte's theory relocates the reflexivity offstage and in a nondiscursive form, in the intuition of active *Ichheit* which can come into view only in so far as the perspective of a domain of consciousness is not merely contemplated but occupied through being *enacted*.

### III

Just as Fichte's *Wissenschaftslehre* may be regarded as describing the transcendental structure which comes to light when we probe the given, so too may the opening moves of Hegel's *Phenomenology of Spirit*.

The *Phenomenology* begins with a consideration of "the way in which" the object is "present in" the most rudimentary objectual consciousness, *wie er in ihr vorhanden ist*,[33] and advances by putting explicatory pressure on that notion. Consciousness in the immediacy of apprehension (*Auffassen*) is described as either "reaching out" to (*hinausgehen*) or "entering into" (*hineingehen*) the object.[34] These terms recall imagery employed in the Introduction to the *Phenomenology*, where Hegel reported that natural consciousness conceives the relation of cognition as either a "tool" by means of which one "takes hold" of the object or a ray of light by means of which the object "reaches" us, who "receive" it.[35] The target of the sense-certainty chapter is not, however, the commonsense conception of cognition, but the attempt (associated, for Hegel, above all with Jacobi) to ground cognition on the object's sheer immediacy.

Hegel allows it to be supposed for the sake of argument that *hinaus-* or *hineingehen* are candidates for the foundation of cognition, and proceeds to show that all that can be claimed by way of constituting *that which* we "reach out" or "enter into," is "pure" and empty being, not the being *of* anything in particular, not even that of the object purportedly cognized.[36] The conclusion that immediate consciousness construed as mere *hinaus-/hineingehen* fails to qualify as genuine, nonempty cognition lays the ground for Hegel's positive claim, elaborated in the course of the chapter, that genuine, i.e. determinate, cognition requires *begreifen*, conceptual grasping.

To the extent that our interest lies in the justification of knowledge claims, the lesson of Hegel's critique of sense-certainty is therefore simply that cognition demands conceptualization. But while Hegel does of course wish to reaffirm this Kantian thesis, his ultimate interest in exhibiting the "poverty" or "emptiness" of cognition reduced below the level of conceptual grasping lies again – like Kant's theory of synthesis and Fichte's theory of object-positing – with the *prejuridical* conditions of the possibility of givenness, the more fundamental order which precedes and underpins the relation of justification constitutive of ordinary empirical consciousness. What will transpire eventually – after consciousness, through multiple twists and turns, has achieved "the representation of *reason*," the certainty that consciousness "is all reality"[37] – is that the given must be conceived as embedded within a heavily modified, concept-based version of Fichte's subject–object identity, and the sense-certainty chapter aims to provide the first step in Hegel's argument to that conclusion.

This becomes clear when we note Hegel's innovation to transcendental theory of the given and the departure that he thereby makes from Kant and Fichte. Midway through the dialectic of sense-certainty, a point is reached where putatively immediate consciousness is endeavoring to hold fast to what it "means" – i.e. its intended object – in the face of the challenge posed by reflection, which asks *which particular* object is intended, and it has also learned that neither consciousness itself nor the object on its own can do the work needed. Immediate consciousness then redefines itself "as a *whole* which stands firm within itself as *immediacy* and by so doing excludes from itself all the opposition which previously took place."[38] This "pure immediacy" or "pure intuiting" is sealed within itself: Hegel says that it refuses to "come forth" when other objects are drawn to its attention and that it allows "no distinction whatever" to "penetrate" it.[39]

In the next moment of the dialectic – in which we endeavor to explicate vicariously this mute, autistic consciousness which has turned its back on the demands of reflection – we "approach it" and "point to" its object on its behalf.[40] Here then two standpoints which were previously identified – that of the (natural) consciousness under observation, and that of the (philosophical) consciousness which observes it – have been separated out.

The next twist of the dialectic alerts us to the puzzle which we now confront.

The phenomenological observer realizes that, in order for him to point to the *correct* object – the one that immediate consciousness has in mind – he needs to "enter into," to allow himself to be "made into," the very same singular point of immediate consciousness as he is observing.[41] The result of such an identification, however, would be to merely *repeat* the experience of stultification, since the phenomenological observer would then *share* immediate consciousness's inability to articulate itself.

We appear, therefore, to have arrived at an impasse: we began with the apparently unproblematic idea, enshrined in Kant's concept of intuition, of a subject directly presented with an object *in its particularity*, but reflection on this idea has revealed a contradiction: on the one hand, the standpoint of phenomenological observation must collapse itself into that of the immediate consciousness under observation in order to understand what it "means," i.e. identify the object it intends, while on the other hand, this same end requires that it hold itself apart, i.e. locate itself outside and oppose itself to the consciousness observed.

What this aporia compels us to recognize, Hegel supposes, is that when we (phenomenological observers) conceive consciousness as related immediately to a particular object, we must be bringing to bear some structure, some richer set of materials, than is disclosed from *within* the perspective of immediate consciousness, and since this structure is not an inner aspect of the object's givenness, Hegel supposes that it cannot be intuitional. The remainder of the sense-certainty chapter begins to lay out this nonintuitional, hence conceptual structure: Hegel argues that "this," "here," "now," and other indexicals must be understood as "universals," and concludes his analysis with the claim that sense-certainty "is nothing but" the "history" of its "movement,"[42] a structure which incorporates negativity and the holistic interrelation of its elements – *this* "Here" is *not* that "Here," yet belongs to a "simple ensemble of many Heres," etc.[43]

With this talk of sense-certainty as a conceptual "movement," Hegel's thesis of the autonomy of conceptuality has begun to show itself, and since his doctrine of the Concept of course opposes Kant and Fichte, it is important to grasp exactly how the discussion of sense-certainty has invited it in.

As already indicated, Kant and (more explicitly) Fichte conceive transcendental theory in perspectival terms; repeatedly, Fichte explains that the philosopher in constructing the *Wissenschaftslehre* is merely reenacting, and constructing a model of, the "acts of mind" of the *Ich*.[44] Now Hegel agrees that transcendental theory must be taken to represent what is internal to subjectivity – else it fails to model a genuine cognitive achievement of the subject's – but the fact that the structure must be *realized in* the perspective of the subject does not entail that it *arises from* it, and Hegel's claim is that there is no pressure for us to think so. In the *Phenomenology* Hegel employs the duplex structure of observed and observing consciousnesses in such a way as to create space for his thesis of the autonomy of the conceptual, in a way that contrasts with Fichte's account of the method of the *Wissenschaftslehre*: on Hegel's account, when we observers recognize that, in order for the aporia in our construal of sense-certainty to be resolved, a conceptual structure must be brought into play, then that structure should be understood as self-subsistent and directly authoritative.

Hegel's absolute idealist metaphysics of reason and subject–object identity occupies therefore, in terms of its bearing on the question of the possibility of the given, the same role as Kant's theory of synthesis and Fichte's theory of object-positing. The crucial difference is that, if Hegel is right, then the theory need not and should not be regarded as specifically anchored in, restricted to, or validated by the perspective of the subject, since it merely spells out what is already in play, implicitly, when "the perspective of the subject" is made the object of philosophical scrutiny. This means that – though there is of course much further to go, because many other contexts need to be worked through – Hegel has in the sense-certainty chapter, if his argument works, broken the back of subjectivism: philosophical reflection is to be conceived henceforth not as attempting to show us how we can, from the inside, "get outside" of ourselves – a conception of the philosophical task to which Kant and Fichte continue to subscribe – but as retrieving and making explicit structures which must be regarded as immanent within the perspective of the subject and yet do not owe their validity to the subject's, nor to any other, mere "perspective."

Hegel's point may be put in focus by returning once again to Reinhold. *Vorstellung* is treated by Reinhold as necessarily revealing in our acquaintance with it an intrinsic transparency and unconditional intelligibility. The unraveling of this assumption provokes Fichte, we saw, to embed *Vorstellung* within the encompassing orbit of the absolute *Ich*. The different and more radical conclusion which Hegel extracts involves a reflexive realization on the part of philosophical consciousness: it is not merely that there must be more to the domain of presentation than Reinhold supposes; rather the philosophical conception of the domain of presentation *as* primitive, as entitled to methodological *primacy*, is *itself* a version of the Myth of the Given, or in Hegel's language, "immediacy," from which it follows that Fichte's proposal, whatever its improvement over Reinhold, is ultimately equally ill-conceived.

Hegel's relation to the transcendental standpoint of the domain of presentation is thus double-edged. Hegel does not foreswear the Kantian–Fichtean transcendental starting point: reflection on the given initiates the argument of the *Phenomenology*, and gives us our first, vital lesson in the method employed in that work and the metaphysics which accompanies it. But the moral of that reflection is an antisubjectivism.

## IV

Supposing the nature of transcendental treatments of the given, as found in Kant and German idealism, to have been made at least roughly clear, to what extent is that model followed also by the existential phenomenologists? Again the topic is huge, so I will need to be extremely brief. What I hope to make plausible is that, despite massive departures from "classical" transcendentalism, existential phenomenology retains distinctive transcendental traits.

In his seminal commentary on *Being and Time*, Dreyfus claims that Heidegger's understanding of fundamental ontology can be glossed adequately in terms of "intelligibility" and our "making sense of things."[45] The claim is contentious but vital for Dreyfus's purposes, since it allows him to treat Heidegger's account of Dasein as self-standing and as at least pointing in the direction of the concerns of philosophy of mind:[46] for if to ask about the meaning of Being just *is* to ask *how we make sense* of the world, then "fundamental ontology" and "analysis of Dasein" are effectively interchangeable.[47] If, however, an independent and prior grasp of the *Seinsfrage* is necessary in order to understand the specific problem which the analysis of Dasein is intended to address, and if furthermore the *Seinsfrage* conditions the very sense of that analysis and its results, then the question must be raised whether NCEC, as Dreyfus formulates it, can be a thesis of Heidegger's at all.

In the *Letter on Humanism* Heidegger comments on a locution that he employs on one occasion in *Being and Time*: "Es gibt Sein."[48] Heidegger explains that *es gibt* is used in *Being and Time* "purposely" and should be understood literally as "it gives" (for which reason the French *il y a* does not provide an accurate translation): "For the 'it' which here 'gives' is Being itself."[49] Why speak in this manner? Heidegger explains that he writes "es gibt Sein" in order to avoid "Being is," because the verb "is" is appropriate to entities but not to Being itself – to use "is" of Being would be to misrepresent Being as an entity. "Es gibt Sein," by contrast, renders the "primal mystery" of Parmenides' "For there is being" – the word "gibt" designates the essence of being as "granting its truth."[50] In a still later text, *On Time and Being*, Heidegger revisits the notion that "es gibt Sein," now saying that the task is to bring into view the "It" and its "giving," *das Es und sein Geben in die Sicht zu bringen*.[51] This task, he says, breaks with Western metaphysics, which thinks Being but not the *Es gibt* "as such."[52]

The issue surrounding *Es gibt Sein* derives, as phenomenological method demands, from consideration of the given. Whether or not it creates a problem for their accounts, as Schelling alleges, and as Jacobi claims that it does for any form of idealism, one dimension of the given which neither Fichte nor Hegel put in explicit focus consists in the *existential awareness* which the given necessarily incorporates. Heidegger, in this respect as in many others standing close to Schelling, maintains that the existential component of the given cannot be regarded as merely supervening on the object's being posited (Fichte), nor as merely the first term of conceptual mediation (Hegel).[53] The Being of beings, Heidegger supposes, must be a further fact, distinct from the fact that beings are intelligible and make sense to us, and from the (equivalent) fact that beings are encountered with determinate features; otherwise there would be nothing for *Es gibt Sein* to register. The question of the ground of the existential component of the given – in Heidegger's preferred terms, the question concerning the nature of the "It" which "gives" – comprises an explanandum of the same manifestly transcendental rank as those addressed by Kant, Fichte, and Hegel. Heidegger's analytic of Dasein – the account of care, equipmentality, and so on, within which everything that Heidegger has to say about practical activity is nested – should thus be regarded as an attempt to illuminate this fact, i.e. to address the question of how Being can "give," or of how anything can be given *as being*. And if we look back to Heidegger's texts of 1927, we find it explained quite clearly that the constitution of Dasein is formulated as a theme for philosophical enquiry *only* in so far as Dasein is regarded as relaying the meaning of Being via its "understanding of being," i.e. in so far as Dasein is that to which Being is given, the site where the *Es gibt* of Being comes to light (its "Lichtung.")[54] Equally clear, from, for example, Heidegger's repudiation of "anthropology, psychology, and biology" in §10 of *Being and Time*, is the internal connection of the analytic of Dasein with the *Seinsfrage*.[55]

In all of this, skilled coping behavior as a *psychological* explanandum is nowhere in sight: embodied coping is of interest to Heidegger, not under that ("ontic") description as such, but in so far as – by way of Interpretation – it belongs to a transcendental explanans.[56] NCEC, in the form Dreyfus gives it, could not play that explanatory role. This is not yet enough to show that NCEC cannot be a thesis of Heidegger's at some very subordinate level, but pending an account of how NCEC can be connected logically with a transcendentally oriented theory of Dasein, the claim should be regarded with skepticism.

If this is correct, then Dreyfus, by isolating and foregrounding the theme of skilled coping behavior in *Being and Time*, may be considered to have interpolated a set of concerns which (at the very least) do not lie at the core of Heidegger's philosophy, and which are properly regarded – to the extent that our business with Heidegger is not a matter of radical reconstructive surgery – as inseparable from transcendental concerns, from which they lie firmly downstream.

Parallel remarks apply to Dreyfus's recruitment of Merleau-Ponty. While NCEC is a thesis concerning the nature of the mental content to be adduced in the explanation of skilled behaviors, at the end of the day Merleau-Ponty, as I read him, is not in this line of business at all: part of the point of *Phenomenology of Perception* is I think to persuade us to withdraw human subjectivity at large altogether from psychological-explanatory contexts.[57] As I read him, Merleau-Ponty's strategy of playing off empiricist and intellectualist explanations against one another is designed, not to create space for a *third* type of explanation competing on the same level, but to show us the need to extract perception altogether from that context and to relate it instead to the transcendental, non-empirical fact of there being given to us a differentiated object world, which comprises the real explanandum of the *Phenomenology*. The metaphilosophical design of the *Phenomenology* – to demonstrate the necessity of our shifting up from a psychological-explanatory to a preobjective transcendental appreciation of perception, by showing that empiricism and intellectualism jointly lead objective thought into antinomies – is not acknowledged by Dreyfus. Dreyfus believes that he follows Merleau-Ponty in seeking to steer perception out of objective thought, but this requires Dreyfus's deflationary interpretation of preobjectivity, which becomes on his account indistinguishable from the sorts of subpersonal inputs theorized by empirical psychologists; Dreyfus reduces preobjectivity to a property of information states – their merely being incompletely processed[58] – whereas Merleau-Ponty regards preobjectivity as correlatively and equally an attribute of the *world*, carrying antirealist metaphysical implications.

Later I will say more in support of my claim that Dreyfus has cut himself loose from the historical Merleau-Ponty, and reconstructed in his place a figure whose concerns fit onto the agenda of contemporary analytic philosophy of mind. For now it should just be noted how Dreyfus reduces the "job of phenomenologists" to the business of merely "get[ting] clear concerning the phenomena that need to be explained."[59] Since Dreyfus retains from phenomenology none of the elements which are required in order for it to offer anything that might count as philosophical *explanation* – Husserl's thesis of the absoluteness of transcendental consciousness, Heidegger's conception of Dasein as the site of *Sein*'s self-unconcealing, Merleau-Ponty's idealism of preobjective being: all these Dreyfus sacrifices through either explicit rejection or deflationary interpretation of the relevant concepts – nothing remains for phenomenology except a task of close observation and cataloguing of data due to receive their explanation elsewhere.[60] It is consequently puzzling when Dreyfus announces that phenomenologists "owe us an account" of how the conceptual emerges from the nonconceptual,[61] since his conception of phenomenology makes it hard to understand how it could give an account which is not merely descriptive but genuinely explanatory of anything as philosophically large scale as conceptuality.[62]

## Dreyfus, McDowell, and transcendentalism

### I

My historical survey has touched on a number of issues. It will help to review these, and to say something about what circumscribes transcendental philosophy, before returning to Dreyfus and McDowell.

I have argued that three distinguishable philosophical projects may be engaged in reflection on the given: (i) epistemology in the narrow "juridical" sense defined earlier; (ii) philosophy of mind, which takes the mind as an empirical content of empirical reality or nature; and (iii) transcendental enquiry, which seeks to determine the preempirical explanatory grounds of the empirical sphere.[63] Though combinable in various ways, it is important to be clear about which of these project(s) is (are) being pursued in any given case.

Paramount for transcendental philosophy is the denial that a theory of mental content can take the place or do the work of a transcendental explanation: from the transcendental standpoint, the attempt to grasp in the form of an empirical configuration the structure which defines the domain within which empirical forms can appear repeats Reinhold's mistake of suppressing perspectivity. Transcendentalism as such does not, however, impose a veto on philosophical consideration of the mind as an empirical object: it implies only that the project of philosophy of mind occupies a secondary place in the full philosophical picture, simply in the sense that transcendental concerns are more fundamental. The two philosophical projects come into conflict only if either (1) the transcendentalist denies, in addition, that there *is* any cogent sense in which the mind can be ascribed empirical reality (the position of Heidegger and Sartre, for example, but not of Kant or Hegel); or (2) the working assumption of the philosophy of mind that the mind is to be considered an empirical object is raised up and asserted as a final metaphysical fact, one which there is no need, and which it makes no sense, for us to attempt to get behind or ground transcendentally. The latter is a claim that many philosophers of mind will of course wish to make, but it is not a presupposition of the philosophical analysis of mind as an empirical object.

The relation of transcendental philosophy to epistemology is more complex, since justificatory concerns – though weakened by the time of existential phenomenology – are of course what originally, in Kant, motivates the transcendental turn, and they remain central in German idealism. Again, the important point for present purposes is that transcendental treatment of epistemological themes extends beyond what is required in order to settle juridical issues. Thus in the case of the given, the full transcendental aim includes determining the conditions which make it possible for something to be given in advance of and in abstraction from the given's justificatory role. Accordingly, transcendental enquiry goes beyond claims to the effect merely that the empirical sphere necessarily has a certain form,[64] and transcendental arguments of the austere Strawsonian type do not exhaust its ambitions.

Transcendental enquiry may affirm, but is not committed to, the existence of a nonempirical or metaphysical subject numerically distinct from the empirical subject, nor to idealism of the strength found in Kant. What it does maintain is that empirical subjectivity requires explication, in the sense that insight must be achieved into how the subject, from a preempirical basis, comes to grasp itself as a content of empirical reality, to the extent that it does so. The refusal to take the subject's empirical reality for granted *ab initio* is complemented by a commitment to idealism only in the weak sense that representation of the world is held to stand in necessary interconnection with preempirical features of the subject.

That the primary object of transcendental enquiry is not the mind, as contemporary philosophy of mind understands it, raises the question: If not about the mind, what then, if anything, *are* transcendental claims "about," and what makes them *true*? Without pretending that talk of articulating the structure of the domain of presentation does anything very much to answer this 64-million-dollar question, the appropriate thing to do in the present context, in which the aim is only to circumscribe transcendentalism as a certain broad type of philosophical endeavor, is just to point out that the metaphilosophical question of the status and truth conditions of transcendental claims has been central to the *internal* business of transcendentalism. Following a line of descent from Reinhold's abstraction of *Vorstellung* from the mind as such, and Fichte's theory of a genetic deduction of ordinary consciousness, down to Heidegger's theory of formal indication and Merleau-Ponty's deictic conception of phenomenological truth, the issue of how transcendental claims should be theorized – whether as "purely formal," "virtual," "regulative," "postulative," "metaphysical," "transcendental psychological," "ontological," or whatever – has been high on the transcendentalist agenda.

## II

How does Dreyfus stand in relation to transcendentalism? This is fairly clear-cut, for there is I think little to distinguish Dreyfus metaphilosophically in transcendentalist eyes from mainstream analytic naturalism, and that when Dreyfus declares that the wall is finally down, the prospect of union with analytic philosophy on the terms envisaged by Dreyfus is one that transcendentalist continental philosophers should balk at.

This is perhaps clearest when Dreyfus gives his view of the nonconceptual ground level which, he believes, lies beyond the reach of McDowell's conceptualist imperialism.[65] In the course of their debate, McDowell reveals the plasticity of his notion of conceptuality, obliging Dreyfus to dig ever deeper in order to locate a stratum on which conceptuality cannot plausibly be supposed to encroach. This, however, threatens to recast the whole debate in terms of the older argument in the philosophy of mind between those (like McDowell and Jennifer Hornsby) who affirm and those (like Daniel Dennett) who deny the autonomy and explanatory self-sufficiency of personal, as opposed to subpersonal, explanation. The debate between Dreyfus and McDowell is, however, surely intended by both parties to bear on what lies at the personal level: Dreyfus wishes to argue, not for nonconceptual *sub*personality, but for nonconceptuality as a dimension of *personal*-level being (Dreyfus's alignment with Heidegger depends on this). Now Dreyfus asserts not merely that we discover as a matter of (phenomenological) *fact* a dependence of conceptuality on nonconceptuality; he also offers – in his critique of what he calls "representationalism"[66] – arguments which parallel closely the subpersonalist's standard strategy of arguing that there simply *must* be some machinery ticking over below the personal level, on the grounds that propositional attitudes and other such folksy mental entities are insufficiently robust to stand on their own two feet. The question thus arises of what distinguishes Dreyfus's ground floor from subpersonal territory, and I suggest that when Dreyfus takes as his paradigm of nonconceptuality something as relatively microscopic as my hand's adjusting itself to the shape of the doorknob,[67] the personal-level status of his nonconceptualism is not secure. The doubt is reinforced when we are told that "subjectivity," "reference to a subject," awareness of oneself "even in some minimal way," are altogether stripped out of nonconceptuality,[68] from which the very distinction of subject and object is missing.[69] If, however, Dreyfus's counter to McDowell does resolve itself into the claim that the execution of personal-level actions involves certain unconceptualized subpersonal occurrences, then (presumably) this is a point that McDowell can accept, for it was never part of the brief of conceptualism to maintain the conceptuality of elements which are subpersonal components of the *execution* of coping, but not themselves *instances* of coping.[70]

Dreyfus's specific claim that his thesis of nonconceptualism is found in the existential phenomenologists assumes that they share his conception of what it is to be either "conceptual" or "nonconceptual," as if these were universal terms of art. But it needs to be asked if one and the same idea is in play in the discourses of phenomenology or classical German philosophy and contemporary philosophy of psychology. The conceptual/nonconceptual distinction is after all not part of the equipment of commonsense psychology: we introduce it in order to do specific theoretical work, and what makes the property of "being conceptualized" or "involving concepts" definite is a surrounding philosophical apparatus. Thus, for example, Kant's thesis of the dependence of objective experience on a priori conceptuality is well defined, and it makes sense to ask, as commentators do, whether Kant upholds certain specific subtheses concerning (for example) the dependence of the synthesis of the imagination on that of the understanding, whether intuition independently of the understanding has objectual reference, and so on. The same applies, in their own terms, to Fichte's and Hegel's accounts of the involvement of concepts in the given. Present-day philosophy of mind, however, is not concerned with issues as formulated in classical German philosophy, and it cannot be simply taken for granted that historical figures have anything to say about the conceptualism versus nonconceptualism debate in the philosophy of mind, since the terms in which it is cast are foreign to transcendental philosophy's starting and end points.[71] When the contexts of philosophical theses – the sorts of reasons given in their support, the problems which they are intended to resolve, the constraints to which they are subject, the implications which they are held to carry – diverge so widely, the notion that an identical philosophical thesis ("all content is conceptualized") can travel across contexts begins to disintegrate.

To illustrate and support the point just made: Dreyfus is most confident that Merleau-Ponty fits the bill of a nonconceptualist (Heidegger, Dreyfus acknowledges, seems partly or at times of McDowell's view).[72] To be sure, Merleau-Ponty thinks that intentionality extends down very far indeed from self-conscious self-determining subjectivity, and he can afford to do so without for a moment worrying that he has tipped over the edge and abandoned intentionality for mere mechanical nature, because he considers that human subjectivity is ontologically continuous with a preobjective reality which (his *Phenomenology* indicates and later writings make clear) has all of the strangeness of a *naturphilosophisch* absolute-idealist reprise of Leibniz's metaphysics of active force. But does the fact that Merleau-Ponty upholds the merely *negative* claim that the *specific* kind of conceptuality which marks out what *he* calls objective thought fails to percolate all the way down mean that he thereby holds the *same* view as certain contemporary cognitive scientists occupied with subpersonal information-processing? To suppose so is again to take a very relaxed view of the criteria of sameness for philosophical theses.

Examination of the *Phenomenology* shows that Merleau-Ponty's thesis of preobjectivity is in any case not in fact squarely opposed, in the manner of Dreyfus's NCEC, to Kant's claim concerning the necessity of understanding or McDowell's CC. At some points Merleau-Ponty may appear to draw a straight contrast of understanding with perception, but also and equally he talks of a "reform" of the understanding: the rediscovery of preobjectivity means, Merleau-Ponty says, that the understanding (*l'entendement*) "needs to be redefined, since the general connective function ultimately attributed to it by Kantianism is now spread over the whole intentional life and no longer suffices to distinguish it."[73] The opposition of "perceptual life" and "concept" can gain application, Merleau-Ponty says, *only* when analytical reflection has falsely dissected the intentional tissue of sense experience into two reified classes, a collection of sensory atoms and a set of connecting principles.[74] Other passages reiterate and amplify the thought that the task is to reconceive the *necessary* relation of perceptual and motor contents with the understanding or "symbolic function."[75]

Now if preobjectivity involves the understanding, as Merleau-Ponty redefines it, then this shows one of two things. If we suppose that *l'entendement* entails conceptuality, then we must say that on Merleau-Ponty's account conceptuality *is* present in preobjectivity, and so that it must be uncoupled from objective thought, which should be defined in terms of a *specific* form of conceptual representation, one generated by analytical reflection.[76] Alternatively, we may conclude that Merleau-Ponty's thesis of preobjectivity is not concerned at all with the *empirical* property of being conceptualized in Dreyfus's sense of the material or functional constitutional infiltration of experiential content by concepts; from this it would follow that NCEC – since it sits within a realist framework and involves no recognition of preobjectivity in Merleau-Ponty's metaphysical sense – is not an alternative to objective thought but a form of (in Merleau-Ponty's sense) empiricism. Either way, the line that Dreyfus draws between "conceptual" and "nonconceptual" does not align with Merleau-Ponty's central distinction.

## III

McDowell's relation to the historical legacy of transcendentalism is at once much closer and much harder to pin down.

On the one hand, McDowell's prioritization of the issue of justification and explicit engagement with the central transcendental explanandum concerning the possibility of a concept's having an object or a belief's having objective purport,[77] along with his (apparent) ascription of a transcendental role to "second nature" as a Hegelian successor to Kantian synthesis and Fichtean positing, and his inclusion of nature within the space of reasons, may all seem to show him pursuing straightforwardly transcendental aims.[78]

Yet also central to McDowell's project are the quietist, diagnostic–therapeutic, exorcistic elements from Wittgenstein, which appear to give a compelling reason for regarding McDowell as, to the contrary, declining the transcendental project: McDowell maintains that "[m]oves in the language of traditional philosophy can be aimed at having the right not to worry about its problems, rather than at solving those problems,"[79] and describes *Mind and World* as aiming to give explanations which unmask as illusion our seeming "to be confronted with philosophical obligations of a familiar sort."[80] Such remarks imply that what may appear to be transcendentalist theses in McDowell should be read (at the end of the day) not as answers to, but as refusals of, transcendental questions. If accordingly McDowell's engagement with transcendentalism is quasi-deconstructive, a provisional adoption of transcendentalist ways of thinking for the purpose of demonstrating how they, by their own lights, yield to an enriched conception of nature, then the *kind* of meaning possessed by McDowell's seemingly transcendental assertions will depend on which sector – whether pre- or post-exorcism – of philosophical thought we occupy.[81]

It is worth noting one fundamental respect in which McDowell's transcendentalism must in any case be regarded as scaled down. In my account of the transcendental project, I emphasized its pursuit, over the horizon of justification, of preempirical grounds. McDowell's inclusion of nature within the space of reasons may seem to satisfy this description. McDowell himself does not, however, regard that claim as entailing any sort of metaphysical commitment, and this seems plausible, in so far as the conception of a reason operative in McDowell – the notion of what a reason as such *is* – is restricted to that of something we can *give*, *employ*, or *use* to a normative end, something the being of which is exhausted in the *justificatory role* it can play *for us*.[82] Thus McDowell cites Sellars's identification of the space of reasons as the space "of justifying and being able to justify what one says."[83] Reflection on what goes on *within* the space of reasons so defined does not, however, equip us with an account of the space of reasons *itself*. In Kant's terms, McDowell's juridically defined space of reasons is merely the space of the understanding, which needs to be located in turn within the space of (theoretical and pure practical) reason, and in Hegel's too, it remains that of the mere *Verstand*, not that of *Vernunft* – it spans the rational relations involved in our cognizing determinate objects, but does not articulate the ground of those relations.[84] The shortfall, measured by traditional transcendental lights, consists in McDowell's silence regarding the nature and status of the space in which we do our reason-giving, and the metaphysical issue of how the space of reasons is grounded – how it either gets to be launched, or supplies its own ground. To draw an analogy with Kant's treatment of space in the Transcendental Aesthetic, it is as if McDowell stops with the proofs of space's a priori necessity and declines to take up the further question of space's transcendental reality or ideality.

The next question is whether this truncation of the transcendental project supplies the basis for a criticism of McDowell. In place of the detailed discussion which would be required in order to return an answer to this question, I wish just to describe a general respect in which McDowell's position may be considered open to transcendentalist criticism. The key question is whether McDowell is entitled to turn his spade or shrug his shoulders at points where the transcendentalist rolls up his sleeves.[85] McDowell embraces the overarching transcendental explanandum, since he affirms that the possibility in general of a relationship between thought and object – "objective purport" – is something that demands explanation. The question, accordingly, is why McDowell interprets the task which is thereby set in relatively constricted terms: if the possibility of objective purport deserves explanation, then why does this not involve positive substantial accounts of (i) the conceptualizedness which makes possible the immediate thinkability of given objects, (ii) the bare possibility (questioned by Maimon) of an intelligible relation between the sensible and the conceptual, (iii) the a priori necessary properties of *Bildung* in virtue of which it can lead us into a space of reasons with a sound title to objectivity, (iv) the properties of first nature in virtue of which it invites our empirical cognition, (v) the unity and differentiation of first and second nature, and so forth?[86]

McDowell has replied to critics on these sorts of points, and since there is no space here to discuss his responses, let me just assume that the issues are not settled, and move on to the following point. The classical transcendentalist will insist that in order to rationalize his position, McDowell needs at the very least to explain the general, principled basis on which the reach of transcendental explanation is, on his account, properly determined. The suspicion must be allayed that what determines McDowell's restricted interpretation of the transcendental task is his prior and independent commitment to the avoidance of what he calls (rampant) Platonism: for if a prior substantial commitment to naturalism is what in fact dictates the degree of McDowell's involvement with transcendental questions, then the transcendentalist will reasonably object that things have been got back to front, and that the projected exorcism relies on an insufficiently wholehearted appreciation of our transcendental-philosophical obligations. McDowell will then have failed to unsettle the transcendentalist's belief in the necessity of pursuing the transcendental task, once taken up, all the way to its bitter Platonic end.

## IV

The puzzle with which I began consisted in the fact that, in the *Inquiry* debate, the distinction between transcendental and a posteriori claims appears to have been erased, contrary to what the avowed historical allegiances of Dreyfus and McDowell lead one to expect. If my characterization of transcendental philosophy is on the right track, then Dreyfus and McDowell should be credited with very different orientations with respect to the post-Kantian legacy: Dreyfus in effect abjures the transcendental project in order to undertake the task – wholly legitimate in its own terms, once freed from accompanying historical claims – of recasting themes in phenomenology for broadly naturalistic purposes, while McDowell proposes a quasi-deconstructive reformation of the transcendental tradition. The disagreement of Dreyfus and McDowell reflects this divergence: McDowell's transcendental orientation, qualified as it may be, leads him to prioritize normative considerations and thence to CC, while Dreyfus's post-transcendental outlook makes room for his nonconceptualism.

While this historical contextualization sheds some light on Dreyfus and McDowell's disagreement, it does not directly help to resolve it, and it may even seem to imply that the argument cannot be resolved at the non-metaphilosophical level at which it is pursued in the *Inquiry* exchange. This is a plausible conclusion, in so far as the sorts of alleged counterinstances to CC adduced by Dreyfus tend (I argued) to subpersonality, while McDowell's prioritization of normativity – which to Dreyfus appears arbitrary – in any case makes it hard to see how any accumulation of putatively nonconceptual phenomenological or other a posteriori data could, by McDowell's lights, undermine CC.[87] That said, I want to indicate a respect in which there is I think scope for an effective criticism to be made of McDowell's conceptualism from Dreyfus's standpoint, on the condition that an important modification is made to the latter.

Given that for McDowell as much as for Dreyfus, what we arrive at ultimately, once our transcendental anxieties have been dispelled and the standpoint of premundane subjectivity which motivates skeptical reflection has been closed down, is an understanding of ourselves as natural entities in a (ontologically rich) natural world, it is unclear why it should be necessary to arrive at this all-important truth via a specifically *transcendental* route. This is not to say that the route to that truth should involve instead, as Dreyfus proposes, an account of how conceptuality and rationality "arise from" or "grow out of" nonconceptuality; Dreyfus's commitment to telling a story of the "genesis" of conceptuality, it seems to me, is a burden that does not assist the case for NCEC. But there is another way in which we can think of ourselves as coming into possession of the all-important truth that Dreyfus and McDowell agree on, which involves nothing more abstruse than direct confrontation with the manifest *fact* of our being-in-the-world, appreciation of which (to the extent that it is needed) is assisted by immersing ourselves in the sort of Heideggerian picture which Dreyfus teases out of Division I of *Being and Time*.[88]

McDowell may object that this is too blunt, too external, too sideways on, to give satisfaction, and that it therefore makes no contribution to the problem at hand. But in making any such reply – and indeed simply by dint of having adhered to the traditional transcendental path – McDowell exposes himself to the objection that he reveals himself to lie still under the influence of the assumption of first-person privilege and the correlative necessity of domain-of-presentation theorizing. In other words, Dreyfus may object that it is only when one's basic conception of the *nature* of justification is unduly conditioned by transcendentalism that one will see fit to abstract "experience" from the world and to reify it as a "tribunal," yielding the subject–object problematic with which *Mind and World* begins. The fantasy of extramundane existence which this conception incorporates, Dreyfus may assert, is better confronted and extirpated at root than indulged. Proceeding in this way, Dreyfus can point out, avoids being saddled with McDowell's thesis of the inclusion of the world within the space of reasons – a thesis which, however often McDowell may remind us that it is "only a reminder," does not seem to shed its spookiness.[89]

And with transcendental worries laid to rest, there is scope for instating nonconceptuality. If there are no longer any transcendental roles to be played, then there is no longer anything to be feared from NCEC: nonconceptual content, just as it cannot be invoked to help explain conceptuality, cannot threaten to interpose an epistemic barrier between mind and world or otherwise reactivate transcendental anxieties; it can have no transcendental bearing, either negative or positive. With the transcendental pressure off, the existence or not of nonconceptual content can be allowed to become a purely phenomenological or otherwise a posteriori matter.

In sum, Dreyfus may argue that McDowell's conception of exorcism as operating from the *inside* of the illusion targeted is bound to leave it at least half alive – in so far as, for example, the image of nature as lying within the conceptual realm seems forever on the verge of a Fichtean or Hegelian reinflation – and so has less to recommend it as a therapeutic measure than the alternative, which involves nothing more than insistently ostending the fact of our being "always already" in the world.

What allows the criticism of McDowell just outlined to be made, it should be noted, is the fact that McDowell distinguishes between the two aims of (a) providing therapy for our anxieties, and (b) exhibiting transcendentally the rationality of the mind–world relation, and that he subordinates the latter to an overarching therapeutic context, to that extent denying the autonomy of transcendental concerns. The denial is essential if McDowell is to represent the transcendental ladder as something to be kicked aside once it has been climbed, i.e. if we are to avoid thinking of transcendental assertions as instances of "constructive philosophy."[90] It is, however, just this degree of standing back from the transcendental agenda, this refusal to grant the sheer rational inexorability of transcendental problems *ab initio*, which makes room for the objection that McDowell's chosen method of internal exorcism to achieve his therapeutic aim is (at best) undermotivated. That the therapeutic, post-transcendental aspect of McDowell's position should create a vulnerability will be regarded by the classical transcendentalist as evidence of the rub between the two aspects of McDowell's project.

It goes without saying that from this nothing follows regarding the vindication of classical transcendentalism. Indeed, to the extent that McDowell's assumption that we must at all costs avoid "rampant" Platonism remains unchallenged, no such result is in the offing. My intention here has just been to indicate how McDowell may be thought to be squeezed from two sides, and so to emphasize the fineness of the line that McDowell's ingenious departure from transcendental orthodoxy requires him to tread.

I have sought to cast doubt on the assumption that transcendental conclusions about "the mind" are in principle intertranslatable with conclusions arrived at in the philosophy of mind. The mind should not be regarded as a given, ready-made philosophical topic, on which we can alight without having already made broad metaphysical decisions which crucially predetermine the kinds of results that enquiry can arrive at. The coming into coincidence of post-analytic and post-Kantian continental philosophy is not exactly a myth, but it ought, I think, to be viewed as problematic, and not yet realized in a complete and systematic form. McDowell comes as close as anyone to an integration of the two traditions, but I have argued that considerably more is at stake in this than, as McDowell sometimes puts it, "domesticating" the rhetoric of post-Kantianism. Fostering the interaction of analytic and continental philosophy does not after all, we should remind ourselves, require us to make their unification a regulative ideal.

## Notes

1 Dreyfus, "Overcoming the Myth of the Mental."
2 Ibid., p. 49.
3 Ibid., p. 58.
4 Ibid., p. 59.
5 Ibid., p. 61; reiterated in "Return of the Myth of the Mental," p. 364.
6 Dreyfus, "Overcoming the Myth of the Mental," p. 61.
7 Ibid., p. 61.
8 That the synthesis story should be dispensed with is a conclusion reached also by Mark Sacks, from an angle more internal to Kant. Sacks argues that a reconstruction of the Deduction which presupposes synthesis but not atomism yields only conclusions too weak for Kant's purposes (Sacks, *Objectivity and Insight*, pp. 71–75, 98–111), while a reconstruction which presupposes perceptual atomism in addition, though it delivers the desired conclusions, is flawed by its presupposition of a specific model of the mind, a doctrine which is contestable and frustrates the deeper insight in transcendental idealism (pp. 76–87, 111–29, 268–72, 312). Scheler's objections to Kantian synthesis overlap with Sacks's; see Scheler, *Formalism in Ethics and Non-formal Ethics of Values*, pp. 65–67.
9 Kant, *Critique of Pure Reason*, Axvi–xvii.

10 In this connection, see Sacks, "Nature of Transcendental Arguments."
11 See McDowell, "Avoiding the Myth of the Given," p. 1, referring to Sellars, "Empiricism and the Philosophy of Mind," p. 127.
12 Fichte, "[First] Introduction to the *Wissenschaftslehre*," §1, 422–24, pp. 7–9; standard edition page reference precedes that of the translation.
13 Ibid., §4, 428, p. 13.
14 Ibid., §2, 424–25, p. 9.
15 Ibid., §4, 428, p. 14.
16 See Sacks, *Objectivity and Insight*, pp. 228–35.
17 *wandern*: Kant, *Prolegomena to Any Future Metaphysics*, §9, 4:282.
18 See Allison, *Kant's Transcendental Idealism*, pp. 10, 83–85, 165.
19 The opening paragraph of the Transcendental Aesthetic (A19/B33) may be read as asserting the *necessity* of the immediately thinkability of objects given to us. Kant distinguishes (i) the necessity, for all and any cognition, of *Anschauung*, the element in cognition by means of which it *relates immediately* to objects, from (ii) the specific necessity, for cognition in subjects of *our* sort, that the intuited object be *given*. Kant furthermore identifies cognition's immediate relatedness to the object with thought's achieving the "end" towards which it is "directed as a means," *worauf alles Denken als Mittel abzweckt*. It is thus implied that, when an object is given to us, thought finds itself in direct possession of the object. Kant is thus rejecting as inconceivable a scenario in which a thinker lacks anything which it can recognize as its experiencing or intuiting of objects. Interestingly, Merleau-Ponty suggests that such alienation from objects is exactly the condition of the thinking subject implied by "intellectualists," but if so, it is an implication that Kant sought to avoid (as Merleau-Ponty partly recognizes).
20 See Guyer, *Kant and the Claims of Knowledge*, pp. 258–59 and 303–5; Guyer refers to Allison's explicit denial (*Kant's Transcendental Idealism*, p. 297) that Kant is concerned with "conditions of the justification or verification of particular knowledge claims." Despite some appearance to the contrary, arising from his avowed focus on the "means" of knowledge and disengagement from skeptical challenges, the conception of conditions of possibility in Cassam is restricted similarly to juridical grounds of belief or knowledge: Cassam takes the scope of an account of "how knowledge is possible" to be set by the removal of "obstacles," and these are identified in terms of threats to relations of justification (see Cassam, *Possibility of Knowledge*).
21 McDowell, "What Myth?," p. 346.
22 A distinction between narrower and broader senses of epistemology is drawn by McDowell in "Having the World in View," pp. 435–37, and Kant is aligned with the latter, but McDowell's broader sense remains narrower than that just defined.
23 What follows relates to the *Elementarphilosophie* in its earlier, historically influential version of 1789–90.
24 Maimon, *Essay on Transcendental Philosophy*, p. 240. In order for there to be real cognition, it must be the case that "the understanding does not subject something given *a posteriori* to its *a priori* rules; rather it lets it arise [*läßt entstehen*] in accordance with these rules (which I believe is the only way to answer the question *quid juris?* in a wholly satisfactory way)" (81–83, p. 48).
25 See Reinhold, *Versuch einer neuen Theorie des Vorstellungsvermögens*, bk. II.
26 See e.g. ibid., pp. 181–84.
27 See Fichte's "Review of *Aenesidemus*," in *Early Philosophical Writings*, and Fichte's letter to Reinhold, 2 July 1795, in ibid., pp. 399–400: to say that the elements of the manifold "*are given*" means that "*you do not know*" how they are arrived at (p. 400). I single out one of Fichte's criticisms of Reinhold from among several.

28 Fichte, "[First] Introduction to the *Wissenschaftslehre*," §4, 428, p. 14.
29 See *Outline of the Distinctive Character of the Wissenschaftslehre with Respect to the Theoretical Faculty*, §V "Sensation Must Be Posited," in Fichte, *Early Philosophical Writings*, p. 260.
30 Reinhold, *Versuch einer neuen Theorie des Vorstellungsvermögens*, p. 205.
31 Ibid., pp. 196, 199–200.
32 Schulze, *Aenesidemus*. Sacks states the requirement on transcendental theory that the structure of experience not be determined as transcendentally real (*Objectivity and Insight*, p. 235n27).
33 Hegel, *Phenomenology of Spirit*, §94.
34 Ibid., §91.
35 Ibid., §73.
36 Ibid., §99.
37 Ibid., §230.
38 Ibid., §103.
39 Ibid., §§104–5.
40 Ibid., §105.
41 Ibid.§105.
42 Ibid., §109.
43 Ibid., §110.
44 See especially Fichte, *A Crystal Clear Report to the General Public*.
45 See e.g. Dreyfus, *Being-in-the-World*, p. 3.
46 See ibid., chs 1–2.
47 This alone is not enough to show NCEC to belong to Heidegger's analysis of Dasein, but it is a necessary step in Dreyfus's argument.
48 Heidegger, *Being and Time*, §43(c), p. 255; "Letter on Humanism,", pp. 254–55.
49 Heidegger, *On Time and Being*, p. 5.
50 Heidegger, "Letter on Humanism," p. 255.
51 Heidegger, *On Time and Being*, p. 5. In this work, Heidegger denies that "Being" adequately identifies the "It," and the place of Being is taken by "Ereignis."
52 Ibid., p. 8.
53 Heidegger's thesis is reaffirmed, and made much of, by Sartre.
54 See Heidegger, *Being and Time*, §§4–5, pp. 32–40, and *Basic Problems of Phenomenology*, pp. 227–29. The existential analytic of Dasein proceeds "with explicit orientation towards the problem of Being," whence it receives its "existential justification" (*Being and Time*, p. 37).
55 The most that I can see, which might seem to favor the opposite view, is Heidegger's admission that there is *continuity* of analysis of Dasein with *philosophische Anthropologie*, in *Being and Time*, §28, pp. 169–70.
56 The notion of transcendental explanation – and perhaps of *any* form of philosophical *explanation* – is sacrificed in the later Heidegger, but in *Being and Time* it retains its purchase.
57 Argued in Gardner, "Merleau-Ponty's Transcendental Theory of Perception." See e.g. Merleau-Ponty, *Phenomenology of Perception*, p. 63: "psychological considerations" are merely what lead us from the natural attitude to "the transcendental problem." Note also the numerous places in which Merleau-Ponty opposes "third-person" misconceptions: pp. 55, 75, 79n2, 80, 120, 123, 174–75, 198, and his reservations concerning "explanation," e.g. pp. xx, 433.
58 See Dreyfus, "Return of the Myth of the Mental," p. 359, concentrating on the theme of the "indeterminacy" of content.
59 Dreyfus, "Overcoming the Myth of the Mental," p. 50; and see p. 53.
60 Ibid., pp. 49–50 and 53.

61 Dreyfus, "Return of the Myth of the Mental," p. 364.
62 The value of phenomenology is a central topic in Dreyfus's exchange with John Searle. On the presently relevant point – philosophical explanatoriness – I do not see that Dreyfus answers Searle.
63 For a succinct characterization of transcendental explanation, see Bell, "Is Empirical Realism Compatible with Transcendental Idealism?," §2.
64 Scheler makes clear the distinction of "the facts of the a priori," from "attempts to make the a priori *understandable* or even to explain it," p. 65.
65 Dreyfus, "Return of the Myth of the Mental," and "Response to McDowell."
66 See the analysis of Dreyfus's arguments in McManus, "Rules, Regression and the 'Background.'"
67 Dreyfus, "Return of the Myth of the Mental," pp. 361–62; "Response to McDowell," pp. 374–75. Hudin brings out the subpersonality of Dreyfus's conception in "Motor Intentionality and Its Primordiality," pp. 578–82.
68 Dreyfus, "Response to McDowell," pp. 373–74. Dreyfus's appeal to Sartre in this context goes awry, since even in *The Transcendence of the Ego* prereflective object-consciousness is a nonpropositional consciousness of itself, "conscience (de) soi," a self-synthesizing unity which is for itself a subject opposed to an object.
69 Dreyfus, *Being-in-the-World*, p. 5: "being-in-the-world ... cannot be understood in subject/object terms."
70 See McDowell, "Avoiding the Myth of the Given," pp. 12–13.
71 Thus Kant treats the topic of empirical psychology under the heading of anthropology, a "pragmatic" discipline.
72 Dreyfus, "Response to McDowell," p. 377n4.
73 M. Merleau-Ponty, *Phenomenology of Perception*, pp. 49, 53; see also e.g. p. 144, the comments on rationality on pp. xix–xx and 430, and Merleau-Ponty's "new definition of the *a priori*" (p. 220).
74 Ibid., p. 53.
75 See esp. Merleau-Ponty, *Phenomenology of Perception*, pp. 126–27, which talks of the need to conceive a "dialectic of form and content" in which neither is reduced to the other. To which corresponds Merleau-Ponty's new conception of the relation of the a priori and a posteriori, pp. 220–22.
76 This is exactly how Merleau-Ponty explains his position in "Primacy of Perception and Its Philosophical Consequences," pp. 18–19: "One of Kant's discoveries, whose consequences we have not yet fully grasped, is that *all our experience of the world is throughout a tissue of concepts* which lead to irreducible contradictions *if we attempt to take them in an absolute sense* or transfer them into pure being, and that they nevertheless found the structure of all our phenomena, of everything which *is for us*" (italics added); Kant's limitation is that his "philosophy itself failed to utilize this principle fully." See also Merleau-Ponty, *Phenomenology of Perception*, pp. 218–22, on intellectualist versus phenomenological conceptions of reflection.
77 In McDowell, *Mind and World*, pp. 41–44 and 95–104, "the transcendental framework" is associated with Kant's erroneous positing of things in themselves outside the space of reasons, but in later writings ("Having the World in View," p. 445, and "Responses," pp. 209–10) "transcendental" is what concerns "the objective purport of our conceptual activity" or (equivalently, for McDowell) what is needed to "vindicate the legitimacy" of objective experience.
78 And, correlatively, taking metaphysical worries at face value: see McDowell's "Response to Bilgrami" in MacDonald and MacDonald (eds), *McDowell and His Critics*, pp. 66–68.
79 McDowell, *Mind and World*, p. 155n30.

80 McDowell, "Knowledge and the Internal," p. xi; see also pp. xx–xxi.
81 Note the echo here of Hegel's "overcoming" of the domain of presentation by means of immanent critique, described earlier; McDowell departs from Hegel in denying that we are thereby carried forward to a new, contentful philosophical thesis.
82 This follows from his rejection of "(rampant) platonism": see McDowell, *Mind and World*, p. 77.
83 Sellars, "Empiricism and the Philosophy of Mind," p. 169; McDowell, Introduction to *Mind and World*, 2nd edn, 1996, p. xiv, and "Avoiding the Myth of the Given," p. 1.
84 On how Hegel's agenda and ambitions exceed McDowell's, see Stern, "Going Beyond the Kantian Philosophy," pp. 259–64, and Halbig, "Varieties of Nature in Hegel and McDowell."
85 See e.g. McDowell, *Mind and World*, p. 178.
86 On these various points, see e.g. Halbig, "Varieties of Nature in Hegel and McDowell"; Larmore, "Attending to Reasons"; Rödl, "Eliminating Externality," and Sacks, *Objectivity and Insight*, pp. 166–68.
87 The dialectic accordingly goes as follows. For McDowell it is axiomatic that our first move in considering world-directed states and episodes should be to put them "in a normative context" (McDowell, Introduction to *Mind and World*, 2nd edn, 1996, pp. xi–xii). Dreyfus protests that on the evidence "perception has a function more basic than justification" (Dreyfus, "Overcoming the Myth of the Mental," p. 16). But the function cited by Dreyfus, namely of "opening onto a world," is one that McDowell's conceptualism can assimilate, on the basis that all modes of openness to the world involve rationality (McDowell, "What Myth?," pp. 343–44). See also R. T. Jensen's conclusion, in "Motor Intentionality and the Case of Schneider," p. 387.
88 Note that such an approach may declare itself to be innocent of the "interiorization of the space of reasons" which according to McDowell underpins much epistemology, and be equally remote from the annihilation of the space of reasons entailed, in McDowell's view, by "full-blown externalism"; McDowell, "Knowledge and the Internal."
89 These comments echo some of what is said in Rorty, "Very Idea of Human Answerability to the World."
90 As McDowell points out ("Responses," p. 225), the ladder is not kicked aside as *nonsensical*; but if anything distinguishes philosophical therapy from philosophical problem-solving, it must nonetheless undergo *some* sort of semantic deflation.

## Bibliography

Allison, H., *Kant's Transcendental Idealism: An Interpretation and Defense*, New Haven: Yale University Press, 1983.

Bell, D., "Is Empirical Realism Compatible with Transcendental Idealism?", in R. Schumacher (ed.), *Idealismus als Theorie der Repräsentation?*, Paderborn: Mentis, 2001.

Cassam, Q., *The Possibility of Knowledge*, Oxford: Oxford University Press, 2007.

Dreyfus, H., *Being-in-the-World: A Commentary on Heidegger's Being and Time, Division I*, Cambridge, MA: MIT Press, 1991.

——, "Overcoming the Myth of the Mental: How Philosophers Can Profit from the Phenomenology of Everyday Expertise," *Proceedings and Addresses of the American Philosophical Association* 79, no. 2 (2005): 47–65.

——, "Response to McDowell," *Inquiry* 50, no. 4 (2007): 371–77.

——, "The Return of the Myth of the Mental," *Inquiry* 50, no. 4 (2007): 352–65.

Fichte, J. G., *A Crystal Clear Report to the General Public Concerning the Actual Essence of the Newest Philosophy: An Attempt to Force the Reader to Understand* (1801), trans. J. Botterman and W. Rasch, in E. Behler (ed.), *Philosophy of German Idealism: Fichte, Jacobi, and Schelling*, New York: Continuum, 1987.

——, *Early Philosophical Writings*, trans. and ed. D. Breazeale, Ithaca, NY: Cornell University Press, 1988.

——, "[First] Introduction to the *Wissenschaftslehre*" (1797), in *Introductions to the Wissenschaftslehre and Other Writings (1797–1800)*, trans. and ed. D. Breazeale, Indianapolis: Hackett, 1994, pp. 2–35.

Gardner, S., "Merleau-Ponty's Transcendental Theory of Perception," in M. Sacks, S. Gardner, and M. Grist (eds), *The Transcendental Turn*, Oxford: Oxford University Press, forthcoming.

Guyer, P., *Kant and the Claims of Knowledge*, Cambridge: Cambridge University Press, 1987.

Halbig, C., "Varieties of Nature in Hegel and McDowell," in J. Lindgaard (ed.), *John McDowell: Experience, Norm and Nature*, Oxford: Blackwell, 2008, pp.72–91.

Hegel, G. W. F., *Phenomenology of Spirit* (1807), trans. A. V. Miller, Oxford: Oxford University Press, 1977.

Heidegger, M., *The Basic Problems of Phenomenology* (1927), trans. and ed. A. Hofstadter, Bloomington: Indiana University Press, 1982.

——, *Being and Time* (1927), trans. J. Macquarrie and E. Robinson, Oxford: Blackwell, 1978.

——, "Letter on Humanism" (1947), trans. F. Capuzzi, in *Pathmarks*, ed. W. McNeill, Cambridge: Cambridge University Press, 1998.

——, *On Time and Being* (1962), trans. J. Stambaugh, Chicago: University of Chicago Press, 2002.

Hudin, J., "Motor Intentionality and Its Primordiality," *Inquiry* 49, no. 6 (2006): 573–90.

Jensen, R. T., "Motor Intentionality and the Case of Schneider," *Phenomenology and the Cognitive Sciences* 8, no. 3 (2009): 371–88.

Kant, I., *Critique of Pure Reason* (1781, 2nd edn 1787), trans. P. Guyer, Cambridge: Cambridge University Press, 1998.

——, *Prolegomena to any Future Metaphysics* (1783), trans. and ed. L. W. Beck, Indianapolis: Bobbs-Merrill, 1980.

Larmore, C., "Attending to Reasons," in N. H. Smith (ed.), *Reading McDowell: On Mind and World*, London: Routledge, 2002.

Lindgaard, J. (ed.), *John McDowell: Experience, Norm, and Nature*, Oxford: Blackwell, 2008.

MacDonald, C. and MacDonald, G. (eds.), *McDowell and His Critics*, Oxford: Blackwell, 2006.

Maimon, S., *Essay on Transcendental Philosophy* (1790), trans. A. Welchman, H. Somers-Hall, M. Reglitz, and N. Midgley, London: Continuum, 2010.

McDowell, J., "Avoiding the Myth of the Given," in Lindgaard (ed.), *John McDowell*, pp. 1–14.

——, "Having the World in View: Sellars, Kant, and Intentionality," *Journal of Philosophy* 95, no. 9 (1998): 431–92.

——, Introduction to *Mind and World*, 2nd edn, Cambridge, MA: Harvard University Press, 1996.
——, "Knowledge and the Internal," *Philosophy and Phenomenological Research* 55, no. 4 (1995): 877–93.
——, *Mind and World*, Cambridge, MA: Harvard University Press, 1994.
——, "Responses," in Lindgaard (ed.), *John McDowell*, pp. 200–69.
——, "Response to Dreyfus," *Inquiry* 50, no. 4 (2007): 366–70.
——, "What Myth?" *Inquiry* 50, no. 4 (2007): 338–51.
McManus, D., "Rules, Regression and the 'Background': Dreyfus, Heidegger and McDowell," *European Journal of Philosophy* 16, no. 3 (2008): 432–58.
Merleau-Ponty, M., *Phenomenology of Perception* (1945), trans. C. Smith, London: Routledge & Kegan Paul, 1962.
——, "The Primacy of Perception and Its Philosophical Consequences" (1946), trans. J. M. Edie, in J. M. Edie (ed.), *The Primacy of Perception and Other Essays on Phenomenological Psychology, the Philosophy of Art, History and Politics*, Evanston, IL: Northwestern University Press, 1964.
Reinhold, K. L., *Versuch einer neuen Theorie des Vorstellungsvermögens*, 2nd edn, Prague and Jena: Widtmann und Mauke, 1796.
Rödl, S., "Eliminating Externality," *Internationales Jahrbuch des Deutschen Idealismus* 5 (2007): 176–88.
Rorty, R., "The Very Idea of Human Answerability to the World: John McDowell's Version of Empiricism," in *Truth and Progress: Philosophical Papers*, vol. 3, Cambridge: Cambridge University Press, 1998.
Sacks, M., "The Nature of Transcendental Arguments," *International Journal of Philosophical Studies* 13, no. 4 (2005): 439–60.
——, *Objectivity and Insight*, Oxford: Oxford University Press, 2000.
Scheler, M., *Formalism in Ethics and Non-formal Ethics of Values: A New Attempt toward the Foundation of an Ethical Personalism* (1966), 5th edn, rev., Evanston IL: Northwestern University Press, 1973.
Schulze, G. E., *Aenesidemus oder über die Fundamente der von dem Herrn Prof. Reinhold in Jena gelieferten Elementar-Philosophie*, Helmstedt, 1792.
Sellars, W., "Empiricism and the Philosophy of Mind," in *Science, Perception and Reality*, London: Routledge & Kegan Paul, 1963.
Stern, R., "Going Beyond the Kantian Philosophy: On McDowell's Hegelian Critique of Kant," *European Journal of Philosophy* 7, no. 2 (1999): 247–69.

# 6

# NEVER MIND

## Thinking of subjectivity in the Dreyfus–McDowell debate

*Lee Braver*

> All this we can do only if, *before* considering the question that is seemingly always the most immediate one and the only urgent one, What shall we do? we ponder this: *How must we think?* For thinking is genuine activity, genuine taking a hand, if to take a hand means to lend a hand to the essence, the coming to presence, of Being.[1]

> Thinking does not become action only because some effect issues from it or because it is applied. Thinking acts insofar as it thinks. Such action is presumably the simplest and at the same time the highest, because it concerns the relation of Being to man. ... Thinking ... lets itself be claimed by Being so that it can say the truth of Being.[2]

The debate between Professors McDowell and Dreyfus centers on the role that concepts and reason play in human perception, thought, and action. McDowell argues that these three activities can only conduct smooth transactions among themselves because "our perceptual relation to the world is conceptual all the way out";[3] sharing a common conceptual currency allows perceptions to interact with rational judgments as more than just brute causes.[4] Dreyfus believes that this position denies "the more basic perceptual capacities we seem to share with prelinguistic infants and higher animals," capacities fundamentally heterogeneous with reason.[5] Dreyfus ranks the discovery of this subrational competence among the highest achievements of Heidegger, Merleau-Ponty, and, to a lesser degree, Wittgenstein, and he has spent a great deal of his career studying it through a unique combination of textual exegesis, empirical data, and his own phenomenological analyses.[6] His conclusion is that for the most part, our behavior and perception are not only bereft of concepts, but even of mindedness. When we are smoothly interacting with the world, there is neither we nor world but just smoothly flowing activity.

Dreyfus marshals an impressive assortment of evidence and arguments for this unorthodox conclusion. Exhibit A, as detailed in *What Computers Still Can't Do*, is the slow, stubborn, but steady implosion of cognitivist AI. Computer scientists have done philosophy a great service by trying to build intelligence on the model Dreyfus sees as the fulfillment of "Plato's vision, refined by two thousand years of metaphysics,"[7] namely, the view of intelligence as the manipulation of representations according to strict rules. The most powerful computer's inability to comprehend what a four-year-old grasps with ease amounts to a *reductio* of this conception of intelligence, demonstrating the need for a better model. Exhibit B, explained primarily in *Mind over Machines*,[8] is his empirical study of skill acquisition which suggests that exposure to a vast and diverse set of experiences imbues experts with a flexibility of judgment that concepts could never yield. Furthermore, the speed of response in chess grandmasters and second basemen makes the additional step of consulting representations implausible,[9] and the centipede syndrome, which might from now on become known as the poor chuck disorder,[10] shows that performance actually degrades when thinking interferes, thus indicating its absence from skillful activity.[11] Exhibit C, mainly found in the commentary *Being-in-the-World*,[12] consists in phenomenological descriptions of hammering, reaching for doorknobs, running for streetcars, etc. Readers are asked to resist the temptation to retroactively misconstrue their experience in order to uncover the "preobjective/presubjective world"[13] that underlies and supports the objective world that philosophy generally studies.

This preworld forms the ground floor of absorbed embodied coping skills, and it is where Dreyfus likes to work. These skills are direct responses to solicitations, unimpeded by concepts, representations, or inferences, thus placing them outside or perhaps beneath the space of reason. The soliciting objects withdraw, the responding agent exists, as Sartre says, in "a pure mode of losing myself in the world, … drunk in by things as ink is by a blotter,"[14] and appropriate behavior ensues. Disruptive circumstances can change us into subjects reasoning about context-free objects, but this is the exception rather than the rule. Furthermore, this disengaged state – taken as basic by most philosophers – depends on the ground floor in at least two ways: (1) coping skills must have opened the world in the first place in order for entities to present themselves as functioning and a fortiori as malfunctioning, and (2) coping skills must continue in the background for me to maintain my grip on this objective world. Thematic attention and reason "[bring] about a radical transformation,"[15] and Dreyfus's central problem (which coincides with the point motivating McDowell's analysis) lies in connecting the ground floor with these higher, very different levels.

The motto guiding this analysis is: "mindedness is the enemy of embodied coping."[16] By showing how these modes conflict with each other,

Dreyfus demonstrates their heterogeneity which suggests that, *contra* McDowell, embodied coping is not minded; since mindless coping is both superior (for most tasks) and a necessary condition for mindedness, it is the more basic. This also indicates where Dreyfus's loyalty lies: although detached reason can do some things very well,[17] he generally follows "the existential phenomenologist's view that human beings are at their best when involved in action."[18]

Dreyfus's work illuminates both difficult philosophical texts and inconspicuous daily experience. It has also been the single most effective tool for convincing analytic philosophers that continental philosophy has something to offer, or even that it can rise above self-indulgent obfuscation.[19] That he has achieved this with Heidegger makes his contribution all the more impressive and, in my opinion, valuable.[20] Of course, one lesson we have learned from Heidegger's analyses of interpretation, as well as his own readings of other philosophers, is that we always bring our own questions to a work, questions which shape what we find there. Boldly pursuing deep questions brings out dimensions otherwise invisible, but at the same time covers up other aspects. This is a more hermeneutic way to read Heidegger's line, "he who thinks greatly must err greatly,"[21] than the more common reading as a weak excuse for his participation in the Nazi party.

I think we can view Dreyfus's reading of the early Heidegger as an example of this kind of strong or "violent" reading. It took someone with his knowledge of and interest in AI and skill acquisition to appreciate the significance of Heidegger's work for this topic, borne out by the number of Heideggerian researchers into philosophy of mind and cognitive science. These implications may very well have remained hidden, or at least considerably more obscured, without Dreyfus's probing examination. On the other hand, his reading is, as all readings must be, selective in focus and emphasis; we need look no further than the fact that his groundbreaking commentary on *Being and Time* delves deeply into almost every corner of the first division while giving short shrift to the second.[22] For those who consider the architectonic of the book nearly Kantian in its organization and unity, such an approach can only appear limited, even if tremendously helpful within those limits. When approaching a strong reading like this, it is good to both gratefully gather its insights and to look for what has been left out, to investigate the areas cast in shadow by the bright light of the intense focus.

As we have seen, Dreyfus considers skillful coping to be at its best when the agent is mindlessly absorbed.[23] Certainly, Division I of *Being and Time* sets up a contrast between the absorbed, engaged use of tools and detached theoretical "just staring at" objects, with a clear preference for the former. However, this initial opposition does not exhaust Heidegger's treatment of the matter; Division II emphasizes phenomena that knock us out of our unreflective routine such as breakdowns, resistance, and unfamiliarity.

Dreyfus's account incorporates breakdowns, but only as subordinated to further and better absorbed coping since Heidegger firmly rejects any kind of transcendent escape from the occupations of this world.[24] These pauses offer the coper an opportunity to step back from the standard behavior of her past and her community to discover new and better practices, often reviving marginal or lapsed behaviors. Both of Division II's fundamental breakdowns do this: anxiety frees Dasein from slavish conformity to what one does so that she can "see new possibilities in the most ambiguous and conflicted situations," while resoluteness towards death can stimulate radically new practices which have the potential to transform an entire culture.[25] The ultimate goal in all of this is to become what we are at our best – mindless copers – so that even authenticity becomes a form of "ongoing, unreflective ... coping,"[26] just one that has gone through the crucible of reforming one's identity.[27] Dreyfus applies this scheme to Heidegger's later work as well; for instance, earth in "The Origin of the Work of Art" resists full articulation in order to preserve lapsed cultural practices which can reemerge or inspire new ones.[28]

Dreyfus is certainly right that Heidegger favors mindless coping over theoretical analysis, but we must remember that these are not the only options. Division II's authenticity presents something of an *Aufhebung* of Division I's antitheses by marrying coping's engagement to theory's attentiveness. He consistently worries about familiar behavior's tendency to lull us into autopilot, a state he calls fallenness and consistently connects to the unthematic absorption in the world that is Dreyfus's highest state.[29] Although Heidegger does indeed rule out any transcendent content beyond worldly roles for us to take up, living authentically entails a Kierkegaardian change in the *way* we are in-the-world from mindless going with the flow to explicit, passionate choosing.[30] Authenticity contrasts with theory's pretense of disinterest and distortive casting of all beings into the mode of presence-at-hand, but it also contrasts with the mindless preoccupations we flee into when shaken by premonitions of meaninglessness and death.[31] A couple of years after *Being and Time*, Heidegger anticipates and rejects interpretations that excessively favor Division I's focus on everyday tool use: "there I took my departure from what lies to hand in the everyday realm, from those things that we use and pursue. ... It never occurred to me, however, to try and claim or prove with this interpretation that the essence of man consists in the fact that he knows how to handle knives and forks or use the tram."[32]

After the *Kehre*, Heidegger emphasizes lucid experiences of Being which must be wrested from forms of mindlessness (rescue Being from oblivion, recollect it from forgottenness, etc.), consistently describing his project in terms of explicitly focusing our attention on what we usually don't notice, precisely the kind of thematic attention that breaks the spell of absorbed coping. "Although we do remain always and everywhere in correspondence to the Being of being, we, nevertheless, rarely pay attention to the appeal to Being. The correspondence to the Being of being does, to be sure, always remain our abode. But only at times does it become an unfolding attitude specifically adopted by us."[33] We are always already in the clearing, but we generally ignore it because we're so preoccupied by our occupations. By drawing our attention from using beings to wondering at Being, he wants us to realize that "of all beings, only the human being, called upon by the voice of being, experiences the wonder of all wonders: *that* beings *are*."[34]

The absorbed use of familiar tools inhibits this awareness, as suggested in *Being and Time* but more explicitly asserted in the later work, as readiness-to-hand (still pretty much the same in "The Origin of the Work of Art," for instance) evolves into technological *Bestand*, the contemporary source of forgetfulness. "Forgetting the truth of being in favor of the pressing throng of beings unthought in their essence is what 'falling' [*Verfallen*] means."[35] The problem is that the more familiar beings become and the more we master their use, the more they recede, just as Dreyfus describes. Although this greatly improves our performance, it means that we take for granted the most important thing – that they are at all and that we are aware of them. Instead of familiarity and mastery, Heidegger consistently prioritizes the moments when things don't run smoothly, precisely because these jarring experiences shock us out of our mindless absorption so that we can become aware of awareness itself. Instead of efficient, skilled productivity, Heidegger values intensity of awareness. What is important about anxiety – the complete breakdown of the projects that enable us to use tools – is not that it allows us to reenter our usual mindless absorption with new projects or practices, but that it can turn us towards Being: "an experience of being as that which is other than all beings is bestowed in anxiety."[36] Certainly tools withdraw when all goes smoothly, but this tendency to thoughtlessness represents an obstacle to the goal rather than the goal itself.

Focusing cultural practices is a significant aspect of Heidegger's treatment of artworks, as Dreyfus claims, but even more important is the way their strife "restrain[s] all usual doing and prizing, knowing and looking, in order to stay within the truth that is happening in the work."[37] Indeed, "The Origin of the Work of Art" explicitly contrasts this experience with smoothly functioning inconspicuous equipment:

> [T]he simple *factum est* is to be held forth into the open region by the work: namely this, that unconcealment of a being has happened here ... or that such a work *is* at all rather than is not. ... To be sure, "that" it is made is a property also of all equipment that is available and in use. But this "that" does not become prominent in the equipment; it disappears in usefulness. The more handy a piece of equipment is, the more inconspicuous it remains that, for example, this particular hammer is. ... The more essentially the

work opens itself, the more luminous becomes the uniqueness of the fact that it is rather than is not.[38]

Equipment's withdrawal is why "the making of equipment never directly effects the happening of truth"[39] whereas the artwork's disruptive strife lights up what is usually transparent. The bumps in the road that jolt us awake may allow us to revive marginal practices as Dreyfus points out, but Heidegger is most interested in how we can become aware of the world's opening to us at all, to become thankful in thinking it. "Startled dismay means returning from the ease of comportment in what is familiar to the openness of the rush of the self-sheltering. ... Startled dismay lets man return to face *that* a being *is*, whereas before a being was for him just a being. Startled dismay lets man return to face that beings *are*."[40]

Heidegger and Dreyfus agree that wondering at beings' presence interferes with using them mindlessly: "subsequent to the initial wonder, beings increasingly lose their strangeness, are pushed into the domain of expertise. ... The incipient wonder is overpowered by the growing familiarity of beings."[41] The difference is that Dreyfus privileges expert absorption, whereas Heidegger, especially in his later work, considers the hiatus of wonder far more important. While Dreyfus hails a practitioner's improvement in performance as she moves from initial self-conscious hesitant manipulation to mastery, Heidegger places the emphasis on the initial roughness precisely because it forces us to be mindful. This "bracketing" is not just a helpful break for discovering new practices, but allows us to experience Being itself, the fundamental goal of his later work. Hence, we might add another motto to accompany Dreyfus's: mindless absorption is the enemy of the awareness of Being. Portraying Heidegger as the philosopher of mindlessness works best when confined to Division I of *Being and Time*, ignoring the decades spent trying to awaken thinking.

Although Heidegger wants us to think Being – after all, this is the "task for thinking" that remains after the "end of philosophy" – this does not amount to cognitivism or conceptualism, Dreyfus's main targets. Along with the importance and difficulty of the task, Heidegger constantly emphasizes the way thinking Being fundamentally departs from traditional conceptions of representational thinking. And here we can benefit from Dreyfus's analyses by applying them to a topic he did not. Both Heidegger and Wittgenstein develop radically new conceptions of thinking in their later work, which bear a strong resemblance to Dreyfus's embodied coping.[42] The difference is that they apply this model to thinking itself, even the contemplation of highly abstract issues, whereas Dreyfus restricts it to bodily interactions with physical objects.[43] I will briefly outline three points of similarity.

First, apropos of the debate with McDowell, thinking of Being is neither conceptual nor representational. We use concepts for beings, but the ontological difference prevents the application of such ontic devices to Being. There can be no concept of Being since there are no individuals to subsume under it;[44] also, we must remain open to profoundly new ways of thinking which would get closed off by a representation of the goal (or conditions of success).[45] This does not preclude thinking and speaking of it, however, as long as these can be freed from conceptual representations.

TEACHER: Any description would reify it.
SCHOLAR: Nevertheless it lets itself be named, and being named it can be thought about ...
TEACHER: ... only if thinking is no longer re-presenting.[46]

Heidegger argues that although language and thought always run the risk of conceptualizing when forced into the form of propositional logic,[47] they are not condemned to this fate by their very nature. While Dreyfus allows for nonconceptual language in immediate reactions to a practical situation ("this hammer's too heavy – hand me that one, would you?"),[48] Heidegger sees much broader possibilities, especially in thinking and poetry. Thinking can employ nonpropositional forms of language such as provocative questions and tautologous statements like "the world worlds," "the thing things," or "Being is"[49] to formally indicate phenomena without nailing them down; poetry evokes the unique features of its subjects.[50] Heidegger agrees that conceptual representational thinking distorts phenomena, but this leads him to explore new forms of thinking and speaking which escape this problem rather than passing over them in mindlessness.

Second, Dreyfus argues that our skilful coping behaviors are "direct and unreflective"[51] without even implicit inferences going on beneath the surface. Reaching for a doorknob is fundamentally different from making an argument and should not be described with explanatory devices such as beliefs, goals, desires, or explicit thoughts.[52] Wittgenstein's later work views the most abstract intellectual actions such as doing philosophy or math as continuous with embodied physical interactions. We often just react without even a tacit network of presuppositions underlying our behavior, and this happens in response to ideas as well as doorknobs. In fact, Wittgenstein models our "intellectual" reaction to skepticism on Dreyfus and Sean Kelly's example of reaching for something:[53]

> If I say "Of course I know that that's a towel" I am making an *utterance*. I have no thought of a verification. For me it is an immediate utterance. ... It is just like directly taking hold of something, as I take hold of my towel without having doubts. And yet this direct taking-hold corresponds to a *sureness*, not to a knowing. But don't I take hold of a thing's name like that, too?[54]

Wittgenstein portrays an epistemological move as similar to the unthinking embodied act of reaching for a towel. The counterpart to this in his famous analysis of rule-following would be the "way of grasping a rule which is *not* an *interpretation*, but which is exhibited in what we call 'obeying the rule' and 'going against it' in actual cases."[55] As he emphasizes over and over again, no representation or conscious thought of any kind need accompany intelligent actions. All higher-order thought processes rest on noninferential faculties which he considers to be "something animal,"[56] the way Dreyfus argues that we share our embodied coping skills with animals. Indeed, conscious rule-following *must* bottom out in an immediate know-how in order to escape an infinite regress of rule interpretation.[57]

Dreyfus makes many of these points in his work on AI, but only in relation to common sense and mundane behavior. I take Wittgenstein to be making the more radical claim that even in abstract, contemplative subjects like logic and math, *ceteris paribus* applies to what seem like absolutely clear, rigid rules,[58] making the determination of relevance an open-ended matter of judgment. Logic and math only appear noncontextual and univocal because they take place within prepackaged "microworlds" of thought, i.e. simplified realms which have already been edited for relevance, etc. Thinking, on the other hand, operates outside these guardrails, which, Heidegger says, is why "thinking does not begin until we have come to know that the reason that has been extolled for centuries is the most stubborn adversary of thinking."[59]

Finally, and most importantly, Dreyfus defines embodiment as "involvement in responding to a world of solicitations."[60] Rather than having a representation of our goal, the situation draws responses from us, pulling our arm to the doorknob or coffee mug. Heidegger describes thinking like this, as succinctly captured in the title, *Was Heist Denken*, i.e. what calls for or to thinking. With the proper experience and training in place, the premises "Socrates is a man" and "All men are moral" solicit the conclusion from us as much as a chocolate bar entices us to eat it or, to use a Levinasian example, a face forbids us to harm it. Heidegger wants to change how we think of thinking, to take "the step back from the thinking that merely represents – that is, explains – to the thinking that responds and recalls."[61] He applies this view to all thinking, not just engaged, embodied activities, because we can only notice and think about "the sorts of things that are suggested by what is addressed ... what the addressed allows to radiate of itself."[62] In particular, philosophers can only express how they are struck by ideas, how things appear to them. So, for example, "Nietzsche's thought has to plunge into metaphysics because Being radiates its own essence as will to power."[63] Certain lines of reasoning compel us, and our responses often fit Dreyfus's description of *phronesis*: "simply *seeing* the appropriate thing to do and responding without deliberation."[64] This is why Heidegger defines all speaking and thinking as responding.

Perhaps a brief excursus into the topic of free will can help explicate this point. Discussions traditionally divide into two slippery slopes which end up as opposing absurdities. On the one hand, motivations and enticements to act such as one's habits or recognition of one option's clear superiority make action intelligible but, in so doing, seem to congeal into determinism. How can we freely choose if it is our personality or qualities in the objects that force us down one or the other path? On the other hand, the agent's disengagement from all motivating factors secures a genuine moment of choice, but at the cost of turning it into an arbitrary opting, e.g. Lucretius' swerve or Sartre's fundamental project. At the bottom of this slope, any reason we might have for choosing one option as opposed to another becomes a cause, thus compromising the freedom we're trying to preserve. If virtue is virtuous because the gods love it, then they can have no reason for loving it, making the affair a superficial infatuation. If the gods love it because it is virtuous, then they suffer a passion imposed upon them by something else, lessening their divinity.

In his relatively ignored 1936 lectures on *Schelling's Treatise on the Essence of Human Freedom*, Heidegger takes up this debate. In keeping with his usual *modus operandi*, he wants to disassemble the terms in which the debate has taken place these many centuries.

> Pure arbitrariness does not give a determining ground for decision. Mechanical force does not give a determining ground for what it is supposed to, for decision. ... Necessity belongs in any case to freedom itself, ... freedom itself *is* necessity. ... True freedom in the sense of the most primordial self-determination is found only where a choice is no longer possible and no longer necessary. ... There is nothing compulsory in this fundamental experience of one's own being, simply because a compulsion cannot be there, but rather necessity is freedom here and freedom is necessity.[65]

Rejecting both extremes as logical and phenomenological nonsense, Heidegger opts for a form of compatibilism or soft determinism. We rarely experience a moment of pure *apatheia* like Buridan's ass, with no inclination one way or another. Such a situation would feel more like flipping a coin than genuine freedom. This is why

> the inclination, that is, various directions of being inclined, are the presuppositions for the possibility of the decision of a faculty. If it could not and did not have to decide for one inclination or the other, that is, for what it has a propensity to, decision would not be decision, but a mere explosion of an act out of emptiness into emptiness, pure chance, but never self-determination, that is, freedom.[66]

Choices are motivated, generally by qualities that phenomenology locates in the objects (the tastiness of a pie, the needs-to-be-savedness of a drowning puppy). Far from compromising freedom, such inclinations are the conditions for the possibility of real choice, even though we cannot choose these preferences themselves but are thrown into them. Heidegger is thinking of the dilemma's traditional horns of blind flailing or mechanical motion in the first sentence of "Letter on Humanism": "we are still far from pondering the essence of action decisively enough."[67]

I find much of value in Dreyfus's analyses, but his restriction of engaged, solicited coping to embodied interactions with the physical environment ends up looking like a vestigial Cartesian mind–body split, where the body is intelligent precisely where the mind is stupid and vice versa.[68] The unfortunate but unsurprising result is that the two cannot be brought together, as Dreyfus admits. Heidegger wants to reform our understanding of both embodied skills like hammering and abstract thinking like philosophizing, showing us that we actually do philosophize as with a hammer. He applies many of the features of engaged coping to philosophical contemplation, as Wittgenstein does to mathematics and logic, some of the most intellectual pursuits around. This strikes me as phenomenologically right: I do respond immediately to words, even to arguments. Although Dreyfus says that he allows for intellectual coping, his repeated example is chess playing which gets reduced to "direct responses to familiar perceptual gestalts."[69] I am arguing that we are skillfully solicited by "purely" intellectual topics as well.

McDowell offers one "architectural plan" which Dreyfus correctly criticizes as upper floors all the way down, meaning that it is too rationalistic in viewing the world as already formed into facts within an inferential scaffolding to which we annex bits of language.[70] I agree that McDowell's picture has serious phenomenological problems. Dreyfus offers the alternative of a lower floor of embodied coping skills supporting separate upper floors of rational representational subjectivity, but he himself criticizes this structure as disconnected. Let me offer a third plan: basement all the way up. Getting rid of the class divisions between the genteel upper floors and the servant's quarters below eliminates the problem of discontinuity but in the reverse direction of McDowell's solution.

Dreyfus and McDowell agree that in "attentive, deliberate ... action an ego is always involved."[71] When we disengage from our behavior to monitor it, we do so as a traditional rational subject facing bare objects. Let me play the old game of challenging a debate's common assumption and question whether we ever are this subject. Retrospective reconstruction distorts practical engagement;[72] it could very well be doing the same thing to reflection. When we are not acting in the world, when we do resort to detached reasoning, what actually happens when we try to think? I propose that even then, we are still responding to solicitations, just intellectual rather than bodily ones. Ultimately, rational representational thinking is and must be a reaction to how ideas strike us: "we are," Heidegger says, "constantly addressed by, summoned to attend to, grounds and reason."[73] We must find an idea in need of justification or explanation to be moved to seek one, and what we find to be an acceptable answer, what appeals to us as plausible and persuasive, is not and cannot be up to our decision.

Now this may sound like it reduces reason to mere subjective whim; indeed, Heidegger's rejection of "the reigning and never-challenged doctrine of 'logic'"[74] is part of what alarmed Carnap. But logic itself is not harmed, we just gain a different (I would say more sophisticated) understanding of justification. Heidegger's oft-used phrase, "groundless ground," means that while these ultimate notions form the foundation or ground for our thought, they themselves cannot be grounded.[75] This doesn't rob these laws of their legitimacy; indeed it is the only possible source of legitimacy.[76] On the one hand, our ways of thinking cannot receive the kind of absolute justification conferred by God, eternal perfect Forms, or more recent versions of Forms such as Frege's. On the other hand, however, they do provide us with our ways of thinking which are as legitimate as legitimacy gets. Heidegger draws this lesson from Kant, who admits that our forms of intuition and concepts of understanding are ultimately arbitrary and unjustifiable since we draw our very modes of justification from them, and yet the knowledge they give us should be regarded as genuine.[77] For Heidegger, to be a finite creature means that we are thrown into what we must be and how we must think. In the later work, our understandings of Being change across history for reasons not entirely explicable, but once ascendant, they determine that epoch's form of legitimation.

We cannot choose how ideas will strike us, since *that* choice would have to rest upon preferences and ways of thinking that themselves could not have been chosen, on pain of infinite regress. This is why thrownness wins out over projection in the later work: "every decision, however, bases itself on something not mastered ... else it would never be a decision."[78] This applies to logic and reflection as much as it does to opening doors: we do not decide what can and should be negated, for example; propositions present themselves to us as negatable.[79] The possibility of negating them must occur to us for us to *consider* doing it, and it must appeal to us as the right thing to do for us to *do* it. We can formulate rules governing proper negation but, as Wittgenstein demonstrates, it is still up to us to accept them, as well as determining when and how to apply them. If it were really up to us to decide how to think and what to value in the absence of all attraction or repulsion, as portrayed by modern subject-centered philosophy like Sartre's fundamental project, we would be as paralyzed as Buridan's ass. Deciding for one way of thinking or living over another requires that I *find* one preferable to the other, that it attracts me. As Heidegger says, "I cannot exist at all without constantly responding to this or that address in a thematic or unthematic way; otherwise I could not take so much as a single step, nor cast a glance at something."[80]

Wittgenstein gives a wonderful description of a linguistic breakdown which forces him to intentionally search for the right word:

> how do I find the "right" word? How do I choose among words? Without doubt it is sometimes as if I were comparing them by fine differences of smell: *That* is too ... , *that* is too ... , – *this* is the right one. – But I do not always have to make judgments, give explanations; often I might only say: "It simply isn't right yet." I am dissatisfied, I go on looking. At last a word comes: *"That's it!" Sometimes* I can say why. This is simply what searching, this is what finding, is like here.[81]

Even during a breakdown – where Dreyfus and McDowell agree that we revert to a clumsy conscious application of rules – we must wait for the right answer to occur to us. Wittgenstein starts by describing the process as an immediate aesthetic reaction, and then discards even that for the idea that the word and its rightness just strike us. "We never come to thoughts. They come to us."[82] I find that this describes thinking even at its most deliberate and abstract,[83] which is why Heidegger insists that "to think is before all else to listen, to let ourselves be told something."[84] When students ask me a difficult question in class, there is sometimes a moment of blank panic when I have no idea what to say, then, something internal shifts, tension releases and I know that I can respond. I open my mouth even though I don't really know what I'm going to say – I certainly don't know how I arrived at the thought – but I know that a response is waiting to emerge from my mouth, one which I'm as curious to hear as anyone. As Wittgenstein says, "In many cases of voluntary speech I don't feel an effort, much that I say voluntarily is not premeditated, and I don't know of any acts of intention preceding it."[85]

Wittgenstein likes to trace the roots of philosophical theories back to a particular picture or image suggested to us by certain turns of phrase or recurrent experiences. I think that the picture that gives rise to the traditional rational subject occurs when I am being careful in how I phrase something, trying hard to avoid any mistakes. My hesitance in expressing the thought leads to the feeling that I am keeping it inside in order to inspect it scrupulously before allowing it out in public. This inspection is done by my mind, imagined as an internal mini-me, a kind of homunculus turning the idea or wording over in his small monkey-like hands. This inner self may rest dormant when I relax and let words whoosh by him on their way out, but if I concentrate, I can submit everything to his alert, watchful approval, passing all thoughts before this tribunal of reason in a less formal version of Descartes's doubtful inspection which founded modern philosophy. Wittgenstein makes the point that simply being "inner," itself a problematic term, confers no magical powers. My inner homunculus's ratiocination can never exceed mine; he too must find certain general rules persuasive and must apply them, ultimately, unthinkingly. In other words, referring the process to my inner mind operating rationally with rules just pushes the question of how I do this back one step without actually explaining anything. Phenomenological description does not support this traditional notion of the subject, even in disengaged or rational activities; it too should be thrown out as one more myth.[86]

## Notes

1 Heidegger, "The Question Concerning Technology," in *Question Concerning Technology and Other Essays*, p. 40.
2 Heidegger, "Letter on Humanism," in *Basic Writings*, pp. 217–18. See also p. 262.
3 McDowell, "What Myth?," p. 338.
4 "I claim that we can coherently credit experiences with rational relations to judgment and belief, but only if we take it that ... experiences have conceptual content" (McDowell, *Mind and World*, p. 162).
5 Dreyfus, "Overcoming the Myth of the Mental," p. 47.
6 In 2000, Dreyfus described "what I am beginning to see as my philosophical method (I did not know I had one): look to Heidegger's and Merleau-Ponty's distinctions for a clue to the phenomena in question and then to those phenomena to test and further develop Heidegger's and Merleau-Ponty's distinctions" ("Responses," in Wrathall and Malpas, eds, *Heidegger, Coping, and Cognitive Science*, p. 314).
7 Dreyfus and Hall (eds), *Heidegger*, p. 72. See also pp. 176, 192; and Dreyfus and Dreyfus, *Mind over Machine*, p. 99.
8 And "Current Relevance of Merleau-Ponty's Phenomenology of Embodiment," and "A Phenomenology of Skill Acquisition as the basis for a Merleau-Pontyian Non-representationalist Cognitive Science," University of California, Berkeley, n.d., <http://socrates.berkeley.edu/~hdreyfus/pdf/MerleauPontySkillCogSci.pdf>.
9 This insight fueled much of Rodney Brooks's robotics work.
10 This refers to the story of Chuck Knoblauch that Dreyfus discusses in "Return of the Myth of the Mental," pp. 354–55.
11 See Dreyfus, "Response to McDowell," p. 374.
12 And Dreyfus and Wakefield, "Intentionality and the Phenomenology of Action."
13 Dreyfus, "Return of the Myth of the Mental," p. 360.
14 Sartre, *Being and Nothingness,*, p. 348..
15 Dreyfus, "Overcoming the Myth of the Mental," p. 61; "Return of the Myth of the Mental," pp. 353, 360.
16 Dreyfus, "Return of the Myth of the Mental," p. 353.
17 See Dreyfus and Dreyfus, *Mind over Machine*, p. 160.
18 Dreyfus, "Response to McDowell," pp. 372–73. Stepping back and reflecting is not "our most pervasive and important kind of freedom" and, in so far as we exercise it, "we are no longer able to act in the world" ("Return of the Myth of the Mental," p. 354). Instead, the "truly pervasive human freedom" is "to let ourselves be involved" (ibid., p. 355, see also p. 363). "'Embodied coping skills' at their best, are not, as McDowell claims they must be, 'permeated with

conceptual mindedness'" (ibid., p. 361). See also "Response to McDowell," p. 373; Dreyfus et al., *Disclosing New Worlds*, pp. 66–67.
19 See my "Analyzing Heidegger."
20 See John R. Searle's praise: "Dreyfus has probably done more than any other English-speaking commentator to make the work of Heidegger intelligible to English-speaking philosophers. Most philosophers in the Anglo-American tradition seem to think that Heidegger was an obscurantist muddle-head at best or an unregenerate Nazi at worst. Dreyfus has usefully attempted to state many of Heidegger's views in a language which is, for the most part, intelligible to English-speaking philosophers. For this, we are all in his debt" ("Limits of Phenomenology," in Wrathall and Malpas, eds, *Heidegger, Coping, and Cognitive Science*, p. 71).
21 Heidegger, *Poetry, Language, Thought*, p. 9.
22 In the Preface, Dreyfus writes that Division I is "the most original and important section of the work," while Division II's "'existentialist' side ... was, for good reasons, later abandoned by Heidegger himself," and its work on temporality is "much less carefully worked out than Division I and, indeed, [has] some errors so serious as to block any consistent reading" (*Being-in-the-World*, pp. vii–viii).
23 Dreyfus, "Return of the Myth of the Mental," p. 361; "Response to McDowell," p. 373.
24 See Dreyfus, "Responses," in Wrathall and Malpas (eds), *Heidegger, Authenticity, and Modernity*, pp. 308–9; Dreyfus, *Being-in-the-World*, p. 305.
25 Dreyfus, "Could Anything Be More Intelligible Than Everyday Intelligibility?," pp. 16, 18; see also Dreyfus, "Responses," in Wrathall and Malpas (eds), *Heidegger, Authenticity, and Modernity*, pp. 318–19. As radically new behaviors, their incommensurability makes comparison with accepted practice impossible to spell out in advance.
26 Dreyfus, *Being-in-the-World*, p. 302.
27 Rather than *radical* breaks, anxiety and death get reincorporated as subordinate moments within the circuit of skillful coping as means for superior practices. One way to put the point is to say that Dreyfus's reading turns *Being and Time* from a general economy into a restricted one, to use Derrida's terminology (see Derrida, "From Restricted to General Economy").
28 See Dreyfus, "Heidegger on the Connection Between Nihilism, Art, Technology, and Politics," in Guignon (ed.), *Cambridge Companion to Heidegger*, pp. 345–72, and "Heidegger's Ontology of Art," in Dreyfus and Wrathall (eds), *Companion to Heidegger*.
29 "That in which concern has *fallen* at any given time is not thematically perceived, not thought, not known" (Heidegger, *History of the Concept of Time*, p. 193). See also pp. 185, 259, and 267, and *Being and Time*, pp. 107/76, 149/113, 163/125, 220/175, 229/184, and 233/189.
30 Anxiety reveals the world as a whole (*History of the Concept of Time*, p. 291, see also p. 313; *Being and Time*, p. 233/189; "What Is Metaphysics," in *Basic Writings*, pp. 103, 109), which lets me consciously choose my roles (*History of the Concept of Time*, p. 318; *Being and Time*, pp. 232/188, 312–13/268). Dreyfus argues that Heidegger improved Kierkegaard's unsuccessful solution to ethical decisions by rejecting notions of will or choice. He reads resoluteness the way later Heidegger retroactively interprets it, as openness to the unique Situation which eliminates the role of choice (Dreyfus, *Being-in-the-World*, pp. 302–3, 318–21).
31 Dasein's fallenness represents "the *flight of Dasein from itself*, a flight from itself into the world discovered by it" (*History of the Concept of Time*, p. 282, see also pp. 277, 291–93, 316).

32 Heidegger, *Fundamental Concepts of Metaphysics*, p. 177. See also *Pathmarks*, p. 370n59.
33 Heidegger, *What Is Philosophy?*, pp. 73–75. See also *Question Concerning Technology*, pp. 44–45, 180; "The Origin of the Work of Art," in *Basic Writings*, pp. 181, 445; *Mindfulness*, p. 217; and *Poetry, Language and Thought*, p. 190.
34 Heidegger, "Postscript to *What Is Metaphysics*," in *Pathmarks*, p. 234. "It is necessary for thinking to become explicitly aware of the matter here called clearing" ("The End of Philosophy and the Task of Thinking," in *Basic Writings*, p. 442). See also "What Is Metaphysics?," in *Basic Writings*, pp.103, 109.
35 Heidegger, "Letter on Humanism," in *Pathmarks*, p. 253. See also "What Is Metaphysics?," in *Basic Writings*, p. 104; "On the Essence of Truth," in *Basic Writings*, p. 131; and *Early Greek Thinking*, p. 122. Dreyfus himself pointed out in an early essay ("Heidegger's History of the Being of Equipment," in Dreyfus and Hall (eds), *Heidegger*) that the treatment of equipment in *Being and Time* represents a step towards technology, the bête noir of Heidegger's later thought. Gerold Prauss makes a similar point (*Knowing and Doing*, p. 10).
36 Heidegger, "Postscript to *What Is Metaphysics*," in *Pathmarks*, p. 233. For death, see *Contributions to Philosophy (From Enowning)*, p. 199; *Principle of Reason*, p. 112.
37 Heidegger, "Origin of the Work of Art," in *Basic Writings*, p. 191.
38 Ibid., p. 190.
39 Ibid., p. 189.
40 Heidegger, *Contributions to Philosophy (From Enowning)*, p. 11, see also pp. 32, 272; *Introduction to Metaphysics*, pp. 178–79; *Principle of Reason*, p. 56.
41 Heidegger, *Mindfulness*, p. 242. "Where beings are not very familiar to man and are scarcely and only roughly known by science, the openedness of beings as a whole can prevail more essentially than it can where the familiar and well-known has become boundless, and nothing is any longer able to withstand the business of knowing, since technical mastery over things bears itself without limit. Precisely in the leveling and planning of this omniscience, this mere knowing, the openedness of beings gets flattened out into the apparent nothingness of what is no longer even a matter of indifference, but rather is simply forgotten" ("On the Essence of Truth," in *Basic Writings*, p. 129). See also "Origin of the Work of Art," in *Basic Writings*, p. 150; *Discourse on Thinking*, pp. 56; *Mindfulness*, p. 184; *Principle of Reason*, p. 68. *Contra* even the hypothetical self-sufficiency of mindlessness, Heidegger insists that "we humans cannot come to be who we are without attending to the world that determines us" (*Principle of Reason*, p. 37).
42 I discuss this in detail in *Groundless Grounds*.
43 Obviously, my discussion is a rational reconstruction of the situation, since there are no objects in the flow, just solicitations. See Dreyfus, "Overcoming the Myth of the Mental," p. 60.
44 "For beings are always individually occurring beings and thus multifarious; contrary to this, being is unique, the absolute singular in unconditioned singularity" (Heidegger, *Principle of Reason*, p. 84). See also *Being and Time*, pp. 22–23/3.
45 Success conditions would also reinforce our willing by setting the goal to be striven for. "An example of an outstanding non-objectifying thinking and speaking is poetry. … Poetic thinking is being in the presence of … and for the god. Presence means: simple willingness that wills nothing, counts on no successful outcome. Being in the presence of … : purely letting be said the god's presence" (Heidegger, *Piety of Thinking*, p. 30). See also *Discourse on Thinking*, pp. 62, 68. Dreyfus addresses the problems with anticipated success conditions in "Primacy of Phenomenology over Logical Analysis."

46 Heidegger, *Discourse on Thinking*, p. 67, see also p. 58; *Piety of Thinking*, p. 27. "There is a saying that is specially engaged with what is said without, however, reflecting on language and thereby turning it too into an object" (*Off the Beaten Track*, p. 237, see also p. 23; "On the Question of Being," in *Pathmarks*, p. 310; *Principle of Reason*, p. 62; *Contributions to Philosophy (From Enowning)*, p. 342).

47 "All 'dialectic' of 'propositions' and 'concepts' moves constantly within objects and blocks every step towards mindfulness" (*Mindfulness*, p. 17, see also p. 186; *Schelling's Treatise on the Essence of Human Freedom*, p. 135).

48 See Dreyfus, *Being-in-the-World*, pp. 208, 220; "Responses," in Wrathall and Malpas (eds), *Heidegger, Coping, and Cognitive Science*, p. 317.

49 See Heidegger, "The Way to Language," in *Basic Writings*, pp. 414–15; *Poetry, Language, Thought*, pp. 179–80; *What Is Called Thinking?*, pp. 153, 172.

50 This might address the concern Dreyfus raises in response to Joseph Rouse's discussion, which bears a partial similarity to mine (Dreyfus, "Responses," in Wrathall and Malpas, eds, *Heidegger, Coping, and Cognitive Science*, pp. 317–18).

51 Dreyfus, "Return of the Myth of the Mental," p. 355.

52 See Dreyfus, "Responses," in Wrathall and Malpas (eds), *Heidegger, Authenticity, and Modernity*, p. 339; "Responses," in Wrathall and Malpas (eds), *Heidegger, Coping, and Cognitive Science*, p. 316.

53 See, for example, Sean Kelly, "Grasping at Straws: Motor Intentionality and the Cognitive Science of Skilled Behavior," in Wrathall and Malpas (eds), *Heidegger, Coping, and Cognitive Science*, pp. 173–75.

54 Wittgenstein, *On Certainty*, §§510–11.

55 Wittgenstein, *Philosophical Investigations*, §201, see also §506.

56 Wittgenstein, *On Certainty*, §359, see also §475.

57 "Don't always think that you read off what you say from the facts; that you portray these in words according to rules. For even so you would have to apply the rule in the particular case without guidance" (Wittgenstein, *Philosophical Investigations*, §292). John Haugeland made a similar point in his comments on the Dreyfus–McDowell debate at the 2006 Eastern APA meeting which he kindly let me see.

58 See Dreyfus and Dreyfus, *Mind over Machine*, pp. 80–81; Dreyfus, *What Computers Still Can't Do*, pp. 56–57.

59 Heidegger, *Off the Beaten Track*, p. 199.

60 Dreyfus, "Return of the Myth of the Metal," p. 353.

61 Heidegger, *Poetry, Language, Thought*, p. 181. "To think 'Being' means: to respond to the appeal of its presencing. ... The responding is a giving way before the appeal and in this way an entering into its speech" (*Poetry, Language, Thought*, pp. 183–84). See also "Introduction to *What Is Metaphysics?*," in *Pathmarks*, p. 279; *Discourse on Thinking*, p. 74.

62 Heidegger, "Way to Language," in *Basic Writings*, p. 409. See also *What Is Called Thinking?*, p. 6.

63 Heidegger, *Nietzsche*, vol. 4, p. 181, see also vol. 3, pp. 5, 188; *Question Concerning Technology*, p. 54; *What Is Called Thinking?*, p. 46; *Principle of Reason*, pp. 23–24; *Early Greek Thinking*, pp. 19, 55. Similarly, "being proffers itself to the thinking of Kant as the objectness of the objects of experience" (*Principle of Reason*, p. 87) and "man does not have control over unconcealment itself, in which at any given time the actual shows itself or withdraws. The fact that it has been showing itself in the light of Ideas ever since the time of Plato, Plato did not bring about. The thinker only responded to what addressed itself to him" ("Question Concerning Technology," in *Basic Writings*, p. 323).

64 Dreyfus, "Overcoming the Myth of the Mental," p. 51. I discuss these topics at greater length in *A Thing of This World*, esp. pp. 305–25.

65 Heidegger, *Schelling's Treatise on the Essence of Human Freedom*, pp. 154–55.
66 Ibid., pp. 148–49.
67 Heidegger, "Letter on Humanism," in *Basic Writings*, p. 217.
68 McDowell makes a somewhat similar objection in "Response to Dreyfus," p. 369, but for a very different purpose.
69 See Dreyfus, "Current Relevance of Merleau-Ponty's Phenomenology of Embodiment," §40; "Merleau-Ponty's Critique of Husserl's (and Searle's) Concept of Intentionality," p. 46. His discussion of carrying on a conversation is much closer to what I am describing here. See also Dreyfus et al., *Disclosing New Worlds*, p. 18.
70 See McDowell, "What Myth?," p. 347, and Dreyfus, "Return of the Myth of the Mental," p. 359.
71 Dreyfus, "Response to McDowell," p. 374, see also p. 373; "Responses," in Wrathall and Malpas (eds), *Heidegger, Coping, and Cognitive Science*, p. 329.
72 See Dreyfus, "Return of the Myth of the Mental," p. 359.
73 Heidegger, *Principle of Reason*, p. 3. See also "On the Question of Being," in *Pathmarks*, p. 293.
74 Heidegger, "What Is Metaphysics?," in *Basic Writings*, p. 97, see also pp. 105, 108; *Being and Time*, pp. 166–67/129.
75 See Heidegger, *Principle of Reason*, p. 111; "Postscript to *What Is Metaphysics?*," in *Pathmarks*, p. 234; *Discourse on Thinking*, p. 83; *Mindfulness*, p. 73. Cf. Wittgenstein: "this seems to abolish logic, but does not do so" (*Philosophical Investigations*, §242; see also §108).
76 See Heidegger, "Letter on Humanism," in *Basic Writings*, pp. 251, 264; "Postscript to *What Is Metaphysics?*," in *Pathmarks*, p. 235.
77 See Kant, *Prolegomena to any Future Metaphysics*, p. 65/319.
78 Heidegger, "Origin of the Work of Art," in *Basic Writings*, p. 180. Heidegger uses this argument to free us from the technological attitude which depicts us as in complete autonomous control of our thought and activities ("Question Concerning Technology," in *Basic Writings*, pp. 323–24; *Mindfulness*, p. 152; Wittgenstein *The Blue and Brown Books*, p. 89; and Braver, *A Thing of This World*, pp. 314–25).
79 See Heidegger, "What Is Metaphysics?," in *Basic Writings*, pp. 104–5; "Letter on Humanism," in *Basic Writings*, p. 260.
80 Heidegger, *Zollikon Seminars*, p. 217. See also "Question Concerning Technology," in *Basic Writings*, p. 330; "Building, Dwelling, Thinking," in *Basic Writings*, p. 361.
81 Wittgenstein, *Philosophical Investigations*, II.xi, p. 218, see also §335; *Blue and Brown Books*, p. 41.
82 Heidegger, *Poetry, Language, Thought*, p. 6. See also Nietzsche, *Beyond Good and Evil*, §17.
83 My best thinking happens when ideas simply occur to me; my worst when I try to force and control it. Artists often describe inspiration like this and Heidegger accepts such an account of artistic creation (see "Origin of the Work of Art," in *Basic Writings*, p. 200). This is one reason why "the work is the origin of the artist" rather than the other way around (ibid., p. 143).
84 Heidegger, *On the Way to Language*, p. 76. See also *Principle of Reason*, pp. 47, 96; "Origin of the Work of Art," in *Basic Writings*, pp. 200, 220; "Way to Language," in *Basic Writings*, pp. 410–11, 418, 423; *Nietzsche*, vol. 3, pp. 187, 214, vol. 4, p. 200; *Piety of Thinking*, pp. 25–27; *Poetry, Language, Thought*, pp. 181, 209; "Postscript to *What Is Metaphysics*," in *Pathmarks*, p. 236; *Contributions to Philosophy (From Enowning)*, §265, p. 325.

85 Wittgenstein, *Blue and Brown Books*, p. 155. "Think of putting your hand up in school. Need you have rehearsed the answer silently to yourself, in order to have the right to put your hand up? And *what* must have gone on inside you? – Nothing need have. But it is important that you usually know an answer when you put your hand up" (*Zettel*, §136, see also §44; *Blue and Brown Books*, pp. 4–5, 34; *Philosophical Investigations*, §334).
86 I would like to thank Tim Nulty and Charles Guignon for their helpful comments on this paper.

## Bibliography

Braver, L., "Analyzing Heidegger: A History of Analytic Reactions to Heidegger," in D. Dahlstrom (ed.), *Interpreting Heidegger*, New York: Cambridge University Press, 2011, pp. 235–55.

——, *Groundless Grounds: A Study of Wittgenstein and Heidegger*, Cambridge, MA: MIT Press, 2012.

——, *A Thing of This World: A History of Continental Anti-realism*, Evanston, IL: Northwestern University Press, 2007.

Derrida, J., "From Restricted to General Economy: A Hegelianism without Reserve," in *Writing and Difference*, trans. Alan Bass, Chicago: University of Chicago Press, 1978, pp. 251–77.

Dreyfus, H., *Being-in-the-World: A Commentary on Heidegger's Being and Time, Division I*, Cambridge, MA: MIT Press, 1991.

——, "Could Anything Be More Intelligible Than Everyday Intelligibility?: Reinterpreting Division I of *Being and Time* in the Light of Division II," in J. Falconer and M. Wrathall (eds), *Appropriating Heidegger*, Cambridge: Cambridge University Press, 2000.

——, "The Current Relevance of Merleau-Ponty's Phenomenology of Embodiment," *Electronic Journal of Analytic Philosophy* 4 (Spring 1996).

——, "Merleau-Ponty's Critique of Husserl's (and Searle's) Concept of Intentionality," in L. Haas and D. Olkowski (eds), *Rereading Merleau-Ponty: Essays beyond the Continental–Analytic Divide*, Amherst, NY: Humanity Books, 2000.

——, "Overcoming the Myth of the Mental: How Philosophers Can Profit from the Phenomenology of Everyday Expertise," *Proceedings and Addresses of the American Philosophical Association* 79, no. 2 (2005): 47–65.

——, "The Primacy of Phenomenology over Logical Analysis," in M. Wrathall and H. Dreyfus (eds), special issue, *Philosophical Topics* 27, no. 2 (Fall 1999): 3–24.

——, "Response to McDowell," *Inquiry* 50, no. 4 (2007): 371–77.

——, "The Return of the Myth of the Mental," *Inquiry* 50, no. 4 (2007): 352–65.

——, *What Computers Still Can't Do: A Critique of Artificial Reason*, Cambridge, MA: MIT Press, 1992.

Dreyfus, H. and Dreyfus, S., *Mind over Machine: The Power of Human Intuition and Expertise in the Era of the Computer*, New York: Free Press, 1986.

Dreyfus, H. and Hall, H. (eds), *Heidegger: A Critical Reader*, Cambridge, MA: Blackwell, 1992.

Dreyfus, H. and Wakefield, J., "Intentionality and the Phenomenology of Action," in E. Lepore and R. van Gulick (eds), *John Searle and His Critics*, Cambridge, MA: Blackwell, 1991.

Dreyfus, H. and Wrathall, M. (eds), *A Companion to Heidegger*, Malden, MA: Blackwell, 2005.
Dreyfus, H., Spinosa, C., and Flores, F., *Disclosing New Worlds: Entrepreneurship, Democratic Action, and the Cultivation of Solidarity*, Cambridge, MA: MIT Press, 1997.
Guignon, C. (ed), *The Cambridge Companion to Heidegger*, New York: Cambridge University Press, 1993.
Heidegger, M., *Basic Writings*, rev. edn, ed. D. F. Krell, San Francisco: HarperSan Francisco, 1993.
——, *Being and Time*, trans. J. Macquarrie and E. Robinson, Oxford: Blackwell, 1962. (Page references are to the Macquarrie and Robinson translation and their marginal, *Gesamtasusgabe* page.)
——, *Contributions to Philosophy (From Enowning)*, trans. P. Emad and K. Maly, Bloomington: Indiana University Press, 1999.
——, *Discourse on Thinking*, trans. J. M. Anderson and E. Hans Freund, San Francisco: Harper Torchbooks, 1966.
——, *Early Greek Thinking: The Dawn of Western Philosophy*, trans. D. F. Krell and F. A. Capuzzi, San Francisco: HarperSanFrancisco, 1975.
——, *The Fundamental Concepts of Metaphysics: World, Finitude, Solitude*, trans. W. McNeill and N. Walker, Bloomington: Indiana University Press, 1995.
——, *History of the Concept of Time*, trans. T. Kisiel, Bloomington: Indiana University Press, 1985.
——, *An Introduction to Metaphysics*, trans. R. Manheim, New Haven, CT: Yale University Press, 1959.
——, *Mindfulness*, trans. P. Emad and T. Kalary, New York: Continuum, 2002.
——, *Nietzsche*, 4 vols, ed. D. F. Krell, San Francisco: HarperSanFrancisco, 1979–82.
——, *Off the Beaten Track*, trans. and ed. J. Young and K. Haynes, New York: Cambridge University Press, 2002.
——, *On the Way to Language*, trans. P. D. Hertz, San Francisco: HarperSanFrancisco, 1971.
——, *Pathmarks*, ed. W. McNeill, Cambridge: Cambridge University Press, 1998.
——, *The Piety of Thinking*, trans. J. G. Hart and J. C. Maraldo, Bloomington: Indiana University Press, 1976.
——, *Poetry, Language, Thought*, trans. A. Hofstadter, New York: Harper & Row, 1971.
——, *The Principle of Reason*, trans. R. Lilly, Bloomington: Indiana University Press, 1991.
——, *The Question Concerning Technology and Other Essays*, trans. W. Lovitt, New York: Harper Torchbooks, 1977.
——, *Schelling's Treatise on the Essence of Human Freedom*, trans. J. Stambaugh, Athens: Ohio University Press, 1985.
——, *What Is Called Thinking?*, trans. J. G. Gray, New York: Harper & Row, 1968.
——, *What Is Philosophy?*, trans. J. T. Wilde and W. Kluback, New Haven, CT: New College and University Press, 1956.
——, *Zollikon Seminars: Protocols – Conversations – Letters*, trans. F. Mayr and R. Askay, Evanston, IL: Northwestern University Press, 2001.
Kant, I., *Prolegomena to Any Future Metaphysics*, with introduction by Lewis White Beck, New York: Macmillan Publishing Company, 1950. (Cited by translation and the Akademie edition page.).

McDowell, J., *Mind and World*, 2nd edn, Cambridge, MA: Harvard University Press, 1996.
——, "Response to Dreyfus," *Inquiry* 50, no. 4 (2007): 366–70.
——, "What Myth?," *Inquiry* 50, no. 4 (2007): 338–51.
Nietzsche, F., *Beyond Good and Evil*, trans. W. Kaufmann, New York: Vintage Books, 1989.
Prauss, G., *Knowing and Doing in Heidegger's "Being and Time,"* trans. G. Steiner and J. S. Turner, Amherst, NY: Prometheus Books, 1999.
Sartre, J.-P., *Being and Nothingness: A Phenomenological Essay on Ontology*, trans. H. E. Barnes, New York: Washington Square, 1992.
Wittgenstein, L., *The Blue and Brown Books: Preliminary Studies for the Philosophical Investigations*, Malden, MA: Blackwell, 1969.
——, *On Certainty*, ed. G. E. M. Anscombe and G. H. von Wright, trans. D. Paul and G. E. M. Anscombe, New York: Harper Torchbooks, 1969.
——, *Philosophical Investigations*, 3rd edn, rev. trans. G. E. M. Anscombe, Malden, MA: Blackwell, 2001.
——, *Zettel*, ed. G. E. M. Anscombe and G. H. von Wright, trans. G. E. M. Anscombe, Berkeley: University of California Press, 1970.
Wrathall, M. and Malpas, J. (eds), *Heidegger, Authenticity, and Modernity: Essays in Honor of Hubert L. Dreyfus*, vol. 1, Cambridge, MA: MIT Press, 2000.
——(eds), *Heidegger, Coping, and Cognitive Science: Essays in Honor of Hubert L. Dreyfus*, vol. 2, Cambridge, MA: MIT Press, 2000.

# Part III

# INTELLECTUALISM AND UNDERSTANDING

# 7

# CONCEPTUALISM AND THE SCHOLASTIC FALLACY

*Taylor Carman*

Phenomenology is *hard*, in part for the obvious reason that describing anything just right is always hard, but also in part because the *phenomena* of phenomenology are always interwoven with the means we have at our disposal in describing them. Often, though not necessarily, the phenomenon in question is something like human *experience* (taking that word, for now, in as broad and theoretically neutral a sense as possible). When we try to describe experience as such, we can't get it at arm's-length, so to speak; we can't detach ourselves from it and render it objective. And if we *do*, we have virtually by definition failed to describe it from the point of view of the person having the experience, namely *as* experienced, *as* lived.

This situation would pose no problem if experience were what philosophers in a broadly Cartesian tradition have supposed it to be, namely an inner domain of mental phenomena – ideas, representations, sensations, thoughts – denizens of a private subjective space cut off from the (so-called) "external" world. If that were the case, we could, as early modern philosophers (even Husserl) thought we could, simply look into our own minds and report what we see there.

But experience is not like that. Instead, as many thinkers in the twentieth century (including Husserl) came to realize, experience is fundamentally world directed. Sartre's description is the most vivid, certainly the most dramatic. Consciousness, he writes, is

> a strong wind. There is nothing in it but a movement of fleeing itself, a sliding beyond itself. If, impossible though it may be, you could enter "into" a consciousness, you would be seized by a whirlwind and thrown back outside … for consciousness has no "inside." … [It is] a connected series of bursts that tear us out of ourselves, that … throw us beyond them into the dry dust of the world, on to the plain earth, amidst things.[1]

Likewise, for Merleau-Ponty, perception is not an internal mental state, but a sensorimotor orientation in the world. To be aware of things in the world is to be absorbed in a situation. The effect of this is that our very attention to ourselves gets systematically redirected away from experience as such and, as Sartre says, "thrown back outside," back into the world. This is no accident, Merleau-Ponty says, for "it is the essence of consciousness to forget its own phenomena."[2] Like a vortex, perception constantly pushes us away from itself, and so, as often happens in philosophy, we lose our grip on the phenomena, "the things themselves."

Small wonder, then, that philosophers and psychologists have found perception so hard to describe, or even think about clearly, for it is part of its very nature to *deflect* thought. Perception is elusive precisely because its function is to draw us out into the world. Consequently, Merleau-Ponty writes, "Nothing is more difficult than knowing precisely *what we see*," for "perception hides itself from itself."[3]

Not only that. Reflection often modifies the experience we reflect on, reorganizing and reconstructing it. In particular, when we reflect, we think, and thinking typically involves conceptualizing content that might not already have been conceptual. We are thus subject to a retrospective illusion, namely that experience, to be available to thought at all, must already have had the rational structure we seem to find in it once we stop and think about it. In a word, reflection *rationalizes*.

This observation of the inherent rationalizing tendency of reflection suggests a diagnosis of intellectualism, that is, the assimilation of all experience to thought or judgment. Intellectualism is not a wholly arbitrary theoretical error, but rather the theoretical expression of an inclination built into reflection itself, which is geared precisely to the conceptual articulation and rational reconstruction of unreflective experience. This is just part of what reflection is in the business of doing, and it isn't illegitimate. After all, reflection often manages to clarify and refine attitudes that really are best viewed as coarse, unfocused, or confused anticipations of clear ideas. Reflection isn't always wrong, even when it retrospectively idealizes its object.

Like the appetites, however, it is prone to excess. Or better, as a counter-image to Kant's metaphysical dove, which thinks it might be able to fly more easily without the hindrance of air beneath its wings, we might say reflection wants to dig back down beneath the ground of experience that it needs to support itself.[4] The hubristic dove is an emblem of what Kant calls "transcendental illusion" (*Schein*) – not itself an error, but an ineluctable standing temptation to error. The retrospective rationalizing effect of reflection is a kind of phenomenological illusion too, a standing temptation to the error of intellectualism.

Following this same diagnostic line of thought, Pierre Bourdieu traces intellectualism in the social sciences to what he calls the "scholastic fallacy," namely the projection of the theorist's own institutionally facilitated attitude of "studious leisure" into the object of study, so that, for example, unreflective social practice gets construed either as the surface appearance of a complex system of unconsciously implemented rules, as in structuralism, or as a text needing to be read and interpreted properly, à la hermeneutics and deconstruction.[5] In either case, the result is a reification of the theoretical attitude of the reflective observer at the expense of the concrete lived phenomenon. Recognizing the scholastic fallacy allows us to see why intellectualism has been and will probably remain a perennial temptation not just in humanistic and social scientific inquiry, but in everyday life.

Consider one of the most celebrated arguments in recent analytic philosophy in defense of an intellectualist conception of experience, namely John McDowell's *Mind and World*. Not unlike existential phenomenologists, especially Heidegger and Merleau-Ponty, McDowell wants to get beyond the Cartesian and Kantian dualism of reason and nature. More specifically, he wants to forestall what he sees as an impasse inherent in a still-dominant conception of ourselves as divided between the mechanical, "disenchanted," law-governed nature of Galilean science, on the one hand, and the realm of rationally binding norms, on the other. In perception, the fatal dichotomy is between a supposedly brutely given, nonconceptual sensory content and free, rationally articulated belief; in action, it is between the exercise of autonomous practical reasoning and mere bodily movements occurring in a physical nature altogether devoid of meaning and purpose.

McDowell's strategy is to avoid the impasse by insisting that human experience and action must already be infused with reason, that "we need to see ourselves as animals whose natural being is permeated with rationality,"[6] which is to say spontaneous and autonomous, that is, self-instigating and self-governing. We are, as Aristotle said, naturally rational animals, so there is no gap between nature and reason, or world and mind. Not that the Galilean conception of physical nature is wrong in itself, only that it misses an essential dimension of *our* nature, namely our initiation into the space of reasons through language and culture. Culture, which embodies meaning and rationality, is itself an aspect of human nature.

For McDowell, then, there is no dualism between nature and reason. But this is only because there is, for him, a very sharp distinction between *natural laws* and *rational norms*. This distinction, it seems to me, afflicts him with a different kind of theoretical blind spot, for while he recognizes the rational component of our nature, rightly refusing to elevate reason to the level of something supernatural, he fails to acknowledge the *sub*rational regions in the space of meaning within which we find ourselves in the world, beneath the threshold of conceptual rationality.

McDowell himself tends to run together a number of different terms, all of which characterize what he likes to call, following Kant, our "spontaneity." Now that term seems to me very obscure, for it might in principle designate any number of doings or initiatives we readily recognize not just in ourselves but in other animals, too. What McDowell has in mind, however, is not just any old doing or initiative, but specifically autonomous rational activity, the kind of freedom involved in reasoning, judging, inferring, and deciding. The idea of spontaneity, he says, is "the idea of an active undertaking in which a subject takes rational control of the shape of her thinking."[7]

For McDowell, reason and spontaneity also go hand in hand with concepts and conceptuality. Debates about nonconceptual content, which McDowell denies we have in our experience of perceiving and acting, can sometimes sound like verbal disputes about how to use the word "concept." So, for example, McDowell thinks I have a *concept* of a given shade of red, even if all I can think or say about it is that it is *"that* shade." All that matters for his theory is that I can retain and make use of such a concept in my subsequent thoughts, inferences, judgment, and deliberations. Thus, he writes, "the topography of the conceptual sphere is constituted by rational relations. The space of concepts is at least part of ... 'the space of reasons.'"[8]

So, while McDowell insists that "conceptual capacities are drawn on *in* experience,"[9] that in "actualizations of our sensibility ... conceptual capacities are passively drawn into operation,"[10] his notion of conceptuality is not neutral with respect to the distinction between receptive experience and spontaneous thinking. It is not as if, according to him, perception and thought both just happen to have conceptual content. Rather, McDowell *defines* conceptuality in terms of the spontaneity of thinking, and then extends the reach of that spontaneity, as it were, into the sphere of perceptual receptivity as well. This is why in most cases he does not just say that *concepts* permeate perception, but that *spontaneity* does: "spontaneity permeates our perceptual dealings with the world, all the way out to the impressions of sensibility themselves."[11] McDowell, that is, conceives of the empirical content of experience generally in terms of its conduciveness to rational reflection: "To understand empirical content in general, we need to see it in its dynamic place in a *self-critical activity*," namely thinking.[12]

This is also why McDowell draws such a sharp distinction between human and "mere animal" perception. He concedes that the two have something in common, yet it seems, on his view, such a something cannot be a kind of content. Not that he thinks mere animal experience has *no* content, only that whatever content it can be said to have cannot be the kind of content *we* have as rational subjects in *our* experience. For in order to be nonconceptual, our experience would have to be in principle unavailable to thought, as he seems to think mere animal perception is, while in order to have experience with conceptual content, an animal would have to be capable of autonomous rational thought, like us.

Critics have objected – rightly, in my view – to this sharp distinction between human and "dumb animal" perception and action, but I think they have not put the objection in quite the right way, or with quite the right phenomenological considerations fully in view. Hubert Dreyfus, for instance, objects that McDowell still believes too much in the reflexive self-awareness or ego-ownedness of experience. Dreyfus's charge is "that subjectivity ... is the lingering ghost of the mental; that the necessity of 'practical self-awareness in action' haunts McDowell's account of involved activity."[13] In this vein, Dreyfus appeals to Sartre's observation that engaged, unreflective awareness involves no reference to a self or owner of experience. Sartre writes,

> When I run after a streetcar, when I look at the time, when I am absorbed in contemplating a portrait, there is no I. There is consciousness *of the streetcar-needing-to-be-overtaken*, etc., and nonpositional consciousness of consciousness. I am then plunged into the world of objects; they constitute the unity of my consciousness, they present themselves with values, with attractive and repellant qualities – but me, I have disappeared.[14]

Like Dreyfus, I find Sartre's description of absorbed, unreflective awareness compelling. But I don't consider it the final word on the status of the self in experience, nor do I think it poses a threat to McDowell's conceptualism.

For one thing, as Sartre himself realized, at least by the time he wrote *Being and Nothingness*, the absence of a robust transcendental ego, construed as an abiding anchor or pole of awareness internal to consciousness, says nothing against the weaker Fichtean–Brentanian notion (which might still be wrong) that consciousness as such always involves a reflexive, "nonpositional" awareness – not of an ego, but of itself. Indeed, in the passage he quotes from *The Transcendence of the Ego*, Dreyfus elides Sartre's passing remark that even in running for the streetcar or gazing at the painting, there is still what he calls "nonpositional consciousness of consciousness." That weaker sort of self-awareness is not awareness of an ego or owner of experience, but rather awareness of awareness itself, which I take it means awareness of the *contents* of one's awareness. Sartre's faith in the rational transparency of the subject, whether McDowell shares it or not, might be enough to sustain the idea that human action always involves necessarily thinkable content, for it seems to guarantee that the contents of consciousness are always available to it, namely the subject, even though the subject does not appear to itself as an ego.

In fact, even someone who rejected that picture of the reflexive transparency of consciousness could still accept Sartre's phenomenological observation as describing a kind of episodic blindness we undergo in those instances when we cease to be aware of ourselves as owners of our experience or as spontaneous agents, initiators of our actions. But this leaves open the question whether we *are* essentially spontaneous agents, even if we are not constantly aware of ourselves as such. I'm often not aware of being in a mood, but that doesn't mean I'm not in one. The experience Sartre describes is genuine all right, and he describes it brilliantly, but I don't think it amounts to a definitive indication of the structure of the self or the nature of agency.

The episodic diminution of subjective self-awareness is therefore not a strong enough counterexample to what I think Dreyfus rightly regards as McDowell's intellectualism. In whatever ways the intentional contents of our experience may ebb and flow, or go in and out of focus, from our own subjective standpoint, what matters for McDowell's theory is just that those contents are in principle available to the subject, that they *can* be fitted into her rational deliberations, that they already somehow occupy the space of reasons. What McDowell requires is not that the "I think" (or "I do") *does* accompany all my representations, but only, as Kant said, that it *can*.

In a different line of argument, Dreyfus appeals to the kinds of bodily skills we share with other animals, skills not governed by cultural norms, but shaped by physiology and instinct: we walk forward instead of backward; we keep our balance by shifting our weight from one foot to another; we crane our necks or squint to get a better look at something.[15] Already early in childhood, such natural gestures begin to exhibit culturally specific characters. And yet, interestingly, some habits you might be tempted to chalk up to cultural idiosyncrasy turn out to be biological dispositions common to more than one species: the "elevator effect" (standing still and looking down to avoid eye contact in close quarters), for example, can be observed in rhesus monkeys and chimpanzees, not just alienated urban dwellers.[16]

These kinds of motor skills are fascinating and important, but McDowell can reasonably argue, as John Searle has, that many of them are not really *actions*, but mere motor components of actions.[17] I don't need conceptual content describing, or even demonstratively indicating, the movement of my legs as I walk, since what I'm *doing* is not moving my legs, but *walking*. And when we do regard, say, walking through a doorway as an action, not just a component part of an action, then it is arguably different for dogs and for us, for human beings appear to be unique in their responsiveness to the norms governing such actions. We are, as McDowell says, capable of acknowledging reasons "as such." I think McDowell is onto something important and right when he says that what we have, and other animals lack, is something like the ability to respond to norms *as* normative (or not), that is, to recognize something like the *normativity* of norms: we nod our heads in assent, shake our heads in disgust, raise our eyebrows in perplexity or doubt, and sometimes act counternormatively, either in jest or in defiance – not of force, but of authority. I don't know whether such gestures require language, but they might. In any case, what we do, and what other animals apparently do not do, is *express* ourselves, where "expression" means not just blind reflex, but a way of taking a stand on the norms we recognize as governing what we do.

I don't think any of this shows, however, contrary to McDowell, that we do not have much of the same kind of intentional content as mere animals. Dreyfus is right that McDowell's minimal requirement, that intentional content be merely "in principle" available to thought, is much too weak to support his claim that the content of mere animal perception and action must differ essentially from ours. Again, debates about nonconceptual content can seem merely terminological. On the one hand, if "conceptual" just means whatever (*je ne sais quoi*) somehow allows perceptual experience to be a source of belief with empirical content, then we might as well say that our experience has only conceptual content, since anything less would by definition render it inaccessible and irrelevant to our empirical beliefs.[18] But then we are in no position to say that the perceptual states of mere animals must be nonconceptual, for even if we grant that mere animals cannot think, it doesn't follow that their perceptual states lack whatever it is (*je ne sais quoi*) that *would* allow their beliefs to have empirical content, if they *could* think. For example, McDowell concedes that, like us, animals perceive Gibsonian "affordances" – obstacles, threats, opportunities, and so on. If it turned out that the perception of affordances is sufficient for supplying belief with empirical content for creatures capable of thinking and believing, then the content of mere animal perception would have to count as conceptual. But McDowell denies this.

On the other hand, if we agree with McDowell, as I think we should, that the content of mere animal perception is nonconceptual, then it seems to me there is no good reason to deny that much of our experience is nonconceptual, too. It is not enough to say, as McDowell does, that the crucial difference between us and mere animals is that, unlike them, we *can* reflect, believe, judge, deliberate, and decide; that the "I think" (or the "I do") *can* accompany our representations. It *can*, yes. Sometimes. Can it *always*? Must it be able to? I don't see why. In short, the mere potential for the exercise of reason by itself tells us very little a priori about the nature of the perceptual content that figures into our beliefs and decisions.[19]

Of course, McDowell intends the link to rationality to be much stronger than this talk of a mere potentiality suggests. Nor by "conceptual" does he just mean whatever (*je ne sais quoi*) somehow allows beliefs to have empirical content. Instead, for him, conceptuality means *already established conduciveness to autonomous rational reflection*. So, his debate with Dreyfus, and indeed the crucial difference between Merleau-Pontyan anti-intellectualism and McDowellian conceptualism, turns neither on whether we are continually conscious of our putative status as rational agents nor on the kind of content minimally necessary for animal behavior, but on whether there are specifically human experiences and actions that exhibit a kind of intentional content importantly different from that which figures paradigmatically in exercises of autonomous reasoning.

Merleau-Pontyan anti-intellectualist phenomenologists like Dreyfus (and me) therefore need a stronger counterexample to combat McDowell's conceptualism. We need more than a kind of experience that just happens to be momentarily egoless, or even altogether (if only temporarily) unconscious,[20] and we need more than behavioral capacities we share with other animals, which taken in isolation arguably fall below the threshold of full-fledged intelligent action altogether. What we need is an experience that has a kind of intentional content that differs in some important way from the *conceptual* content that figures, by definition, in rational thought.

I said earlier that McDowell tends to run together a number of different terms, all of which he uses to characterize autonomous rationality. One term that I think should *not* be lumped together with the others is "meaning." In *Mind and World* "meaningful" more or less coincides with "conceptual," which McDowell in turn defines in terms of reason, reflection, deliberation, thought. Accordingly, he explicitly equates what he calls "the kind of intelligibility that is proper to *meaning*" with "the kind of intelligibility we find in something when we place it in the space of *reasons*."[21]

The crucial question is thus: is *meaning* exhausted by the rational structure of thought, even if we grant that such rational structure can manifest itself, not just in the actual spontaneity of the intellect, but also in the receptivity of perceptual experience? Heidegger, Merleau-Ponty, and Bourdieu have in different ways insisted that rational intelligibility is only part, indeed a derivative part, of the kind of meaning that falls outside the rational intelligibility of the natural sciences, or in McDowell's words, the kind of intelligibility "we find in a phenomenon when we see it as governed by natural law."[22] Is there a kind of experience that exhibits a kind of content worth distinguishing from the content of thought?

Often enough, of course, actions we perform unthinkingly remain readily accessible to reflection. Sartre, for example, says that although he may be unselfconsciously absorbed in counting his cigarettes, so that "I do not 'know [*connais*] myself as counting,'" still, "if anyone should ask, 'What are you doing there?' I should reply at once, 'I am counting.'"[23] The ease of the reply, I take it, makes McDowell's point that, at least in this case, the content of the absorbed *counting* consciousness is already the conceptual content of the reflectively articulated belief *that I am counting*.

In other cases, though, reflection cannot so easily appropriate the content of unreflective experience. Consider the kind of bodily understanding Bourdieu ascribes to what he calls the "*habitus*," that is, the "durable, transposable dispositions" to act appropriately in a variety of situations in a familiar social field.[24] We know, for instance, how far to stand from someone while having a conversation: we have a feel for the "right" distance, and we unthinkingly, often unconsciously, adjust, moving closer or further away to maintain the proper "equilibrium," as Merleau-Ponty says.[25]

This is a nice example of unreflective intelligence, but I don't think it demonstrates the presence of anything McDowell would have to acknowledge as genuinely nonconceptual content. For it is open to him to say, as Sartre does, that if someone were to ask me how far you should stand from someone in a conversation, though I might not be able to specify a distance in inches or centimeters, I might be able to indicate it ostensively, for example, by taking up what strikes me as more or less the right position and saying, "About like *this*." McDowell will count that as supplying a demonstrative concept, and his point in calling it a "concept" is just that I can retrieve it, if only with the words "*that* distance," in my subsequent thinking.

I said I *might* be able to indicate the proper distance ostensively. Can we do so reliably? I suspect so, but that is an empirical question. If not, then conceptualism is in trouble. And indeed, other aspects of ordinary conversational skill are more obviously threatening to McDowell's view. As Merleau-Ponty says, practical tasks generally elicit the necessary movements from us in an immediate, unreflective way,

> just as the phenomenal forces at work in my visual field elicit from me, without calculation, the motor reactions that establish the best equilibrium between them, or as the conventions of our milieu, or our group of listeners, immediately elicit from us the words, the attitudes, the tone suited to them.[26]

Just as we naturally squint or lean forward to get a better look at something, so too we know when it's appropriate to strike up a conversation and when it isn't, when to respond and when not to respond to someone addressing us, when to speak up in (or out of) turn in the right way, and how to steer a conversation toward pertinent and agreeable subjects and away from irrelevant or potentially upsetting issues.

The art of conversation as a whole is a lot like the distance standing that often accompanies it, in that our conduct need not be governed by explicit rules or general concepts. But it also differs crucially, since it is less conducive to the demonstrative form of identification that McDowell deems sufficient for conceptual content, which in turn he takes to be necessary for grasping meaning at all. Could we, if pressed, specify – even demonstratively – *when* it is appropriate to speak or remain silent, or precisely *how* the tone or mood of a conversation has become disturbing or inappropriate? As in the case of distance standing, we sometimes have an uneasy, perhaps barely conscious sense that things are going subtly wrong: the other person is talking too much or too little, or the conversation is drifting into subjects that are irrelevant or threatening. *How* to put things right? *When* to do so, even if it means interrupting, talking out of turn, or withholding the affirmative or reassuring gestures that often keep a conversation on a friendly footing? At what point do I stop smiling, contradict the person I'm talking to, create a diversion with a joke, or simply end the conversation?

The advantage this example has over Dreyfus's appeal to the kinds of motor skills we share with animals, it seems to me, is that conversation is a uniquely human capacity, yet it seems to involve something very different from conceptual content, even on McDowell's broad understanding of that notion. Of course, conversing requires rationality, yet it also involves a kind of intelligent sensitivity to nuances of tempo, reciprocity, mood, duration, and subject matter that are arguably not *already* as such conducive to conceptual recognition and rational reflection. The point is not that such nuances are altogether unavailable to thought, but that thinking about them often requires a significant shift or modification in the content of our initial sensitivity to them in order to render them thinkable, to conceptualize them – in short, to rationalize attitudes that were not in the first instance thoughts at all, but intelligent, intuitive "feels" for how things were showing up and how well or badly we were coping with them.

Of course, in good scholastic fashion, a determined conceptualist might appeal once again to the many obvious successes of reflection, such as Sartre first being absorbed in counting his cigarettes, and then, when questioned, easily and correctly reporting that what he was doing was counting his cigarettes. But all that shows is that unreflective awareness *sometimes* has conceptual content; it doesn't show that it *always* does or that it *must*.

When something goes awry in a conversation, often all we feel is a vague sense of unease, like when we literally lose our balance, or more generally when we lose that sense of comfortable equilibrium that normally keeps us engaged in what we're doing. The conversation is not going well. Topics come up and then fall flat. There are awkward silences. You and your interlocutor find yourselves interrupting each other or talking at cross-purposes. Finally, it might occur to you that something in particular is wrong: this person is too talkative, or sullen (maybe angry), or too inquisitive, or long-winded, or self-indulgent. You have now undergone a discernible shift from the intuitive, intelligent sensitivity that was allowing you to keep the conversation going, to a belief you have subsequently formed about what went wrong, or how or why. We make such diagnostic judgments only once we have in some sense *withdrawn* from the conversation, even if we're still going through the motions and speaking and listening awkwardly and uncomfortably. As long as we're really *in* the conversation, in the proper sense – when our "hearts" are in it, as we say – we are trying to make it work, and that means precisely *not* judging, not even recognizing, what we might later identify as the source of the trouble. Keeping a conversation going, indeed any absorbed activity, requires that we preserve certain gaps or blind spots in our field of attention, just as we tune out distractions that would otherwise destroy our concentration.

The kind of intelligent sensitivity we normally exercise in conversation, however, involves more than the momentary lapse in attention or self-consciousness we see in Sartre's examples of running for the streetcar or counting his cigarettes. For those cases leave open the question whether the content of the experience is essentially conceptual or nonconceptual. In the case of the conversation gone wrong, I want to suggest, there is an important difference in the *kind* of content involved in the engaged and the reflective attitudes, respectively. For the engaged attitude *keeps us in* the conversation precisely by steering us away from potential conversational pitfalls, heading them off in advance, indeed *obscuring* possible sources of trouble and preventing us from even *recognizing* them, until later, when we might find ourselves believing, from a reflective attitude, that some particular thing had indeed gone wrong. It is implausible to construe engaged conversational intelligence as a conceptual or rational recognition of ongoing potential threats to the smooth continuation of the conversation, so that we can always be ready to avoid them. Good conversations, after all, are not freighted with a constant sense of vigilance or defensive anticipation of potential infelicities; they just roll along effortlessly.

Sean Kelly has argued that the content of the "motor intentionality" of our intelligent bodily comportments differs essentially from the content of cognitive attitudes like belief. The difference, according to Kelly, is that whereas the propositional contents of cognitive attitudes are detachable or abstractable from the psychological attitudes in which they are embedded, motor-intentional content is constituted by and dependent on the concrete exercises of bodily skill they inform and govern.[27] My point about the embeddedness of the content of conversational intelligence in conversational performance closely parallels Kelly's argument for the embeddedness of motor-intentional content in the exercise of motor skills. Like motor-intentional content, the content of skillful social intelligence *resists* abstraction and incorporation into purely rational configurations of inference, deliberation, and decision. It is the content it is *owing to* the concrete performances of social skill it governs.

I think the felt transition from engagement to reflection is philosophically significant, and we are in danger of losing sight of it if we commit ourselves, with McDowell, to the assimilation of experiential content to conceptual content, or in his words "empirical content in general" to "its dynamic place in [the] self-critical activity" of rational reflection.[28] That commitment is, I suspect, yet another product of the scholastic fallacy, the illicit projection of the structure and content of reflection into unreflective experience, motivated (understandably) by our already having adopted a reflective attitude by the time we stop and think.

## Notes

1 Sartre, "Intentionality," p. 383.
2 Merleau-Ponty, *Phenomenology of Perception*, p. 67.
3 Ibid. Cf. Merleau-Ponty, *Visible and the Invisible*, p. 213.
4 Kant, *Critique of Pure Reason*, B8. My metaphor here is akin to Hubert Dreyfus's comparison of John McDowell's conceptualism to the idea that, in supporting "the edifice of knowledge," "human experience is upper stories all the way down." Dreyfus, "Overcoming the Myth of the Mental,", p. 47.
5 Bourdieu, "Scholastic Point of View," p. 381. Bourdieu borrows the phrase from J. L. Austin's withering critique of sense-data theory as "a typically *scholastic* view," mired in decontextualized language, "an obsession with a few (and nearly always the same) half-studied 'facts,'" in short, "over-simplification, schematization, and constant obsessive repetition of the same small range of jejune 'examples.'" *Sense and Sensibilia*, p. 3.
6 McDowell, *Mind and World*, p. 85.
7 Ibid., p. 60.
8 Ibid., p. 5.
9 Ibid., p. 9.
10 Ibid., p. 120.
11 Ibid., p. 69.
12 Ibid., p. 34.
13 Dreyfus, "Response to McDowell," p. 373. The embedded quotation is presumably referring to the sentence, "Self-awareness in action is practical, not theoretical." McDowell, "Response to Dreyfus," p. 367.
14 Sartre, *La transcendance de l'ego*, p. 32.
15 See Dreyfus, "Response to McDowell," p. 375.
16 de Waal, *Our Inner Ape*, p. 174.
17 In skiing, for example, according to Searle, "the body takes over and the skier's Intentionality is concentrated on winning the race." Searle, *Intentionality*, Cambridge: Cambridge University Press, 1983, p. 151.
18 Again, I limit the discussion here to the kind of content that actually figures in experience. As McDowell says, a notion of intentional content might play a very different role in cognitive science, where we needn't assume its availability, even in principle, to consciousness or reason. I might have no *experience* at all of the content a cognitive scientist is justified in attributing to me "from sideways on," as McDowell puts it. McDowell concedes that mere animals have that kind of content, too, but he doesn't seem to think they have anything worth calling "experience." This is the drastic, and I think disastrous, conclusion that follows from his insistence that experience, to be a source of belief at all, must already be "permeated with rationality." McDowell, *Mind and World*, p. 85.
19 Dreyfus makes this same point in his "Response to McDowell" when he charges that the "pervasiveness claim" rests on a category mistake, since "Capacities can't pervade anything." Dreyfus writes, "I don't see an argument for the move from the reasonable claim that attentive experience with its attendant ego is *sometimes exercised* to the claim that this capacity is *always operative*" (pp. 372, 376). For similar objections to the cognitivist account of first-person attitudes in Richard Moran's *Authority and Estrangement*, see my "First Persons," pp. 395–408.
20 Permanently or recalcitrantly unconscious content, being in principle unavailable for rational reflection, could not play the role definitive of conceptual content in McDowell's sense.
21 McDowell, *Mind and World*, p. 74 (emphasis added).

22 Ibid., p. 71.
23 Sartre, L'Être et le néant, p. 19; Being and Nothingness, trans. H. E. Barnes, p. 13.
24 Bourdieu, Logic Practice, p. 53.
25 Merleau-Ponty, Phenomenology of Perception, pp. 123–24, 106, 122, 179, 153, 177, inter alia.
26 Ibid., pp. 123–24, 106, 122.
27 Kelly, "Merleau-Ponty on the Body."
28 J. McDowell, Mind and World, p. 34.

## Bibliography

Austin, J. L., Sense and Sensibilia, Oxford: Oxford University Press, 1962.
Bourdieu, P., The Logic Practice, trans. R. Nice, Stanford: Stanford University Press, 1990.
——, "The Scholastic Point of View," Cultural Anthropology 5, no. 4 (1990): 380–91.
Carman, T., "First Persons: On Richard Moran's Authority and Estrangement," Inquiry 46, no. 3 (2003): 395–408.
de Waal, F., Our Inner Ape: A Leading Primatologist Explains Why We Are Who We Are, New York: Penguin, 2005.
Dreyfus, H., "Overcoming the Myth of the Mental: How Philosophers Can Profit from the Phenomenology of Everyday Expertise," Proceedings and Addresses of the American Philosophical Association 79 (2005): 47–65.
——, "Response to McDowell," Inquiry 50, no. 4 (2007): 371–77.
Kant, I., Critique of Pure Reason (1781, 2nd edn 1787), trans. P. Guyer, Cambridge: Cambridge University Press, 1998.
Kelly, S. "Merleau-Ponty on the Body," Ratio (n.s.) 15, no. 4 (2002): 376–91. Reprinted in M. Proudfoot (ed.), The Philosophy of Body, London: Blackwell, 2003.
McDowell, J., Mind and World, Cambridge, MA: Harvard University Press, 1994.
——, "Response to Dreyfus," Inquiry 50, no. 4 (2007): 366–70.
Merleau-Ponty, M. Phenomenology of Perception (1945), trans. C. Smith, London: Routledge & Kegan Paul, 1962.
——, The Visible and the Invisible, trans. A. Lingis, Evanston: Northwestern University Press, 1968.
Sartre, J.-P., Being and Nothingness: A Phenomenological Essay on Ontology, trans. H. E. Barnes, New York: Washington Square Press, 1956.
——, L'Être et le néant, Paris: Gallimard, 1943.
——, "Intentionality: A Fundamental Idea of Husserl's Phenomenology," trans. J. P. Fell, in D. Moran and T. Mooney (eds), The Phenomenology Reader, London: Routledge, 2002.
——, La transcendance de l'ego, Paris: Librairie Philosophique J. Vrin, 1981.
Searle, J., Intentionality: An Essay in the Philosophy of Mind, Cambridge: Cambridge University Press, 1983.

# 8

# ON OVERINTELLECTUALIZING THE INTELLECT

*Alva Noë*

## 1

According to an old and tired idea, the scope of experience is fixed by what projects to our eyes, or to the sensory periphery of our bodies. Experience, then, is something that happens inside us as a result of our being so affected by the world around us. I reject this way of thinking about experience and its scope. We see much more than projects to the eyes. We experience what is hidden or occluded (the tomato's back, for example); we experience the nature of things (what they are – telephones, say, or other people); we perceive emotion and meaning (the intensity of a person's concentration; what she is saying).

Of course, there are constraints on what shows up for us in experience; and these constraints have to do with our physical, embodied, spatial relations to things. But it is impossible even to begin to make sense of what shows up in terms of a one-way causal influence of the things around us on our nervous system.[1]

Instead of thinking of what we experience as fixed by the way the world projects to us, giving rise to events of consciousness inside of us, we should think of what is experienced as what is *available* to a person, as what is available to a person *from a place*. The seeing does not happen in the head. Rather, the experience is achieved or enacted by the person. We do it *in the world*. The scope of experience is a matter of what is available to us. And what is available to us depends on not only what there is, but also, crucially, on what we can do. What we can do depends in turn on understanding, know-how, but also on tools and technology (pictures, language, the telephone, the pencil), and on where we find ourselves and what environmental or social resources are available to us.

What is available is that to which we have access, and the ground of access is knowledge, understanding, and skill. Mere sensory projection is neither necessary nor sufficient. It is understanding that brings the world into focus for perceptual consciousness.

## 2

One of reason why art matters to us, I think, is that it provides opportunities for us to recapitulate this basic fact about ourselves: understanding and skill enable us to bring the world into focus for perceptual consciousness.

Consider what sometimes happens when you encounter unfamiliar artwork. Every song on the new record (for example) may sound more or less the same, each coming across flat, or unengaging. Every painting in the gallery presents its face to you, but only as a face in a crowd, with no discernible features. Sometimes we encounter the work, but it is as if we don't see it, or can't see it, or don't see any meaning in what we see.

But suppose you don't give up. You listen to the record again and again; you begin to notice different qualities in the different songs. As you familiarize yourself with them, they begin to engage your attention, and offer you comfort, or excitement, or stimulation, or pleasure. Perhaps you discuss the music, or the paintings in the gallery, with a friend, and she draws your attention to patterns or devices or lyrics. Whereas before the works – the songs, the paintings – were flat, opaque, undifferentiated, now they reveal themselves to you as structured and meaningful, as deep and involving. Each song, or each painting, now shows you its very own distinctive face. You make its acquaintance.

If you have spent time around art, you have probably had this experience. To a child all "classical music" sounds the same, just as every white-haired figure presented in eighteenth-century garb "looks like" George Washington. We don't differentiate well among the unfamiliar; this partly explains why the rural Nigerian border guards thought my girlfriend and I looked so much alike that we must be brother and sister. Or consider the case of literacy: to an illiterate person, the text might as well be invisible. The consciousness of the person who can read, in contrast, is captured by the text and by all that it affords.

We gain knowledge, and familiarity, and skill, and so we are able to bring the world into focus for perceptual consciousness.

## 3

Some philosophers think of perception as nonintentional and nonconceptual. These philosophers are empiricists. Empiricism holds that perception is basic in our cognitive lives. Perceptual experience, for empiricists, is prior to and independent of our ability to think and talk about objects. First we perceive, then we frame concepts so that we can represent what we perceive in thought and refer to what we perceive in speech. For empiricism, perceptual consciousness (awareness, experience – I use these interchangeably) does not depend on possession of concepts or knowledge of the reference of terms; it is what first makes the latter possible. Empiricism is realistic and it is foundationalistic. The basic constraint on what we can see is what there is; our perceptual sensitivity to objects and their basic properties such as size, shape, and color is the foundation of our cognitive lives.

In this chapter, and in all my work, I advance an antiempiricism that denies that perceptual experience is prior to thought and talk. I do not claim that we need to be able to think of things prior to our encounter with them in experience; what I urge is that the conditions on encountering a thing in experience are also conditions on encountering that very thing in thought. Perceptual experience can enable us to be aware of things only given the coinvolvement of understanding. Perception and thought arrive at the party together. Thought is not prior to experience; experience is itself a kind of thought. But then thought itself, as we have seen, at least sometimes, is a form of perceptual consciousness.

From the standpoint of empiricism, the conception of experience as thoughtful and active that I defend here overintellectualizes experience. For to suppose that perceptual experience relies on the exercise of the understanding, as I do, might seem to threaten to treat perception as if it were judgment or categorization. Certainly it does not ring true to suggest that we see things, as it were neutrally, and then subsume them under concepts. Such a view would overintellectualize perceptual experience, presenting seeing as if it were a kind of contemplative detachment.

What is sometimes unnoticed is that this line of criticism is itself guilty of an act of overintellectualizing. But what is overintellectualized, on this line of criticism, is the intellect itself – as if the only legitimate exercise of the understanding was in a deliberative act of bringing things under concepts. If we think of understanding that way – as the exercise of deliberative judgment – then it is hard to take seriously the idea that experience rests on the understanding in the way I have urged.

Nothing compels us to think of the understanding in this detached, deliberative way. We can find an alternative conception in Wittgenstein. For Wittgenstein, understanding is akin to an ability. Understanding a concept is having a skill. One way to exercise the relevant conceptual skills is in explicit deliberative judgment; but that is not the only way. There is a distinctively perceptual mode of exercise of intellectual and conceptual (and also sensorimotor) skills. This is nicely illustrated by the phenomenon of linguistic perception. When you know a language you can perceive words, sentences, even meanings; when you don't know a language you are unable even to discriminate these linguistic objects. They are not dependent for their existence on your knowledge, but your knowledge – your fluent, skillful mastery – is a condition on them showing up for you.

Wittgenstein's discussion in *Philosophical Investigations*, especially the discussions of rule following, elucidates the idea that understanding is like a practical skill. In particular, as I read Wittgenstein, he discovered that it is psychologism to hold that my actions can be rule governed only if I explicitly entertain the governing rule in mind. Crucially, as Wittgenstein argued, following a rule is only one of the different ways for rules to govern what we do. The novice uses the rule as a draftsman uses a ruler, as an active guide. The expert no longer has any need for such explicit reliance on the rule. He has learned how to act in accordance with the rule without any need to consult the rule in thought (even in unconscious thought). But that doesn't mean that the behavior is no longer rule governed. The expert's skill allows for fluency and automaticity, but the zone of fluency is not one where the rules lose their force and relevance. The master acts in accord with the rules without thinking of them deliberately, precisely because he or she has mastered them. We see this in the chess grand master whose play is a free and spontaneous expression of understanding.

## 4

Hubert Dreyfus has a different conception.[2] He contrasts the detachment of thought and reason with the engagement of what he calls absorbed coping. The novice is a thinker: detached, attentive, conscious, deliberate. The expert is involved in the activity and has left the conscious mind behind. The expert is in the groove; for the expert, what matters is the flow. This analysis is supported by empirical findings to the effect that the expert's performance is disrupted by focused attention on the execution of the task, whereas the performance of a novice improves when attention is brought to bear in this way. For Dreyfus, the assumption that the grand master's play flows from an understanding of rules is a giveaway of a shaping idea that he has called "the Myth of the Mental," the idea that engaged, skillful coping requires the backing and support of robust, regulating cognition.

Dreyfus urges that grand masters, in the groove, don't make moves for reasons. They just act, responsive to the demands of the situation. Dreyfus is right about the immediate responsiveness of experts. But this doesn't mean that there is no place for thought or reason in an account of what the expert does. We can agree with Dreyfus that the fact that the grand master is able to tell you why she acted, after the fact, no more shows that she acted from a reason than the fact that the refrigerator light is on whenever you look shows that it is always on (as Sean Kelly has remarked). But it would be a mistake to think that the question whether she acted for a reason depends on whether she entertained reasons (even unconsciously) before acting. That presupposition is tantamount to the psychologism that Wittgenstein warns against. What mastery (or understanding) of rules enables is for one's actions to involve the rules without needing to think about them in any explicit, deliberative way. Again, language is a good object of comparison. There are rules that govern our use of words. Our skillful linguistic behavior expresses our knowledge of these rules. But there is certainly no requirement that we consider the rules that would justify our usage while we are caught up in the stream of linguistic activity. And so with chess, and action more generally.

Nor does one's inability to make explicit the rule that would have justified one's move (or one's speech behavior) show that one's action was not the skillful expression of mastery of a rule. Perhaps I can say nothing more articulate about why I moved as I did than: "this is a weak pawn structure; in a case like this you need to try to strengthen your defenses," or some such. Dreyfus is inclined to say, of this sort of case, that it shows that understanding, reason, thought, have left the building; the player is responding to context, to situation, to the brute solicitations of the state of the board. But this reply ignores a better alternative: that it might be essential to our conceptual and intellectual skills, as it is essential to every other kind of skill, that their deployment be context sensitive and situation dependent. The fact that the chess master can't give a context-free, situation-independent statement of the principle that governed her action does not show that understanding and reason were not at work.

It is to overintellectualize the workings of the intellect to suppose that every exercise of understanding requires a deliberate act of contemplation of an explicitly formulated rule. Such an overintellectualized conception of the intellect leaves out the possibility that intellectual skills themselves may admit of expertise and effortless exercise. Dreyfus is right to attack what he has variously labeled cognitivism, rationalism, representationalism. But he aims his attack at the wrong aspect of these doctrines. They do not go astray because they cite rules, justifications, reasons, and understanding in offering an account of action and experience. They go astray, rather, because they take for granted that the intellect's operation is always deliberate and detached. And this is Dreyfus's mistake as well. Like the views he attacks, Dreyfus takes for granted that there can be no operations of the intellect that belong, as it were, to the engaged mode. That's precisely the way of thinking about the intellect made available by Wittgenstein. Our understanding, our thinking, our deliberations themselves, always only take place in a context, against a background, and for certain purposes.

## 5

I turn now to a line of objection that has been leveled against the sort of conception of experience as skill-based access that I develop here; it has also been pressed against Gibson. To bring the objection into view, recall that for Gibson affordances are the possibilities for action provided by things. A tree stump affords sitting; Gibson argued that we perceive affordances.[3]

The way traditional cognitive science understands this, the idea would be that we see the tree stump, say, and represent it as affording sitting.[4] In this way, perceiving the affordance is, in effect, an act of categorizing or classifying the tree. To see the tree's sit-upon-ability is, in effect, to bring the object under the concept of seat. It may not seem to us, when we see the tree's affordance property, that this is what we are doing. But phenomenology, it is observed, is not a reliable guide to cognitive psychology.

Gibson's own theory of affordances was advanced as an alternative to this perception-as-classification idea. This is what he had in mind when he said that we see affordances directly.

It is usually supposed that there is something special about affordances, for Gibson, in virtue of which we can see them directly. And then the question is, what is it about the fact that a thing affords me the possibility of action that allows me to see it in a way that I could not otherwise see it? John Campbell has criticized Gibson on this sort of ground. Campbell writes,

> suppose, for example, that an unfamiliar piece of apparatus appears on a workbench. I have no idea what this thing is for. I don't know if I can touch it – maybe I will be electrocuted, or the thing will blind me, if I do that. Or maybe it is simply the latest kind of television, or a paper weight. So I don't see it as affording anything in particular. In that case, by Gibson's theory, the thing should be simply invisible; I should be able to see it only when I am told what it is for. But that is not a persuasive conclusion; it seems perfectly obvious that we can see things without knowing what they can be used for.[5]

As I read Gibson he is not committed to such a conclusion, for it is not Gibson's view that we only see affordances, or that we can only see objects in so far as we can see their affordances. Gibson's point comes earlier: that we can see affordances. The significance of his thought is this: for Gibson, perceptual consciousness is not confined to so-called categorical (or categorial) properties of things, such as shape, say, or size, or qualities like color. Gibson is advancing "the radical hypothesis" that "the 'values' and 'meanings' of things in the environment can be directly perceived."[6]

This is just what Campbell denies. As Campbell writes, the

> natural view to oppose to Gibson is that visual experience does not provide us with knowledge of affordances. It provides us with the knowledge of the categorical properties of objects which are the reasons why objects have the affordances they do.[7]

And he continues:

> This is particularly compelling when you consider shape properties. ... It surely is plausible that ordinary experience of the shape

of an object does not provide you merely with the endless opportunities for various types of action made possible by its having that shape. It confronts you with the categorical shape property itself, the reason why the object provides all those properties.

As I interpret Campbell, his charge is that Gibson gets things precisely backwards. We don't see things by seeing what they are for; we see things and so, on that basis, learn about what they are, or might be, for. A very similar line of criticism can be (and has been) framed against the sort of conception of perceptual experience as constituted in part by the exercise of what I have called "sensorimotor understanding" or "sensorimotor expectations" (that is, by expectations about the way sensory stimulation varies as a function of movement). Sensorimotor expectations cannot be constitutive of perceptual awareness of an object, for it is the antecedent perception of an object, with its stable, independent nature, that gives rise to and justifies sensorimotor expectations in the first place, so the objection goes. My sense of how the appearance of something will change as I move is simply the wrong sort of thing to serve as the ground of my successful perceptual contact with the object itself. For how can a wealth of contingencies of this sort give one access to the underlying basis of those contingencies, to the object itself? And where do we even get the idea that the object is there independently of how we experience it?[8]

I have already mentioned that it isn't Gibson's view that, as Campbell puts it, the experience of the shape of an object provides you "merely with the endless opportunities for various types of action."[9] Nor is it my view that what we really experience are patterns of appearance and the way they change as a result of movement. Neither Gibson nor I wish to deny that ordinary experience is a confrontation with objects themselves. What I deny – I don't want to speak for Gibson here – is that we can just take the fact that objects and their so-called categorical properties show up in experience for granted. It is our unavoidable perceptual predicament that there is no such thing as a perceptual encounter with the object that is not also an encounter with it from one or another point of view; there is no such thing as seeing an object from every point of view at once; so objects of perception always have hidden, undisclosed parts or aspects. What I have called the problem of perceptual presence is that of explaining how a merely perspectival glimpse of something can disclose its nature when that nature transcends what is contained in a single glimpse alone. In this essay, and in my other writing, I have offered a solution: what enables us to achieve perceptual contact with objects despite the limited and partial character of our perceptual situation is our understanding (sensorimotor and otherwise). Sensory events alone, without skill and understanding, are blind.[10]

## 6

I suspect that Campbell and other empiricists suppose that affordances, or appearances, are not real, or at least, that they are not sufficiently basic. Animals perceive danger and sexual availability and opportunities for concealment, it would be admitted, but they do so thanks to a more basic ability to represent shapes and sizes and movements of things. There are two big, and by now familiar, problems with this line of response.

First, as already stated, we cannot take for granted our perceptual access to objects and their shape and size. The problem of perceptual presence – namely, the problem of what our perceptual sense of the presence of features that are manifestly out of view or hidden consists in – arises for every perceptual object or quality, whether we think of it as categorical or dispositional.

Second, the contrast between categorical and dispositional properties tends to collapse. Among the things I can learn from what I see are how things are with respect to shape and size, but I can also find out about how things look. Indeed, it belongs to our perceptual predicament that in visual perception I must learn about how things are by looking and so by making sense of how things look. The empiricist tradition has tended to assume that looks are subjective dispositions of one kind or another. They are effects in us; matters of sensations. In an effort to break with what Putnam has called the "interface" conception of experience,[11] it might seem that we need to do away with the idea that we are aware of looks (for example). But that is dogmatic and unreasonable. We need to rethink what looks and other appearances are. They are not "in here," and it is not our burden to get from them, somehow, to what is "out there." Nothing forces that interface conception on us. I have argued that appearances are environmental properties. If we want to think of them as dispositions, then they are the ways objects affect their environment, not ways they affect our sensations. Perception is an activity of learning about things by learning about how they affect the world.[12]

Similar remarks go for affordance properties. The grass can show up for me in perceptual consciousness as a place to rest; the animal can show up for me as a threat, or as a desirable mate. The fact that the perceiver's nature and other environmental conditions are factors determining what something affords me does not mean that a thing's affordances are not among what I can directly perceive.

What enables objects and their properties to show up for us in experience is the fact that they exist and that we have access to them. A theory of direct perception requires a theory of access.

This is what I have been trying to provide: remarks towards a general theory of access.

What enables us to bring objects into focus for perceptual consciousness, and also their affordance properties or other forms of significance, is our understanding (sensorimotor and otherwise). This is something that Gibson, no less than Campbell and (for rather different reasons) Dreyfus, seem to have been unwilling or unable to allow. Concepts and sensorimotor skills get applied in perceptual experience in the distinctively perceptual mode. That is, we don't use conceptual or sensorimotor rules to categorize objects or to represent them in our minds. Conceptual and sensorimotor skills are not means of representation; they are means of achieving access to things. Indeed, a theory of direct perception requires us to appreciate anew the role played by skills and understanding in perceptual experience. The object's nearby existence does not suffice to enable the object to show up for perceptual consciousness. To achieve contact with the object and its different kinds of properties requires skill – skills of a sensorimotor as well as intellectual variety. Conceptual skills, along with sensorimotor skills and other kinds of understanding, belong to the means by which we accomplish perceptual contact with reality. In perceptual application, we don't use concepts to represent things in thought, or to categorize; concepts are part of the adjustments whereby we bring what is present, but absent, into view. Since everything is always in some degree absent or remote, understanding is necessary for perceptual consciousness.

## 7

At the outset (in §2) I called attention to the way in which aesthetic experience – the experience of the work of art – is an achievement of the understanding. The bare exposure to the song, or to the painting there on the wall in the gallery, is not yet the aesthetic experience. Aesthetic experience is achieved by interrogating what is there before you. To bring the work into focus, we need to acquire the skills needed to do this. And this we do on the fly, *in situ*, with the resources the world (the artwork) provides. Through looking, handling, describing, conversing, noticing, comparing, keeping track, we achieve contact with the work/world. We achieve an appreciation of the way the piece hangs together – what the work is – through activities I will refer to collectively as aesthetic discourse, or better, criticism. We achieve the sort of understanding that consists in seeing connections, what Wittgenstein characterized as a perspicuous overview of the whole.[13] We learn our way around in a space of possibilities that the piece opens up.

Aesthetic criticism is thus a necessary accompaniment of the kind of perceptual achievement in which aesthetic experience consists. Criticism is the way we make the adjustments needed to make sense of what is before us. Aesthetic experience happens against the background of criticism.[14] This was Kant's conception. Aesthetic experience – for example, the sort of experience he characterized as that of the beautiful – has intersubjectively valid content. Our aesthetic experience of the work of art reflects our sense of what the work demands, not only of us, but of anyone. Our response thus reflects our sense of how one ought to respond to the work. Aesthetic experience happens only where there is the possibility of substantive disagreement, and so also the need for justification, explanation and persuasion. The work of art is only experienced when it is experienced as making claims on us, claims we need to adjudicate.

Kant was also clear that despite the fact that aesthetic experience is a thoughtful recognition of what the work demands – we must regard the experience as a cognitive achievement – it is nevertheless the case that aesthetic response is always also and fundamentally a matter of feeling, of responsiveness, rather than a matter of judgment. We don't engage in explicit deliberative reasoning to decide whether something is beautiful. There is literally no possibility of such reasoning. We can't convince ourselves or others of the beauty of a work. Rules, algorithms, criteria, have no place here.

And yet – crucially – we can try. We have to try, if we are to take our own aesthetic responses (our own aesthetic *judgments*) seriously. What we need to see is that there is a deployment of our cognitive faculties that is at once rigorous, and rational, but that does not require that it eventuate in a QED. We aim at persuasion, at clarification, at motivation, and indeed justification. I can't prove to you that something is beautiful, but I can teach you to see its beauty, and I can fault you for being unable or unwilling to do so.

Whether or not this is exactly Kant's view, it seems that Kant, like Wittgenstein, offers a picture of the way the intellect enlivens aesthetic experience which shows us how, to use John McDowell's Sellarsian phrasing, aesthetic experience is in the space of reason, even though, at one and the same time, there is no sense in which it is attached to explicit deliberative judgment. Crucially, as I would put it, the critical inquiry that the artwork occasions and requires is the very means by which we exercise the understanding that brings the work of art into focus and so allows us to feel it, to be sensitive to it.

The pleasure of aesthetic experience, on my approach, is the pleasure of "getting it." It is the pleasure of understanding, of seeing connections, of comfortably knowing one's way about. It is the pleasure that comes from recognizing the purposiveness (*Zweckmässigkeit*, as Kant would have it), or integrity (as Dewey put it), or meaning, of the work. This meaning or purposiveness was there all along, but hidden in plain sight.

And so there can be no charge here of overintellectualizing. What we need to admit, finally, is that there is a nonjudgmental use of concepts, a deployment of concepts in, as I put it earlier, a perceptual or experiential mode. We can say more about this here. Building on the idea that understanding is akin to an ability, I propose that we think of concepts as tools for picking up features of the world around us, or techniques for grasping things, features, aspects, qualities. To learn a concept is to learn to grasp something (it is to acquire a *Begriff*; it is to learn to do something, *etwas befgreifen*). What criticism affords is the cultivation of the understanding, the development and so the procurement of the conceptual tools that enable us to pick up what is there before us. Concepts are ways of achieving access to the world around us.

8

Art and philosophy are one. Philosophy aims at the kind of understanding that lets us find our way about and make contact with the world. Philosophy aims at the sort of understanding that an artwork occasions and that aesthetic criticism produces. Philosophical discussion is a modality of aesthetic discourse; it is a species of criticism. Philosophical arguments, no less than aesthetic ones, never end with a QED. This troubled Plato in the *Meno* and it has continued to puzzle philosophy all along. Philosophy – and again, the same is true of art – is always troubled by itself, always seeking better to understand its project. The solution, I think, is in the recognition that the value of philosophical conversation, like aesthetic conversation about a work of art, consists, not in arrival at a settled conclusion, but rather the achievement with a new understanding that enables one to bring the world, or the artwork, or one's problems, into focus. We seek this transformation in philosophy and in art.

We also see that the conception of aesthetic experience I am articulating here – incorporating as it does elements from Kant and Wittgenstein – is really a conception of perceptual experience *tout court*. All perceptual experience is a matter of bringing the world into focus by achieving the right kind of skillful access to it, the right kind of understanding. Art matters because art recapitulates this basic fact about perceptual consciousness. Art is human experience, in the small, and so it is, in a way, a model or guide to our basic situation. Art is philosophy. And all perceptual experience, viewed correctly, is rather a kind of aesthetic experience.

And so, the encounter with the world, like the encounter with a work of art, unfolds against the background of aesthetic conversation. Perception is not a matter of sensation; it is never a matter of mere feeling. Perceiving is an activity of securing access to the world by cultivating the right critical stance, that is, by cultivating the right understanding.

It is easy to lose track of the thoughtful and rhetorical structure of human experience. For example, it is sometimes noticed that contents of experience do not enter into logical relations with other contentful states. Perception does not entail belief; and belief does not rule out countervailing perceptual experience. This is sometimes taken to show that experience and belief have different kinds of content, that the content of the former cannot be conceptual in the way that the latter is. Examples like the Müller–Lyer Illusion are sometimes adduced to demonstrate this.[15] The fact that the lines can look different in length even when I know they are the same is thought to show that the content of the perceptual experience cannot be logically structured in the way that the corresponding belief is structured.

But this is a gross mistake. Nothing requires us to say that concepts are brought into play in the one case, but not the other; all that we are compelled to say, rather, is that there are different ways for them to be brought into play. To suppose that the contents are truly incommensurable, rather than in conflict, say, is not to explain the phenomenon of conflict between what we see and what we know. It is to explain it away, or really, to deny the phenomenon.

The big mistake is that we overlook the aesthetic, or critical, context of all experience. There is no such thing as how things look independently of the larger context of thought, feeling, and interests. What we know and what we see push and pull against each other, and they move each other and guide each other and tutor each other. This is plain and obvious when we think of the experience of art. It is no less true in daily life. What makes it almost impossible to appreciate this in the present case – the Müller–Lyer illusion – is the cartoonish simplicity of the case. The rhetorical context is so impoverished that it seems, mistakenly, as if we are uncovering something deep and primitive in the workings of the visual system, its cognitive impenetrability. But really, the psychologist has pulled a fast one on us.

## 9

An important upshot of taking aesthetic experience to be the very paradigm of a perceptual experience is that it lets us see our way clear to a better conception of the nature of phenomenology. Consider three puzzles about phenomenology as traditionally or conventionally construed.

First, introspection is fuzzy. Traditional approaches take for granted that experience is a matter of introspection, for they take for granted that the experience is something that happens inside you that supports and accompanies your action. But introspection is a we-know-not-what. What are we supposed to be looking for? And how do we know when we've found it? How can we be sure we are describing it accurately? These unanswered questions befuddle any attempt to take introspection seriously as a method. Anyway, once we give up the idea that experiences are internal events, we can more or less leave introspection aside.

Second, there is a familiar worry about transparency. When we turn our attention to our experiences of seeing, hearing, touching, we almost inevitably turn our attention to what we see, or hear, or touch. It seems that the experience is invisible to us, for it is transparent and we find ourselves seeing right through it to the other side, to the world itself. A similar problem arises when we try to think about the visual field. If we turn our attention to the visual field, we almost inevitably end up turning our attention to that which is before us, to the world. Several philosophers have noticed this.[16] So our question is, then: given the transparency of experience, such as it is, what is there left for us to investigate, if we seek to investigate the character of our own experience?

Third, Dreyfus, Sean Kelly, Sartre, and others have emphasized a certain phenomenological paradox, to wit, that when we turn our attention to our experience, we actually modify the character of our experience. In the free flow of experience, there is only, for example, the bus I am trying to catch, or the painting on the wall I want to see. We naturally and spontaneously respond to the world and we do so in a way that shows we are sensitive to the world's solicitations. We step back to achieve the point of optimum grip on the picture; we lunge around the passersby in our effort to capture the bus driver's attention. But nowhere does the experience itself, as an episode in consciousness, show up for me. Indeed, I am myself absent from the story. And when we stop and contrive to think about what we saw and felt and "experienced," well, then we are in a completely different, reflective, contemplative, detached domain. No matter how sensitively I try to make explicit why or how I adjusted myself to get a better view of the picture on the wall, I cannot be making explicit that which was implicitly operative in my consciousness. For even to frame the question is to alter the experience.

We can begin to see our way clear to a new way of responding to these puzzles. Phenomenology does not require that we turn our attention away from the world, that we introspect, or that we try to defeat experience's transparency. Phenomenology requires, rather, that we turn our attention to what we are doing, to our engaged activity. And we actually have a paradigm of what it would be to do this: aesthetic criticism.

Experience is not something that happens in us. It is something we do. Experience itself is a kind of dance – a dynamic of involvement and engagement with the world around us. To study the experience, we must study the dance. The aesthetic task of bringing a dance itself into focus for perceptual consciousness – the task we undertake when we grapple with live performance, for example, whether as a member of the audience or as a performer – is exactly the same as we confront when we wish to investigate our own experience. Aesthetic criticism serves as our model.

The phenomenological stance, then, is the aesthetic stance, and the aesthetic stance is available to us both as performers (or agents) or as critics (or members of the audience, as it were). Dreyfus and Sartre are right that I can't contemplate my experience of running for the bus, as I run for the bus. But there is no call for this sort of self-monitoring (neither on the part of the performer nor the critic). Paying attention to yourself, or to what is going on inside you, is one thing, and paying attention to the task at hand, to what you are doing, is another. And *that* is what is required of the aesthetic stance: a critical awareness of and sensitivity to what you are doing.

## 10

To summarize what we have accomplished so far: experience is active and it is thoughtful; it is intellectual, but it is also sensual; it is rule governed, and the question of which rules govern us, why and how, always arises. But that does not mean that we must in fact always be able to give a certain answer or that we can make it all explicit.

I want now in closing to address a worry that stems from a problem about animal minds. If experience is always aesthetic, if it always takes place in a setting where criticism and philosophy are also in place, then can there be any sense at all to the idea that nonhuman animals have experience? What is aesthetic criticism in the life of the dog? Or the whale? This question has a certain urgency for me, since, after all, part of what has motivated me to develop a practical, active, tool-like conception of concepts and the understanding (in chapter 6 of *Action in Perception*) was precisely to open up the possibility of appreciating the continuity between animal and human minds. By locating experience in the setting of a narrative drama of a striving to achieve skill-based access to the world, have I not simply reintroduced the necessity of there being a very sharp line between them and us all over again?

The problem of consciousness, as I understand it now, is that of understanding how the world shows up for us. The problem of consciousness is the problem of the world's presence to mind. How the world shows up for us depends not only on our brains and nervous systems, but also on our bodies, our skills, our environment, the way we are placed in and at home in the world. The world shows up for us thanks to what we can do – to the way we can achieve access – and this depends not only on us (on our brains and bodily makeup), but also on the world around us and our relation to it. We make complicated adjustments to bring the world into focus.

This is so for animals as well as humans. We move and peer and squint and reach and handle and respond and so we skillfully take hold of what there is around us. We achieve access to the world. We enact it by enabling it to show up for us. Sometimes we fail. There are different ways we can fail to achieve access to the world; there are different ways the world can fail to show up for us. If the skills needed to pick up a feature are absent, then the feature is not present in our experience. If I don't have the relevant skills of literacy, for example, the words written on the wall do not show up for me. I can't see them, even though they are there. I lack the skills. This is just the way the words can fail to show up for infant children, or for my dog.

But there is a way we adult humans can get lost, or confused, a way we can fail to secure the world, which is not available to children or animals. We can find the very techniques, technologies, skills, and practices that open up the world for us in the first place to be the source of puzzlement. As Heidegger put it, we can be a problem to ourselves.

Adult human persons are smarter than animals and children. At least some of them are. We are smart enough to be not only skillful, but ironic. We are smart enough to be confused by the complicated choreographies of our own transactions with the world around us. And so we are driven to philosophy and art. For philosophy and art – as we have seen, these are really one – are our main way of grappling with the anxiety caused by our predicament.

Animal and infant experience is no less complicated; it is no less enacted than our own. It's just that animals, children, and perhaps some grown-up humans, are not able to perceive the puzzling character of our own being. They aren't anxious. They aren't a problem to themselves.

I readily admit that what I have said here is simply to redescribe what we already know: that human adults have intellectual and mental lives unlike those of animals and children. What I try to secure, through this redescription, is an appreciation of the fact that perceptual consciousness – experience – is what we share with other living creatures, and not something we possess apart. It is precisely the aesthetic character of experience – that it is performed in dynamic exchange with the world around us – that brings this fact about our mutual nature into focus.

## Notes

1 I defend this claim in *Out of Our Heads*, and also in *Action in Perception*.
2 See, for example, his "Myth of the pervasiveness of the mental" (Chapter 1, this volume). This is a central and animating theme of Dreyfus's thought.
3 Gibson, *The Ecological Approach to Visual Perception*.
4 See, for example, Fodor and Pylyshyn, "How Direct is Visual Perception."
5 Campbell, *Reference and Consciousness*, pp. 43–44.
6 Gibson, *The Ecological Approach to Visual Perception*, p. 127.
7 Campbell, *Reference and Consciousness*, p. 44.
8 See, for example, John Campbell's contribution to an American Philosophical Association symposium on my *Action in Perception*: "Sensorimotor Knowledge and Naïve Realism." See also my reply to Campbell: "Reply to Campbell, Martin and Kelly."
9 Campbell, *Reference and Consciousness*, p. 114.
10 For more on the problem of perceptual presence, see my *Action in Perception*, as well as *Varieties of Presence*.
11 Putnam, *Threefold Cord*.
12 This is not to deny that how things are *with me* or *in me* sometimes makes a difference to how things look. For example, as Putnam has observed, I may notice that how things look is different when I look with one eye than when I look with the other. Nor is it to deny that one can experience blurs or gleams or

brilliancies and highlights. It is tempting to describe these as differences in my experience to which there are no corresponding properties in the environment. And this would be right, so long as we recognize that our experience is not itself *in us*, but is rather something we undertake in relation to the world around us. Blurs and gleams arise from our relation to, and transaction with, the world around us. It is also critical to remember that blurs, gleams, or other "sensations" are not the foundations of perceptual experience, but modalities of it. One's sensitivity to a thing's color, for example, is a sensitivity to a feature of the world around me; it is not to be explained in terms of sensations. I thank Hilary Putnam, Jim Conant, and John McDowell for discussion of this point at the March 2007 meeting at University College Dublin, held in honor of Putnam's eightieth birthday.

13 L. Wittgenstein, *Philosophical Investigations*, §122.
14 This point is important. The existence of critical conversation about art is not a mere accidental by-product of art practices themselves, but an essential constituent of those practices.
15 See, for example, Evans, *Varieties of Reference*.
16 For example, G. E. Moore and Gilbert Ryle.

## Bibliography

Campbell, J., *Reference and Consciousness*, Oxford: Oxford University Press, 2002.

——, "Sensorimotor Knowledge and Naïve Realism," *Philosophy and Phenomenological Research* 76, no. 3 (2008): 666–73.

Evans, G., *Varieties of Reference*, Oxford: Oxford University Press, 1982.

Fodor, J. A. and Pylyshyn, Z. W., "How Direct Is Visual Perception: Some Reflections on Gibson's 'Ecological Approach,'" *Cognition* 9 (1981): 139–96. Reprinted in A. Noë and E. Thompson (eds), *Vision and Mind: Selected Readings in the Philosophy of Perception*, Cambridge, MA: MIT Press, 2002, pp.167–227.

Gibson, J. J., *The Ecological Approach to Visual Perception*, Hillsdale, NJ: Lawrence Erlbaum, 1979.

Noë, A., *Action in Perception*, Cambridge MA: MIT Press, 2004.

——, *Out of Our Heads: Why You Are Not Your Brain and Other Lessons from The Biology of Consciousness*, New York: Farrar Straus & Giroux, 2009.

——, "Reply to Campbell, Martin and Kelly," *Philosophy and Phenomenological Research* 76, no. 3 (2008): 691–709.

——, *Varieties of Presence*, Cambridge, MA: Harvard University Press, 2012.

Putnam, H., *The Threefold Cord: Mind, Body, World*, New York: Columbia University Press, 1999.

Wittgenstein, L., *Philosophical Investigations*, trans. G. E. M. Anscombe, Oxford: Blackwell, 2001.

# 9

# INTELLECTUALISM, EXPERIENCE, AND MOTOR UNDERSTANDING

*Charles Siewert*

### Introduction

Intellectualism is by definition a vice – the vice of overstating the role of intellect in experience and action, of seeing reason (or inferences, or concepts) where they are not. In what follows I find some justification for Dreyfus's charge that McDowell's views are intellectualist in this sense. But my reasons leave me room to agree with McDowell: our rational capacities also do, in a way, "pervasively shape" our experience, and this can make it misguided to look for some "core" of experience we share with sentient creatures that lack them.

My criticism is rooted in a recognition that our experience is also "pervasively shaped" by something we certainly *do* share with other animals – namely, a capacity for *movement*. Such movement, I will argue, makes for changes in how things appear to us that cannot be completely captured in concepts of those things that the appearances afford. So, in this sense, concepts do *not* completely "pervade" our experience; experience by nature "runs ahead" of the thought that it makes possible. Further, this dynamic structure of appearance, shaped by motor activity, makes objects apparent to us; it is sufficient to yield "object directedness" – to give us experience *of space* – even absent the powers of "self-critical rationality" that McDowell deems essential. So we can share this spatial *form* of experience with animals that lack our intellectual self-consciousness, even if things never look to them quite as they do to us.

Explaining these ideas will occupy roughly the first two-thirds of this chapter. In the remainder, I will further develop these themes of self-consciousness and sensorimotor activity by considering how Merleau-Ponty figures in the Dreyfus/McDowell dispute. I will absolve him of McDowell's charge that he subscribes to some risible "Myth of the Disembodied Intellect." My interpretation of the "impersonal existence" Merleau-Ponty says we lead as perceivers will credit him with a more interesting view. It will find him engaged in a serious effort to meet the challenge that animates much of McDowell's own work, that of how best to integrate a conception of ourselves as "active thinkers" with an understanding of our embodied, sentient nature. Altogether, my remarks here will, I hope, contribute to an understanding of just where intellectualist pitfalls lie, and of where alternatives to them may be sought.

## Dreyfus versus McDowell

Let me start by sketching some features of the disagreement between Dreyfus and McDowell. Consider this gloss on two central ideas found in McDowell.

1 *The pervasiveness of concepts.* Our perceptual experience is pervasively shaped or permeated by concepts.[1]
2 *The pervasiveness of self-consciousness.* Our experience and actions are both inextricably bound to a kind of critical self-consciousness.[2]

Dreyfus opposes both of these forms of pervasiveness as intellectualist myth (what he calls the "Myth of the Mental").[3] According to Dreyfus, *neither* the use of concepts nor even an *implicit* self-awareness is much involved in our everyday activity. Against (1) he says, an "as-structure" – and thus concepts – are often absent from our activities. As he puts it, "most of our activities don't involve concepts at all ... they don't have a situation-specific 'as-structure.'"[4] This is illustrated with reference to that beloved example of the everyday – going in and out of doors. Dreyfus remarks: "I don't see the doorknob as a doorknob when I am absorbed in using it."[5] And what goes for doorknobs goes for much of what we skillfully cope with as we go about our lives: we do not perceive it *as* anything, and thus a conceptualization of what we perceive is not involved. Therefore, contrary to thesis (1), concepts do not pervade our experience.

Against (2), he says that when we are involved or absorbed in activity, typically, he says, no "ego," no "I," is present. As he puts it, "in fully absorbed coping, there is no immersed ego, not even an implicit one."[6] Perception is a "skilled bodily accomplishment that goes on without an explicit or implicit sense of an 'I' who is doing it."[7] In this connection Dreyfus endorses a remark of Sartre's:

> When I run after a streetcar, when I look at the time, when I am absorbed in contemplating a portrait, there is no I ... I am then plunged into a world of attractive and repellant qualities – but me, I have disappeared.[8]

Dreyfus also cites (though with some ambivalence) a quotation from Merleau-Ponty – a passage on which, as we shall see, McDowell also seizes. According to Colin Smith's English translation, quoted by Dreyfus[9] and McDowell,[10] Merleau-Ponty says:

> In perception we do not think the object and we do not think ourselves thinking it, we are given over to the object and we merge with this body which is better informed than we are about the world.[11]

In line with his criticisms of McDowell, Dreyfus takes Merleau-Ponty to be saying ("albeit poorly") that in perception we allow ourselves to be "drawn into" an "absorbed coping" and "involvement" with things, which is a fundamentally nonconceptual response to environmental "solicitations," one in which there is "no 'I' present," and no experience of *this body* "as mine."[12]

McDowell counters partly by emphasizing the modesty of his claims. He offers us the example of catching a Frisbee – something either humans (who are rational agents), or dogs (who are not) might do. McDowell asks: "[W]hat difference does it make, according to me, for activity to be permeated with rationality … ?"[13] "The point of saying that the rational agent, unlike the dog, is realizing a concept in doing what she does is that what she is doing … comes within the scope of her practical rationality – even if only in that, if asked why she caught the frisbee, she would answer, 'No particular reason; I just felt like it.'"[14]

Thus conceptual pervasiveness is exhibited in such unexceptionable facts as these: a human agent is prepared to give some such rationalization of her behavior, as a dog, for instance, is not. And insofar as a readiness to rationalize what one is doing in this way constitutes a readiness *to think of oneself as an agent*, open to evaluation in the light of norms of rationality, this observation brings along with it the idea that there *is* a practical self-awareness involved in ordinary activity – whatever Sartre may have had to say about chasing streetcars.

McDowell also shifts to the offensive by hurling the "myth" talk back at Dreyfus and his "hero" Merleau-Ponty. They are allegedly under the spell of a mythological "dualism of embodiment and mindedness."[15] They think that in absorbed coping there is no experience of an "I" doing anything, but only *this body* responding to solicitations. This, McDowell says, makes the body into a second "person-like" thing, distinct from (intellectual) me. And here McDowell objects:

> *I* am the only person-like thing (person actually) that is needed in a description of my bodily activity. If you distinguish me from my body, and give my body that person-like character, you have too many person-like things in the picture when you try to describe my bodily doings.[16]

And, with reference to the just-quoted passage from Merleau-Ponty, McDowell chides:

> Once I have separated *me* – the thinking thing I am – from *this body*, it is too late to try to fix things by talking about the former merging into the latter. No one but a philosopher would take seriously the thought that in perception, or in action for that matter, I merge into my body. The fact is that there is nothing for me to mean by "I" ... except the very thing I would be referring to (a bit strangely) if I said "this body" ... If I give "this body" the reference it must have in Merleau-Ponty's context, it is wrong to say I merge into that; I simply *am* that. This is mere sanity.[17]

For McDowell the attempt to isolate in human experience a nonconceptual "ground floor" of embodied coping, quite distinct from the rational, conceptual activity of the intellect, promotes an absurd alienation of body and mind. Better, then, to recognize from the start that human experience is inextricably pervaded by concepts.

## How concepts shape our experience: the modest thesis

Let's have a closer look at McDowellian thesis (1). It seems to me that talk of the "pervasiveness" of concepts is importantly ambiguous; right away I want to distinguish two claims. One of these seems more suitably put by saying that our concepts pervasively "shape" our experience: how we experience things – i.e. how they *appear* to us – *depends on* what conceptual capacities we have, or are exercising, and on what sorts of reasons we do or would give for what we're doing. That is: things would have (for example) *looked* differently to me than they actually do, if I hadn't had certain conceptual capacities I actually do, or hadn't been acting (as I was) in ways contingent on my being disposed to offer or accept certain reasons for what I was doing.

Now this seems to me quite correct, for reasons I will explain shortly. But there is another thesis (for which the "pervasiveness" talk is perhaps better suited) that I take to be distinct from this, and stronger. This is the claim McDowell puts by saying that "all content" of "world-disclosing" experience ("every aspect" of it) is "present in a form in which it is suitable to constitute the content of conceptual capacities."[18] This strikes me as much more questionable.

So: the two "Pervasiveness of Concepts" theses I want to distinguish are these:

(1a) *Conceptual shaping*. Our experience is conceptually shaped – that is, often or almost always, how we (normal adult human beings) experience things (e.g. how they look to us – and broadly speaking, how they *appear* to us) depends on what conceptual capacities we have, or are exercising.

(1b) *Conceptual readiness*. All experiential content is present in a form in which it can be the content of a process in which corresponding conceptual (i.e. inferential) capacities are exercised. Every aspect of experiential content is "conceptually ready" – i.e. ready to figure distinctly in conceptual thought.

Now first, what are we to make of (1a), the "shaping" claim? Whatever its merits, it does not seem that examples like McDowell's Frisbee catching adequately support it. Granted, I am typically ready, if asked, to offer some reason for what I'm doing. But it is not clear how that is supposed to show that the concepts expressed in my answer were somehow previously shaping the content of my experience. Nevertheless, we can make it clear, in various ways, that things typically would not appear to us as they do, were we not exercising some conceptual understanding at the time. If this modest thesis is what is meant by saying that concepts are "shaping" our experience, then I think it will be hard to deny.

Here is one way of making the point. It is not unusual for me to be looking for something. I don't just mean that I am often *searching for something I've lost* – although sadly that is common enough too. I just mean that as part of what I am doing when I go about my mundane activities (e.g. sorting the laundry, retrieving my suitcase from the baggage carousel, getting ready to leave the apartment, waiting at the intersection, preparing to exit the freeway), I am looking for something: the matching sock, the suitcase, my keys, a change of the traffic-light, the University Ave exit. This needn't involve a reaction to some failure in my normal ways of getting things done. In such circumstances, I'm coping about as skillfully as I ever do. But still, how things look to me depends on what I am looking for and how I am looking for it. And *that* I am looking for what I am looking for depends on my being disposed to give and consider reasons for what I am doing – e.g. reasons involving the concepts of sock, suitcase, keys, traffic-light, and so on. Thus things would not have looked to me as they did, had I not been doing something that involved my grasp of concepts.

We may put the idea more generally (and without talk of "looking for" something). What I look *at* varies with the *task* in which I am engaged. Since *how things look to me* depends on what I look at, it follows that my tasks shape how things look to me. And typically I would not be engaged in these tasks, if I were not inclined to give or accept various *reasons* for what I am doing. But that involves dispositions to employ *concepts* in various ways. So it follows that how I am disposed to deploy concepts shapes my experience.

But even if this upholds a modest version of McDowell's pervasiveness of concepts thesis (1a), does it support (2) – the pervasiveness of self-consciousness? Here again I think it's important to distinguish (at least) two theses.

(2a) *Rational-pragmatic self-consciousness.* Normal human beings, when awake and active, are typically disposed to cite some reason for what they are doing that involves referring to themselves, and absent such dispositions, would not be doing what they are doing.
(2b) *No spatial experience without self-criticism.* Perceptual experience has content at all and constitutes "outer experience," "awareness of aspects of the world," only if subjects of perceptual experience can think about whether conditions are suitable for judging how things are by how they appear to them.[19]

I think (2a) is fairly unobjectionable, for reasons similar to those already mentioned. It seems to me that, typically, I wouldn't be looking for what I am looking for (in the sense earlier invoked) if I did not take myself to have reasons to do this, and that involves a readiness to *think thoughts about myself*. Though we have to qualify such claims by recognizing there are cases in which people merely confabulate reasons for what they're doing, I don't think a broad skepticism here will get very far. (Usually, when I *think* I'm looking for my keys so I can use the car, *I really am*.) So I do not contest (2a). However, again, (2b) seems to me much more worrisome. Later I will return to this, and to the issue of self-consciousness. But first, I want to examine the pervasiveness of *concepts* theses a little more.

## But do concepts *constitutively* shape experience?

One may be willing to go along with my rationale for accepting the modest sort of "conceptual shaping" asserted in (1a), but fear that this fails to address an important part of what is at issue. To get clearer about this, we should turn to some of Dreyfus's criticisms – in which he denies that concepts are ordinarily involved in experience, because it commonly has no "as-structure." This will help us to recognize further distinctions needed to navigate the controversy.

Just what might I mean by saying I perceive (or see, or experience) something *as* something, or that it appears to me *as* something? Here's one way of interpreting this. Usually, awake, eyes open, I am looking at things before and around me. That is not to say that I am always *examining* or *scrutinizing* them – just that I am generally looking at something or other as long as I am seeing. In the ordinary course of events, I am often looking (even if only glancingly) at things in my environment (say) a doorknob (or a glass, a pen, a spoon), and they look somehow to me. So, for example, commonly enough I look (at least briefly) at what I reach for. Further, were I asked, about one of these things, what *that* was, then (unless I had reason to think otherwise) I would have said "a doorknob" ("a glass," "a pen," and so on) – without much further ado, that is, without any need to examine the thing in question, or get a much *better* or *closer* look at it. (Though in order to grasp the reference of "that" I would likely *continue* to look at, or *look back at*, the thing in question.) But it seems that my ability to *identify in thought* what I was looking at is secured by how it had *already* looked to me. Where I do identify, or am merely able (and ready) to identify, something as Φ from how it looks to me, without needing to do anything to make *more* of it apparent to me, I see no objection to saying that it has *appeared to me as* Φ, or that I have *seen it as* Φ. Is it unusual for me to be able to visually identify things I have looked at? It seems fairly common. And insofar as many of the thoughts that actually spontaneously occur to me in the course of my day – spoken aloud or kept to myself – involve thinking something *about what I then happen to be looking at*, and these thoughts only manifest abilities of visual identification that were already there, this sort of "appearing-as" will not be unusual. This is not to say that, for every period during which things appeared somehow to you, there is some definite and numerous list of values of "Φ" answering to the question, "*As what* did things appear to you, during this time?" Still, it is common for us to have at least some such dispositions to classify what appears to us from how it appears.

Here is a second way to take "appearing as" talk. The way I look at things as I go about my business, how my gaze "locks onto" them or "travels over" them, plays a part in how they look to me, and *thereby* in how I am *treating* them – what I am treating them *as*. So the way I look at a door in front of me as I approach my apartment, or the way I look at what lies on the table where I'm sitting before I reach for things there, or how I look at what's in the kitchen drawer as I prepare breakfast, or at the traffic-light as I approach the intersection, will make the doorknob, the glass, the pen, the spoon, or the light appear somehow to me – and in such a way that I am able to *treat* them *as* a doorknob, *as* a glass, and so on. (For instance, in each of these cases the appearance to some extent facilitates my reaching for the items in question and handling them in a manner suitable to things of each one's type.) And when something *appears to me in such a way as to facilitate my treating it as* Φ, it seems to me we might also speak of something's being seen as, or appearing as Φ.[20]

Now we can admit this second, *practical* sort of "appearing as Φ" does not entail the first, (let's say) "*doxic*" sort of "appearing as Φ," which is involved in visual identification. (The doorknob could appear to you in such a way as to enable you to treat it as a doorknob, though you are at a loss to classify it as such.) But *radical* dissociations are unusual in this sense: a person who regularly had practical appearing-as- Φ; with *little or no* doxic appearing-as- Φ would be suffering from visual agnosia, which is uncommon.

So I would propose we recognize and distinguish these sorts of "appearing as":

> Something *doxically appears to me as* Φ just when I am disposed (should the question arise, and absent a reason for doubt) to identify it in thought *as* Φ from how it appears to me, without needing to make it *more* apparent to me (e.g. without needing to "look harder at it").
>
> Something *practically appears to me as* Φ just when the manner in which it appears to me (e.g. how it looks to me) facilitates my treating it as Φ.

The distinction is rough and invites many further questions.[21] But the idea seems defensible that *some* sorts of "as-structures," understood along these lines, are pretty common in our experience. So I can't entirely join with Dreyfus's criticisms of McDowell, since – to focus on Dreyfus's example – it seems to me I do, in some sense, ordinarily see doorknobs as doorknobs. For how they appear to me commonly prepares me to identify them as doorknobs without further ado, and helps me in other ways to treat them in a manner befitting doorknobs.

Still, it's not clear how deeply this sets me at odds with Dreyfus. I will come back to this. But first, the claim that "doxic appearing-as" is common contains a further ambiguity that needs to be flagged. One might agree that doxic appearances are commonplace, but think also that there's a sense in which it is at least conceptually possible that things might look to someone just as they do to me as I do my laundry, drive to work, and so on, even though he is *entirely without my conceptual capacities*. You might think this, because you think that what I've labeled doxic appearing-as can ultimately be cleanly factored into two components: a "purely sensory" manner of appearance independent of all conceptual capacities, and an intellectual component, conceptual in nature.

Now I certainly want to distinguish between something's *visually appearing as* Φ to me, and my *judging it to be* Φ (a distinction manifest, for instance, in the phenomena of blindsight and visual illusion). And I do want to allow that things can visually (more broadly: sensorily) appear somehow to creatures who lack conceptual capacities in any demanding sense. But it is not clear to me that the sort of "factoring" view just sketched is correct. However, this is not because I am convinced by the McDowellian criticism that such a view must leave unaccountable how sensory appearances could serve to warrant belief. Admittedly, I can (for example) justify my belief that *this is a nail* (and that *this one's longer than that one*), only if I can make judgments about (and thus exercise some concept of) how it looks to me – a justification I might give by saying something like, "I think this is a nail (and this one's longer than that one), since *that is how it looks to me.*" But it is left unclear just why such remarks can succeed as justifications of belief only if the manner in which the nails appear, from which I judge them to be a certain way, could not have been experienced by those whose lack of inferential abilities would deprive them of any *concepts* of nail or length. Why, for example, can't something appear constant in size and shape, in a manner typical of nails, to someone without the relevant inferential capacities? And why not suppose it is *that* very manner of appearance of which someone speaks, when using the phrase "how it looks to me" in the context of the sort of justification just illustrated? For I may say something looks to me "like a nail" when it appears to me (visually) constant in size and shape in a manner typical of nails – i.e. it looks to me the way nails look.

Nevertheless, I do doubt that the "factoring" view of doxic appearance is correct. It is not correct, I believe, if the following is true. First, there is often a difference between how something appears to you when you *recognize it as* $\Phi$ and when you don't (think of the experience of recognizing – as momentarily you did not – a face, a partly occluded object, the Gestalt in a drawing). And for something to appear to you as *recognizably* $\Phi$ in a given context is more than for it to appear to you shaped and situated in a manner that a $\Phi$ typically would. Second, the manner of appearance on which judging something to be $\Phi$ is based is just such a "recognitional" appearance. And finally, at least some capacities for such sensory recognition require the possession of concepts, because they can arise only through acquiring abilities to make judgments that deploy these concepts. (Consider e.g.: "That tone of voice sounds *sarcastic*"; "This looks like an *antique*"; "This tastes *metallic*"; "That looks like a *chess set.*") The idea would be that these may rightly be considered reports of *recognitional appearances* whose *range* (the variety of instances thus recognizable) depends on having acquired a grasp of the concepts expressed in the judgments they afford.

These matters are not straightforwardly resolved. But what we've said allows us to distinguish two "conceptual-shaping" claims, of different strengths.

(1a (i))  *Modest shaping.* Commonly, if we did not have or were not exercising certain conceptual capacities, things would not have appeared to us as they do.
(1a (ii)) *Constitutive shaping.* Necessarily, if some creatures lack our conceptual capacities, things do not appear to them in just the manner things commonly do appear to us, and on the basis of which we classify them.

I endorse the first, modest thesis because of what I said about the common connections between: *how things look to us, what we're looking at, what we take ourselves to be doing.* And since I accept that doxic appearances are widespread, I would also endorse even the stronger, constitutive thesis, provided that a thoroughgoing "factoring" view of them is shown to be mistaken. (However, I do not claim to have shown that here; it needs more investigation.) In any case, I am disinclined to contest (1a) – "shaping" claims – of either strength. And I have already indicated I have no quarrel with (2a) – rational-pragmatic self-consciousness. So my suspicions will instead be trained on McDowell's pervasiveness (1b) – the conceptual readiness thesis and (2b) – no spatial experience without self-criticism.

## Is all experience "conceptually ready"?

According to pervasiveness (1b), every distinct content of normal, adult human perceptual experience is present in a form in which it is ready to figure distinctly in the exercise of conceptual capacities. For all such content is presumably the content of a "world-disclosing" experience, as McDowell understands this notion. And (1b) says all such content ("every aspect" of it) is "conceptually ready." There is a question about how to interpret talk of "content" here. One might think: the *content* of experience is, in some sense, *what* you experience, but is not simply to be identified with all that the things you experience *in fact are*; rather it somehow has to do with *how you experience them*. (The things you experience can have features or aspects that don't figure in the content of your experience of them.) The content of perceptual experience would then in some sense be a *manner* in which what perceptually appears to you does appear to you. Now ways of appearing (thus the "contents") I mean to discuss in connection with (1b) are not mere sense impressions, uninterpreted sensations, or the like, but something sufficient for a kind of perceptual intentionality, understood as "object directedness," an experience of things in space. (The notion of *representation* I will leave to the side.) What I will argue is that there are varying manners of visual appearance we commonly enjoy, accessible in reflection, in virtue of which experience is directed at spatial objects, but which are not ready to serve as the diverse contents of the exercise of correlatively distinct conceptual capacities.

I have already appealed to the notions of "looking at" and of "how things look." Let me recall and expand a little on the phenomenology I have presented. How things look to you (e.g. your surroundings as you stand on the street corner) almost always depends on what you're looking *at* (say, the oncoming cars) which often depends on what you're looking *for* (say, a break in the traffic, so you can cross). What you're looking at (hence how things look) is undergoing frequent change. But to the extent we can speak (if only roughly) of what you're looking at during a given time, *more* appears to you (looks somehow to you) than just what you're looking *at*. When you look at that car coming towards you, you're not looking at anything *right around it*. And you're also not looking at the driver's door, or the right headlight. But both are in an area that looks somehow to you. And (obviously) what you are not looking at does not appear to you *in nearly as much detail* as what you are looking at (not as much of what appears is apparent to you). We may speak of the area apparent to you over a given time as your "visual field," as long as we do not pretend that this entitles us to assume that area has precisely delineated boundaries, and as long as we do not forget that this "field" is typically in flux with the direction of your gaze, and that what you are looking at within it appears very differently than what you are not looking at.

Some will want to mark this difference in appearance by speaking of "visual focus" and "periphery." But I find this misleading. For "periphery" suggests something at or near an *edge*, located as far away as one can get from what you are looking at, without venturing into the realm of what is *hidden, nonapparent*. However, the apparent-but-not-now-being-looked-at area is not confined to some "border region." The so-called "periphery" is found *throughout* the visual field – *within* what one is looking at, as well as *right around it*. (Similarly, it could be misleading to speak of the nonfocally apparent as "background," inasmuch as it sounds odd to say the apparent area *within* the seen "figure" lies in the "background.") So instead of speaking of what appears "peripherally" (or in the "background"), I will just speak of what "nonfocally" appears, and the way it appears.

So: during a given time, some of what appears to you is *focally* and some is *nonfocally* apparent, and what *had been* nonfocal *is becoming* focal, and vice versa. That is, I want to say, a fact about the *structure* of visual appearance, in the following sense. First, your experience is characterized by this feature even as how things appear to you *otherwise* differs enormously, and that variation consists in different ways of being a changing focal/nonfocal appearance – different determinates of that determinable, different ways of "filling out the structure," so to speak. (So e.g. the specific focal/nonfocal change in appearance involved in looking at a fork will differ from that involved in looking at a spoon.) Second, episodes of experience *not* possessed of this character – either because the appearance is too homogeneous to offer anything to look at (a ganzfeld), or because one holds one's gaze fixed (or nearly so) for several seconds or more – are *atypical*, and *functionally inferior* to ordinary vision. (That is to say: to do much with vision you need variety in what you look at, and you need to look around a bit.)

Now the fact that visual appearance exhibits this structural character can be sufficient to give it *intentionality* on a reasonable construal of what that requires. For one central (if vague) understanding of intentionality takes it to involve a *directedness to objects* – a particular way in which an experience may be said to be *of an object*. And the notion of intentionality is also connected with a certain family of contrasts in terms of which what has intentionality is assessable: truth and falsity (for judgments or beliefs); satisfaction and frustration (for desires or intentions); accuracy/correctness and inaccuracy/incorrectness/illusoriness (for perceptual experience). Visual experience can count as intentional by these standards just in virtue of being a determination of the kind of dynamic structure I've described (the movement to and fro from nonfocal to focal appearance). For when something nonfocally apparent is looked at and becomes focally apparent, and when it again recedes into nonfocal appearance as one's gaze then shifts elsewhere (only to become focally apparent once more when looked at again), there is a kind of perceptual *object constancy*. That is, the way something appears to you changes, but because of the *manner* of change in appearance, what appears itself appears to remain the same. There is some sort of stability in what appears to you (or can appear to you) through change in appearance that is sufficient for you to enjoy an appearance "of an object," for you to have experience "directed at" it, in the sense labeled "intentional." Moreover, as something's appearance thus changes from nonfocal to focal and back, it is better apparent to you, or appears to you not as well (you see it better or more poorly). And for something to be better apparent to you, when you get a better look at it, is for it to appear to you accurately or correctly (in some respect, to some extent). And sometimes when it better appears to you, the way it now appears is incompatible with the way it had appeared to you (when you had not as good a look at it), so that this prior manner of appearance is revealed to have been somehow inaccurate, incorrect or illusory.

The overall point is this. Object constancy is inherent to typical ways of filling out the structure of appearance I have identified, which are also inseparable from certain kinds of normative assessability – "better" and "worse" appearances. It follows that having appearance with this structure is commonly sufficient for having experience that is object directed and assessable for accuracy in a sense reasonably deemed adequate for talk of "intentionality" to be apt. We are thus concerned here with a manner of appearance, with a kind of experiential "content," which is enough to give experience intentionality, so that the content in question is "intentional" on a reasonable construal, and the experience is *of things in space* – "outer" experience.

The question I now want to ask first is: are the variations in manner of appearance to which I have just drawn attention always *present in a form in which they can variously figure in distinct exercises of my conceptual capacities*? For this I will assume the following condition must be met.

> For every such variation in manner of appearance I enjoy, I must be able to identify in thought a difference in *"as what"* something

appears to me; that is, I must be able to distinguish the ways of appearing so as to show them to be different *doxic* appearances. (For only then is the specific content of experience always present in a form in which it can be the content of my exercise of a correlative *conceptual* capacity.)

Now, I can distinguish in thought all manners of appearance doxically only if I can do this for variations in *nonfocal* appearance. But how will I accomplish this feat? I will take one of three courses. (A) I will *look at* what had nonfocally appeared and identify *as what* it *then focally* appears to me, assuming that this is also *as what* it had *nonfocally* appeared. (B) I will keep my gaze steadily fixed on something that focally appears and try to identify *as what* something then *nonfocally appears* to me. (C) I will let my gaze roam normally and try to identify *as what* things nonfocally appear *while the way what is before me appears rapidly altered.*

If I take route (A), then the target manner of appearance has been altered, and the doxic appearance I thus identify is not the *original nonfocal* appearance, but a *new focal* appearance brought into being by the direction of my gaze. The assumption will often be unwarranted that the target (nonfocal) manner of appearance was the same (doxic) appearance as that which ensued on looking at what had appeared nonfocally. For it's often the case that, for some values of "Φ," you will need to look *at* something (and thereby change its appearance) if you are to identify it as Φ, from its appearance.

If we shift to option (B), we also run into problems. First, it's *unusual* to stare truly fixedly at something before us. And if I do this, in an effort to identify *as what* things *nonfocally* appear to me, the resultant nonfocal appearance will typically not be identical to some appearance more briefly experienced, when I let my gaze pursue its normal, restless course. (Let us assume here that, as is typically the case, the appearance of the nonfocal area is far from homogeneous in the way a uniformly lit and colored flat surface would be.) So, I might consider, say, the appearance of what I'm not looking at when faced with a page full of text. The word I now *stare* at does not present an appearance that matches the interior nonfocal appearance of that word when I read it normally, as I scanned across the line. It inevitably now becomes more apparent to me than it did then; it appears in more detail somehow. Nor is it clear to me that the appearance of what *surrounds* what I'm looking at matches some normal fleeting, nonfocal appearance. So I should not trust attempts to identify *as what* things nonfocally appeared to me before in normal vision, by resort to some nonfocal appearance later experienced while *staring* at some bit of the same scene.

Second, when I stare at a word on the page and struggle to keep my *gaze* from illicitly straying where I cast my *thoughts*, I am scarcely able to identify *as what* anything variously *nonfocally* appears to me. I may, of course, say to myself something like, "That (entire) area appears to me as containing *these* distinct shapes in *these* distinct locations." But I really have no idea just *which* distinct shapes and locations would be specified by these "these's." This is clear, when, with my gaze still rigidly fixed, I try to break up this identification, saying, ostensibly about the variously nonfocally apparent: "*That* appears to me as *this* shape *there*, *that* appears to me as *this* shape *there*, *that* appears ... etc." This would be a sham identification; I find I literally do not know what I'm talking about in mouthing those words. In vain would I pretend to identify in such manner, for use in thought, some set of distinct shapes and locations matching the heterogeneity of nonfocal appearance, as I stare fixedly at some word on the page. I am aware of differences in how some area nonfocally appears to me. But I cannot in thought identify *what those differences are*, by means of predicates whose interpretation reflects the variation in appearance so as to express correspondingly various thoughts that may distinctly figure, at least briefly, in my inferential capacities.

Well, why don't I *stop staring*, and take option (C)? Why don't I try, as I am reading a page of text, to identify *as what* things nonfocally appear to me *as this changes*? This is hopeless. There is such rapid change in this nonfocal field of appearance that any attempt to quickly fix in thought constantly altering sets of identifications specifying *as what* things nonfocally appear, supposedly covering the entire heterogeneous flux of this appearance, is plainly futile. If I couldn't perform such an identification even when staring – freezing change in nonfocal appearance as much as possible – how in the world am I supposed to do it when change in appearance is enormously *speeded up*?

If these remarks stand, they yield an argument that manners of appearance that structure vision, sufficient for intentionality, are not conceptually ready. To see this, first note also: there is no definite boundary between the focally and nonfocally apparent that would allow us to isolate the one from the other in a course of actual experience, without any change in the character of appearance. In natural vision, the two aspects of appearance are inseparable parts of a dynamic whole: something's becoming better apparent to you. Thus the nonfocal appearance is inseparable from a *structure* of appearance that (if my earlier remarks are correct) brings intentionality along with it. However (as we have just seen), the very character of differences in nonfocal appearance means that these are not *in a form* suitable for functioning in conceptual capacities. Nonfocal appearances need to be *transformed*: they must give way to (and form a temporal whole with) an appearance of a *different* character. Often, only as one looks at what had been apparent-but-not-looked-at can a different manner of appearance arise that would allow one to identify in thought what appears as $\Phi$ – and thus deploy a concept of $\Phi$. The conclusion is that there are nonfocal variations in appearance, which (because they cannot occur but in the context of a structure sufficient for intentionality) are sufficient for a kind of "intentional content" (spatial experience), but which are *not conceptually ready*: they are not in a form in which they can serve as the contents of distinct conceptual capacities.[22]

Now this will count against McDowell's (2b), if we assume (as seems reasonable) that that spatial experience that we have, to which my argument applies, is also what he calls "world disclosing." For then it will be false that every aspect of the content of world-disclosing experience is conceptually ready, as (2b) claims. One might try to deflect my objection by recalling that, according to McDowell, "world-disclosing" experience is necessarily "categorially unified" in some Kantian sense, and proposing that only what I have called "doxic appearings as Φ" are to count as "categorially unified experiences." But this wouldn't really help, even if some sort of *constitutive* shaping holds. For assuming the manner of doxic visual appearance requires the sort of structure I said makes object constancy possible, and that necessarily includes varying *nonfocal* appearance, still the doxic appearance will always include *some* manner of appearance, essential to its intentionality, which *isn't* conceptually ready. So again, it's not true that *every aspect* of the content of experience is conceptually ready.

The basic point I'm making here concerns a structural (and thus "pervasive") fact about appearance, and locates a difficulty in McDowell's position just where it was supposed to draw its strength. McDowell argues that we must recognize the pervasiveness of concepts in experience, or else we will not be able to make sense of the epistemic role of experience in supporting beliefs about the things experienced. But now it emerges that, on the contrary, to make sense of this we must recognize an important way in which concepts do *not* pervade experience. For it is precisely through this movement back and forth between nonfocal appearance and focal appearance, involved in looking at things and in thereby making them *better apparent* to us, that we are able to identify them in thought and so make use of appearances in our conceptual capacities. And yet it is essential to this very structure of appearance that it always contain manners of appearance that are not concept ready. Further, this same structure of appearance is required for the *justification* of perceptual judgments. For it is through making things better apparent to us, by getting a better look at them, that we *confirm and correct* our judgments about them. Thus, the epistemic function of experience can be fulfilled only if, in a sense, experience always *outruns* the application of our concepts and the operations of the intellect, *transforming* itself in such a way as to make that application and those operations possible.

Now that I have, in this section, turned from indicating where I can agree with McDowell (on (1a) and (2a)), to arguing for my divergence from him (on (1b) – conceptual readiness), it may seem that I am also beginning to sidle up to Dreyfus. My reasons for opposing that thesis differ from his. But I believe they could be extended so as to make closer contact with his concerns, by appeal to my distinction between doxic and practical "appearing-as." (Though doing this will require we agree not to confine the use of "as" talk to doxic appearances [as it seems Dreyfus wants to do].)

First recall that appearing *practically* as Φ does not entail appearing *doxically* as Φ. And we can find the two coming apart when we consider what nonfocally appears. Here is a simple example. Remember: how things look to me depends on what I'm *looking at*, which often depends on what I'm *looking for*, which depends on *what reason* I take myself to have for what I am doing. Suppose what I'm looking *at* is the kitchen drawer – and then, what's *in* the drawer. And what I'm looking for is a fork, and the reason I take myself to have for doing this (and other things I'm doing) is: *I'm setting the table*. How do things then appear to me? Well, when I open the kitchen drawer what appears to me does not right away *doxically* appear to me as a fork. (My kitchen drawer is a mess, and I am not, as yet, disposed to identify as a fork what appears to me there, from how it looks.) And yet my gaze is drawn to where, in an area *nonfocally apparent* to me, a fork lies awaiting discovery. We may say that here something nonfocally apparent *practically* appeared to me as a fork, since it appeared to me in a manner that facilitated my treating it as a fork, by, in the first instance, enabling me to look at it so as to recognize it as a fork. (For looking at something *is* a way of treating it.) We may say generally that whenever the nonfocally apparent "attracts" our gaze so as to make it look to us recognizable as Φ, this will count among what was practically, but not (yet) doxically, apparent as Φ. (The initial practical appearance as Φ may *culminate* in a doxic appearance as Φ.) In terms more congenial to Dreyfus, I might say that the nonfocally apparent appears to me so as to "solicit" my gaze. This sort of response to the "solicitations" of what I see, when engaged in some everyday task, is commonplace; it is pervasive.

Thus there is a way in which my earlier argument against the conceptual readiness thesis can be extended to support Dreyfus's claim against it, which (as I understand it) holds that *what we perceive* typically includes things *soliciting the exercise of our skills*, as this is appropriate to our tasks. For the highly specific manner of solicitations perceived that arise in the context of our activity is not in a form suited to be the content of our conceptual capacities – contrary to McDowell's claim. To put things a bit more in my terms, the apparent *aspect* under which things attract my gaze and facilitate other activities (i.e. specifically *as what* they are practically apparent to me) – this is often nothing I am disposed to *identify in thought*. To further join my argument to Dreyfus's, I would need to add that often enough, for some values of "Φ," even when something is *focally* apparent to me as Φ (I am looking at it, and it appears to me as Φ), it is only practically, not doxically, thus apparent to me. For example, something may focally – but (merely) practically – appear to me *as an obstacle*, or *an opening*, or *reachable*, or *out of reach*. For I may just happen to have no inclination to *think* of what thus appears to me *in these terms*. But that doesn't matter to the appearance.

It may be that Dreyfus will decline my overtures, since he wants to avoid "as" talk in connection with perceiving "solicitations." However, I am not convinced this is more than a terminological problem. But here I will mention a qualm I have (which maybe Dreyfus doesn't share). Notice that I do not oppose McDowell over conceptual readiness by affirming that vision has "*nonconceptual* content." For, as I understand it, the same manner of appearance that enables me to identify something in thought as Φ may also enable me *otherwise* to *treat* it as Φ. I do not claim to discern within this manner of appearance some special, distinct *component* (and some "layer of content") which, when isolated, is unable to motivate conceptual identification, but adequate for other jobs. I would not be interested in defending (and would be suspicious of) the idea that the way something looks to me when it doxically appears to me as Φ includes *as a proper part*, a merely practical appearance as Φ. If anything, I would want to say that doxic appearances are just a special case of practical appearances that generally involve a certain use of language. In any case, I do not base my objections to McDowell on the notion that the content of sensory experience is either wholly nonconceptual or can be analyzed into conceptual and nonconceptual parts.

## Is self-critical rationality required for spatial experience?

I now turn to the pervasiveness of self-consciousness claim (2b). Again, I have no beef with (2a): I do agree that we are generally disposed to offer some reason for what we are doing, which involves a propensity to think first-person thoughts, and otherwise, we wouldn't be doing what we actually do. So I accept the idea that there is *some* sort of practical self-consciousness implicit in our ordinary activities. But I am much less sanguine about (2b), the claim that "outer experience" requires self-critical rationality. Here too (as with (1b)) I think there is a genuine problem of intellectualism.

Recall that McDowell points out that something more than mere "receptivity" is needed for sensory or perceptual content. Merely to register "impressions" – whether we think of these as subjectively discernible *sensations* or as causal impacts on our sensory receptors – is not to perceive or to experience things in any sense that makes talk of (intentional) *content* in order. I would certainly agree with that. And I would agree that it's still not enough for intentionality if we just add to the sensory stimuli some regular discriminatory response to them. But it's far from clear that (as McDowell holds) nothing but self-critical rationality will do to fill this gap – that one won't have genuine visual *content*, until one has a concept of (e.g.) what constitutes "suitable conditions" for seeing the color, shape, size, or position of things, a capacity to consider whether these conditions obtain, and to withhold judgment that things are as they appear, when one believes suitable conditions are absent. Unless McDowell has shown that nothing short of this will give one perceptual intentionality, or experiential content, then we lack reason to accept (2b). And I do not see how the gap would be filled by consideration of the ways in which concepts "pervade" our (normal, human, adult) experience. So there is inadequate support for the notion that outer experience requires self-critical rationality. Actually, the previous discussion helps us to see that we can go further: we have reason to think this (2b) thesis is mistaken.

To show this, we need only make clear that there is something less than self-critical rationality that is enough to make sense experience intentional (and to make it "outer") in some recognizable sense. If what I said earlier was on the right track, we may speak of a kind of perceptual content and intentionality where we find certain forms of *object constancy* in experience.[23] Through changes in how things appear to one, an unchanging shape, or position, or size, or distance is apparent. Where there is such object constancy, we may say (in the case of vision) that one sees something's shape, position, or size *well* or *poorly*, its shape (etc.) is *better apparent* in some conditions than others, and that it appears to us *accurately* or *inaccurately*, *correctly* or *incorrectly*. And so we have, in some sense, "outer experience," "an awareness of aspects of the world." The question then is whether there is something *more* than mere "impressions" or "sensations," but *short of* McDowellian self-critical rationality, which will make a creature's experience exhibit such constancies and be suitable for such assessment.

I propose that the right ability for *movement* is sufficient to get us beyond mere impressions to object directedness. The idea is already latent in my discussion. I have emphasized that how things look to us depends on how we look at things, and that the continual upheaval in appearances wrought by this activity of looking – of making the nonfocal focal and losing the focal to the nonfocal as the gaze shifts – renders the appearance of objects and their identification in thought possible. It now may be explicitly pointed out that this activity consists partly in *bodily movement*. An ability to move (one's eyes, head, whole body) is part of the ability to "get a better look" at something – to move in such a way as to make its shape, movement, size, or location *better apparent* to one. Thus we have a kind of activity (not mere "receptivity"), which is sufficient for sensory intentionality, but which doesn't require self-critical rationality. So my claim is, first, that there is such a capacity for generating sense experience by movement, which is sufficient for making things appear to one in a way fairly regarded as an experience of space. And second, the exercise of such sensorimotor skills does not require one to be disposed to endorse, consider, or reconsider *reasons* for acting this way or that, or for judging that something is the case.

*Sensorimotor* skills sufficient to make shape, location, motion, etc. apparent to you thus do not require self-critical rationality in McDowell's sense. So (2b) is false.[24]

McDowellian concerns seem to me likely answerable. Suppose someone objects that we can identify no "common core" of *content* shared between beings who are and those who are not possessed of active self-critical rationality. This can simply be granted. We can say that while both sets of beings are capable of making the shape, size, position, movement, and distance of things apparent to themselves through their own movement, the way things appear to the two may never be just the same. For the way things appear to the self-conscious reasoners will inevitably be shaped by interests and activities not available to the other group, in the manner suggested when I argued for pervasiveness (1a). So if talk of the "content of our experience" is meant to get at the way things appear to us, there will inevitably be a difference in content. But this is quite compatible with the alternative I have proposed to McDowell's (2b).

Will someone here raise the specter of a "recoil into the Myth of the Given"? Just what alleged errors go by the label, and which really *are* errors, needs more explicit, detailed consideration. I have already indicated some doubts on this score. But here I will just add that there is no incoherence in maintaining that we who have the capacity to make assertions about how things appear to us in justifying our claims about how things are, and creatures who *don't* have the wherewithal to engage in justification can all share a capacity to make our spatial environments better apparent to us through our movements.

This conception of "outer experience" I propose allows us to preserve a distinction between the sensory and intellectual, but without depriving the sensory of intentionality or degrading it to the status of mere sensation. We can say that what suffices for *sensory* intentionality are sensorimotor abilities, and what is necessary and sufficient for *intellectual* intentionality are classificatory, analogical, and inferential abilities – and a creature can have the first, without the second. To have the second is (in McDowell's words) "to know your way around the space of reasons." To have the first is just to know your way around the space in which you *literally live*.

This way of keeping the distinction between the sensory and the intellectual seems to me to have certain advantages over McDowell's picture. First, it does without the dubious notion of "raw" sense impressions, and obviates the problem of how to get sensory intentionality – an experience of space – by somehow adding distinctively conceptual abilities to "uninterpreted" sensory whatnots. Second, it better allows us to honor our kinship and continuity with (while respecting our difference from) other animals, and our own younger selves. We can all have "outer experience" on a sensorimotor basis, even if only relatively mature humans are active self-critical thinkers.[25]

However, a doubt may loom. We might maintain the conviction (perhaps at work in McDowell) that it makes sense to hold some creature to *norms* – even to speak of its seeing *correctly* or *accurately* or getting a *better* or *worse* look at things – only if that creature *also* itself has *some* appreciation of the norms by which it is assessed. (Unless of course those norms are simply imposed on it by other normatively assessable creatures, as humans impose standards that determine e.g. what makes a "good racehorse.") But how could normative "appreciation" be found in anything but a capacity for self-critical thought, alive to the demand for justification? Now I don't think it goes without question that normative assessability requires normative self-consciousness. But we also should not too quickly conclude that the criticism of McDowell I have just aired leaves one no way to hold onto this idea in some form, if indeed we should. How this might be so will emerge in the course of the next section.

## Self-consciousness and the "anonymity" of motor understanding

I now want to return to Merleau-Ponty, and offer an interpretation of the passage (earlier quoted) that figures in the Dreyfus/McDowell dispute. I do this partly because I don't want to see interest in Merleau-Ponty's views dimmed by disfigurement, but also because I believe their judicious interpretation can enrich the dialogue in ways that do not emerge in the Dreyfus/McDowell exchange. I wish to show not only that Merleau-Ponty does *not* subscribe (as McDowell thinks) to an embarrassing dualism of "person" and "lived body" – a form of the "Myth of the Disembodied Intellect." I will also argue that Merleau-Ponty is, in a way, more Kantian than either McDowell or Dreyfus recognize – though Merleau-Ponty's "Kantianism" (if you can call it that) is determinedly nonintellectualist. To explain why I say this will add another twist to my discussion of the pervasiveness of self-consciousness theme. To anticipate: for Merleau-Ponty there *is* a form of (what we might call) self-consciousness generally bound up with perceptual experience – though not the sort of *intellectual* self-consciousness involved in McDowell's "self-critical rationality." To see how this is so we will need to grasp an expanded sense of "understanding."

A thorough defense of my interpretation of Merleau-Ponty would require many more words than I could reasonably ask for here. So I will have to be somewhat schematic, leaving more detail to another occasion. But I hope that what I can say now will be enough to make my interpretation plausible and enhance its philosophical interest.

Readers familiar with *Phenomenology of Perception* may be puzzled that McDowell finds Merleau-Ponty's crucial error in some doctrine that sunders the person I am from some "person-like" thing that is my body. One might have thought him passionately concerned to *contest* just such dualist notions. Doesn't he famously assert "I am my body"?[26] Of course, Merleau-Ponty's view *may* be profoundly inconsistent, or even – as McDowell hints – insane. But before reaching such dire conclusions we should see if we can find some more coherent position in his book.

McDowell's view that Merleau-Ponty subscribes to a dualism of (intellectual) person and (bodily) person-like thing derives from the passage cited in translation, where Merleau-Ponty is made to say that "in perception, we *merge* into our body." The picture here seems to be that two previously *distinct* entities occasionally *fuse* into one – and (since this is "in perception") either one *perceives* the "merger" transpiring, or it's somehow arranged *by means of* perception. That is a peculiar view, to say the least. But another translation (and interpretation) is possible and preferable. Let's reexamine that passage quoted by Dreyfus and McDowell a bit more fully, with an alternative translation, set beside the original.

> Dans la perception nous ne pensons pas l'objet et nous ne nous pensons pas le pensant, nous sommes à l'objet et nous nous confondons avec ce corps qui en sait plus que nous sur le monde, sur les motifs et les moyens qu'on a d'en faire la synthèse. ... Dans cette couche originaire du sentir que l'on retrouve à condition de coïncider vraiment avec l'acte de perception et de quitter l'attitude critique, je vis l'unité du sujet.[27]

> In perception we do not think the object and we do not think ourselves thinking it, we are given over to the object and we are one with this body that knows more than we do about the world, and about the motives and the means we have for its synthesis. ... In this primary layer of sense experience that one discovers only if one really coincides with the act of perception and leaves the critical attitude, I experience the unity of the subject.

Three points I wish to make about this – let's call it the "unity" passage – straight off. First, the fact that Merleau-Ponty says "I experience the unity of the subject" should keep us from supposing that he banishes self-consciousness entirely from ordinary perceptual experience. On the contrary, he is saying (rightly or wrongly) that I have the "lived" experience of myself as a perceptual subject. To be sure, this does not mean that in perception I am, either explicitly or implicitly, *thinking about myself* – it's not *that kind* of self-consciousness. For (as he asserts in the passage) perception is distinct from thinking, and does not include some self-regarding thought: "In perception we do not think the object and we do not think ourselves thinking it." Thus if (like Dreyfus) we wish to attribute to Merleau-Ponty the view that there is "no ego present" in ordinary experience, I think this had better just mean that often I entertain no "I-thought" as I engage in my activities – chasing streetcars, or whatever.

Second, notice that my translation dispenses with the worrisome implication of Smith's, that we have here two distinct items somehow blending ("merging") together. Rather the idea is simply that we (perceptually) experience our unity or oneness with our bodies. This does not mean, bizarrely, that sometimes I am something distinct from my body, with which I then mysteriously *mingle*, when I start *perceiving*. No, it just means that the sort of self-consciousness I have that is specific to *thought* may not be an experience of my oneness with my body – but *in perception* I *do* have such experience.

Third, while my translation does not excise the troublesome phrase "the body that knows more than we do" – which may be taken to imply that we are distinct from our bodies – there is a way to fix this problem too. (And this route is again preferred on the grounds that it preserves Merleau-Ponty's coherence and sanity.) When he speaks of "this body that knows more than we do about the world and the motives and means we have for its synthesis," he is being (not uncharacteristically) elliptical, sacrificing precision and explicitness for rhetorical flow. To be more explicit, he could have said something like: "this body that knows more (in a bodily i.e. *sensorimotor way*) than we know (in an *intellectual way*) about the world and the motives and means we have for its synthesis." The point is not that we are not our bodies (again that would go dead against other passages). The point is rather that our bodies, through their activity, exhibit a kind of (bodily) knowledge or understanding distinct from that which we exhibit (and more commonly recognize) in our *thought*. Merleau-Ponty would admit that the truth of this claim is not obvious, and runs counter to traditional philosophical assumptions. But he thinks he has made the case for it in the couple of hundred pages preceding.

I believe the translation I suggest is preferable to Smith's on both linguistic and hermeneutic grounds. I leave discussion of the linguistic points to a note.[28] But here I will say something about the hermeneutic point – why my take on the unity passage makes better sense of its place in the argument of Merleau-Ponty's book. This will help elucidate its philosophical interest.

We need first to remind ourselves of where the passage occurs. It comes about a quarter of the way into Part II of Merleau-Ponty's *Phenomenology* ("The World as Perceived"). Building on the results of Part I ("The Body"), he has just been arguing for and applying a way of understanding the distinction between the senses and the intellect – between, as he puts it (using Kantian and Husserlian language), sensory "consciousness" and "synthesis" on the one hand, and intellectual "consciousness" and "synthesis" on the other.[29] This is in partial fulfillment of the general project of Part II, which is to bring the lessons of Part I, and its view of the "habit body" and the experience of one's own body, to bear on the broad ambition (in some sense shared with Kant and Husserl) of explaining *how consciousness of objects is possible for us* – or, as he puts it, heightening its problematic character – how there is "for us" an "in itself."[30] As applied to the visual case, for example, this challenge is, in part: "[to] try to understand how vision can be brought into being from somewhere without being enclosed in its perspective"[31] – how vision can be *constrained by* perspective without being *confined within it*; how it can make apparent to us things that "transcend" their perspectively shifting appearances. Thus, much of Part II is concerned with how to make sense of the phenomenon of perceptual constancy, in light of Part I. But before he gets very far into this, he wishes to deal with an objection he sees arising for his way of understanding sense experience.[32] And the unity passage occurs in the context of trying to meet the challenge. Thus, to understand that passage, we need to understand what way of viewing sensory consciousness/synthesis he has proposed, and what challenge he's trying to meet.

Part of what Merleau-Ponty finds distinctive of the sensory is its "anonymity." He also speaks, relatedly, of what is "prepersonal," "impersonal," or (mysteriously hedging) "almost impersonal." Now one might guess that by saying sense perception is somehow "anonymous" or "impersonal" he is asserting a sort of "no ownership" view: perceptual experience is *no one's*, i.e. no *person's*. And this would suggest the sort of person/body dualism that McDowell finds absurd. But if we go back to where Merleau-Ponty introduces the idea of this anonymity/impersonality in Part I, we will find that what's put in play is the notion that perception commonly functions in a way that doesn't involve *personal choice* – that is, in a way that doesn't involve an agent's *reasoned or rationalizable choice of a means to a goal*.

The personal/impersonal contrast first rears its head when Merleau-Ponty argues that even fairly primitive animals exhibit a kind of adaptiveness in their behavior that is to be understood in teleological terms, though the types of movements they make are not chosen by them as means to an end. He gives the example of a beetle that substitutes the activity of a second limb for that of an amputated one in a manner that preserves functional equivalence.[33] It is assumed the beetle did not deliberate about how to achieve the same end by different means – it was thus not a matter of "personal choice."[34] And Merleau-Ponty proceeds to argue that a similar mode of behavior can be observed in beings such as ourselves that *are* capable of personal choice. He claims that human amputees experiencing phantom limbs sometimes attempt to use their phantoms (to walk, for example), even though they clearly believe that they *literally have no leg to stand on*.[35] And he argues[36] that this is best understood, if we do not suppose that the patient has *chosen* to move a (nonexistent) leg as a means of accomplishing some task. For then we couldn't satisfactorily account for why his belief that he lacked a limb didn't impede such practical reasoning. So we should say he acts "impersonally" (or "in the light of an impersonal being"), from *habit* – and with the kind of generality that comes with habit. Merleau-Ponty goes on to say that actually we *ordinarily* exercise just such capacities for "impersonal" (or at least, not fully personal) movements at the service of our tasks. That is, our movements are for the sake of those aims, but we cannot correctly rationalize our actions by appeal to choices of these specific movements as means to those ends. "[M]y life is made up of rhythms which have not their *reason* in what I have chosen to be, but their *condition* in my ordinary surroundings. Thus there appears round our personal existence a margin of *almost* impersonal existence, which can be practically taken for granted, and which I rely on."[37] Merleau-Ponty further reinforces his view by appeal to cases of *selective deficits* in motor abilities. He notes that brain damage can severely impair one's ability to undertake "movements to order," even when one can quite readily perform similar movements in familiar situations, as the task at hand requires. This, he thinks, is best understood if we recognize that ordinary goal-directed motion does not depend on the *representation* and *choice* of one's movements as means.[38]

I cannot now try to reconstruct and evaluate this argument in more detail. For now I simply want to emphasize Merleau-Ponty's use of "anonymous" or "impersonal" to mark a mode of activity that can exhibit the hallmarks of *teleology*, even though it is *not rationally chosen* by one, and so is not something that, in the fullest sense, *one did*, that is, something for which one took *responsibility* by one's deliberative choice. Now Merleau-Ponty argues (and this gets us closer to the challenge that motivates the unity passage): one's capacities for such "anonymous" unreasoned bodily movement – one's motor "habits" – are organized – they form a kind of *system*. One can experience one's own body in terms of a *system* of postures and movements functionally equivalent relative to one's tasks (e.g. answering the telephone) – one has what he calls a "body schema."[39] Further he says, acknowledging this will be controversial, that moving in these functionally equivalent task-oriented ways constitutes a form of *understanding*. Understanding, then, is not to be confined *behind* movement in some inferential engine (be it soul or brain) that issues orders to the body. It is to be found *in the very movements of our eyes and hands*. This movement *is* understanding in action, no less fundamentally than the classifications and inferences we make in thought. And such understanding he takes to include the sorts of movements alluded to in the previous section, whereby objects are made apparent to us: the sensorimotor basis of spatial perception.

Now – as I interpret him, Merleau-Ponty believes it is right to say our movement *is* understanding for (at least) the following three reasons.

(i) It exhibits a general *spontaneous adaptiveness relative to our goals*, which is characteristic of understanding.

(ii) In ordinary perception we *experience the "harmony" of our performance with our goals*.[40] (As I read this: we sense when we're moving as we should (relative to our goals) – and when we're not – so it involves a kind of *normative sensitivity*, characteristic of understanding.)[41]

(iii) The truth of (i) and (ii) is not to be accounted for by postulating *some more basic activity of mind* in which these movements are represented, chosen, and commanded, and the results monitored – so that understanding could then be said only truly to reside in that separate "inner" mental activity. So the movement is not to be construed merely as the *effect* or *product* of understanding.[42]

Thus, according to Merleau-Ponty, one's own bodily movements constitute a genuine (but nonintellectual) form of understanding.

It would be desirable to reconstruct in more detail, and so to assess, this (complex, if underdeveloped) case for what we might call "motor understanding." That is impossible here. But we can now more fully comprehend Merleau-Ponty's claim near the beginning of Part II, that part of what distinguishes sensory (as opposed to intellectual) "synthesis" and consciousness is their "anonymity/impersonality." What this comes to is the idea that sensory consciousness and synthesis are effected by the operation of a fundamentally *motor* form of understanding whose specific adaptive modulations are not properly regarded as governed by *reasons* commensurate with them. And now we can also see what sort of objection to this Merleau-Ponty saw coming from the philosophical tradition. Early on he considers the worry that this proposed enlarged sense of "understanding," which (in a certain way) detaches it from reason, may seem absurd. On traditional assumptions, how can this be genuine *understanding* at all? And how can *one's own body* intelligibly be said to *understand* anything?[43] Much later he elaborates on a similar concern, by invoking the idea that genuine consciousness must be intelligible to itself in self-consciousness of its own unifying activity, or else it would not be consciousness at all. But (according to the objector) to speak of *perceiving* with one's eyes and hands, to make the *body* the subject of consciousness, or to attribute to it some kind of *knowledge*, is therefore incoherent. The body can be no more than a "material instrument" of knowledge, the site of its causal preconditions.[44]

To such concerns Merleau-Ponty responds partly by arguing[45] that we are not entitled just to assume that all consciousness is epistemically in "possession of itself" in the way some have argued rational *thought* must be. And we should not *expect* that the sort of reflective self-consciousness that may be bound up with thought should reveal to us the body-subject of perception, and its motor-understanding ways. For, as he has been arguing, *perception is not thought*, and *perceptual* synthesis is not *intellectual* synthesis. However, what we might still find, *in perception*, is an experience of one's own body engaged in a kind of motor understanding, including an experience of the "harmony" of performance with aim, which would constitute a form of consciousness of oneself *as subject*. And (as I interpret him) that is just what he believes we do find. For this brings out the point of the unity passage: "In perception, we are one with this body. ... In sense experience, I experience the unity of the subject." Thus for Merleau-Ponty, ultimately something like a Kantian connection between consciousness and self-consciousness is preserved, but transposed in a sensorimotor key.[46]

This also gives us a glimpse of how we might see the experience of space as due to the exercise of nonintellectual motor skills (in something like the way suggested above, in the previous section, while still paying respect to the thought that some kind of normative self-consciousness is required if one's performances are to be genuinely normatively assessable. The idea is that the experience of one's own body in motor understanding can involve an experience of the suitability of one's movement to one's aims, even absent a responsiveness to the demand for justifying reasons. We can also here see the Merleau-Pontyan account responding to McDowellian Kant-inspired concerns in this general way. Where McDowell[47] tries to preserve a Kantian picture of ourselves as enjoying the "spontaneity" of thought, even as we also belong to the natural world – not with Kantian appeal to a noumenal realm, but by resort to an (Aristotelian) *"second nature"* – so also, with a rather similar end in view (but greater wariness of intellectualism), Merleau-Ponty employs his notion of *motor habits and understanding*.

To bring all this back now to the worry about "merging" with our bodies: we should see Merleau-Ponty as here distinguishing – not *two subjects* (an "I" and a "habit body") that may merge and separate – but *two ways of being a subject*. He writes, "The one who, in sensory exploration, gives a past to the present and directs it to a future, is not myself as an autonomous subject, but myself insofar as I have a body and am able to look."[48] But this is not to say that there are two numerically distinct "myselves" – one who is a body (with motor understanding) and one who is an intellect (with rational autonomy). Rather, the point is: *being a sensorimotor subject* is distinct from *being an autonomous subject*. But this does not preclude my being both a "body-subject" (who understands things through movement) and a person (who by considering reasons, decides what to do and believe, and takes responsibility for this). And – even more importantly—*the kind of body-subject I am may be deeply enmeshed with the kind of person I am*. That they are (and how they are), would be partly recognized in the truth of conceptual pervasiveness (1a). And as I read Merleau-Ponty, he would not reject as intellectualist *this* sort of "conceptual shaping" of experience. Rather, he could (and should) recognize that this belongs to how one perceives the world as "polarized" by one's "projects," so as to motivate the responses these require.[49] And, if one's *personal choices* in this way structure the experience of one's situation so as to engage one's motor skills, we arrive at an idea of how to connect rational deliberation with motor understanding.[50]

Still, this does not preclude some creatures' being body-subjects (of a sort) without making "personal choices" – without being *persons* – at all. Presumably many nonhuman animals are like this. This, again, is why pervasiveness of self-consciousness (2b) should be rejected. However, again, there *is* a durable insight in the tradition linking consciousness with self-consciousness. But to preserve it, we must be careful to distinguish sensory from intellectual consciousness properly. Then we will not say (with McDowell) that the sensory experience of things requires intellectual self-consciousness. Rather we will say (with Merleau-Ponty) that much as there is, arguably, a kind self-critical rationality bound to the intellectual form of consciousness, so there is a kind of *bodily self-experience*[51] bound to its sensory form.

Much more would need to be done to explain and defend the view I am here attributing to Merleau-Ponty. Of course, it may be mistaken. But, though it is certainly something "only a philosopher" would say, it is hardly crazy.

## Summary

What I find amiss in McDowell's view is not the claim that our status as self-critical reasoners pervasively shapes our perceptual experience, and is implicit in much of our activity. That, I believe, is basically correct. Where things go wrong, I have argued, is with the idea that the intentionality of perceptual experience requires some sort of permeation by concepts whose presence in experiential content distinguishes every manner of "outer" appearance, and whose possession is presumed to require a capacity for self-critical reflection.

To further our understanding of these issues (while saving Merleau-Ponty from undeserved ridicule), I have reconstructed in outline his view that there is, in sensory life, a nonintellectual form of understanding at work. He puts this by saying there is something "anonymous" or "impersonal" in our existence as perceivers. But he supposes this is true, not because ordinarily perception and sensorimotor activity are *no one's*, still less because a person is a disembodied intellect that occasionally "merges" into a merely "person-like" body. He speaks of "impersonality" here because he assumes rational choice is part of what it is to be a person, and holds that the specific ways we move in our everyday activities and in making things apparent to ourselves are – though intelligently adaptive to the demands of our tasks – often not *chosen for reasons*.

But, according to Merleau-Ponty, we persons are not just rational agents who can correct our judgments and decisions by citing norms aimed at truth and rightness. And we are not just this, *plus* a locus of causal mechanisms. We are also, in a way that *joins* our rationality to our participation in nature: embodied subjects who understand our world and ourselves through situation-sensitive, goal-oriented movement which, while governed by our intentions, eludes reconstitution in reasoned choices of thought. *This*, at least, is a view worth taking seriously as an attempt to achieve what McDowell himself strives for: a conception of ourselves that *integrates* – and does not just awkwardly juxtapose – our rational capacity to make up our minds with our unchosen, embodied existence.[52]

## Notes

1 Some characteristic statements of this theme in McDowell: "Our perceptual experience is permeated with rationality" ("What Myth?," p. 339). "[O]ur relation to the world, including our perceptual relation to it, is pervasively shaped by our conceptual mindedness … if a perceptual experience is world-disclosing … any aspect of its content is present in a form in which it is suitable to constitute the content of a conceptual capacity" (ibid., p. 346).
2 On McDowell's view, perception has content and constitutes "outer experience," "awareness of aspects of the world," and is distinguishable from the mere "receptivity" of "sense impressions," only if it is "permeated with concepts" in a way that implies self-critical rationality is "operative" in it. For example, to perceive things as colored – to have experience with that content – it would not be enough to produce color words correctly in response to a sensory stimulus. One needs in addition a "self-conscious conception of how [one's] experience relates to the world" – e.g. "the concept of visible surfaces of objects and the concept of suitable conditions for telling what color something is by looking at it" (McDowell, Mind and World, pp. 46–47, 50). McDowell's claim that a kind of practical self-consciousness is also ubiquitous in human experience is explained at McDowell "Response to Dreyfus," pp. 368–69.
3 Dreyfus, "Overcoming the Myth of the Mental." In my usage "mind" and "mental" do not connote "intellectual" or "conceptual" as they apparently do in Dreyfus's. So I will frame the issue here as one of a potentially worrisome aggrandizement of *intellect* rather than of *mind*. But I regard this as a terminological matter.
4 Dreyfus, "Response to McDowell," p. 371.
5 Ibid., p. 375.
6 Ibid., p. 374.
7 Ibid., p. 375.
8 Cited by Dreyfus, ibid., p. 373.
9 Dreyfus, "Return of the Myth of the Mental," p. 355.
10 McDowell, "What Myth?," p. 350.
11 Merleau-Ponty, *Phenomenology of Perception*, p. 227; *Phénoménologie de la perception*, p. 275.
12 Dreyfus, "Return of the Myth of the Mental," pp. 355–56.
13 McDowell, "Response to Dreyfus," p. 368.
14 Ibid., p. 369.
15 Ibid.
16 Ibid.
17 McDowell, "What Myth?," p. 350.
18 Ibid., pp. 346–48.

19 Passages cited in note 2 divide between these theses.
20 Some might worry that my idea (that appearances facilitate our treatment of what appears) conflicts with the theory, influentially advanced by Goodale and Milner (*Sight Unseen*) of "two visual systems," one for visual identification (they say "perception"); the other for visual guidance of action, assuming we say (as they do) the second sort of vision is *unconscious* (and we take this to entail it does not involve visual *appearance*). Now I do not intend to deny here that there are fine differences in visual stimuli to which we quickly adjust movements (of e.g. our hands) even where these are not differences in how the stimuli *look* to us. But it does not follow (and I am not persuaded the research shows) that visually apparent differences make *no* significant difference to the initiation and direction of visually guided movement. And only this second claim would be in conflict with what I am maintaining here.
21 Among these questions are: What do I mean by (i) "you identify something in thought as $\Phi$"? (ii) "you identify something as $\Phi$ from how it looks"? (iii) "you treat something as $\Phi$"? As a start, I would say this. For (i) it would be sufficient that you verbally judge that something is $\Phi$, or that verbalizing your thought would involve a reference of the form "the $\Phi$" or "that $\Phi$." For (ii), it would be enough that (i) is true, because of how something looks to you – and *not* because you are disposed to *infer* something is $\Phi$ from its being $\Psi$. As for (iii), it would be sufficient for *your treating something as $\Phi$ that*, because of how it appears to you, what you did to it or with it is *what $\Phi$s are for* (e.g. you opened the door with the doorknob because of how it looked to you). More broadly, we might say you treat something as $\Phi$ when you do something to or with it for the sake of some goal, and being $\Phi$ is explanatorily relevant to your doing that for this end. And a common way for it to be relevant is via the manner of appearance something $\Phi$ presents to you. And that warrants our speaking of its (practically) appearing to you as $\Phi$.
22 This is to be distinguished from the fineness of grain argument for nonconceptual content, which McDowell contests (*Mind and World*, pp. 46–60, 160–66). McDowell's appeal to "type demonstratives" to answer this argument won't help here. The problem I'm raising is not that the appearances are somehow too finely specific to be captured conceptually (as if some level of visually discernible "fineness" in determinables like color and shape inherently elude conceptualization). The problem is that reflection reveals that efforts to match the heterogeneity of nonfocal appearance with distinct demonstrative thoughts simply fail to provide one with intelligible distinctions that may function, even briefly, in one's conceptual capacities in a distinct fashion. This is compatible with allowing that type demonstratives afford us thoughts as finely discriminating as any focal appearance of color or shape.
23 To some extent my concerns parallel Tyler Burge's criticism of McDowell's (and many others') intellectualism in *Origins of Objectivity*: contrary to what some would-be followers of Kant suppose, object constancy is enough for experience of objects; you don't also need self-conscious reflection. But Burge's criticisms, as I understand them, arise against the backdrop of a conception of object constancy different from that I invoke, and accord no special role to sensorimotor activity.
24 Why do I confine myself to saying the exercise of these sensorimotor capacities is sufficient for experience of space? Why not: sufficient *and necessary*? To evaluate this stronger claim we need to consider whether there is something else, short of such motor capacities, whose exercise would be sufficient for sensory intentionality (of the sort that comes with focal/nonfocal dynamic structure) – even without self-critical rationality.

25 It's true that McDowell acknowledges something *in between* mere sense impressions and reason-permeated experiential content: we share with nonrational animals a "perceptual sensitivity" to features (Mind and World, pp. 50, 64), and certain perceptual "competences," relating to the perception of "affordances" (e.g. experiencing a space as big enough to get through) ("What Myth?," pp. 343–45). But I think one needs to say more than this. One needs somehow to link such shared competences to *object perception*, and to the *experience of space* in something like the manner I propose. If one takes this step it will at least seem highly misleading to say, like McDowell in Mind and World, that "outer experience" is confined to creatures possessed of rational self-consciousness.
26 Merleau-Ponty, Phenomenology, pp. 231, 239.
27 Merleau-Ponty, Phénoménologie, p. 275.
28 One may say (for instance) that two tributaries of a river *se confondent* – and so say that they *merge into* one another. But to say we (*nous*) *confondons* something *avec* (with) something is not to speak of *merger*, but standardly, of *confusing or mistaking* one thing for another. And in fact, Colin Smith translates the phrase "nous confondre avec" in that very way at the start of the same chapter (Phenomenology, p. 241; Phénoménologie, p. 241). In that passage, Merleau-Ponty says intellectualists will find it absurd to say we see "with our eyes," but he suggests that, given their views, they will have a hard time accounting for how we should ever have been so confused as to think we did. He asks there: "How can we ever confuse ourselves with our bodies?" ("Comment pouvons-nous jamais nous confondre avec notre corps?") His implicit suggestion is that the intellectualist's assumption that really we see with our *mind and not our body* is wrong: we are *not* mistaken in thinking we see with our eyes, and so we have not *confused* ourselves with (i.e. mistaken ourselves for) our bodies – in some way indeed, we *are* our bodies. We can thus see why Smith didn't employ a similar ("confuse") translation of *confondre* a few pages later, for the unity passage. We don't want to have Merleau-Ponty assert there, in his own voice, that we *mistake ourselves for (or confuse ourselves with) our bodies.*

But there *are* alternatives to both "merge" and "confuse." Smith adopts one in *another* passage in which *se confondre avec* occurs, where he translates it as "identify oneself with" (Phenomenology, p. 94; Phénoménologie, p. 97). It may seem to bring us somewhat closer to what Merleau-Ponty means in the unity passage to say: *in perceiving I identify myself with my body*. But then we might hear "identify" as involving a form of *thought*, so that the point would be that in perception I *think of myself and my body as one and the same* – which is clearly *not* the point at all. Thus it seems the best solution would be to take Merleau-Ponty to be saying, as I do: in perception, *I am one with my body*. (I owe this suggested translation to Béatrice Longuenesse, to whom I am also indebted for discussion of the French Kantianism in which Merleau-Ponty was steeped during his philosophical formation.)
29 Merleau-Ponty, Phenomenology and Perception, p. 250; Phénoménologie, pp. 249ff.
30 Phenomenology, p. 83; Phénoménologie, p. 86.
31 Phenomenology, p. 78; Phénoménologie, p. 82.
32 Phenomenology, pp. 275–76; Phénoménologie, pp. 274–75.
33 Phenomenology, p. 90; Phénoménologie, p. 93.
34 Mark Okrent (*Rational Animals*) has recently developed in detail an account of goal-directed animal behavior partly inspired by Merleau-Ponty's (more prominent in his *Structure of Behavior*), and partly similar in its aims.
35 Merleau-Ponty, Phenomenology, p. 93; Phénoménologie, p. 96.
36 Phenomenology, pp. 93–95; Phénoménologie, pp. 96–98.

37 *Phenomenology*, p. 96; *Phénoménologie*, p. 99. It may be implicit in Merleau-Ponty's hedging that he wants to distinguish a fully *im*personal mode of existence (such as nonhuman animals have) from the *pre*personal ("*almost* impersonal") mode we humans have. We act rarely, if ever, *totally impersonally*, since even our unchosen adjustments in motor activity occur in the service of *some* personal choice, some governing intention, and against the background of a *world* structured by our projects, not a mere *environment* (*Umwelt*) shaped by biological needs (see *Phenomenology*, pp. 100, 381; *Phénoménologie*, pp. 103, 379). (I am grateful to Clinton Tolley for discussion of this issue.)

38 *Phenomenology*, pp. 118–19; *Phénoménologie*, pp. 119–20. From this it should be clear just how dissimilar Merleau-Ponty's view is to that which McDowell attributes to him in "Response to Dreyfus," p. 368.

39 See Merleau-Ponty's general (but unfortunately mistranslated) characterization of "body schema" (*Phenomenology*, p. 163; *Phénoménologie*, p. 164).

40 *Phenomenology*, p. 167; *Phénoménologie*, p. 169.

41 I do not take Merleau-Ponty to mean that one commonly *focuses one's attention on one's movements* (as one might, for example, in doing yoga, or in certain forms of dance), so as to *monitor* how well they accord ("harmonize") with one's aims. It is rather a question of experiencing the "fittingness" of one's movements *in the situation*. For this, attention is not *withdrawn* from one's surroundings. Perhaps here someone will object: "There is no experience of harmony when things are going *well*, only an experience of *dis*harmony when things go awry." But would we say the same about hearing literal, musical harmony? That we never hear the harmony of the singers' voices – *only* their discord?

42 A standard move would be to resist Merleau-Ponty here by insisting that there really are representations, selections, and monitoring lying behind all skilled bodily movements – but this is all done "unconsciously" at the "subpersonal" level (which is not the same as Merleau-Ponty's "impersonal" level). However, we should not be too quick to assume that burying intellection in subpersonal modules answers all reasonable concerns. We should ask, for example: if certain practical reasoning is "too intellectual" to credit to an animal as a whole, just why would it be less problematic to attribute this to its *subsystems*? And if we conclude that goal-directed *animal* movements don't need such intellectual guidance, why suppose ours always do? Further, notice that in our own case we would not want to make the subpersonal planning allegedly controlling our movements *impenetrable* to personal-level belief and planning (on pain of denying effective personal choice altogether). Now, as Merleau-Ponty's cases somewhat exotically illustrate: we are persistently moved by habit sometimes (but not always) in defiance of what's obvious to belief. And often (but not always) we are worse at executing our movements when we *think* about them than when we do not. Just how are we to account for these phenomena, in the way Merleau-Ponty's cognitivist opponent wants, as *peculiarly selective failures of communication among internal planners*? We could (and maybe should) remove this sort of difficulty by rejecting the premise on which it is based: there is no puzzling *failure* of internal communication to account for, because there is really no subpersonal inner planner with which to "communicate." It is no surprise that one's belief doesn't impede the practical reasonings that it should rationally undermine, because the postulated reasonings *simply don't occur in the first place*. And it is no wonder that one's motor competence can still thrive even when the power to generate "abstract" movement to order is hobbled – if the latter is not (even unconsciously) a normal part of the former to begin with.

43 Merleau-Ponty, *Phenomenology*, p. 167; *Phénoménologie*, p. 169.

44 *Phenomenology*, pp. 253–54, 275–76; *Phénoménologie*, pp. 252–53, 274–75.
45 *Phenomenology*, pp. 254, 276; *Phénoménologie*, pp. 253ff., 275ff.
46 In an illuminating discussion of a Kantian distinction between awareness of oneself "as object" and "as subject," which compares Kant's own views with Cassam's, Longuenesse ("Self-Consciousness and Consciousness of One's Own Body") notes similarities between Cassam and Merleau-Ponty that set them apart from Kant on this matter. But noting certain *dissimilarities* is also crucial to appreciating Merleau-Ponty's position. For Merleau-Ponty (unlike Cassam), what makes my experience of my body a consciousness of myself "as subject" is not that it involves "ascribing" perceptual or other mental states to myself. Nor is this at bottom explained as a matter of an "immunity to error through misidentification" (at a time and through time). As I read Merleau-Ponty, what's crucial (and basic) here is rather: how one's perceptual experience of one's own bodily activity makes it at once both *definitive of one's own perceptual perspective* on the world and *constitutive of a form of understanding*. That is why such experience is a consciousness of oneself "as subject."
47 McDowell, *Mind and World*, pp. 110–11.
48 Merleau-Ponty, *Phenomenology*, p. 279; *Phénoménologie*, p. 277.
49 As he describes at pp. 128–29 and 156–57 of the *Phenomenology* (*Phénoménologie*, pp. 129–30 and 157–58).
50 This only hints at how to elaborate Merleau-Ponty's account of perception and motor skills into a satisfactory philosophy of action. What needs elucidation: how do one's tasks (given in part by one's choices) configure appearances in terms of what is *to be done* (requirements) and *what can be done* (opportunities), so as to translate reasoned decision into action? And how is our freedom reflected in the extent to which our actual circumstances constrain the possibilities we can see in our situation? Romdehn-Romluc's ("Merleau-Ponty and the Power to Reckon with the Possible") piece challenging Dreyfus, together with Dreyfus's response ("Reply to Romdehn-Romluc"), help illuminate the difficulties in this area, and possible modes of resolution.
51 I borrow this expression from Thompson, *Mind in Life*.
52 For questions and comments in response to earlier versions of this chapter, I would like to thank participants at the 2008 Asilomar conference of the International Society for Phenomenological Studies, and the 2008 conference of the California Phenomenology Circle. I would also particularly like to express gratitude for discussions with David Cerbone, Steve Crowell, Hubert Dreyfus, William Hasselberger, Paul Hoffman, Béatrice Longuenesse, Wayne Martin, Samantha Matherne, Mark Okrent, David Pitt, Komarine Romdehn-Romluc, Joseph Schear, Clinton Tolley, and Mark Wrathall.

# Bibliography

Burge, T., *Origins of Objectivity*, Oxford: Oxford University Press, 2010.
Dreyfus, H., "Overcoming the Myth of the Mental: How Philosophers Can Profit from the Phenomenology of Everyday Expertise," *Proceedings and Addresses of the American Philosophical Association* 79, no. 2 (2005): 47–65.
——, "Reply to Romdehn-Romluc," in T. Baldwin (ed.), *Reading Merleau-Ponty: On Phenomenology of Perception*, London: Routledge, 2007, pp. 59–69.
——, "Response to McDowell," *Inquiry* 50, no. 4 (2007): 366–70.
——, "The Return of the Myth of the Mental," *Inquiry* 50, no. 4 (2007): 352–65.
Goodale, M. and Milner, D., *Sight Unseen*, Oxford: Oxford University Press, 2004.

Longuenesse, B., "Self-Consciousness and Consciousness of One's Own Body: Variations on a Kantian Theme," *Philosophical Topics* 34, nos 1 and 2 (2006): 283–309.
McDowell, J., *Mind and World*, Cambridge, MA: Harvard University Press, 1994.
——, "Response to Dreyfus," *Inquiry* 50, no. 4 (2007): 366–70.
——, "What Myth?," *Inquiry* 50, no. 4 (2007): 338–51.
Merleau-Ponty, M., *Phénoménologie de la perception*, Paris: Gallimard, 1945.
——, *Phenomenology of Perception*, trans. C. Smith, London: Routledge & Kegan Paul, 1962.
Okrent, M., *Rational Animals: The Teleological Roots of Intentionality*, Athens, OH: Ohio University Press, 2007.
Romdehn-Romluc, K., "Merleau-Ponty and the Power to Reckon with the Possible," in T. Baldwin (ed.), *Reading Merleau-Ponty: On Phenomenology of Perception*, London: Routledge, 2007, pp. 44–58.
Thompson, E., *Mind in Life*, Cambridge, MA: Harvard University Press, 2007.

## Part IV

# EXPERIENCE, CONCEPTS, AND NONCONCEPTUAL CONTENT

# 10

# THE GIVEN

*Tim Crane*

### The given, and the Myth of the Given

In *The Mind and the World Order*, C. I. Lewis made a famous distinction between the immediate data "which are presented or given to the mind" and the "construction or interpretation" which the mind brings to those data.[1] What the mind receives is the datum – literally, the given – and the interpretation is what happens when we bring it "under some category or other, select from it, emphasize aspects of it, and relate it in particular and unavoidable ways."[2] So although any attempt to describe the given will inevitably be an interpretation of it, this should not give us reason to deny its existence: "no one but a philosopher could for a moment deny this immediate presence in consciousness of that which no activity of thought can create or alter."[3]

Whatever those outside philosophy might think, Lewis was certainly right about what philosophers were prepared to deny. His conception of the "given" is without question one of the targets of Wilfrid Sellars's influential critique of the notion of the "whole framework of givenness."[4] One of the things Sellars was attacking was the idea that something that was merely given by the senses could put one in a position to be justified in making a judgment about the empirical world. The "given" in this sense is a myth because one cannot be given what one is not in a position to receive. In the case of experience, Sellars's point is that one's experience cannot serve as the justification for one's empirical beliefs unless one is able to bring the experience, in some way, into the "space of reasons."

In his Presidential Address to the American Philosophical Association in 2005, which inaugurated his exchange with John McDowell, Hubert Dreyfus reminisces about how as a student at Harvard he attended C. I. Lewis's lectures on epistemology, where Lewis gave epistemological arguments for the existence of the given.[5] Dreyfus himself accepts the Sellarsian critique of the given, as does McDowell, and as do many others. But Dreyfus thinks that even those who, like McDowell, reject the "Myth of the Given" nonetheless fall under the influence of another myth: the Myth of the

229

Mental. This is the idea that our fundamental way of interacting with the world in experience is intellectual or rational in character. Dreyfus argues that this is a myth because it ignores the more fundamental enactive engagement with our world, which he calls "embodied coping."

McDowell has responded to Dreyfus's charge that there is no reason why his conception of experience cannot fully accommodate an account of embodied coping. I think McDowell is right: there is nothing in his views that makes it impossible for him to recognize the phenomenon of embodied coping and fully incorporate it within his conception of the mind. But it seems to me that a deeper disagreement between McDowell and Dreyfus lies not in their attitudes to embodied coping, but in their attitudes to experience. Despite his rejection of the given in the mythical sense with all its works and empty promises, it is clear that in recent work McDowell does accept something like a distinction between what is given to us, and what we bring to experience. This is not meant as a criticism of McDowell; later in this chapter I will defend a similar distinction. But it is important to emphasize that what McDowell is saying here is very different from Dreyfus's view of experience: there is something like a given, for McDowell, as he himself acknowledges.[6] In order to set the stage for this, I must first briefly explain the developments of McDowell's views about experience.

In *Mind and World*, McDowell had argued that the challenge posed by Sellars can only be met if experience has conceptual, propositional content. An experience is an experience *that things are thus and so*, and *that things are thus and so* is something one can also judge (a proposition). *That things are thus and so* is the propositional content of the judgment, and a judgment's having this content is an actualization of the conceptual capacities of the subject. Likewise, McDowell argues, when an experience has the propositional content *that things are thus and so* this too is an actualization of the conceptual capacities of the subject. Because experience involves the exercise of conceptual capacities, experiences *themselves* – and not just the beliefs based on them – can be relevant to a subject's standing in the "space of reasons" and therefore can act as justifiers of a subject's beliefs.

McDowell has changed his mind recently on certain details of this account, under pressure from objections from Charles Travis.[7] He now rejects the idea that experience has propositional content, and replaces this with a conception of experience as "intuition" in a Kantian sense, which has a nonpropositional content. An intuition in this sense is defined as "a having in view."[8] Let's assume, to borrow one of Travis's examples, that seeing a pig underneath an oak is an example of having something in view, and therefore of an intuition. This experience has a certain content, which should not be understood as representing something "as so," since that would be propositional.[9] But neither should experience be understood as some understand it, simply as relating us to objects – the pig and the oak.[10] Rather, the content of an intuition is something structured, it has a *unity*.[11] The details of this proposal are complex, but at their core is the Kantian proposal that the content of an intuition – what is presented in the experience – is structured by (for example) formal categories of object and property.

The view is not, however, that in experiencing the pig under the oak, we "apply" the concept of an object to the pig. This would confuse the content of the intuition with the content of the "discursive activity" which it can give rise to – for example, when describing the thing under the oak as a pig or as an animal. So there is a distinction between the content of an intuition and the content of a judgment or an assertion which is based upon it. McDowell no longer thinks that what one can see is also what one can judge. Nonetheless, he still insists that the content of an intuition is conceptual, in the sense that "every aspect of the content of an intuition is present in a form in which it is already suitable to be the content associated with a discursive capacity."[12] What it is for content to be conceptual, then, is not for it to be conceptualized – in the sense that one has to be actually exercising a conceptual capacity when in a state with such a content – but for it to be conceptualizable.

Travis's own picture is somewhat different.[13] He thinks that there is no need to think of experiences as having "content" at all. Seeing a pig under an oak is simply an awareness of some portion of the visible world, our visible surroundings. If we have the concept of a pig, or the ability to recognize pigs, then we can judge that the pig is under the oak on the basis of this experience plus our ability to recognize that what we experience is an instance of a thing of a certain kind. Concepts for Travis involve generality – in his terminology, they "reach" beyond the particular situation of (e.g.) seeing something. Making the judgment that the pig is under the oak involves asserting that this particular situation is a situation of a certain kind (a pig-under-an-oak kind). And if the situation *is* one of this kind, then this experience can "bear for you" on what you should think.

McDowell claims that Travis's picture – although correct in some respects – ultimately involves a commitment to the Myth of the Given. McDowell's charge is that on Travis's view, "having things in view must be provided for by sensibility alone."[14] However, this is not something that should worry Travis. Having things in view – seeing, experiencing – *is* provided for by sensibility alone, since he conceives of seeing "as seeing what is there (roughly before the eyes) to be seen."[15] So if something is before one's eyes, one's visual capacities are working as they should, one sees it: it is "in view." Travis answers the distinct question of how seeing justifies one's belief – of how, in Travis's own words, it "bears, for us, on what to think" – by claiming that one can recognize what is seen as an instance of a general kind of thing, and that this role is carried out by the application of concepts, or reason.[16]

Although McDowell thinks that this correctly describes one way in which experience is related to conceptual judgment, he argues that this is not the only way.[17] This is because what has to be in view is not just what is there to be seen – the pig under the oak – but the pig "present to one through the presence to one of some of its properties, in an intuition in which concepts of those properties exemplify a unity that constitutes the content of a formal concept of an object."[18] It is only if this is so that "one is thereby entitled to judge that one is confronted by an object with those properties."[19] Both Travis and McDowell, then, accept that at a certain point in the description of justification, we arrive at a connection between two kinds of fact, and this connection is what justification consists in. For McDowell, the connection is between the unified nonpropositional content of an intuition and the propositional content of the judgment which one makes. For Travis, the connection is between what is seen and the judgment which one makes by applying concepts to what is seen. The difference between them concerns whether there is any role for something like the "content of an intuition" in describing this connection. But they both agree that there is a connection, and that once this connection is made, the Myth of the Given is avoided: neither view involves saying that one can be given something which *justifies* that one is in no position to receive. For neither view says that *what justifies* you in believing that there is a pig under the oak is *mere* sensibility: on each view, you can only be justified if you bring concepts to bear on what you see.

It is not clear to me what remains of the Sellarsian attack on the given for someone who has the conception of the relationship between seeing and conceptualizing which Travis has. If seeing is an encounter with some portion of reality, and making a judgment about what is seen is applying one's concepts to what one sees on the basis of this seeing, then I see no obstacle to the claim that seeing something can justify one's judgment.[20]

Suppose, then, we put the debate about the Myth of the Given to one side. Is there still any point in talking about what is given in experience, or about the distinction between what is given and what is brought to experience? In the rest of this chapter I will try and answer this question. But first I need to introduce some concepts central to the recent debate in the philosophy of perception.

## The content of experience

Apart from the discussions inspired by Sellars, recent philosophy of perception has not had much to say about the idea of the given. Theories of perception talk instead about the "content" of experience, or the representational or "intentional" content of experience. But if there is a question about the given, then surely it ought to be connected in *some* way with the question about representational content. The claim that experiences represent the world is supposed to be a description of the connection between the mind and the world in experience. Surely there must be some link between this and the idea of the given sketched above, if that idea has any value at all?

That experience has "content" is, of course, a piece of philosophical jargon or terminology, and it has meant many different things to different writers. It's worth reminding ourselves of some of them. When G. E. Moore in "The Refutation of Idealism" talks about the view (which he rejects) that the sensation of blue involves blueness as its "content," what he means is that it involves the instantiation of a property.[21] Today this would be better classified as a "qualia" view rather than a content view. Another example is Moritz Schlick's 1932 essay "Form and Content." Schlick says that "the difference between form and content is, roughly speaking, the difference between that which can be expressed and that which cannot be expressed."[22] Schlick was not only talking about the mind, but he does apply the distinction between form and content to things like the experience of colors. He argues that although one can express some truths about the colors of things, "the content itself (e.g., the green of the leaf) ... cannot be grasped by any expression."[23] This is "not because content is too difficult to get at, or because the right method of investigating it has not yet been found, but simply because there is no sense in asking any questions about it. There is no proposition about content, there cannot be any."[24] Again, these remarks would make little sense if "content" had its contemporary meaning; in its inexpressibility at least, Schlick's notion of content again has more in common with the contemporary notion of qualia.

"Content" in these earlier uses referred to something specifically sensory. In contemporary discussions, however, "content" refers to the representational dimension of mental states. One of the merits of Susanna Siegel's 2005 *Stanford Encyclopedia* article, "The Contents of Perception," is that she gives a definition of content of experience which can apply to both the sensory and to the (putative) representational aspects of experience. Siegel defines content as "what is conveyed to the subject by her perceptual experience."[25] On some views what is conveyed to the subject is something sensory ("qualia" or what Moore calls "content"), on some views something representational (an intentional content), while on some views what is conveyed to the subject is simply one's visible surroundings. McDowell's view is something else again: what is given is the content of an intuition, neither a representation nor simply one's visible surroundings.[26]

To my ear, "what is conveyed" sounds rather close to "what is given." So if we adopt Siegel's definition of "content" we can also say that the content of an experience is what is given to the subject in that experience. Not all participants will accept this use of the word: Travis and Brewer, for example, will not describe their position as a view about content, since they take content to be something representational. For this reason, I will use the word "content" as Siegel defines it, and I will use "representational content" to describe the putative feature of experience which Travis and

Brewer think does not exist. Similarly, McDowell thinks that intuitions have content but that this content is not representational.[27] So we can mark this distinction again by distinguishing content in the broad sense from representational content. A common definition is that a state of mind has representational content when it is assessable as accurate or inaccurate: Michael Tye says "any state with accuracy conditions has representational content."[28]

If content is what is given or conveyed to the subject (by definition) then the substantive question is what content is. In other words, what is given or conveyed to the subject in an experience? In the next section I will outline the dominant contemporary answer to this question, which I call "standard intentionalism," and in the section after this I will describe an alternative.

## Intentionalism and propositional content

Intentionalism about the mind is the theory that all mental phenomena exhibit intentionality, the directedness of the mind upon its objects.[29] Intentionalism about experience is the view that experience is (wholly or in part) an intentional state or event. Since it is common to call intentionality mental representation, then we can say that an intentionalist view of experience is that experience is a representational state. The content of an experience, according to intentionalism, is how the world is represented to be by the experience. This again conforms to Siegel's definition: *how things are represented as being* is what is conveyed or given to the subject in an experience.

What I will call the "standard" intentionalist view is the theory that the content of experience is *propositional*. A proposition is something that can be true or false. An intentional state which has propositional content is a propositional attitude; hence perceptual experience is a propositional attitude. As Alex Byrne puts it:

> All parties agree that perceiving is very much like a traditional propositional attitude, such as believing or intending ... when one has a perceptual experience, one bears the perception relation to a certain proposition $p$.[30]

When Byrne says that perceivers stand in a "perception relation" to a proposition, he obviously does not mean that we *perceive propositions* in the sense that we perceive pigs and people. This would be to confuse the representational content of an experience with what it is in the world that we experience (what I would call, following Husserl, the "object" of the experience).[31] What Byrne means is that a subject perceiving a pig should be understood in terms of their being in a representational state which is assessable as true or false. There are well-known reasons for taking such representational states to be *relations* between the subject of the state and a proposition.[32] This "perception relation" then should not be confused with the "perception relation" which holds between a subject and a pig when they perceive a pig. It is unfortunate perhaps that the same name has been given to both relations; but once the distinction is made, confusion should evaporate.

Having said that the content of experience is propositional, the next question that typically arises is what the nature of these propositions is. And here it may seem as if there are already a number of well-established theoretical options. One can take propositions to be "coarse-grained" as Russell did: containing the objects and properties in the world that they (or the states whose contents they are) are about. Or one can take them to be composed of modes of presentation of objects and properties, as Frege did.[33] The Russellian view takes the sentences "Hesperus shines in the evening" and "Phosphorus shines in the evening" as expressing the same proposition; the Fregean view denies this. A position which combines some elements of each is the Lewis–Stalnaker view of propositions as sets of worlds, or related ideas such as centered worlds, or sets of possibilia. This view tries to capture some of the intentionality of the Fregean view while building up propositions only out of ordinary (albeit nonactual) objects and properties.

What is to decide between these different conceptions of propositional content? On the one hand, one might want to choose the Russellian conception because it gives the best account of the fact that perception is "direct": that it directly concerns objects and properties in the world. Or it might be thought to give the best account of the fact that perception seems to be "object involving." On the other hand, one might want to respect the fact that perception has an "aspectual" element: that when one perceives things, one always does so in some limited way; some properties are perceptible while others are not, and even the properties themselves might fall under some "mode of presentation." On the face of it, the Russellian conception would count any perceptual experiences of the same object as having the same properties and as having the same content (the same thing is "conveyed to the subject by the experience"). The Fregean, by contrast, would count experiences as having different contents when they present their objects in different ways (according to the way Fregean modes of presentation are individuated).

Michael Tye has clearly expressed the kinds of reasons someone might have for taking different views on the nature of the propositional content of experience. He asks us to consider his visual experience of the surface S of an object O looking red:

> My visual experience intuitively represents S as having the property of being red. At this level my experience is accurate if and only if S

is red. But my experience also has something important in common with certain other visual experiences not directed at S. Suppose, for example, that O is replaced with another object O' that looks just like O or that I am hallucinating a red surface so that phenomenally it is for me just as it is in seeing S. Intuitively, in all three cases, it seems to me that *there is* a red surface before me. At this phenomenal level, my experience is accurate if and only if there is a red surface before me. This content is existential, not involving S, though it does also include the subject of the experience.[34]

The issue Tye is addressing is when we should count experiences as being the same or different. The three distinct experiences Tye mentions can be classified as having different contents, but also at some other "level" as having the same representational content. There is something to be said for each answer. After all, in the first case, the subject is actually seeing S, so the correctness of the experience should depend on how things are with S itself. But on the other hand, if we should count experiences as representing the world in the same way when they seem the same to the subject, then we should treat the representational content as general or "existential." Which should we choose?

David Chalmers has responded to this tension by adopting a "pluralistic" conception of the representational content of experience:

> One should be a pluralist about representational content. It may be that experiences can be associated with contents of many different sorts by different relations: we can call such relations content relations. For example, there may be one content relation that associates experiences with object-involving contents, and another which associates experiences with existential contents. ... On this view, there may not be such a thing as the representational content of a perceptual experience. Instead, a given experience may be associated with multiple representational contents via different content relations.[35]

The idea is that rather than there being one "perception" relation between the subject and the propositional content of experience, there are many, one for each distinctive kind of content (not just Russellian and Fregean, but for the different kinds of contents within these categories: object dependent, quantificational, etc.). Chalmers's proposal is based on the idea that "associating" different kinds of contents can serve to highlight different aspects of the state in question.

If we think of the representational dimension of experiences in terms of associating different propositions with a concrete event, then content pluralism about experience is plausible, just as it is plausible about attributions of some other mental states. Consider desire: did Oedipus want to marry his mother? In one sense, obviously not; he would not have assented to that sentence, he would not have entertained that thought to himself, and he would have done many things inconsistent with having the desire. So we should say that the sentence "Oedipus wanted it to be the case that he married his mother" has a false reading. But there is also a sense in which it is true that he wanted to marry his mother: his mother is such that Oedipus wanted to marry her; he wanted to marry Jocasta, and Jocasta was his mother. It would be pointlessly dogmatic to insist that these claims are false, or that they serve no purpose in the description of the situation (after all, this was the source of the tragedy).

In struggling to make sense of these phenomena, philosophers have appealed to various distinctions between kinds of attitude ascriptions: for example, it is common to say that in the *de dicto* sense ("Oedipus wanted it to be the case that ... ") it is not true that he wanted to marry his mother, but that in the *de re* sense ("His mother is such that Oedipus wanted ... ") it is true. That there are these two kinds of descriptions *and* that they can make explicit the ambiguities in these situations is very plausible. We might think, then, of different contents (the complete *dictum* in the *de dicto* case, and the incomplete content in the *de re* case) as being associated with Oedipus's state of mind via different "content relations." And this might be the model for perceptual representational contents, as Chalmers has argued.

If an experience literally has multiple contents, and the content of an experience is what is conveyed to the subject, then it follows that multiple contents are conveyed to the subject in an experience. So if my experience conveys to me that Hesperus is shining in the sky, it also conveys to me that Phosphorus is shining in the sky, it also conveys to me that there is something shining in the sky; and so on.

What does it mean to say all these things are "conveyed" to me by my experience? If it is a claim about the information which the experience delivers, or what kind of information can be derived from the fact that I am having this experience, then it is not difficult to make sense of the claim (whether or not the claim is true). But if it is a description of the phenomenology of the experience, of what it is like to have an experience, then it is less clear what it means. When having a visual experience of the planet Venus in the evening, it does not *seem* as if many distinct (and possibly incompatible) contents are being conveyed to me. What is given or conveyed to me is a certain scene, a certain region of concrete reality, which seems like a reasonably unified thing. It does not seem like receiving multiple messages saying different things (even if these messages are relayed by different "content relations").

Or take the Lewis–Stalnaker conception of propositions as sets of possible worlds, and consider my experience of a pig under the oak. What is conveyed by my experience is that there is a pig under the oak. This is the propositional content of the experience, and according to the Lewis–Stalnaker view, this propositional content is the set of all worlds in which the pig is under the oak (we can ignore the details of centering, etc., since these are not relevant to the basic point here). In what sense could what is phenomenologically (consciously) conveyed to me simply *be* this set of worlds? It is hard to see how content pluralism, whatever its other merits, could be a theory of the phenomenology of experience.

But if we take it at its word, standard intentionalism is precisely intended to be a theory of phenomenology. According to Peter Carruthers, for example, "phenomenal consciousness consists in a certain sort of intentional content."[36] And Tye is well known for the claim that phenomenal character is one and the same as representational content.[37] So these intentionalist views are explicitly intended to be views about phenomenology. In fact, even independently of the defense of intentionalism, it is widely assumed that content is supposed to have something to do with phenomenology. Siegel, for example, writes:

> Another commonly-held constraint is that the contents must be adequate to its phenomenology. ... The notion of phenomenal adequacy has considerable intuitive force. This suggests that the contents of experience have to in some way reflect the phenomenology of the experience.[38]

Given how Siegel originally introduced the word "content," it seems like an understatement to say that phenomenal adequacy is simply another "constraint" on content. Content, remember, is what is conveyed to a subject in an experience, and an experience is a conscious state or event. Surely *part* of what is conveyed is how things are consciously?

So the question remains: what has an experience's propositional content got to do with its phenomenology? Part of the answer, presumably, is that what is given to me has a certain form: not just the pig, the oak, but *that the pig is under the oak*. It is in this sense then that what is given to the subject (and therefore what the subject takes in) is something that can be true or false, a proposition in this sense. Certainly the idea that what we *take in* in experience is something with a propositional structure is an idea which is widely defended, even outside the circles of standard intentionalists. This is what McDowell famously argued for in *Mind and World*, even though he has now rejected it. But there he said that "one takes in, for instance, sees, that things are thus and so. That is the sort of thing one can also, for instance, judge."[39]

Nonetheless, it is not easy to make literal sense of the idea that what we take in in experience is what we can judge. When I judge, because of what I can see, that the pig is under the oak, this is something which, in a certain way, abstracts from the real presence of the pig there. The content of the judgment can outlive the experience, it can be the content of others' judgments, things can follow from it (for example, that something is underneath the oak).

What can outlive the experience, of course, is the concrete state of affairs: the pig actually being under the oak. Could this be what is given to the subject? Maybe; but not according to the standard intentionalist account. This is because, for the standard intentionalist, what is given is something that can be true or false. But the pig being under the oak is not something that can be true or false. It is just something that is there. Nor is it something from which things follow. Things follow from truths or propositions; the pig being in the garden is not a truth or a proposition, but something in the world. And things in the world are not true or false.[40]

So we have to distinguish between the propositional content of an experience, and what is phenomenologically given to the subject. The reason for this is the plausibility of content pluralism, plus the implausibility of saying that multiple representational contents are given to the subject. Of course, it is possible to question content pluralism; but I will not examine this route here. Rather, I want to propose a very different way of thinking about the intentionality of perception. I don't think we should abandon the idea of propositional content; but we have to see it as playing a different role.

## A phenomenological conception of content

In "On Sense and Reference" Frege employed an analogy with seeing the moon through a telescope to distinguish between sense, reference, and what he called "idea."[41] The moon is analogous to the reference of a word; the image on the telescope lens is the sense (it is the "property of many people") and the idea is compared to the image on the retina. An idea is something which is dependent on a particular perceiver, a particular subject, at a particular moment. It is, therefore, by definition unshareable.[42]

Standard intentionalism treats the content of experience as something at the level of Frege's sense (whether or not they individuate propositions in the Fregean way). Contents are abstract objects, and intentional states are relations to these objects. But there is no need for intentionalists to deny the existence of Fregean ideas, just because they accept Fregean sense. Moreover, intentionalists need not treat ideas as simple "qualia" in the usual sense of that word: nonrepresentational conscious mental properties. An idea is plausibly construed – like an image on the retina, with which the analogy is made – as a representation. But it is a representation which is concrete and particular, specific to this person, this time and this place.

Fregean ideas are a model for what I want to call the content of experience in the phenomenological sense – what is phenomenologically given or conveyed to subjects in their experience. This particular way of representing the world in this experience is what we might call (following Husserl, *Logical Investigations*) the "real content" of the experience. *Real* here is contrasted not with *unreal*, *fake*, or *imaginary* but with *ideal*. Ideal objects are what contemporary Anglophone philosophers would call "abstract" objects: objects without a location in space and time. In order to identify content in the "real" sense, we need to make a distinction between the particularity of any perceptual episode, and the "abstract" or "general" nature of propositional content. By abstract here, I mean: not tied to any particular moment of thinking or experiencing. It is because of this that a proposition does not have a spatiotemporal location: it can be the content of many acts of thinking, even if it is an indexical proposition that represents a certain particular time. Contrast this with the mental representation of this particular pig at this particular moment. This representation is tied to this moment; although another event could represent the same pig, in the same way, it would not be this particular representation – just for the reason that this particular representation is an unrepeatable, dated, located "concrete" occurrence.

The distinction between a concrete, particular act with what I am calling its "real" content, and the abstract, "general" content which can be assigned to the act, should be fundamental to the theory of intentionality. The propositional content which can be assigned to an act is "abstract" not just in the sense that it is an object which has no spatiotemporal location, but in the sense that it "abstracts" from some of the concrete reality of the experiential episode. If the propositional content of the act is something that can be shared between different subjects, or something that can be shared in different acts of the same subject, then it is something which abstracts from the particularity of the subject's own condition. The real content, however, is unrepeatable because essentially linked to the state and time of the act's occurrence, and specific to its bearer. In this sense of content, no one other than me can have mental episodes with the content of my mental episodes. Someone could have a very similar experience, of similar things, or even an experience which seemed exactly the same. But that would be to generalize across different concrete experiences, and *describe* the sense in which they are the same. Describing is relating the experience to a propositional content. But this description is an attempt to capture some aspect of how the representation represents the world. It – the description – is not the representation itself.

The ideas involved in experiences – particular, conscious episodes – have content, since they are a case of something being given or conveyed to the subject. But what kind of content do they have? I have argued elsewhere that experiences have nonpropositional content, in the sense that their fundamental way of representing the world is nonpropositional. Nonpropositional content ought not to be mysterious. Many pictures have nonpropositional content: they represent objects and their properties but are not the kind of thing you can use to "say" things. Pictures can have correctness conditions, but there is a difference between a representation having a correctness condition expressed as a proposition and its having a proposition as its content.[43]

Experiences construed in this way have something in common with McDowell's "intuitions." They have nonpropositional content, and their content has a certain kind of unity: as McDowell says, "in a visual intuition, an object is present to a subject with those of its features that are visible to the subject from her vantage point."[44] An intuition is a particular event or occasion of something being brought into view. McDowell insists that the content of an intuition is conceptual, but this is consistent with not *every* aspect of the content actually being conceptualized, or thought about, or made the content of a judgment.[45] The view that not everything that is presented in an experience is conceptualized is one I find very plausible; but I would prefer to call it the view that experience has *non*conceptual content! Judgment (or McDowell's "discursive activity") is the conceptualization of the content of experience.[46] Experiences or McDowell's intuitions "reveal things to be as they would be claimed to be in claims that would be no more than a discursive exploitation of some of the content of the intuition."[47] It is useful to think of conceptualization as the "discursive exploitation" of the content of an experience, which is there to be conceptualized but not necessarily so exploited. And it seems to me that many of those who take themselves to believe that experience has "non-conceptual content" can agree with McDowell here.[48]

Where I depart from McDowell, though, is in taking experience to be representational. I need to explain what I mean by this, although the basic line of thought is familiar. We should start with a basic perceptual phenomenon: the case of seeing. When we see the world, it is quite correct to say that we take in concrete reality. The things we see around us present themselves to us from particular perspectives, in particular conditions of illumination, and in concrete relations to things around us. One possible position is to say that this is all we need to understand experience: what is experienced and the relations in which these things stand to us.[49] If this were so, then there would be no difficulty in explaining how experience takes in concrete reality: for that's what experience is, a relation to the layout of concrete reality. This is the "relational" conception of experience.

The basic idea behind intentionalism, however, is that experience could be essentially the same way without the objects of experience being the way they seem to be. Or: concrete reality need not be the way it seems to be in order to be experienced as being this way. It is this simple idea – the idea which lies behind the arguments from illusion and hallucination – which motivates intentionalists to treat experience as essentially representational. Experience may not seem like a representation, they say, but *if* an experience can be essentially the same despite the change or absence of its objects, then a theory of perception should recognize that this is what it really is.[50]

If experience is a representation – and I don't claim to have given an argument for this view – then it is a concrete, particular event or state of affairs. It represents the experienced world in a particular, concrete way: from this perspective, in these conditions. The conditions of the way it represents the world are specific to the way I am experiencing it now. Suppose I am looking at the pig under the oak in my garden. Of course, someone else can see what I see, they can look at what I look at. But my experience on this particular occasion and the way it represents the world to me now, that is specific to me and to this particular experience.

In the quotation above from Chalmers, he talked of "associating" a content with a state of mind. What makes this "association"? Some philosophers will say that the only way in which something can be a representation is if it is *interpreted* as such, if it can be *assigned* a correctness condition. I assume here that this is false. There can be an intrinsic form of representation which is not simply a matter of the *assignment* of a correctness condition by an interpreter, a matter of something being described as representing something. An experience is, on this view, such a representation. What the assignment of a correctness condition does is to specify one or more of the many ways in which the experience represents the world. But the nature of that experience itself as a representation is what is *described* by the correctness condition; it does not consist in the assignment of a correctness condition.

Another way to put this point is to say that it is not part of the fundamental psychological reality of the act that it is a relation to a proposition. The psychological reality of the act is its reality as a representation; a representation is an intrinsic state (of the person, or the brain, or the soul), and this intrinsic state is something which has a specific, concrete nature of its own. This concrete nature does not consist in some unanalyzed relation to a proposition. That is a theoretical, external description of the state, not what it is in itself.

The position I have described might be criticized on the grounds that it ignores the distinction between *vehicle* and *content* of a representation. It might be said that of course there is a distinction between the particular, concrete event of representing something and the propositional content of that event. But this is just the distinction between the concrete vehicle of representation – the "way" something is represented – and its propositional content. And, the objection runs, my observations above about the concrete nature of experiences are only relevant to the vehicle of perceptual representation, not to their content. Just as the same proposition might be expressed by a sentence or by a picture, so the same proposition might be the content of a belief and the content of an experience: the differences noted above are to do with vehicles, not content. So we do not need an additional "phenomenological" notion of content.

Before responding to this objection, I need to make one clarification. The term "vehicle" has been used for (at least) two different kinds of distinction in ways of representing.[51] One is the distinction between the linguistic and imagistic representation. The other is the distinction between ways in which (say) an image or a linguistic representation can be physically realized. An image, for example, can be realized analogically or digitally. Here I am interested only in the first distinction, and use the word "vehicle" to mark the difference between linguistic and imagistic representation. (I admit that it can be used in the other way too.)

My response to this objection is first to point out that we adopted Siegel's definition of "content" as "what is conveyed to the subject in an experience."[52] If what is conveyed to the subject has a phenomenological dimension – as it surely must have – then it cannot be irrelevant to the content of an experience in this sense that what is conveyed is conveyed in a certain concrete *form*. If the way an experience represents the world has something in common with an image, then this fact is relevant to what is conveyed to the subject in an experience. Compare the debate about visual imagination: if visualizing employs something like images, as has been argued, then this fact is not irrelevant to what is conveyed to the subject in an act of visualizing, and therefore not irrelevant to the content of the act, in the present sense.

In other words, if one is trying to characterize the phenomenology of a particular experiential episode, then it is not irrelevant to that phenomenology that the episode involves a specific kind of "vehicle" in this sense. One might even say that where the phenomenological conception of content is concerned, we should not make the distinction between vehicle and content: it is central to the phenomenology of an experience that what is conveyed to the subject includes its specific vehicle.

## The role of propositions

I have argued that if content pluralism is true, then a theory of perceptual experience needs another phenomenological notion of content, something resembling Frege's "ideas" or Husserl's "real" content. But this is not to deny that certain mental states can also be thought of as relations to propositions. There is nothing wrong with this way of thinking, so long as one thinks of it as a theoretical way of characterizing or describing mental states. One way to do this is by using David Lewis's analogy between numbers and propositions.[53] Lewis proposed that we can think of the way in which propositional attitudes are "relations" to abstract propositions as analogous to the way in which physical magnitudes are "relations" to abstract numbers. Just as the weight of a standard bag of sugar can be thought of as a relation ("weight-in-kilos") between the bag and the number 1, so the belief that Mongolia had the second largest empire in the history of the world can be thought of as a relation ("belief") to the proposition expressed by the sentence "Mongolia had the second largest empire in the history of the world." It is true, literally true, that the weight can be related to this number in this way; but this is not what something's weight fundamentally is. Fundamentally, weight is an intrinsic (or near-intrinsic) property of an object. Similarly, it is literally true that the belief is a relation to a proposition; but this is not what the belief fundamentally is.

What is going on here, it seems to me, is that the concrete belief state is being "modeled" by the abstract proposition. Propositional contents can be used to "model" mental states in the way that (e.g.) relations between numbers can model physical systems, or idealized systems can model target physical systems. Abstract objects of various kinds are assigned to mental states; relationships among these objects parallel relations among the mental states. Propositions can be used as part of the model of a mental state – under the proviso, of course, that there is an element of idealization in any model (this is why, for example, we do not expect a system of a subject's real beliefs to exhibit deductive closure).

I call this the "semantic" conception of content. "Semantic" because the standard practice of formal semantics is to assign objects (e.g. functions, sets, properties) to parts of sentences in an attempt to show how relations between these objects determine the semantic properties (truth or falsehood) of the whole sentences. This is what an interpretation is. To take a simple example: an interpretation might assign a particular object to a name, "$a$," and a set of objects assigned to a predicate "– is $F$," and the sentence "$a$ is $F$" is true just in case the object assigned to the name is a member of the set assigned to the predicate. Interpretations become more complex with propositional attitude states, of course, but the overall aim is to let the relationships between the objects assigned by the interpretation determine the intuitively correct truth-values of the sentences.

In the case of intentional states, different assignments of propositional objects highlight different aspects of the mental state being modeled. We can say this consistently with saying that some kinds of propositional objects do better than others in capturing how things seem to the subject. If we want to express how the world seemed to Oedipus in the complex condition he was in, then we will want to assign a proposition to his desire that does not represent his mother as his mother, for example. This is consistent with assigning the state a *de re* content which relates him to his mother herself. There is no conflict here; it is just an aspect of our complex practice of attitude attribution. Nonetheless, it is also possible to hold that the desire itself is an intrinsic state of the subject which has its own representational nature which is only partly captured by the various ways of relating it to propositions.

In the case of perceptual experience, Christopher Peacocke's well-known theory of "scenario content" is a good example of a style of assignment of content which aims to get close to the way an experience represents the world in all its detail.[54] A scenario in Peacocke's sense is a set of all the ways of filling out the space around the perceiver with objects and properties which is consistent with the correctness of the experience. As such, it attempts to describe much more detail of the real content of an experience than (say) a simple subject–predicate proposition does. But it is still a content in the semantic sense.

Treating relations to propositions as models therefore enables us to see why Chalmers's content pluralism is so plausible. Different kinds of propositional objects can be used to highlight or emphasize different aspects of an experience: some might highlight the fact that the state involves an episode of seeing some particular object, others might highlight the fact that things would seem the same if one were experiencing a distinct but indistinguishable object. Content pluralism allows different kinds of contents to be used in different models. It is the best theoretical representation of our practice of attributing intentional states.

## Conclusion

There is, I have claimed, something like a "given" in experience: it is the phenomenological conception of content ("what is conveyed to the subject"). The propositional content of a perceptual experience is also something that deserves the name of "content." But it must be distinguished from content in the phenomenological sense. The content in the phenomenological sense is something spatiotemporal, concrete, particular, and specific to its subject. The content in the propositional sense is not. There are, therefore, two conceptions of the content of experience, the semantic and the phenomenological. I think that the phenomenological conception has a certain priority, since it is part of what is being modeled. Semantic contents can only be "descriptions" of this content.

I'd like to end with a more general moral. Frege and Husserl both rejected psychologism about logic. Logic cannot be the science of human thought, for familiar reasons. Hence logic is better understood as being about abstract ("ideal") relations between items which are timeless, shareable, and abstract. Many contemporary philosophers join Husserl and Frege in rejecting psychologism about logic. But in embracing a purely semantic conception of the content of experience, they go too far in rejecting psychologism about the psychological. Psychologism about logic is an extreme thesis, and surely false. Psychologism about the psychological, on the other hand, is very likely to be true.[55]

## Notes

1 Lewis, *Mind and the World Order*, p. 52.
2 Ibid.
3 Ibid.
4 Sellars, *Empiricism and the Philosophy of Mind*. As is, surely, H. H. Price's view in *Perception*. Sellars studied with Lewis at Harvard, and with Price in Oxford.
5 Dreyfus, "Overcoming the Myth of the Mental."
6 See McDowell, "Avoiding the Myth of the Given."
7 See Travis, "Reason's Reach"; see McDowell, "Avoiding the Myth of the Given."
8 McDowell, "Avoiding the Myth of the Given," p. 260.
9 Ibid., p. 267.
10 See Brewer, "Perception and Content."
11 McDowell, "Avoiding the Myth of the Given," pp. 264–65.
12 Ibid., p. 264.
13 Travis, "Reason's Reach."
14 McDowell, "Avoiding the Myth of the Given," p. 267.
15 Travis,"Unlocking the Outer World."
16 Travis, "Reason's Reach," p. 235.
17 McDowell, "Avoiding the Myth of the Given," p. 266.
18 Ibid., p. 271.
19 Ibid.
20 I am indebted here to unpublished work by Ciara Fairley.
21 When Moore discusses the view that "blue is said to be part of the content of the 'the sensation of blue,'" he compares a sensation of blue to a blue bead or a blue beard, and says that "the relation of the blue to the consciousness is conceived to be exactly the same as that of the blue to the glass or hair: it is in all three cases the *quality* of a *thing*" (G. E. Moore, "Refutation of Idealism," pp. 447–48).
22 Schlick, "Form and Content," p. 291.
23 Ibid., p. 303.
24 Ibid., p. 306. See also Bernard, *Form and Content*.
25 Siegel, "Contents of Perception" (n.p.).
26 McDowell, "Avoiding the Myth of the Given," p. 264.
27 Ibid., pp. 266–67.
28 Tye, "Representationalist Theories of Consciousness," p. 253.
29 See Crane, "Intentionalism."
30 Byrne, "Perception and Conceptual Content," p. 245.
31 See Crane "Intentionalism."
32 See Fodor, "Propositional Attitudes."
33 See excerpts from Russell and Frege in Moore (ed.), *Meaning and Reference*.
34 Tye, "Nonconceptual Content, Richness, and Fineness of Grain."
35 Chalmers, "Perception and the Fall from Eden."
36 Carruthers, *Phenomenal Consciousness*, p. xiii.
37 Tye, *Ten Puzzles of Consciousness*.
38 Siegel, "Contents of Perception."
39 McDowell, *Mind and World*, p. 54.
40 Here I am especially indebted to Charles Travis's "Unlocking the Outer World," though we somehow end up with very different views (*Current and Recent Work*, Charles Travis's website, https://sites.google.com/site/charlestraviswebsite/Home/current-and-recent-work). Mark Johnston ("Better Than Mere Knowledge?") has

raised some similar criticisms of standard intentionalism, a view which Johnston (rather misleadingly) calls "the fact-directed view."
41 Frege, "On Sense and Reference."
42 For making me see the importance of this analogy, I am indebted again to C. Travis.
43 Crane, "Is Perception a Propositional Attitude?"
44 McDowell, "Avoiding the Myth of the Given," p. 265.
45 Ibid., p. 264.
46 Cf. Crane, "Nonconceptual Content of Experience," p. 155.
47 McDowell, "Avoiding the Myth of the Given," p. 267.
48 This is an oversimplification, since it ignores McDowell's view that the unity of the content of an intuition is the actualization of conceptual capacities, albeit employing formal concepts akin to Kant's categories (see McDowell, "Avoiding the Myth of the Given," p. 265). Discussion of this idea must wait for a later occasion.
49 Brewer, "Perception and Content."
50 This is, of course, what is denied by disjunctivists, but I will not deal with this response in this chapter.
51 Crane, *Mechanical Mind*, ch. 4.
52 Siegel, "Contents of Perception."
53 I understand that the analogy derives from Lewis, but it has been illuminatingly discussed by Field, "Mental Representation," Churchland, "Eliminative Materialism and the Propositional Attitudes," Stalnaker, *Inquiry*, and most recently in an important study by Matthews, *Measure of Mind*.
54 Peacocke, "Scenarios, Concepts and Perception."
55 This chapter derives from lectures given at the Universities of Barcelona (to the LOGOS group), Lausanne, Stockholm, Hertfordshire, St. Andrews, Parma, Warwick (the MindGrad Conference) and at the Institute of Philosophy in London. I am grateful to participants on these occasions for discussions, and especially to Katalin Farkas, Pepa Toribio, and Charles Travis.

## Bibliography

Bernard, H., *Form and Content*, Oxford: Blackwell, 1973.
Brewer, B., "Perception and Content," *European Journal of Philosophy* 14, no. 2 (2006): 165–81.
Byrne, A., "Perception and Conceptual Content," in E. Sosa and M. Steup (eds), *Contemporary Debates in Epistemology*, Oxford: Blackwell, 2005, pp. 231–50.
Carruthers, P., *Phenomenal Consciousness: A Naturalistic Theory*, Cambridge: Cambridge University Press, 2000.
Chalmers, D., "Perception and the Fall from Eden," in T. S. Gendler and J. Hawthorne (eds), *Perceptual Experience*, Oxford: Oxford University Press, 2006, pp. 49–125.
Churchland, P. M., "Eliminative Materialism and the Propositional Attitudes," *Journal of Philosophy* 78, no. 2 (1981): 67–90.
Crane, T., "Intentionalism," in A. Beckerman, B. McLaughlin, and S. Walter (eds), *The Oxford Handbook of Philosophy of Mind*, Oxford: Oxford University Press, 2009, pp. 474–93.
——, "Is Perception a Propositional Attitude?," *Philosophical Quarterly* 59, no. 236 (2009): 452–69.

——, *The Mechanical Mind*, 2nd ed., London: Routledge, 2003.

——, "The Nonconceptual Content of Experience," in T. Crane (edn), *The Contents of Experience: Essays on Perception*, Cambridge: Cambridge University Press, 1992, pp. 136–57.

Dreyfus, H., "Overcoming the Myth of the Mental: How Philosophers Can Profit from the Phenomenology of Everyday Expertise," Presidential Address, *Proceedings and Addresses of the American Philosophical Association* 79, no. 2 (2005): 47–65.

Field, H., "Mental Representation," *Erkenntnis* 13 (1978): 9–18.

Fodor, J., "Propositional Attitudes," in *Representations*, Hassocks: Harvester Press, 1980, pp. 177–203.

Frege, G. "On Sense and Reference" (1892), in P. T. Geach and M. Black (eds), *Translations from the Philosophical Writings of Gottlob Frege*, Oxford: Blackwell, 1952.

Harrison, B., *Form and Content*, Oxford: Blackwell, 1973.

Husserl, E., *Logical Investigations* (1901), trans. J. N. Findlay, London: Routledge, 2001.

Johnston, M., "Better Than Mere Knowledge? The Function of Sensory Awareness," in T. S. Gendler and J. Hawthorne (eds), *Perceptual Experience*, Oxford: Oxford University Press, 2006, 260–90.

Lewis, C. I., *Mind and the World Order*, London: Constable, 1929.

Martin, M. G. F., "The Limits of Self-Awareness," *Philosophical Studies* 120, nos 1–3 (2004): 37–89.

——, "The Transparency of Experience," *Mind and Language* 17, no. 4 (2002): 376–425.

Matthews, R., *The Measure of Mind*, Oxford: Oxford University Press, 2007.

McDowell, J., "Avoiding the Myth of the Given," in *Having the World in View*, Cambridge, MA: Harvard University Press, 2009, pp. 256–72.

——, *Mind and World*, Cambridge, MA: Harvard University Press, 1994.

——, "What Myth?," *Inquiry* 50, no. 4 (2007): 338–51.

Moore, A. W. (ed.), *Meaning and Reference*, Oxford: Oxford University Press, 1993.

Moore, G. E., "The Refutation of Idealism," *Mind* 12, no. 4 (1903): 433–53.

Peacocke, C., "Scenarios, Concepts and Perception," in T. Crane (ed.), *The Contents of Experience: Essays on Perception*, Cambridge: Cambridge University Press, 1992, pp. 105–35.

Price, H. H., *Perception*, London: Methuen, 1932.

Schlick, M., "Form and Content" (1932), in *Moritz Schlick: Philosophical Papers*, vol. II: 1925–36, Dordrecht: Reidel, 1979, 285–369.

Sellars, W., *Empiricism and the Philosophy of Mind*, Cambridge, MA: Harvard University Press, 1956. Reprinted 1997.

Siegel, S., "The Contents of Perception," in E. Zalta (ed.), *Stanford Encyclopedia of Philosophy*, 2005, <http://plato.stanford.edu/archives/win2011/entries/perception-contents/>.

Stalnaker, R., *Inquiry*, Cambridge, MA: MIT Press, 1984.

Travis, C., "Reason's Reach," *European Journal of Philosophy* 15, no. 2 (2007): 225–48.

Tye, M., "Nonconceptual Content, Richness, and Fineness of Grain," in T. S. Gendler and J. Hawthorne (eds), *Perceptual Experience*, Oxford: Oxford University Press, 2006, 504–30.
——, "Representationalist Theories of Consciousness," in A. Beckermann, B. McLaughlin, and S. Walter (eds), *Oxford Handbook of Philosophy of Mind*, Oxford: Oxford University Press, 2009, pp. 253–67.
——, *Ten Puzzles of Consciousness*, Cambridge, MA: MIT Press, 1995.

# 11

# WHAT IS CONCEPTUALLY ARTICULATED UNDERSTANDING?

*Joseph Rouse*

The disagreements between John McDowell and Hubert Dreyfus about whether practical–perceptual coping skills are conceptually articulated turn in significant part on their underlying disagreement about what is at issue and at stake in distinguishing conceptual understanding from non-conceptual capacities. Dreyfus and McDowell are not alone in this failure to settle the subject matter of philosophical reflection upon concepts and conceptual articulation. In recent years, for example, a remarkable sequence of prestigious John Locke Lecturers[1] have presented and defended very different accounts of concepts or the conceptual domain. The disconnection among these views is substantial enough that an observer might wonder whether we philosophers have any idea (or at least any one idea) of what we're talking about when we talk about concepts. My aim is therefore to think through the larger terrain in which the Dreyfus–McDowell debates are situated, and sketch an alternative framing of the issue that draws upon both of their primary concerns.

One of the most important dividing lines among philosophical accounts of the conceptual domain is whether to provide a descriptive or a normative account of conceptually articulated content. Descriptive accounts take conceptual content to be something actually present or operative in specific performances by concept users. Jerry Fodor is exemplary of this approach. He began his book on *Concepts* by saying: "the scientific goal in psychology is to understand what mental representations *are*. ... Nothing about this has changed much, really, since Descartes."[2] To use a concept is to have something in mind, or something causally implicated in what one does; in Fodor's specific version, concept use involves having token mental states that possess representational content.

Normative approaches to conceptual articulation, by contrast, identify the conceptual domain with those performances and capacities that are appropriately assessed according to rational norms. The issue is whether various performances are accountable to reasoned assessment, and can sufficiently stand up to it. Whether something is normatively accountable in this way is then itself a normative issue: the question is whether assessment according to conceptual norms is appropriate, rather than whether it actually occurs. Whether certain kinds of representations or structures are actually contained or causally efficacious in a particular thought or action then does not matter, but only whether that thought or action is sufficiently accessible and potentially responsive to conceptual assessment. As we shall see, this distinction provides an illuminating context for understanding Dreyfus's criticisms of McDowell's claim that conceptual understanding must be pervasive in perception.

Dreyfus's primary concern underlying his criticisms of McDowell has been to show that our most basic perceptual responsiveness to our surroundings consists of a kind of "mindless coping" with situations that are meaningful to us as bodily agents. As active perceivers and agents (perceptual receptivity and skillful activity are not separable on his account), we find ourselves already immersed in the world in ways that solicit a bodily responsiveness. Dreyfus's long-standing criticism of artificial intelligence emphasizes a level of intelligent responsiveness to our surroundings that do not require the use of implicit or explicit representations, reflective deliberation, or even self-consciousness (in the form of a Kantian "I think" or even a Merleau-Pontyan "I can"). Such bodily skillfulness responds to our surroundings as a field of attractions and repulsions, experienced as tension and its release, or a smooth, coordinated bodily "flow." A meaningfully configured situation solicits some responses and repels others, and our bodily comportments are attuned to these solicitations.

Such skilled receptive responsiveness typically must be learned, of course. A novice performer of various human activities often does appeal to rules, and must engage in reflection, but the result is typically stumbling, bumbling performance. Expertise is different (for Dreyfus, however, the kind of expert responsiveness to circumstances that characterizes the high-level performances of chess grandmasters or stellar athletes is not fundamentally different from almost anyone's everyday expertise in negotiating their familiar surroundings perceptually and practically). The achievement of expert skill as a perceiver and agent does not involve the internalization of such rules and reflective considerations but instead bypasses them by developing a direct bodily responsiveness to the overall configuration of a situation. As Dreyfus long ago expressed this point,

> In acquiring a skill ... [there] comes a moment when we finally can perform automatically. At this point we do not seem to be simply dropping these [previously deployed] rules into unconsciousness; rather we seem to have picked up the muscular gestalt which gives our behavior a new flexibility and smoothness. The same holds for acquiring the skill of perception.[3]

For Dreyfus, any attempt to insinuate conceptually articulated representations in the midst of everyday practical–perceptual skills or the extraordinary performances of experts would then be doubly mistaken. Conceptual understanding is *superfluous* wherever we have become skillfully responsive to circumstances, since we can be flexibly and appropriately responsive without any intervening conceptualized representations. Reflective conceptual articulation is also *antagonistic* to skilled engagement with the world: in stopping to think, we would dissolve any smooth-flowing skilled bodily attunement to what is taking place.

These concerns are highlighted in two of Dreyfus's most prominent examples in his arguments against McDowell, namely, blitz chess played at a speed of two seconds/move, and the contrast between baseball player Chuck Knoblauch's expert throwing on difficult plays, and his more frequent failure at simple throws. These two examples function together to indicate the absence of conceptual understanding from skillful coping with one's surroundings, and the potentially deleterious effect on bodily performances when explicit reflection and conceptual articulation do interpolate themselves into one's ongoing involvement in the world. The examples thereby highlight the "mindlessness" of expert understanding, and from that Dreyfus infers its nonconceptual character. With some parallels to animals who are "experts" at negotiating their environment as it solicits their response, expert players of chess or baseball do not have a concept in mind, but instead respond directly to the affordances or solicitations of a situation on the board or field. The point I want to emphasize is that these examples, and the underlying concerns that motivate them, are only relevant challenges to *descriptive* accounts of the conceptual domain. The point of the examples is that expert chess players or second basemen need not, and perhaps cannot, have concepts explicitly or implicitly "in mind," and cannot take up a stance of reflective detachment while they perform well.

That Dreyfus's arguments only challenge descriptive accounts of the conceptual domain is highlighted by a contrast to his former student John Haugeland's exact opposite use of chess and baseball examples.[4] For Haugeland, chess played at any speed exemplifies conceptual normativity. No nonhuman animal can play chess, because no animal grasps the relevant concepts; animals can't recognize pieces and moves, the legality of those moves, or their strategic significance toward winning or losing. Moreover, players' perceptual and practical skills at recognizing positions and making moves must be responsive and accountable to those concepts and the norms they articulate. If not, they would not be playing chess. Haugeland would treat baseball (which he once characterized as the all-star example of intentionality) similarly. Knoblauch's grasp of the concepts of a base, an out, and winning a game is on display in his fielding, even when he is "mindlessly" successful. The relevance of concepts here is normative rather

# WHAT IS CONCEPTUALLY ARTICULATED UNDERSTANDING?

than descriptive. Nothing turns on whether one has a concept in mind, or in brain, but only on whether one's performances are, or can be, held accountable to the relevant standards in the right way. Not surprisingly, then, Haugeland comes down on McDowell's side on whether perception is permeated with conceptual understanding. For Haugeland, as for McDowell, if perception is not conceptual, it is not genuinely perception (or at least "objective perception").

Haugeland's and McDowell's concerns are thus orthogonal to Dreyfus's concerns. This point becomes especially clear if we consider how Haugeland's arguments against the possibility of a biologically based understanding of human intentionality (including our ability to play chess and to perceive chess pieces and positions) also provides a decisive consideration against treating expert chess play, and other forms of skilled perceptual–practical responsiveness, as nonconceptual.[5] Haugeland argued that biological functioning can only articulate whatever patterns in the world that it *actually* responds to normally, even if those patterns are gerrymandered from the perspective of a conceptually articulated understanding. For example, a bird whose evolved perceptual responses led it to avoid eating most yellow butterflies, except for one oddly mottled pattern of yellow, would not thereby have made a *mistake* about the color of the mottled yellow ones. Moreover, even if those response patterns were de facto coextensive with conceptually significant features of the world, such that the birds always and only avoided yellow butterflies, those patterns would not display an intentional directedness toward the butterflies' color, for that result would merely be a de facto contingency. For Haugeland, intentional directedness must introduce a possible gap between what is meant and what is actually encountered, such that there is a possibility of error. Even if the avoidance response were actually coextensive with the butterflies' color, a counterfactual query would still be telling: if there *were* to be a shade or pattern of yellow that the birds' normal functioning would not lead it to avoid, would it have any means of self-correction?[6] Haugeland concluded that

> [t]he trouble with the insectivorous birds is that there is no definition of that to which they are *supposed* to respond except as that to which they *do* respond when everything is functionally in order. ... The colors of the butterflies have no normative status at all apart from their involvement in that normal functioning.[7]

Now consider a grandmaster playing blitz chess. The grandmaster's ability to recognize and respond almost instantaneously to complex patterns on the chess board is the outcome of an extended "selective" regime (artificial selection involving study of past games leading to recognition of significant configurations, rather than natural selection operating on a population). To the extent that we are simply talking, as Dreyfus insists we are, about a felt responsiveness to complex perceptual configurations experienced as tensions and solicitations, then the grandmaster's play allows no space for the occasional strategic or even constitutive error. Grandmasters playing blitz chess do make errors, of course. Yet Dreyfus's account of skilled coping as ground-floor nonconceptual intentionality cannot recognize them as errors, but only as responses that are abnormal for grandmasters. They would only be errors if the conceptually articulated regulative and strategic norms of chess play already constitutively governed the pattern-recognition capacities involved. This point would be especially telling wherever there are board patterns that frequently elicit mistakes even from expert players in blitz chess. Just as "there is nothing that the [bird's] response can 'mean' other than whatever *actually* elicits it in normal birds in normal conditions,"[8] so if Dreyfus were right that expert chess play were nonconceptual, there is nothing that a "normal" grandmaster's blitz chess play could mean other than what grandmasters normally do in various actual board configurations. Any patterns that characteristically trouble blitzing grandmasters could only be recognized (from without, by conceptually reflective systems that actually understand and deploy chess concepts and standards) as design limitations in their trained cognitive orientation, rather than errors in play (and of course, the counterfactual case of obscure positions that might not be arrived at in the ordinary run of play would be relevant here as well). Dreyfus takes for granted that grandmasters are playing *chess* at a rapid pace, but he is not entitled to that claim unless their play is informed by and accountable to the conceptually articulated norms of the game. If he were right about expert chess play, then experts would not be playing chess, but only an oddly gerrymandered simulacrum of the game.

Yet precisely because Dreyfus relies upon an entirely different way of thinking about conceptual understanding than Haugeland or McDowell do, their points about these examples are compatible. Dreyfus should agree with Haugeland and McDowell that grandmasters playing blitz chess must *understand* the concepts of rooks, moves along ranks and files, and winning, and must recognize that their play is accountable to that understanding. Haugeland and McDowell could and do agree with Dreyfus that such conceptually articulated abilities can be and often are executed without explicitly attending to or reflecting upon a concept or its application. Moreover, Haugeland does, and McDowell could, endorse a further component of Dreyfus's concern, namely that many of the patterns actually recognizable by grandmasters (and other skilled perceivers) may have no higher-order articulation than that constituted by the ability to recognize them, and hence that such skillful recognition is irreplaceable by any rule-governed system.[9] Indeed, Wayne Martin uses the example of blitz chess precisely to dissociate conceptual normativity and the judgments that express it from explicit or reflective application of concepts:

## WHAT IS CONCEPTUALLY ARTICULATED UNDERSTANDING?

> In [playing speed chess] I make judgments – I reach a conclusion that is in some sense responsive to evidence – even though I don't undertake any conscious deliberation and I experience my judgment as issuing more-or-less instantaneously.[10]

What matters for a normative account of conceptual understanding and judgment, such as those advocated by McDowell, Haugeland, or Martin, is not whether concepts are explicitly represented or employed in the course of one's actual performances. The issue is only whether those performances are accountable and responsive to the relevant conceptual norms. Conceptual understanding involves the possibility of reflection, and subsequent revision and repair of its associated practical/perceptual skills, but it need not be identified with any present component of the exercise of those skills. In that context, Dreyfus's examples would serve a different inferential role than he has proposed. They would not exemplify a domain of skillful practice in which concepts and rational norms are not yet operative. Instead, they would contribute to the phenomenology of conceptual understanding.[11] As such, they would serve as counterexamples to any claim that explicit representation or conscious deliberation is essential to conceptual understanding, ruling out some specific *accounts* of conceptual understanding, rather than limiting the *scope* of conceptual understanding as Dreyfus proposed.

Once we have recognized the extent of McDowell's and Dreyfus's agreement about what centrally concerns each of them, the question still remains of how we should demarcate the domain of conceptual understanding. Why should we choose to give a normative rather than a descriptive account of conceptual understanding? Their disagreement about how to use the term "conceptual" is not merely verbal, despite the extent of the agreement that I have identified between them. At stake here are which phenomena belong together in philosophically significant classifications, and what task philosophers should undertake in thinking about intentionality and conceptual understanding. In what follows, I will use some central considerations from Dreyfus's work to argue for something more akin to McDowell's normative approach to demarcating the conceptual domain. Instead of following Dreyfus in thinking of practical/perceptual coping as a distinct, preconceptual "ground floor" of intentionality, or following McDowell in simply taking our responsibility to conceptual norms to be pervasive even in perception, I shall argue that we should think of conceptual understanding as itself involving practical–perceptual skills in ways that build upon Dreyfus's account.

To begin thinking about the possibility of recognizing how conceptual understanding might itself have a practical–perceptual dimension, consider our ability to utter grammatical, meaningful sentences in a natural language. On anyone's view, I think, uttering sentences in a natural language is an exemplary case of a conceptually articulated performance. One can imitate such performances without grasping conceptual norms – think of Sellars's example of a parrot trained to utter sounds that resemble "that's red" whenever visually confronting something red[12] – but one cannot actually utter a *sentence* without understanding both that it is a meaningful sentence and to some extent what it means (we would thus conclude about the parrot that it makes a noise that resembles the utterance of a sentence, but does not thereby utter the sentence). Yet this familiar practical performance of uttering meaningful sentences offers clear analogs to Dreyfus's examples of blitz chess and overreflective throwing of baseballs. We sometimes speak very rapidly, so much so that we cannot explicitly think about what we want to say, but instead discover what we are saying as we say it. The all too well-known phenomenon of being "tongue-tied" parallels the latter case, and here, too, there is sometimes a connection between reflection and loss of fluency: sometimes we become tongue-tied precisely when we stop to consider our words more carefully. Rapid, fluent conversation is not explicitly "mindful" of the concepts it expresses. Speakers can respond fluently and smoothly to the solicitations of the conversational situation, and often discover what they have to say only when they say it. Such talk is not thereby preconceptual or nonconceptual.

Dreyfus has long been ambivalent about recognizing that the production and consumption of linguistic expressions are practical–perceptual phenomena analogous to other examples of skilled coping. He has on occasion cited examples of learning a second language as exemplary cases of practical–perceptual expertise, and has frequently cited the ability to disambiguate natural-language expressions as an example of the kind of nonformal understanding characteristic of human beings that cannot be reproduced by digital computation.[13] Yet he also strongly resists assimilation of the kinds of practical–perceptual skills involved in recognizing or producing meaningful sentences to those that are involved in other kinds of skilled or even expert performance. Responding "mindlessly" to the solicitations of chess positions in blitz chess with rapid-fire moves, and responding to the solicitations of a conversation with rapid-fire utterances, have to remain distinct kinds of skilled performance for Dreyfus if he is to maintain his preferred distinctions between levels of involvement in a meaningful situation, and especially between preconceptual and conceptually articulated performances.[14] Unless he can maintain a clear and relevant distinction between the kinds of understanding involved in our everyday linguistic performances and those enabling other forms of practical–perceptual coping with one's surroundings, then it will be very difficult to sustain his insistence upon a practical–perceptual "ground floor" of intentionality shared with animals and infants that is distinct from the conceptually articulated and reflective "upper floors" of intentional comportment.

I have elsewhere argued that conversational and other discursive performances should be understood as forms of practical–perceptual responsiveness to circumstances that should not be differentiated from other kinds of "skilled coping."[15] Rather than recapitulate this prior disagreement with Dreyfus, however, I want to situate it in a broader context that might illuminate his debates with McDowell in a more encompassing way. Dreyfus acknowledges that once conceptually articulated linguistic ability is in play, "all coping is permeated by it,"[16] which among other things would enable our perceptual experience to bear evidentially upon our discursive performances.[17] This recognition points toward a high-level parallel between Dreyfus's phenomenological account of intentionality and many advocates of a normative account of conceptual understanding. Both treat conceptual content as a rational form somehow imposed upon a preconceptual, arational material granted us by nature. For Dreyfus, or for his phenomenological fellow-traveler and sometime coauthor Samuel Todes,[18] this preconceptual domain is a skillful bodily responsiveness to already meaningful perceptual affordances or solicitations, and the relevant preconceptual "nature" is biological, marking our common heritage with other animals.[19] For Brandom, Davidson, or even McDowell, conceptual normativity is instead something we bring to bear upon what is also in the space of causes, or the domain of natural law. Nature (or "first nature" for McDowell) in the relevant sense is physical nature, and it is not already meaningful.[20]

Despite this important difference between Dreyfus and these advocates of a normative understanding of concepts, all of these moves nevertheless confront the same kind of familiar but intractable problem. Once a domain is conceived as impervious to conceptual normativity, whether as empiricist Given, skillful coping, Kantian noumena, or natural law, there is no way to bring that domain back into assessable relations to concepts. I will not argue for that claim here. Many versions of this problem are well known, with Sellars or perhaps Hegel as the classical source.[21] A similar claim provides McDowell's central motivation for insisting upon the pervasiveness of conceptual norms. I have argued elsewhere[22] why McDowell is right to attribute this problem to Davidson, and why similar problems arise for Brandom and McDowell in turn, and will not recapitulate those arguments here. I will instead give further consideration to how and why the problem arises, and how we might circumvent it.

Two characteristic issues confront any account of the conceptual domain. Conceptual understanding incorporates both the articulation of conceptual content, and the maintenance of its normative force or authority. Broadly speaking, these two issues correspond to two directions of philosophical approach to the issue. Some naturalistically inclined philosophers trace the normative force of conceptual understanding to causal relations or functional roles within the context of natural selection. Conceptual content must then accrue to whatever elements actually play the relevant causal or functional roles. These approaches yield descriptive accounts of conceptual content, which typically proceed, in Dretske's instructive phrase, by trying to "bake a normative cake out of nonnormative ingredients." I believe that the history of such efforts, and the reflective critical analyses prompted by their recurrent failures, suggest that they will always remain half-baked, but again, I will not argue for that claim here.

An alternative approach, characteristic of most normative accounts of conceptual understanding, begins by explicating conceptual content holistically as an abstractly describable pattern. Familiar versions of this strategy include the patterns emerging from Dennett's intentional stance, Davidson's recursive truth-theoretic radical interpretation, or Brandom's model of discursive scorekeeping. In each case, a merely abstract relational pattern supposedly acquires both genuine *content* and normative force together, through its causal involvement. Causal involvement takes various forms: predictive success for Dennett, token identity for Davidson, or Brandom's incorporation of externalist reliability within his semantic inferentialism. Haugeland tellingly characterized all of these approaches as "interrelationist": to be content-conferring, these patterns must be distinguishable, but inseparable, from their actual causal realization.[23] The intractable problem has been to secure both the causal and normative roles of these interrelations.

Philosophers continue to reiterate these two alternatives of naturalistic reduction or holistic causal–normative interrelation despite what I take to be characteristic and well-known difficulties. I think this persistent recurrence reflects a widespread inability to imagine an alternative apart from reversion to logical or transcendental idealism. Yet I think Dreyfus's and Todes's appropriation and development of Heidegger and Merleau-Ponty on perceptual praxis suggests a different way to circumvent this apparent impasse. They show how practical–perceptual involvement with the world is already normative and reflective teleological.[24] I therefore propose to explore the possibility of understanding conceptual articulation and understanding as itself an extended form of practical–perceptual coping with surrounding circumstances.

As I already noted, Dreyfus resists this possibility, as does Todes's[25] amalgamation of Merleau-Ponty and Kant, each insisting upon a fundamental difference in kind between conceptually articulated thought and nonconceptual perceptual practice. They do so, however, while trying to graft their phenomenological accounts of perceptual praxis to untenable and unsuitable accounts of conceptual understanding. Todes identified conceptual understanding with what Frank Jackson later called "representational structures that somehow effect a partition in the possibilities ... independent of how things are,"[26] such that "the real world is conceived as one sort of world among many other equally possible worlds."[27]

While Dreyfus explicitly invites others to conjoin his view of perception to Sellarsian normative accounts of conceptual sapience, his actual arguments instead presume something akin to Fodor's or Searle's descriptive accounts of conceptual content as occurrent properties of mental states[28] (that is why he argues primarily for the "mindlessness" of practical–perceptual coping, rather than for its independence of the normative authority of conceptual understanding). Neither of these assimilations is promising. Each requires grafting a descriptive–determinative account of conceptual content onto a normative, reflective-teleological account of practical–perceptual coping.

I propose that we consider shifting the form of the problem. We should not start, as Brandom or Davidson do, with a distinguishable structure of conceptually articulated thought, and ask how it is effectively and accountably related to an antecedent, causal or practical–perceptual engagement with the world. The issue is instead to understand how practical–perceptual engagement itself becomes conceptually articulated and thereby contentful.[29] In the remainder of this chapter, I will indicate some of the challenges confronting this way of thinking about conceptual understanding, and some possible directions for how to respond.

This approach shares a "bottom–up" strategy with naturalists like Dretske or Millikan, but from a very different starting point, toward a very different end. I will only briefly mention three aspects of what I take to be required to get the starting point right. The first is to understand organisms teleologically, as directed toward the goal of maintaining and reproducing their characteristic life-cyclical pattern under changing circumstances.[30] Second, that life-cyclical pattern does not distinguish the organism's form of life from its environmental niche, but is instead a unified phenomenon that one might call (by extension from Heidegger) *in-der-Umwelt-Sein*. Neither an organism's environment, nor its characteristic ways of "being-in" it, can be adequately characterized independently. Third, I take from Dreyfus and Todes the recognition that practical–perceptual activity has a reflective rather than determinative teleology: its intentional fulfillment would not be a predetermined goal or condition toward which it aims, but is instead an indefinite exploration toward what Dreyfus sometimes calls an "optimal grip," translating Merleau-Ponty's "maximum prise."

The fundamental difficulty facing any such attempt to understand conceptual articulation as bodily praxis has been succinctly expressed by John Haugeland, in the arguments about biological functionality that I referred to above. The worry is that biological normativity or teleology is incapable of articulating conceptual *content*: "there can be no biological basis for understanding a system as functioning properly, but nevertheless misinforming. ... There is nothing that [a behavioral] response can 'mean' other than whatever *actually* elicits it in normal [organisms] in normal conditions."[31]

Haugeland argues that biological functionality is too closely tied to its actual environments, and thus lacks what Heidegger called transcendence: it cannot intend anything beyond the pattern of its normal responsiveness. I think Haugeland thereby rightly characterized the limits of nondiscursive organisms' practical–perceptual responsiveness to environmental affordances. So I think the challenge is to understand how the emergence of *discursive* practice from nondiscursive activity could make a difference, without in effect magically invoking a *"lingua ex machina."*

Appeals to language in this context often seem like cheating, because most philosophers who exploit the connection between language use and conceptual understanding invoke a very thin conception of language. Language is typically identified with some relatively abstract or formal structure (or an equally abstract interpretive activity). This structure must of course be concretely realized in the actual, situated production and consumption of token utterances, and in its ultimate accountability to the world. But when someone like Brandom insists that "Standard discursive practices are solid (even lumpy)," all he means, as he goes on to say, is "that they involve [relations to] actual objects and states of affairs."[32] The practical–perceptual skills of speakers and listeners, their bodily involvement in the world, and the social-institutional settings in which their skills are exercised, typically play no role in such philosophical conceptions of language. Even relations to objects are often tacked on at the margins as perceptual or practical entrances and exits to language proper, which is conceived as consisting in wholly "intralinguistic" performances treated as if they were disembodied.

What would it mean to understand discursive practice as not merely interrelated with practical–perceptual coping with the world, but to adapt Haugeland's distinction, "intimately" embedded in it, where "the term 'intimacy' ... suggests a kind of *commingling* or *integralness* of mind, body, and world – that is, to undermine their very distinctness."[33] I can discuss this enormous topic all to briefly here, but I will enumerate several prominent aspects of how to approach it.

First, discursive practice must involve the acquisition and exercise of subtle and difficult practical–perceptual skills. Anyone who visits another linguistic community with little or no grasp of the language knows the difficulty of perceiving the semantically significant phonemic articulation of a spoken language, and producing it fluently. Wittgenstein said that if a lion could talk, we couldn't understand him;[34] more importantly, we couldn't even *hear* what he was saying (i.e. recognize the semantically significant sonic patterns), let alone be able to roar back. Acquiring language *is* in significant part acquiring a complex orientation and set of ear, tongue, eyes, and body. Semantics and phonemics are not so readily separable from these practical–perceptual capacities, since part of what enables one to recognize highly variant reproductions as instantiating the same phonemic pattern is grasping its semantic relevance. This point cannot be reduced to the theory-ladenness of perception without begging the question, however, since what I am proposing is that the "theory" in question *is* this practical–perceptual pattern.

Second, language use is also thickly embedded in complex social relations. Consider as just one example the familiar philosophical treatments of names, often thought to be among the simplest discursive phenomena. From early Wittgenstein to Kripke, names have been understood as something like tags conventionally connected to objects. Yet Patricia Hanna and Bernard Harrison remind us that naming requires much more intricately articulated practices:

> To give a name is ... to reveal, in the ordinary way of things, a label that has been used for many years, through occurrences of tokens of it in the context of many naming practices, to trace, or track, one's progress through life. Such [mutually referring practices include] the keeping of baptismal rolls, school registers, registers of electors; the editing and publishing of works of reference of the *Who's Who* type, the inscribing of names, with attached addresses, in legal documents, certificates of birth, marriage, and death, and so on.[35]

Nowadays, of course, Google searches are preeminent among all of these name-tracking practices. But the larger point is that naming and understanding names cannot and does not make sense apart from its embeddedness in such a "name-tracking network" of social practices. Moreover, as Kukla and Lance have powerfully argued, names are also caught up in the essentially second-person indexical character of discursive practice.[36] Perry argued for the "essential indexicality" of location and orientation, without which third-person descriptive facts are free-floating.[37] Kukla and Lance insist upon the equally essentially indexical call-and-response pattern of discursive practice. If I cannot grasp that you are talking to *me* in ways that solicit me to acknowledge and respond (in ways that also impose a defeasible social obligation), I am not a competent discursive practitioner. This vocative character of discourse is a central part of its ineliminably practical–perceptual character.

Third, learning a first language *is* learning to get a distinctive practical–perceptual hold on circumstances. We do not first recognize a certain class of circumstances, and then attach words to them. The ongoing practice of using the word is instead part of the circumstances that we learn to negotiate in picking up on a discursive practice. Wittgenstein highlighted this point in one of the most important passages in the *Investigations*:

> What's it like for him to come? – The door opens, someone walks in, and so on. – What's it like for me to expect him to come? – I

walk up and down the room, look at the clock now and then, and so on. – But the one set of events has not the smallest similarity to the other! ... It is in language that an expectation and its fulfillment make contact.[38]

We overlook this entanglement of our understanding of language and our practical–perceptual grasp of circumstances, in part because we tend to equate language-learning with learning a second language. Second-language learning can be relatively "thin" at first, because the world already has a discursively articulated grip upon us as language users. Only when attending to subtleties do we discover how much a thin conception of a language overlooks among the skills embedded in our practical mastery of its uses in context. Think, for example, of the differences between the uses of prepositions in various natural languages, for which it is hard to disentangle an understanding of which circumstances call for that word rather than another from a native speaker's grasp of which word sounds right to a discursively trained ear.

Philosophers marginalize these phenomena that highlight the practical–perceptual concreteness of discursive practice, perhaps because we have been rightly but overly impressed with the expressive resources of logic and linguistics. The insights from these more formal disciplines encourage a misleading reversal in the order of understanding. Philosophers tend to see formal relations as a framework around which the bodily and socially interactive aspects of discursive practice are built. We should instead understand these powerful expressive resources as abstracted from and presupposing immersion in a natural language as an integral part of the world we inhabit. Sellars and Brandom started this reversal by emphasizing the priority of material inference over formal logic.[39] Formal relations let us say explicitly what we already know how to do in grasping concepts, but cannot substitute for that capacity even in principle. I think we need to extend this move, by recognizing that the material-inferential proprieties that govern our use of words in turn presuppose a rich practical–perceptual grasp of the ongoing discursive practice that constitutes a natural language.

In giving philosophical priority to the practical–perceptual dimension of discursive practice, we would thereby reorient our understanding of language, from a formal structure that *interfaces* with practical–perceptual coping, to an ongoing activity *integral* to the unified phenomenon of skillful responsiveness to a human environment. Biologically, language would thereby show up as a characteristically human form of niche construction.[40] Human beings develop in a world pervaded by discursive performances, and our practical–perceptual capabilities are shaped through that development. This claim philosophically foregrounds the widely known fact that humans do not acquire discursive capacities unless actually exposed to an extant discursive practice during their crucially formative years. Language then becomes a preeminent example of the intimate entanglement of human bodily skills with specific, concrete features of our (historically constructed) human environment; the uses of words are prominent aspects of that environment.[41]

It is not terribly controversial by itself to recognize that language can be understood as developed practical–perceptual coping with a discursively articulated environmental niche. What is controversial is to try to understand the conceptual contentfulness of discursive practice at this level of description. Understood in those terms, why wouldn't language just be a complicated form of biologically adaptive behavior? Our utterances would then be merely noises that, recalling Haugeland's telling remark, "can 'mean' [nothing] other than what normally elicits [them] in normal circumstances."[42] If language and thought are just more complex forms of practical–perceptual coping, how could there be a gap between what our utterances or thoughts mean, and what they actually respond to, or in traditional terms, between sense and reference? The worry is that responses to the utterances of others would then be no more contentful than are the mutually responsive vocalizations within flocks of birds or herds of sheep. Put another way, treating conceptual understanding as practical–perceptual may seem to recapitulate the objective side of the Kantian dualism that sharply separates understanding ourselves in causal–functional terms as objects, from understanding ourselves as thoughtful concept-mongers.

Adequately developed answers to these challenges would require work on a rather different scale than this chapter. I will instead conclude by pointing toward some of the considerations that make it both plausible and promising to treat conceptual understanding not only as pervasive within perception and practical coping with the world, but as practically–perceptually constituted. In doing so, we would follow McDowell in providing a normative account of conceptual understanding (while acknowledging Dreyfus's insistence that this understanding can be deployed "mindlessly" and nonthematically). Yet we would also extend Dreyfus's account of practical–perceptual skillfulness to incorporate the capacities for conceptual articulation that accompany the acquisition of a language. We would only challenge as mistaken Dreyfus's separation of discursive and nondiscursive practical–perceptual skills as coextensive with conceptual and nonconceptual domains.

As a first consideration toward enabling such an account, I note that the difference between animals' responsiveness to their environment and human conceptual understanding is often overstated on both ends. On the one hand, many animals are responsive to fairly high-level environmental affordances, and their responsive repertoire is often quite flexible. The problem is not that there is *no* opening between what their actions and expressions mean or aim for, and what they normally respond to, but only that this opening is vague and unarticulated. As Okrent observed about one famous case, "there is simply no answer to the question of whether the aim of the [frog's flicking of its tongue] is to catch a fly, or an edible flying insect, or an edible insect."[43] As Heidegger put a similar point in very different terms, nonhuman animals are "world-poor," not worldless.[44]

As a second consideration coming from the other direction, many philosophers overestimate the transparency and openness of human conceptual thought. The capacity for understanding is more closely bound to the discriminations and articulations available within extant discursive practices than most philosophers are prepared to recognize. This recognition is a central and not fully assimilated achievement of the tradition stemming from Quine and Davidson, and the different tradition stemming from Heidegger. Philosophers from Jonathan Bennett to Frank Jackson have expressed dismay over Davidson's willingness to "explain *true* in terms of *language I know*,"[45] or Quine's denial that we can "effect a partition of the possibilities independently of how things actually are."[46] Jackson and Bennett would be just as appalled by the emphasis placed by philosophers such as Heidegger or Merleau-Ponty upon the way even conceptually articulated understanding is situated within a bodily involvement in the world that cannot be fully transparent to reflection. Despite these expressions of philosophical dismay at the finitude of conceptual understanding, I think that Davidson, Quine, and Heidegger were right, and that Davidson and Quine, at least, did not take this point far enough.

Yet there remains a genuine issue to confront in understanding the difference between nonhuman animals' vague and inarticulate disclosure of their environment, and our discursively articulated world. Much of the literature on the evolution of human cognition appropriately draws attention to our ability to discriminate and coordinate multiple perceptual cues, and respond to them with extraordinary flexibility.[47] Yet no degree of complexity and flexibility in responsiveness to environmental cues is sufficient by itself to constitute a conceptually articulated grasp. Flexible behavior and high-level affordances complicate what organisms actually respond to, without ever making sense of that responsiveness as directed toward and accountable to possibilities. Three interrelated features of discursive practice nevertheless can take us a long way toward accounting for this difference without abstracting conceptual thought from practical–perceptual embeddedness in the world.

The first of these three important features of discursive practice is the partial decoupling of discursive performances from their immediate nonverbal circumstances. The perceptual and expressive repertoire that one acquires in learning a natural language is extraordinarily large and open-ended, and much of its deployment is cued intralinguistically. Although language use ultimately acquires meaning holistically by contributing to our overall practical–perceptual involvement in the world, any specific

## WHAT IS CONCEPTUALLY ARTICULATED UNDERSTANDING?

utterance is crucially mediated by intralinguistic connections. Here it matters to my proposal that language is not a general-purpose cognitive capacity. Its articulative possibilities are biased toward some domains of human expressive and responsive activity, and our linguistic abilities develop alongside other capacities that are not so readily articulable linguistically. Dor and Jablonka summarize this partiality well:

> The expressive envelopes of different languages are different in interesting and subtle ways, but they all share a common core. ... Interestingly, many of the messages which turn out to be very difficult to communicate through language seem to be very well suited for communication through other means of communication: we can *mime* and *dance* them, use *facial expressions* and *body language* to express them, *paint* and *draw* them, write and play *music*, prepare *charts* and *tables*, write *mathematical formulae*, screen *movies* and *videos*, and so on.[48]

Not only did we start out with nonlinguistic cognitive and expressive capacities alongside the emergence of language, but those capacities have also proliferated and further developed. I think that Dreyfus's own recognition of this important point, coupled with a mistaken inclination to equate conceptual articulation with explicit expression in language, has been an important motivation for his resistance to McDowell's claim that conceptual normativity is pervasive in human engagement with the world.

We can recognize why it would be a mistake to equate conceptual articulation with linguistic expression when we acknowledge that language is not a self-contained practical–perceptual domain. Our linguistic discursive practices open onto and "incorporate" other sensory/cognitive/performative capacities, via recognitive, demonstrative, anaphoric, and indexical locutions, even while they are themselves only intelligible as an integral part of our biological capacities for practical–perceptual interaction with our surroundings. Yet the possibility of understanding of conceptual normativity as practical–perceptual skill depends precisely upon conceiving language as such a semiautonomous practice. The possibility of a gap between what our expressive performances "mean" or "intend," and how those performances are involved with our actual surroundings, depends upon such semiautonomy. We belong to a complex set of practices ("language") that is both based in and accountable to our multiply intra-active involvements in the world, and yet which also enables the extensive articulation of patterns that are initially accountable primarily to other "intralinguistic" performances. The availability of a semiautonomous and open-ended domain of expressive activity is crucial to introducing a gap between what we mean and what we actually or typically do. Yet precisely because discursive practice is embedded within and understood through our overall practical–perceptual life, it does not become a merely self-contained activity, a "frictionless spinning in a void" in McDowell's picturesque phrase.[49] Language makes conceptually articulated understanding possible, and pervasive in human life, but the conceptually articulated normativity that language enables extends far beyond the more localized domain that is readily expressible within language.

The vocative character of discursive practice that Kukla and Lance emphasize[50] is a second crucial feature for understanding how conceptual normativity can be understood as practical–perceptual coping with our surroundings. Discursive performances are addressed to an audience, and can be recognized by competent performers *as* addressing them. Such recognition is itself a complex skill with a richly practical–perceptual dimension. Recognizing the ineliminably vocative dimension of discourse helps overcome the philosophical prejudice that reduces language use to assertion, as Kukla and Lance emphasize throughout. Yet the vocative aspect of utterances also makes their links to past and future utterances internal to what the utterance itself does. These links reinforce the partial decoupling from surrounding circumstances that makes discursive practice semiautonomous. Moreover, vocative ability is integral to normative accountability more generally, allowing us to call others to account and to be called. Finally, this vocative dimension of our utterances combines with the emergence of a reflexive semantic apparatus to allow us a still more finely articulated expressive capacity.

The final and most important feature of discursive practice that I emphasize, however, is its distinctive teleology. What most limits the articulative capacity of animal behavior is its determinative teleology. The relative inflexibility of the goal with respect to which animal behavior is intelligible limits its capacity to *mean* more than what it normally *does*. Here I take seriously Okrent's claim that the goal of an organism's behavior is the ongoing reproduction of its characteristic way of life.[51] In the human case, however, the open-endedness of discursively mediated niche construction is integral to our way of life. Thus, who we are is at issue in our interactions with our surroundings and one another. We do what we do, and are what we are, only with respect to issues that remain unsettled and ahead of us. Thus, human behavior is not merely instrumentally intelligible in its directedness toward a determinate way of "making a living" as an organism. It is expressively intelligible in its collective, interactive, and reflexive directedness toward what Heidegger called a "for-the-sake-of-which." It is this reflexively open-ended teleology of our discursive practical–perceptual capacities that allows us to hold one another and ourselves accountable to conceptually articulated possibilities, rather than just to normal patterns of response to surroundings. Heidegger rightly called attention to practical equipmental contexts as a locus for such purposiveness without a purpose.[52] Yet discursive practice is itself the pervasive equipmental context in human development and activity, without which it would be incomprehensible how we could sustain these other practices that assign roles and appropriate uses to equipment.

In proposing these first steps toward a merger of Dreyfus's account of practical–perceptual coping skills with McDowell's emphasis upon the pervasiveness of conceptual normativity, I have not tried to answer the question of how a freely spontaneous conceptual understanding comes to bear upon perceptual receptivity or skillful practical–perceptual coping. I instead proposed to reformulate that question, by asking how practical–perceptual coping with our surroundings is itself the locus of conceptual articulation. Conceptual understanding is not something external to our practical–perceptual involvement in the world, that would then have to become "operative" in perception. Conceptually articulated discursive practice is a distinctive way in which practical–perceptual bodily skills can develop through an extended process of niche construction and coevolution of languages and language users.[53] If this way of thinking about conceptual understanding can be worked out successfully, then an important way in which the Dreyfus–McDowell debates would matter is by providing philosophical access to this previously unexplored approach to understanding conceptual normativity.

## Notes

An earlier version of this chapter was presented to the meeting of the International Society for Phenomenological Studies (ISPS) in Pacific Grove, California, in July 2007, and some additional passages were drawn from a subsequent presentation to the ISPS in July 2009. I am grateful to the Society for this opportunity for critical responses, and to the audience on both occasions for very helpful comments and criticism.

1 McDowell, *Mind and World*; Fodor, *Concepts*; Jackson, *From Metaphysics to Ethics*; and Brandom, *Between Saying and Doing*.
2 Fodor, *Concepts*, p. vii.
3 Dreyfus, *What Computers Can't Do*, pp. 248–49.
4 Haugeland, *Having Thought*.
5 Ibid., ch. 13.
6 Haugeland himself uses such a counterfactual thought experiment to a similar end at the conclusion of "Objective Perception," in *Having Thought*, by imagining a dog who seems able to recognize and distinguish different members of the same family, but is incapable of responding appropriately to the (impossible) counterfactual situation in which the family members' individual physiognomic properties were redistributed among them. So long as such a system is exposed only to the actual conditions to which its development is already adapted, it can seem intentionally directed (and seem to track conceptually significant differences), but its inability to respond appropriately under extraordinary circumstances exposes the illusion. Haugeland's strategy here ironically parallels Dreyfus's own earlier objections (*What Computers Can't Do*) to the alleged intentional directedness of AI programs like Roger Schank's restaurant scripts, which could not handle counterfactual circumstances for which they were not already

designed (e.g. Schank's restaurant scripts' inability to answer questions about whether the waiter is wearing clothes).
7 Haugeland, Having Thought, p. 314.
8 Ibid., p. 310.
9 Such cases nevertheless only count as "recognition" and as "skill" because of their conformity to the rules of chess, and their conduciveness to successful play. They are conceptually responsive even though there are no extant concepts that express them generically. Cases of recognition skills that do not correlate with already-articulated linguistic terms or phrases are in this respect like colors that we can discriminate, but have not named, which McDowell has often discussed. For McDowell, the conceptual domain extends beyond the explicit classificatory concepts already at our disposal, which is why anaphoric, demonstrative, and indexical expressions are integral to the linguistic expression of conceptual understanding.
10 Martin, Theories of Judgment, p. 2.
11 On several occasions during their conversations, Dreyfus asked McDowell how the pervasiveness of conceptual norms in perception is actually experienced by perceivers. On the line I am suggesting, McDowell's response should be that Dreyfus himself has actually already described that experience on his behalf. In many cases, including Dreyfus's favorite examples, we experience our responsiveness and accountability to conceptual norms as a kind of "mindless coping" in which we are not thematically aware of concepts, or engaged in reflective assessment. Nevertheless, we also understand that our performances are accountable to norms that could be applied reflectively, and how to bring such norms to bear, even when we do not actually do so, and have no concepts explicitly or implicitly in mind.
12 Sellars, Empiricism and the Philosophy of Mind.
13 Dreyfus, What Computers Can't Do; Dreyfus and Dreyfus, Mind over Machine.
14 Dreyfus's most extended and explicit discussion of language as itself a practical perceptual skill occurs in his response to an earlier paper of mine that challenges his distinction between practical coping skills and linguistically articulated understanding. See Dreyfus, "Responses," esp. pp. 317–20.
15 Rouse, "Coping and Its Contrasts."
16 Dreyfus, "Responses," p. 314.
17 Dreyfus's willingness to acknowledge this point does not mean that he is entitled to it. An important reason for McDowell's insistence that conceptual normativity is pervasive in experience is the thought that if there were a preconceptual region of experience, there is no plausible way to understand how it would bear upon conceptually articulated judgments evidentially, or how inferences from such judgments could bear upon our experience or understanding within that preconceptual domain. I endorse McDowell's concern on this point, which extends Sellars's well-known identification of and challenge to the Myth of the Given (Empiricism and the Philosophy of Mind).
18 Todes, Body and World.
19 In calling this capacity "biological," I do not thereby attribute to Dreyfus a naturalistic conception of our perceptual capacities. Although Dreyfus has not extensively discussed this point, I suspect that he would argue for the importance of phenomenological description to characterize both human biology and the ways in which other organisms are responsive to their environments (his extensive debt to Merleau-Ponty, Phenomenology of Perception and Structure of Behavior, suggests that the latter text would be a model for how he would think about animal behavior biologically). Part of what he is arguing is that such a

supposedly preconceptual, bodily responsiveness to meaningful environmental solicitations is part of our common heritage as animals, even though it cannot be explained biologically in ways that would reduce the phenomenological dimension to some objective determination (natural selection might then explain which organisms with which practical perceptual capacities are extant, but could not explain the availability of such variations).

20 I have argued elsewhere (Rouse, *How Scientific Practices Matter*) that McDowell's account thereby renders incomprehensible our understanding of physical nature as the domain of law.
21 Sellars, *Empiricism and the Philosophy of Mind*; Hegel, *Phenomenology of Spirit*.
22 Rouse, *How Scientific Practices Matter*.
23 Haugeland, *Having Thought*, ch. 9.
24 "Reflective teleological" is my term for the kind of "purposiveness without a purpose" that is classically characterized in Kant's account of empirical concept formation in the First Introduction to the *Critique of Judgment*. Working out the parallels between Kant's, Heidegger's, and Dreyfus's or Todes' accounts of such intentional teleology is beyond the scope of this chapter.
25 Todes, *Body and World*.
26 Jackson, *From Metaphysics to Ethics*, p. 53.
27 Quoting Todes, *Body and World*, p. 276.
28 Fodor, *Concepts*; Searle, *Intentionality*.
29 I believe that Heidegger's various accounts of the opening of a clearing or world, such that entities can show up as entities, is one exemplar of this strategy, but again, this is not the place to explore that interpretation. In any case, my proposal below for how to pursue such a strategy differs significantly from his approach.
30 Okrent (*Rational Animals*) provides what I take to be a compelling set of arguments for conceiving of biological teleology in terms of goals (acting for the sake of maintaining a self-constitutive pattern) rather than the more familiar treatment in terms of functions.
31 Haugeland, *Having Thought*, p. 310.
32 Brandom, *Making It Explicit*, p. 632.
33 Haugeland, *Having Thought*, p. 208.
34 Wittgenstein, *Philosophical Investigations*, p. 223.
35 Hanna and Harrison, *Word and World*, p. 108.
36 Kukla and Lance, *Yo! and Lo!*.
37 Perry, "Problem of the Essential Indexical."
38 Wittgenstein, *Philosophical Investigations* I, §§444–45.
39 Sellars, "Some Reflections on Language Games."
40 For a sophisticated contemporary biological exposition of this pervasive phenomenon, see Odling-Smee *et al.*, *Niche Construction*.
41 Noë (*Out of Our Heads*) sketches a broad overview of a similar approach to understanding perceptual and discursive intentionality biologically, although he does not directly take up the central problem of explicating conceptual contentfulness in those terms.
42 Haugeland, *Having Thought*, p. 310.
43 Okrent, *Rational Animals*, p. 173.
44 Heidegger, *Fundamental Concepts of Metaphysics*.
45 Bennett, critical notice of *Inquiries into Truth and Interpretation*, by Donald Davidson.
46 Jackson, *From Metaphysics to Ethics*, p. 53.
47 On this theme, see Sterelny (*Thought in a Hostile World*) as a salient example.

48 Dor and Jablonka, "From Cultural Selection to Genetic Selection," p. 40.
49 McDowell, *Mind and World*, p. 18.
50 Kukla and Lance, *Yo! and Lo!*.
51 Okrent, *Rational Animals*.
52 Heidegger, *Being and Time*.
53 Deacon, *Symbolic Species*, and Dor and Jablonka, "From Cultural Selection to Genetic Selection," offer important and informative treatments of language as coevolved with human neural and social development. With regard to their most crucial point of difference, however, I follow Dor and Jablonka in recognizing language as a special-purpose cognitive capacity rather than a general capacity for symbolic understanding.

## Bibliography

Bennett, J., Critical notice of *Inquiries into Truth and Interpretation*, by Donald Davidson, *Mind* 94 (1985): 601–26.
Brandom, R., *Between Saying and Doing*, Oxford: Oxford University Press, 2008.
——, *Making It Explicit*, Cambridge, MA: Harvard University Press, 1994.
Davidson, D., *Inquiries into Truth and Interpretation*, Oxford: Oxford University Press, 1984.
Deacon, T., *The Symbolic Species*, New York: W. W. Norton, 1997.
Dennett, D., *The Intentional Stance*, Cambridge, MA: MIT Press, 1987.
Dor, D. and Jablonka, E., "From Cultural Selection to Genetic Selection," *Selection* 1 (2002): 33–55.
Dretske, F., *Knowledge and the Flow of Information*, Cambridge, MA: MIT Press, 1980.
Dreyfus, H., "Responses," in M. Wrathall and J. Malpas (eds), *Heidegger, Coping, and Cognitive Science*, Cambridge, MA: MIT Press, 2000, pp. 313–50.
——, *What Computers Can't Do*, 2nd edn, New York: Harper & Row, 1979.
Dreyfus, H. and Dreyfus, S., *Mind over Machine*, New York: Free Press, 1986.
Fodor, J., *Concepts: Where Cognitive Science Went Wrong*, Oxford: Oxford University Press, 1998.
Hanna, P. and Harrison, B., *Word and World*, Cambridge: Cambridge University Press, 2002.
Haugeland, J., *Having Thought: Essays in the Metaphysics of Mind*, Cambridge, MA: Harvard University Press, 1998.
Hegel, G. W. F., *Phenomenology of Spirit*, trans. A. V. Miller, Oxford: Oxford University Press, 1977.
Heidegger, M., *Being and Time*, trans. J. Macquarrie and E. Robinson, New York: Harper & Row, 1962.
——, *Fundamental Concepts of Metaphysics: World, Finitude, Solitude*, trans. W. McNeill and N. Walker, Bloomington: Indiana University Press, 1995.
Jackson, F., *From Metaphysics to Ethics*, Oxford: Oxford University Press, 1998.
Kukla, R. and Lance, M., *Yo! and Lo!: The Pragmatic Topography of the Space of Reasons*, Cambridge, MA: Harvard University Press, 2009.
Odling-Smee, J., Laland, K., and Feldman, M., *Niche Construction: The Neglected Process in Evolution*, Princeton, NJ: Princeton University Press, 2003.
Martin, W., *Theories of Judgment*, Cambridge: Cambridge University Press, 2006.

McDowell, J., *Mind and World*, Cambridge, MA: Harvard University Press, 1994.
Merleau-Ponty, M., *Phenomenology of Perception*, trans. C. Smith, London: Routledge & Kegan Paul, 1962.
——, *The Structure of Behavior*, trans. A. Fisher, Boston, MA: Beacon Press, 1963.
Millikan, R., *Language, Thought, and Other Biological Categories*, Cambridge, MA: MIT Press, 1984.
Noë, A., *Out of Our Heads: Why You Are Not Your Brain, and Other Lessons From the Biology of Consciousness*, New York: Hill & Wang, 2009.
Okrent, M., *Rational Animals: The Teleological Roots of Intentionality*, Athens: Ohio University Press, 2007.
Perry, J., "The Problem of the Essential Indexical," *Noûs* 13 (1979): 3–21.
Rouse, J., "Coping and its Contrasts," in M. Wrathall and J. Malpas (eds), *Heidegger, Coping, and Cognitive Science*, Cambridge, MA: MIT Press, 2000, pp. 7–28.
——, *How Scientific Practices Matter: Reclaiming Philosophical Naturalism*, Chicago, IL: University of Chicago Press, 2002.
Searle, J., *Intentionality: An Essay in the Philosophy of Mind*, Cambridge: Cambridge University Press, 1983.
Sellars, W., *Empiricism and the Philosophy of Mind*, Cambridge, MA: Harvard University Press, 1998.
——, "Some Reflections on Language Games," in *Science, Perception and Reality*, London: Routledge & Kegan Paul, 1963.
Sterelny, K., *Thought in a Hostile World*, Cambridge, MA: MIT Press, 2003.
Todes, S., *Body and World*, Cambridge, MA: MIT Press, 2001.
Wittgenstein, L., *Philosophical Investigations*, trans. G. E. M. Anscombe, Oxford: Blackwell, 1953.

# 12

# A TRILEMMA ABOUT MENTAL CONTENT

*Susanna Schellenberg*

There are good reasons to accept each of the following three claims:

(C1) Nonrational animals and humans can be in mental states with the same kind of content when they are perceptually related to the very same environment.
(C2) Nonrational animals do not possess concepts.
(C3) Content is constituted by modes of presentations and is, thus, conceptually structured.

The three claims form a trilemma. I will discuss reasons for accepting and rejecting each of the three claims and will thereby explore ways to resolve the trilemma. I will suggest that the trilemma is best resolved by giving up (C3). I will argue that we can understand content as constituted by modes of presentations, without understanding content as conceptually structured. In doing so, I hope to shed some light on the nature of perceptual content and its relation to concepts and bodily skills. The larger aim is to address questions of what the very idea of perceptual content could possibly be, what we mean when we say that experience is conceptually or non-conceptually structured, and how basic bodily skills and conceptual capacities relate.

## Rational capacities and perceptual content

The main reason for accepting (C1) of the trilemma is that perception is a cognitively basic capacity that we share with nonrational animals. If we share this capacity with nonrational animals, then it is plausible that the mental state we are in when we perceive bears at least some similarities to the mental states of nonrational animals when they perceive the very same environment. In what way are the mental states similar? One central way in which our perceptual states may be similar is with regard to their content.

Content is a theoretical term that we make use of to describe anything from basic informational states to cognitively rich belief states. It is a term we use to give an account of the mental states of beings to explain potential (mental) actions. There are few uncontroversial characteristics of content. The most uncontroversial one may be that there is a correspondence between content and accuracy conditions: content either determines accuracy conditions or is identified with accuracy conditions. Content may be understood as *determining* accuracy conditions insofar as one can ask with respect to any state, thought, or expression whether things are as they are represented to be. On a more coarse-grained understanding, content can be *identified* with accuracy conditions insofar as the accuracy conditions specify the possible conditions that must be realized for the state, thought, or expression with that content to be accurate. It can be considered a minimal condition on the notion of content that there is a tight connection between content and accuracy conditions. It is possible to question even this condition, but anyone who does so is arguably talking about something quite different than what is normally meant by content in philosophical discussions.

A second characteristic of content that is generally agreed on and which I will consider a minimal condition on the notion in play is that content can be distinguished from the attitude any given being takes towards that content. A content that is accurate if and only if, say, it is raining might be the object of a hope, a belief, a fear, or a perception. One can hope, believe, fear, or perceive that it is raining. More generally, one can have a range of different attitudes towards any given content C.

Over and above these two minimal conditions, there are few points of agreement. Points of disagreement range from how the structure and nature of content should be understood to the relationship between the subject and the content of her mental state. One point of controversy about the nature of perceptual content is whether it should be identified with the way the world seems to the perceiving subject or whether it should be identified with the information received by an informational system. The way the world seems to the perceiving subject and the information she receives differ, since the information received might be distorted at some point in the processing chain. Further points of disagreement include whether content is propositional or nonpropositional, whether it is object dependent or object independent, and whether or not it includes indexicals – to name just a few. For present purposes we do not need to take a stance on these issues. The minimal conditions specified make for a sufficiently determined notion of content to address the relation between perceptual content and rational capacities.

What is it about a perceptual state in virtue of which it has some particular representational content? One way of answering the question is to say that we use the term "content" to characterize internal information-bearing states of beings, where this characterization may or may not involve taking into account the being's environment. This way of thinking about content leaves open just how cognitively rich the information-bearing states are and to what extent the being is conscious of the information that she represents.

Regardless of how we think about the *nature* of content, we can agree that we *ascribe* the very same content to two beings if we are warranted to do so given the criteria we use to ascribe content. Again there are many criteria that can be deemed relevant in ascribing content. If the relevant criterion is simply that two beings are related to the very same environment, then we will ascribe the very same content if and only if two beings are related to the same environment. If the relevant criterion is that two beings are related to the same environment *in the same way*, then things are more complicated. After all, what it takes to be related to the same environment in the same way can be specified in a number of manners. We might say that we are warranted in ascribing the same content if and only if the causal source of the state is the same. Alternatively, one might say that we are warranted in ascribing the same content if and only if the causal source of the state is the same and processed in the same way. Finally, one might say that we are warranted in ascribing the same content if and only if the causal source of the state in fact results in the same mental state.

All responses leave open whether the beings to which we ascribe content are in fact in a mental state with the relevant content. It is one thing to ascribe content to a being's mental state and quite another thing to say that the being is in a mental state with that content. The fact that we make use of a theoretical notion of content to ascribe mental states does not entail that the being to which we ascribe content in fact is in a mental state with that very content. This point becomes particularly salient when we consider the nature of the ascribed content. When we ascribe content to a being we use concepts. So the ascribed content is conceptually structured. While we may typically use different concepts to ascribe content to humans and cats, the ascribed content is at least potentially the same. Certainly, we use concepts in both cases.

If ascribing content to a being would imply that the being is in a mental state with that very content, then the very fact that we use concepts to ascribe content would imply that the relevant beings are in mental states with conceptual content. However, the fact that we ascribe conceptually structured content to a subject does not imply that the subject is in a mental state with content that is so structured. Moreover, the fact that we at least potentially use the very same concepts to ascribe content to humans and cats does not imply that they are in mental states with the very same content.[1] More generally, while we use concepts to ascribe content to beings, this fact does not imply that the being to which we ascribe this content possesses the concepts that we used to make this ascription.

Taking this into account, we can make room for an alternative to (C1), which is compatible with the claims that animals do not possess concepts (C2) and that content by its very nature is conceptually structured (C3):

(C1′)   Nonrational animals and humans that are perceptually related to the very same environment can be *ascribed* the same content.

Now this first way of resolving the trilemma involves staying agnostic about when it is correct to say that a being is in a mental state with a certain content. (C1′) only speaks to the question of content ascription. As such it leaves us unsatisfied. We do not simply want to say that content can be ascribed to perceivers. We want to say that perceivers are in mental states with content and say something about the nature of this content. After all, our cognitive lives and actions are determined at least in part by the content of our mental states. Insofar as the first way of resolving the trilemma speaks only to the question of content ascription, it leaves us wanting.

A second way of modifying the first claim is to argue that nonrational animals and humans share the same enabling conditions for concept possessions:

(C1″)   Nonrational animals and humans that are perceptually related to the very same environment share the same enabling conditions for possessing the concepts that constitute the content of their mental states.

If one takes this approach, one refrains from making a claim about the content of mental states itself, by resorting to a claim about enabling conditions for the mental capacities that constitute content. By making a claim about the enabling conditions one is making a claim about the mental lives of humans and nonrational animals. As a consequence, the agnosticism of (C1′) is avoided. However, by retreating to conditional aspects of mental states, we are not provided with any tangible element that subjects have in common when perceiving the very same environment.

A more satisfying way of resolving the trilemma is to modify (C1) by arguing that humans and nonrational animals have some aspect of content in common. In its original form, (C1) states that nonrational animals and humans are in mental states with the very same content. A weaker and arguably more plausible claim is to say that at least some part of the content of the mental states of beings that perceive the very same environment is the same:

(C1‴)   Nonrational animals and humans that are perceptually related to the very same environment are in mental states that share at least some content.

If we reformulate the third claim of the trilemma and allow that at least some content is nonconceptually structured, then the trilemma can be resolved with (C1‴) in a way that does not require us to be agnostic about the nature of mental content.

While each of the three suggested modifications of (C1) provides a way to identify a common factor between the perceptual state of humans and nonrational animals without positing that they are in mental states with the very same content, they each leave us wanting. The first modification is unsatisfactory in that it requires staying agnostic about the content of mental states. The second modification avoids this agnosticism but only by refraining from making any claim about the content itself. The third modification is the most attractive, but it raises the question of just what aspect of content is the same between rational and nonrational animals and what the relationship is between the aspect of content that is the same and the aspect of content that is different. One might say that the aspect of content that rational and nonrational animals share is the aspect that represents basic perceptual properties of the environment, such as shape and size properties. Positing that there is such a shared content requires arguing either that perception does not represent higher-level properties or that representations of such properties do not cognitively penetrate the representation of basic properties. Both approaches are problematic.[2] The first requires making assumptions about what is represented in perceptual experience and what plays a role only on the level of judgments or beliefs formed on the basis of perceptual experience. The second requires positing that there is a core sensory aspect of perceptual experience that is unaffected by aspects that are not part of this core, be they representations of higher-level properties or background beliefs. I have not shown that these issues cannot be resolved, but the fact that there are these issues makes the search for an alternative worth the effort.

## Concepts, bodily skills, and nonrational animals

Let's consider (C2) of the trilemma. Whether it is correct to say that nonhuman animals possess concepts is largely a question of what notion of concepts is in play. For any given understanding of concepts, it is a matter of empirical investigation to settle whether members of a species possess concepts so understood. On a sufficiently high-level cognitive understanding there is little reason to expect nonhuman animals to possess concepts. If possessing a concept is, for instance, a matter of grasping the inferences that the concept plays a role in, then few, if any, nonhuman animals are likely to turn out to possess concepts. However, if the benchmark for concept possession is lower, such as merely being able to act in a discriminating way, then it is more plausible that humans are not the only beings that can possess concepts.

Suppose concepts are understood in terms of collections of action-oriented abilities. Or suppose they are structured representations of features that allow us to sort and physically coordinate actions with regard to objects in the world.[3] On either understanding of concepts there are good reasons to attribute at least some concepts to nonrational animals. Consider a dog. Let's call him Fido. Fido is able to track his bone. That makes a prima facie case for saying that Fido possesses the concept of being bone-shaped or the concept of smelling like a bone, possibly even the concept of a bone. He tracks the bone in virtue of perceiving the bone. When he perceives the bone, he is in a mental state that represents either the bone or one of its properties. In short, there is a prima facie case for saying that he represents what he is tracking in virtue of employing concepts.

One critical point on which views of concepts differ is what role if any the possession conditions for concepts play.[4] On a practical understanding, the possession conditions for a concept are constituted at least in part by the ability to discriminate the things that the concept picks out from the things that it does not pick out. On an intellectualist understanding, the possession conditions for a concept involve the ability to think about the reference of the concept.

The practical understanding is more basic than the intellectualist understanding. After all, while a being may possess concepts understood in the first way without being able to have thoughts, the converse does not hold. Moreover, the intellectualist understanding cannot be understood independently of the practical understanding insofar as a being that has the ability to think about the referent of the concept, necessarily must have the ability to discriminate the referent from other things. As these considerations bring out, if one has a sufficiently nonintellectualized notion of concept possession, then it is less controversial to say that perception is conceptually structured.

Now, it has been argued that we can only make proper sense of conceptual abilities if we recognize that they are grounded in perception which in turn is grounded in bodily skills, abilities to act, and affordances, where perceptual content is nonconceptually structured.[5] We can all agree that perceiving guides the actions and movements of situated and embodied beings. The claim in question is more controversial. The claim is that conceptual abilities are grounded in the actions and bodily skills involved in perception and that perceptual content is not itself conceptually structured.[6]

Let's assume for the sake of argument that conceptual abilities are grounded in perception and that perception in turn involves bodily skills. Even on this assumption, there is no need to say that conceptual abilities are not themselves constituted by bodily skills and the ability to act. At least for certain concepts, namely perceptual concepts, there are good reasons to think that possessing concepts is constituted in part by bodily skills and the ability to act. If the possession conditions for a concept are constituted at least in part by the ability to discriminate the things that the concept picks out from other things, then perceptual concepts, such as shape and size concepts, arguably involve bodily skills insofar as the relevant discriminatory capacities are a matter of having certain dispositions to act.

One possible way of developing this idea is with regard to perceiving the locations of objects and property instances. In perception, one sees objects as located in certain relations to one's body. What are crucial for determining the coordinates of perception are the spatial locations from which possible movements originate and the directions of the relevant movements. The axes of our egocentric frame of reference are determined by our *dispositions to act* that bring about a *practical* understanding of basic spatial directions.[7] The idea of a practical understanding of basic spatial directions is related to Evans's thought that an understanding of spatial directions is not simply related to the place we occupy, but rather to the possibilities for action that one has by virtue of the way one occupies that location.[8] When I tilt my head, I do not see objects on the verge of sliding off the surface of the earth. The reference of "up" is not determined by the direction of my head, but rather by how I would move, given the position of my body.

It is unproblematic to think of the practical understanding of basic spatial directions in terms of spatial concepts as long as one is willing to ascribe these concepts to any creature capable of object-directed movement. It is unproblematic, since the spatial concepts are not what enable spatially oriented movement and actions. The direction of explanation goes the other way. Dispositions to act bring about the spatial orientation that allows subjects to locate objects in their visual field. This means that one has spatial concepts only insofar as these concepts are grounded in one's dispositions to act. These dispositions to act allow one to have the practical understanding of basic spatial directions that can be expressed with spatial concepts.[9]

I have suggested one way in which one can think of basic concepts as constituted by bodily skills and dispositions to act. If concepts are understood in this way, then it is at least conceivable that nonrational animals possess such concepts. If nonrational animals possess such concepts, then we can resolve the trilemma for at least those perceptual experiences the content of which is constituted solely by such concepts.

However, resolving the trilemma in this way requires adopting a number of controversial ideas about concepts. It requires arguing that basic spatial concepts are constituted solely by bodily skills and dispositions to act. So it requires rejecting the claim that any rational capacities are involved in possessing such concepts. Moreover, while basic spatial concepts may be understood as constituted by bodily skills and dispositions to act, cognitively higher-level concepts surely cannot be understood in this way. So adopting the approach sketched in this section would require relinquishing a unified account of concepts. One would have to argue that while the concepts that are constituted by bodily skills and dispositions to act are the kinds of concepts that nonrational animals can possess, the possession of other concepts requires rational capacities. In short, while understanding certain concepts as constituted by bodily skills and dispositions to act allows for a way to resolve the trilemma for a limited range of cases, it does so only if one adopts controversial views about concepts.

## Perceptual experience and nonconceptual content

A third way of resolving the trilemma is to reject (C3) by arguing that perceptual content is nonconceptually structured. How should one understand the idea that content is nonconceptually structured? One standard response is to argue that content is nonconceptual in that it is constituted by the properties and perhaps the objects to which we are perceptually related. If one holds that content is constituted by Fregean modes of presentations, this response is not an option.[10] After all, modes of presentation are ways of singling out the objects and properties to which we are perceptually related, not the objects and properties themselves. One might argue that on a Fregean understanding of content, it is part of the very idea of content that it is conceptually structured.

How can we understand content to be constituted by modes of presentation in a way that does not imply that it is constituted by concepts? One option is to understand the modes of presentation employed in perception in terms of discriminatory, selective capacities by means of which we differentiate and single out particulars in our environment. The relevant particulars are external and mind-independent objects, events, property instances, and instances of relations. In virtue of employing such discriminatory, selective capacities we represent particulars in our environment in a certain way.

Say we perceive a lush forest. We employ our perceptual capacity to discriminate shades of green from other colors and to single out the various shades of green in our environment. Similarly we employ our capacity to differentiate and single out leaf shapes from, say, flower shapes and tree shapes. It is not clear what it would be to single out an object in our environment without employing capacities of this kind.

Now how should we understand the capacities in play? A discriminatory, selective capacity functions to differentiate and single out, where singling out a particular is a protoconceptual analogy of referring to a particular.[11] So if we possess the discriminatory, selective capacity that functions to differentiate and single out green, we are in a position to differentiate instances of green from other colors in our environment and to single out instances of green. More generally, to possess a discriminatory, selective capacity is to be in a position to differentiate and single out the type of particulars that the capacity concerns, were one related to such a particular. So if we possess such a capacity, then – assuming no finking, masking, or other exotic case is involved – the following counterfactual should hold: if we *were* perceptually related to a particular that the capacity functions to single out, then we *would* be in a position to single out such a particular. There are further analogies between discriminatory, selective capacities and concepts. Like concepts, the capacities in play can be employed in different environments and in this sense are repeatable.

What happens in hallucination? Although such capacities are necessarily determined by functional connections between perceivers and their environment, arguably they can be employed even if one is misperceiving or hallucinating. After all, one could be prompted to employ the capacities due to nonstandard circumstances, such as unusual brain stimulation or misleading distal input. If this is right, then we can employ a discriminatory, selective capacity even if a relevant particular is not present – where a relevant particular is of the type that the capacity functions to single out.

So discriminatory, selective capacities can be employed such that a particular is successfully singled out, or they can be employed without successfully singling out any particular. In this sense, employing discriminatory, selective capacities constitutes accuracy conditions. So employing discriminatory, selective capacities has all the hallmarks of content insofar as it yields something that is entertainable and that can be accurate or inaccurate. So if S is employing discriminatory, selective capacities that constitute the way her environment sensorily seems to her, then S is representing her environment in virtue of employing discriminatory, selective capacities. Indeed, insofar as the content is yielded by employing discriminatory, selective capacities and the discriminatory, selective capacities constitute the experience, the content is a proper part of experience rather than merely ascribed to the experience as on (C1′). So if S is representing her environment in virtue of employing discriminatory, selective capacities, then S has a perceptual experience that is fundamentally a matter of representing her environment as being a certain way.

On this way of understanding content we can acknowledge that perception is a cognitively primitive skill that we share with nonrational animals and moreover explain how to think of the content of perceptual states of animals that do not possess concepts. So thinking of content in this way provides for a good reason to resolve the trilemma by rejecting (C3).

## Notes

1 For a discussion of this set of issues, see Stalnaker, "What Might Nonconceptuality Be?," p. 351ff.
2 For a discussion of this set of issues, see Siegel, "Which Properties Are Represented in Perception?," and Macpherson, "Cognitive Penetration and Color Experience."

3 For these ways of understanding concepts, see Prinz and Clark, "Putting Concepts to Work."
4 Any such notion of concepts must be distinguished from notions on which they are mental representations (e.g. Fodor, *Language of Thought*, and *Concepts*; Jackendoff, *Computation and Cognition*; Laurence and Margolis, "Concepts and Cognitive Science"; Carruthers, *Phenomenal Consciousness*; Prinz, *Furnishing the Mind*) or prototypes (e.g. Rosch, "Principles of Categorization"; Smith and Medin, *Categories and Concepts*).
5 See, for instance, Dreyfus, "Return of the Myth of the Mental," and "Response to McDowell." For a radically different approach, see McDowell, "What Myth?," and "Response to Dreyfus."
6 Dreyfus (in "Return of the Myth of the Mental" and "Response to McDowell") argues moreover that the actions and bodily skills themselves have nonconceptual content.
7 When I speak of action I mean something that involves at least potentially bodily movement. Thinking may be understood as a mental action. I am however using the notion of action in a more restricted sense. For a discussion of dispositions to act, see Mumford, *Dispositions*, and "Intentionality and the Physical."
8 Evans, *Varieties of Reference*.
9 For a detailed development of this approach, see my "Action and Self-Location in Perception."
10 I will not argue here that perceptual content is best understood in terms of Fregean senses. I have done so in "Particularity and Phenomenology of Perceptual Experience," and "Perceptual Content Defended."
11 In some cases, a discriminatory capacity may also function to type the kind of particulars that the capacity concerns, but this is not an essential feature of the capacities in play.

## Bibliography

Carruthers, P., *Phenomenal Consciousness: A Naturalistic Theory*, Cambridge: Cambridge University Press, 2000.
Dreyfus, H., "Response to McDowell," Inquiry 50, no. 4 (2007): 371–77.
——, "The Return of the Myth of the Mental," Inquiry 50, no. 4 (2007): 352–65.
Evans, G., *The Varieties of Reference*, ed. J. McDowell, Oxford: Clarendon Press, 1982.
Fodor, J., *Concepts: Where Cognitive Science Went Wrong*, New York: Oxford University Press, 1998.
——, *The Language of Thought*, Cambridge, MA: Harvard University Press, 1975.
Jackendoff, R., *Computation and Cognition*, Cambridge, MA: MIT Press, 1987.
Laurence, S. and Margolis, E., "Concepts and Cognitive Science," in E. Margolis and S. Laurence (eds), *Concepts: Core Readings*, Cambridge, MA: MIT Press, 1999, pp. 3–81.
Macpherson, F., "Cognitive Penetration and Color Experience: Rethinking the Issue in Light of an Indirect Mechanism," *Philosophy and Phenomenological Research* 84, no. 1 (2012): 24–62.
McDowell, J., "Response to Dreyfus," Inquiry 50, no. 4 (2007): 366–70.
——, "What Myth?" Inquiry 50, no. 4 (2007): 338–51.
Mumford, S., *Dispositions*, Oxford: Oxford University Press, 1998.
——, "Intentionality and the Physical: A New Theory of Disposition Ascription," *Philosophical Quarterly* 195 (1999): 215–25.

Prinz, J., *Furnishing the Mind: Concepts and Their Perceptual Basis*, Cambridge, MA: MIT Press, 2002.

Prinz, J. and Clark, A., "Putting Concepts to Work: Some Thoughts for the Twenty First Century," *Mind and Language* 19 (2004): 57–69.

Rosch, E. "Principles of Categorization," in E. Rosch and B. Lloyd (eds), *Cognition and Categorization*, Hillsdale, NJ: Lawrence Erlbaum, 1978, pp. 27–48.

Schellenberg, S., "Action and Self-Location in Perception," *Mind* 116 (2007): 603–32.

——, "The Particularity and Phenomenology of Perceptual Experience," *Philosophical Studies* 149 (2010): 19–48.

——, "Perceptual Content Defended," *Noûs* 45, no. 4 (2011): 714–50.

Siegel, S., "Cognitive Penetrability and Perceptual Justification," *Noûs* 46, no. 2 (2012): 201–22.

——, "Which Properties Are Represented in Perception?," in T. Gendler and J. Hawthorne (eds), *Perceptual Experience*, Oxford: Oxford University Press, 2005, pp. 481–503.

Smith, E. and Medin, D., *Categories and Concepts*, Cambridge, MA: Harvard University Press, 1981.

Stalnaker, R., "What Might Nonconceptual Content Be?," in E. Villanueva (ed.), *Concepts*, Philosophical Issues 9, Atascadero, CA: Ridgeview, 1998, pp. 339–52.

# Part V

# BODILY SKILLS, RATIONALITY, AND SELF-CONSCIOUSNESS

# 13

# ARE WE ESSENTIALLY RATIONAL ANIMALS?

*Joseph K. Schear*

## 1

John McDowell says "yes." Hubert Dreyfus says "no." Who's right?[1]

Call the thesis that human beings are essentially rational animals *the venerable thesis*. In the first part of the essay I seek to show that the venerable thesis is what the McDowell–Dreyfus exchange, to the extent that it is a real dispute, is about. I then turn to distinguish two of Dreyfus's arguments against McDowell – the argument from critical distance, on the one hand, and the phenomenological argument from the "merging" structure of embodied skillful comportment, on the other. The first argument, I suggest, misfires. The second, by contrast, promises to meet its target; the question of its persuasiveness turns on whether Dreyfus's phenomenology of merging is faithful. Assuming it is, the rationalist such as McDowell might rejoin with a separate argument for our essentially rational way of being that calls attention to our power to ask the question of what, or who, we are. This argument, however, supports only a weak reading of the venerable thesis with which Dreyfus, and certainly Heidegger, need not disagree. Before turning to the arguments, however, let me first guard against a possible misunderstanding of the venerable thesis, and proceed to offer two alternative readings of it.

## 2

The venerable thesis, if it stands *any* chance of being true, must not entail that human beings always think and act rationally. To see that this entailment does not hold, we must distinguish rationality as a property of particular thoughts and actions (often praiseworthy) from rationality as a capacity. Irrational thoughts or actions are defective expressions of the capacity for rationality. Accordingly, the wealth of irrational thoughts and actions in human life, far from refuting the venerable thesis, would serve to support it, so long as we hear "rational" in the capacity sense. After all, it is only a being capable of rationality that can be intelligibly assessed as thinking or acting irrationally.[2]

There are at least two different readings of "*essentially* rational" in the venerable thesis. There are, that is, two different contrasts to the claim that we are merely contingently rational animals. According to the claim that we are contingently rational, it is an accidental fact about us that we are beings possessed of the capacity for rationality; we could do without this capacity and go on perfectly well being what we are. The first contrasting essentialist thesis is this: Rationality is essentially *one* of our capacities. If you believe this, then you think that we have *other* essential capacities that are not the expression of, or otherwise wrapped up with, the capacity for rationality. You might, for example, think human beings are a kind of mishmash of various interacting but not tightly unified capacities, allowing even for structural tensions among the capacities that make up the human. This I will call the the weak reading of the venerable thesis.

The second, and stronger, reading is: Rationality is the form of the human as such, the very essence of being human. The capacity for rationality, on this stronger reading, is our central and defining feature. It is, evidently, what makes us who we are. Everything essentially human is precisely *that* by virtue of being an expression of, or perhaps support for, the capacity for rationality. Rationality is, one might say, the foreground of our being. Anything that is in the background deserves to be in the picture at all only because it is background *to the foreground*, namely rationality.[3]

These two readings of the venerable thesis are very rough formulations, to be sure, but they will suffice for us to turn now to the exchange between Dreyfus and McDowell.

3

In his *Mind and World*, McDowell's central argument against nonconceptualism about experience starts with the thought that our empirical judgments are answerable to the world. What does it take for this to be so? For our empirical judgments to be genuinely answerable to the world, our experience of the world must afford us reasons to judge one way or another. And for experience to afford us reasons to judge one way or another, experience must be informed by conceptual capacities. That is: experience must have the kind of content that can "serve up" *reasons* for judgment, reasons *for* the judging subject. Accordingly, experience must have conceptual content, not nonconceptual content. As McDowell puts it:

> To avoid making it unintelligible how the deliverances of sensibility can stand in grounding relations to paradigmatic exercises of the

understanding such as judgments and beliefs, ... we must insist that the understanding is already inextricably implicated in the deliverances of sensibility themselves.[4]

Dreyfus glosses the argument as follows:

> If I understand him rightly, McDowell accepts the transcendental argument that the conditions of the possibility of the mind relating its content to the world requires conceptual capacities, and these capacities *must be always and everywhere operative* in human experience.[5]

Now McDowell's argument has, at every turn, provoked much rich discussion and objection. But it is worth noting at the outset that, so set out, the argument is invalid, at least insofar as it purports to deliver the conclusion that sensibility must *as such* be conceptually structured. It shows at most that *some* deliverances of sensibility must be already informed by conceptual understanding. It hardly shows that *all* experience must be permeated by conceptual understanding. The argument, to be valid, would have to conclude rather with: experience, *so far as it matters for rational knowledge of objective reality*, cannot be nonconceptual. This conclusion is entirely consistent with a kind of experiential pluralism according to which experience, so far as it matters for *other* (nonepistemic) forms of relation to the world, need not make available reasons for judgment and belief. On such a pluralistic view, experiential life is a part of, but is not exhausted by, epistemic life.

The original context of McDowell's argument, recall, targeted a pair of claims put forward by Evans in his discussion of the relationship between perception and judgment in *Varieties of Reference*. Simplifying madly, the pair of claims is that (i) perception as such has nonconceptual content and (ii) perception is a basis ("input") for judgment and belief. McDowell in effect argued that if Evans wants (ii), as he should, he should not endorse (i). But granting that argument against Evans, one would need further premises to establish the claim that the content of perceptual experience is *all and only* conceptual.

Now return to the venerable thesis. According to the weak reading, rationality is a particular capacity (among others) that belongs to us essentially. The weak reading of the venerable thesis is perfectly adequate to the terms and ambitions of McDowell's argument outlined above. That there is *a* mode of sensory consciousness informed by the understanding, but not that *all* modes of sensory consciousness are so informed, requires only the weak reading. However, Dreyfus's objection to McDowell is indeed a challenge to the thesis that experience is all and only conceptual – that we are, as Dreyfus likes to put it, necessarily "full-time" rational animals. Dreyfus's objection, however, does not challenge the claim that we are necessarily "part-time" rational animals – which is one way of putting the weak reading of the venerable thesis. But the weak reading is all McDowell needs, and all that his argument entitles him to, for the insistence that experience be capable of standing in grounding relations to judgment.

The more modest conclusion that makes the argument valid accordingly leaves open the acknowledgment of forms of experience that do not matter for rational knowledge of objective reality, and thereby need not be conceptual.[6] So what might we conclude, based on what I have said thus far, about the McDowell–Dreyfus dispute? In short, Dreyfus is objecting to a bad argument for a conclusion that McDowell does not in fact need. This sounds like a disappointing result.

## 4

It is worth noting that McDowell basically grants the point at issue in an earlier exchange with Charles Taylor. Taylor, like Dreyfus drawing on the existential phenomenological tradition, introduces what he calls "a background of pre-understanding" – that is, a background of preconceptual embodied coping with the world – that provides a setting for, but does not fall within the scope of, "conceptual, reflective thought." McDowell's reply in that context is instructive:

> [H]ow much would it have helped me if I had made much of a background of pre-understanding? I agree with Taylor that there is something between spontaneity in what he calls "the strong Kantian sense, turning crucially on conceptual, reflective thought," on the one hand, and conformity to Galilean law, on the other. We need this middle ground for thinking about non-human animals, and it is what is supposed to be occupied by pre-understanding even in our case. But the difficulty that concerns me arises because making up our minds about the world is an exercise of spontaneity in precisely the Kantian sense. The problem is how spontaneity in that sense could be rationally constrained by receptivity.[7]

This in effect is a concessive stance to Taylor's background of pre-understanding. Though McDowell hardly presents himself as a convert ("what is supposed to be occupied by"), he himself points out that "pre-understanding" does not bear on his problem about the constraint on spontaneity by receptivity. It is as if he is saying: "I am happy to acknowledge a form of skillful rapport with the world, a mode of receptivity, that does not have to do with reasons for judgment. I am even happy to grant that this form of relation to the world provides an essential setting for, but does not fall within, our power of rational thought. I am happy to do all this, so long as I am granted the variety of receptivity germane to my book's problem, which is precisely what we need to secure the intelligibility of empirical judgment." This stance is available to McDowell in the more recent exchange with Dreyfus, but it is not one he is at present willing to rehearse. If not the imperialism of hostile take-over, McDowell is now keen on a friendly annexation of the kinds of background phenomena that interest Taylor and Dreyfus. Cautionary concession, it seems, has given way to a kind of triumphalism about reason.

## 5

McDowell might respond to the claim that his argument, so far as it purports to demonstrate that experience is all and only conceptual, overreaches by reminding us of the centerpiece of the diagnostic phase of his argument. The diagnostic question, recall, is this: why would a philosopher refuse to acknowledge the very possibility that sensibility can be informed by our rational capacities for thought and judgment? McDowell's answer to this question from Lecture IV ("Reason and Nature") in *Mind and World* is by now familiar. It is because the modern philosopher is in the grip of a dualism of nature and reason. Nature is the realm of Galilean law. Our sensory systems belong within the realm of nature so understood. Contrast our capacity for rationality, which is a capacity for freedom and self-determination and thereby cannot be properly understood as a bit of mere nature. Our sensory consciousness therefore cannot possibly be combined with our capacity for rationality, the anxious modern philosopher insists. McDowell urges that if our conception of what can count as natural is relaxed, to include second nature, we can make room for sensibility as at once a rational and natural phenomenon.

Whatever one's estimate of the promise of that piece of therapy, the point to register here is that the diagnosis does not apply to a philosopher like Dreyfus, who is perfectly happy to grant that sensory experience *can be* informed by conceptual capacities, but who is not willing to grant that *all* modes of sensory experience are, much less must be, so informed. McDowell at times writes as if the philosopher who contests his conceptualism *cannot but* be in the grip of a dualism of nature, or the body, and reason. But diagnosing the inability of some philosophers, purportedly caught in the grip of a bad picture, to appreciate the very idea of rational receptivity does not supply the missing premise for the global conceptualist conclusion. Merleau-Ponty and Dreyfus, and presumably Taylor, need not deny an involvement on the part of conceptual rationality in the phenomenology of embodiment – need not deny that intentions can be *in* action – to claim that the whole story about our bodily being-in-the-world (*être au monde*), and much of what is interesting about that story, is not captured by that involvement.

## 6

The strong reading of the venerable thesis is not supported by, or needed for, the key argument against nonconceptualism about experience, I have argued. But McDowell certainly announces his commitment to the strong reading. As he says, "conceptual rationality is everywhere in our lives in so far as our lives are distinctively human."[8] Following up on the kinship, in his vision of rationality "permeation," between the involvement of conceptual capacities in perceptual experience and their involvement in bodily movement, McDowell writes,

> My claim is that capacities that are conceptual, capacities that belong to their possessor's rationality, are operative not only in reflective thought and action but also at the ground-floor level at which there is absorbed coping and acting in flow. ... Human beings are rational animals. What could be more natural than to hold that the capacities that belong to what differentiates human beings from other animals, their rationality, are operative in activity that is essentially human, including activity at the ground-floor level?[9]

To this question Dreyfus has replied with the following series of challenging questions:

> Rather than take for granted that critical rationality is the defining feature of human beings, we should ask: What is rationality? Is it required? Should it be? Does it permeate all our activity? How does it relate to mastery? If critical distance undermines expertise, we had better not view rationality as a pervasive obligation.[10]

Now *this* sounds like a genuine dispute. I want now to consider two of Dreyfus's central arguments against the claim that rationality prevades all of our activity and experience. The first argument, which I do not believe is persuasive, is what I call the argument from critical distance. The second argument, which I believe promises to meet its target, is what I will call the argument from merging. Part of my aim here is just to distinguish these two arguments (which Dreyfus at times runs together) if only as a way of identifying the precise issues at stake.

## 7

The argument from critical distance starts with the charge of a category mistake. In reply to McDowell's claim that nothing could be more natural than the idea that conceptual capacities, capacities that belong to our rationality, are "operative," or "permeate," or are "in play" in our activity,

Dreyfus replies: capacities cannot pervade anything. Capacities are exercised on occasion. But that does not allow one to conclude that capacities, when they are not exercised, nonetheless pervade or are "operative." To think otherwise, Dreyfus alleges, is to commit a category mistake.[11] If there is anything to the idea that the capacity for rationality permeates activity, it must be that one is constantly exercising it by stepping back reflectively from one's acting in flow. But this would precisely undermine acting in flow, as Dreyfus claims above. Hence Dreyfus's warning that we had better not view rationality as a pervasive obligation.

The distinction between a capacity or power and its exercise is certainly worth recognizing.[12] Consider my capacity to twirl my pencil. On occasion I find myself exercising the capacity to twirl my pencil. Does it follow that the capacity permeates or pervades my activity as such? That obviously seems false.

One might reply that the capacity to twirl one's pencil is indeed pervasive because capacities, as such, are inherently general. Capacities are inherently general because their being is not exhausted by their exercise on a particular occasion. As Kenny puts it: "there are no genuine abilities which are abilities to do things only on one occasion."[13] Consider the absurdity of crediting someone with the ability to ride a bicycle who only can ride a bike on *one* block on a *single* occasion. This inherent generality of capacities, however, does not suffice for pervasiveness. Whatever the pervasiveness of a capacity ultimately amounts to, if it has any sense, it surely has to be more than the idea that a capacity by its very nature is not tied to, or sunk in, a particular occasion of its exercise. To claim the title of "pervasive," a capacity has to be, one wants to say, more *actual* than the mere in principal potentiality of its exercise across a range of diverse occasions.

Let us consider another capacity, the virtue of kindness. This is, very roughly, the capacity to be kind in the right way at the right time in the right circumstances. If someone possesses this virtue, it seems perfectly intelligible, and not a category mistake, to say that the capacity is pervasive. This seems intelligible because the life and ongoing activity of the possessor of the virtue of kindness is pervaded by it. To be kind, after all, is to live in a certain way – namely, with an open-eyed *readiness* for the characteristic circumstances that call upon the exercise of one's capacity for kindness. That is what it is *to be* kind. So here there is sense to the idea of a capacity that is pervasively present where the pervasiveness does not entail the constant de facto exercise of the capacity. One could easily imagine someone, an Ebenezer Scrooge, who had hitherto been thoroughly mean-spirited and petty towards others, consumed by *Schadenfreude* and callous indifference – without the virtue of kindness – who somehow undergoes a conversion, becoming kind. That this kind of global transformation is one in which one's world, one might say, becomes a fundamentally different place further suggests that the capacity for kindness can indeed be faithfully called pervasive.

There is certainly more to say about the distinction between non-pervasive and pervasive capacities. But supposing there is something to it, then Dreyfus's charge of a category mistake is misplaced. The very idea of a capacity that pervades one's activity, indeed one's life, far from being nonsensical, is an idea that makes sense. It hardly has the absurd ring of asking "But where is the University?" after being shown around Christ Church, the Bodleian Library, and the Ashmolean Museum.[14]

The question, then, is: Where does rationality, understood in McDowellian terms as a capacity to be responsive to reasons as such, belong? Is it a pervasive capacity, like kindness, or a merely general capacity, like the capacity to twirl one's pencil? Dreyfus uses evidence of the exercise of the capacity for critical rationality disrupting the flow of absorbed coping to tell against rationality being understood as a pervasive capacity. But if there is a notion of pervasiveness that does not consist in constant exercise, then that evidence does not work.

That is: *While* one is absorbed in the flow of some activity, such as playing a sport at peak performance, engaging in reflection – a paradigmatic exercise of the capacity for rationality – is generally a bad idea, at least insofar as one wants to stay in the flow. After all, to engage in reflection is generally (if not always) to take up a deliberative stance of critical distance, a "stepping back" which tends to take one out of the absorption characteristic of the flow. But here the capacity of rationality is pictured as disrupting the flow because it is pictured as exercised in an actual stepping back, inaugurating a course of reflection, which is not the question. The question is whether rationality *qua* capacity is pervasive, where its pervasiveness does not consist in the process of an ongoing constant exercise (which would indeed be inimical to flow).

I characterized the pervasiveness of the capacity for kindness as living in a certain way, with one's modes of activity and feeling and thought structured by a readiness to be kind when appropriate. If we understand the pervasiveness of the capacity for rationality along similar lines, possessing the capacity for rationality would likewise be a matter of living in a certain way, ready and open to the circumstances that call upon one's capacity to be responsive to reasons. So understood, the presence of the ability to step back and adopt a stance of critical distance with regard to one's activity would not disrupt the flow of absorbed coping. After all, being absorbed in the flow of activity is not generally a characteristic circumstance that invites rational scrutiny. One might further suggest that it is *part* of what it is genuinely to possess the capacity for rationality that one precisely does not *exercise* the capacity to step back in circumstances in which rational deliberation would unduly disrupt the course of the activity at issue. Compare the way in which not behaving kindly in circumstances that do not invite it is precisely part of what it is to be genuinely kind.

Characterizing a capacity as pervasive, then, is no category mistake. And the pervasive presence of the capacity for critical rationality in those who possess it need not disturb or otherwise sabotage the flow of their absorbed activity. This defense of McDowell's position against Dreyfus's argument from critical distance does not, it is worth noting, decide which of the two readings of the venerable thesis we should endorse. For, the very intelligibility of rationality as a pervasive capacity does not in any way decide whether it is one among other essential capacities of the human, or rather *the* core capacity of the human. Recognizing a sense of the pervasiveness of rationality along the lines suggested above at most removes an obstacle that stands in the way of adopting the stronger reading of the venerable thesis.

## 8

There is a separate, and I believe more promising, argument that Dreyfus has offered against the pervasiveness of rationality, understood along the lines of the strong reading of the venerable thesis. So I want now to try and bring that argument into view. The pervasiveness of rationality as a capacity, I have argued, does not entail its constant exercise, in the sense of ongoing engagement in critical reflection. I have also suggested that it is integral to the possession of the capacity for rationality precisely not to "step back" and subject one's flow of activity to rational scrutiny. However, both of these claims are fully consistent with the idea that what *was* going on in the flow of absorbed coping is perfectly available for rational scrutiny, retrospectively, after the flow is over, as McDowell would surely insist. And indeed, in McDowell's hands, the pervasiveness claim does imply that there is no distinctively human activity, however flowing, that is not in principle available to be taken up by the power of critical reflection, if only retrospectively – hence his commitment to our essentially rational way of being in the strong sense. As McDowell once put it: "we cannot put limits on the self-scrutiny of reason."[15] (There may be contingent issues about bad memory, and so on, but there is nothing in principle about the flow of absorbed activity, on McDowell's view, that would prevent it from being taken up by critical rationality.) So, absorbed activity must have the right *form* to be taken up by our power of rationality, on pain of it being ruled out of the court of the distinctively human. Conceptual rationality, after all, is "everywhere in our lives."

And here Dreyfus has offered a phenomenological argument that denies that absorbed coping has conceptual form, the form suitable to our power of rationality. The argument is phenomenological because its key move is the identification of a decisive experiential feature of absorbed coping, namely "merging," that precludes it from falling within the space of reasons. The basic shape of the argument runs as follows, the terms of which I will go on to explain:

(1) The capacity for rationality requires the presence of determinate objects.
(2) The merging character of absorbed coping precludes the presence of determinate objects.
(3) Absorbed coping is thus not available to the capacity for rationality.
(4) Therefore, it is not the case that human beings are essentially rational in the strong sense.[16]

Rationality requires the presence of determinate objects. Consider two paradigmatic exercises of the capacity for rationality, making a judgment and acting intentionally. When one makes a judgment, there is an object, a determinate identity, present to one as one's topic. So, for example, when one judges *that Spring has begun*, there is present to one a thinkable element (*Spring*) that can figure, if challenged (say), in one's reasons for judgment. Likewise, when one acts intentionally, there is something, a determinate object, that is present to one that one is (oneself) doing or bringing about – the object of one's intention. So, for example, when one is walking across the street or building a house, one's walking across the street or the house one is building figure as thinkable elements fit to serve in reasons one could give for acting as one does. In judging, one is *taking* something to be true about a determinate object. In acting, one is *making* a determinate object true. Both judging and acting are forms of rational engagement with the world that involve the presence of determinate objects to the subject of rational engagement. The engagement is rational because determinate objects can figure in reasons to which one is responsive, and which one can in principle offer, in the context of justifying or otherwise considering one's judgment or one's action.

What, more concretely, is the presence of a determinate object? We can title such presence subject–object presence. Subject–object presence is a way in which aspects of the world are presented to one, and correlatively, a way of being present to, or aware of, oneself as being presented with the world this way. Subject–object presence is the presence characteristic of rational agency, the two basic forms of which are judging and acting. What, we may ask, is the phenomenology of subject–object presence? How, that is, do determinate objects "show up" in rational agency, in the broad sense of making judgments and acting intentionally?

John Haugeland once characterized the notion of an empirical object as "autonomous, authoritative, accessible."[17] This characterization was offered in an inquiry into the possibility of empirical truth. (I'll turn to action in a moment.) First, an object is autonomous because it presents itself as independent of my relation to it. An object is given to me as *other* than me, *already there*, out there on its own. Kant characterizes this autonomy in terms of the finitude of intuition.[18] Second, an object is authoritative because it occupies a position of authority over my judgment: the independent object "says" whether my judgment about it is true or false; the object is "the boss" of my judgment. It shows up to me, one might say, as the thing that could show me up. This feature of being an object, its standing over against the subject, is what McDowell stresses in his demand, against Davidsonian coherentism, for intelligible "constraint" by objects, i.e. constraint *on* the subject position to make judgments.[19] Kant characterizes this authority in terms of the relation of cognition to its object "carrying something of necessity with it."[20] And third, an object is accessible in that it is *there* for me, poised to play its role as an autonomous authority vis-à-vis my judgment. McDowell characterizes this in terms of the visible object "speaking" to one, as if to say, "see me as I am."[21] These features of being an object – an autonomous, authoritative, accessible – well capture the structure of awareness and object at work in empirical judgment. This is the subject–object presence of judgment – or, in McDowell's terms, the subject–object presence of the receptivity of experience that constrains judgment.

Subject–object presence is not limited to conceptual experience and judgment, for it applies to intentional action as well, only the terms are reversed. When I act, I bring about some change in the world. I make a difference, even if only a difference in my own location by moving. For this to happen, I must of course be in the world. However, in acting I am present to myself as in a sense standing apart from things, autonomous, insofar as I am capable of *intervening* in the world – realizing "the thing to do" – and thereby making things happen in the world. Second, in acting, *I* am the authority (not the object), to the extent that the world is supposed to measure up to my intention. In successfully realizing my intention I make true some state of affairs that hitherto did not exist. And lastly, I am "accessible" to the world, insofar as the world, or at least aspects of it, can be affected, or shaped, by my action – that is, can serve as the "patient" of my agency. In intentional action, then, as in judging, we have the form of consciousness characteristic of rational agency. By this I mean a consciousness of oneself as a distinct existent in an independent world of determinate objects – in the broad sense that includes the world as it is, and the world as it is to be. These determinate objects are, on the one hand, the truthmakers of one's judgments, and, on the other hand, the objects of one's truthmaking endeavors (i.e. one's intentions).

It is helpful to characterize subject–object presence in terms of a form of *distance* between the subject and its world. Let me guard against two possible misunderstandings. The distance here is *not* the skeptical distance that plagues much modern epistemological reflection on our relation to the world. This is the sense of distance according to which our thoughts, it is feared, are all false (for all we know) since some of them are false, or perhaps simply because they are *our* thoughts. McDowell rightly diagnoses and debunks this sense of skeptical distance: "of course thought can be distanced from the world by being false, but there is no distance from the world implicit in the very idea of thought."[22] To think otherwise is to fall prey to what Hegel characterized as "what calls itself fear of error reveals itself rather as fear of the truth."[23]

Secondly, the distance at issue is *not* the distanced posture of the contemplative subject pondering things, detached and disengaged, adopting the critical gaze *du Penseur*. Just as there is no skeptical distance from the world implicit in the very idea of thought, there is nothing in the very idea of perceiving or making judgments about objects, much less *acting*, that entails a contemplative distance of disengagement or detachment.[24]

Rather, the distance at work in subject–object presence is more basic than any kind of detached style of being in the world. The distance I mean characterizes the structure of awareness and object as such, which *any* form of reason-responsive engagement with the world, detached or not, presupposes. What *this* sense of distance involves is the appreciation of the very distinction between the subject and her thinkable objects, on the one hand, and the very distinction between the agent and her objects of intention, on the other. Without appreciating these distinctions, the very intelligibility of a *gap* between a (possibly false) thought and its object, or a *gap* between a (possibly unfulfilled) intention and its object, would not make any sense. And without the appreciation of the possibility of such gaps, the very idea of rational thought and intention would fall apart. For, any recognizable notion of responsiveness to reasons as such – reasons *for* the subject – presupposes determinate objects present as distinct from the reasoning subject, the kinds of things that can be cited in the practice of discovering what is, or what is not, reason for what.

Subject–object presence, then, is an independent reality of determinate objects – the world as it is, or is to be – present to a rational subject in a position to judge and act for reasons. The second premise of the argument above is that the merging character of absorbed coping precludes such presence. By "merging," Dreyfus means, negatively, the absence of the characteristic structure of subject–object presence. This absence is what Dreyfus draws from Merleau-Ponty in the football passage that Dreyfus makes so much of, particularly with the key phrase "faire corps avec lui":

> For the player in action the football field is not an "object." It is pervaded by lines of force ... and is articulated into sectors (for example, the "openings" between the adversaries), which call for a certain mode of action. The field itself is not given; ... the player becomes one with it [*fait corps avec lui*]. ... At this moment

consciousness is nothing but the dialectic of milieu and action. Each maneuver called forth from the player modifies the character of the field and establishes new lines of force in which the action in turn unfolds and is accomplished, again altering the phenomenal field.[25]

In this description of merging, the relevant contrast is between the field as an object that is *given* to be known or acted upon versus the field as a vortex of forces with which the player "becomes one." "Lines of force" – or what Dreyfus calls a "shifting field of attractions and repulsions" that solicit one's skillful comportment – are precisely *not* given as determinate objects affording opportunities for knowledge or manipulation. Correlatively, the player does not experience himself as in any sense distinct from a domain to be known or acted upon (e.g. made different than it is). Rather, he experiences himself as *one* with a field, at most a dynamic "moment" in a dialectical whole. So, insofar as reason-responsive engagement requires the presence of determinate objects, and the presence of determinate objects is subject–object presence, the merging at work in at least a certain form of skillful comportment, with its absence of subject–object presence, is not adapted to the demands of reason-responsive engagement. Not every aspect of experience, then, is present in a form in which it is suitable to constitute the content of conceptual capacities (to mimic one of McDowell's key formulations). Lines of force, or the shifting phenomenal field of attractions and repulsions, are not determinate objects of thought or intention, Dreyfus suggests, for they are not items one can so much as single out and hold still. They simply do not have that kind of determinate identity or persistence. They are nothing apart from their dynamic place in the throes of embodied comportment. And without having a determinate (or determinable) identity, they cannot serve as topics with which to reason. Accordingly, reason does not have its characteristic material with which to operate (not even retrospectively). So if the phenomenology of merging presence is accurate, absorbed coping does not have the right form to figure in reasons, marking the limits of reason's scope. McDowell would thus be mistaken in his claim that there is no form of human activity that is not in principle available to be taken up by the power of critical reflection. And the strong version of the venerable thesis, that all distinctively human activity is pervasively rational, would be false. If the argument from merging can be made to stick, rationality may necessarily be one of our capacities, but it does not pervade our activity as such, and therewith could not be *the* form of our life.

That, then, is the basic shape of the argument from merging. Clearly much more would need to be said to fill it out. My main aim is simply to present the argument so as to bring it *into view*. Questions that arise include: What precisely is a "line of force," or an "attraction" or "repulsion"? What is the metaphysics of such things, if not determinate objects that can figure in reasons? It is no accident that Dreyfus characterizes his project in terms of describing the "nonconceptual *world* of absorbed coping." The denial of the presence of determinate objects in at least a certain form of skillful comportment is a claim entered in the ontological investigation of the world, not merely a claim limited to the study of our way of relating to the world. (This, as I read him, is faithful to Merleau-Ponty's intentions in the *Phenomenology of Perception*.)

Those sympathetic to the venerable thesis will rightly ask: Is it really the case there is no way a line of force can figure in a reason? Suppose the football player is watching a videotape of the match, after it has concluded, with his fellow players and coaches. Could not a line of force in some sense be pointed out, or somehow cottoned onto, in the context of strategic deliberation about how things went during some stretch of the match, in the service of how things might go in future matches? If so, isn't that sufficient for it to be a determinate object, and thereby capable of figuring in a reason for action? Dreyfus's basic thesis about merging is that the lines of force are *only* available as *bodily* solicitations in the dynamic flow of activity: without that form of solicitation, the line of force simply ceases to be, disappears, vanishes. The field of attractions and repulsions is accordingly not composed of elements that could be held onto and reidentified retrospectively in the envisaged football deliberation. They are literally unthinkable, at least for the discursive intellect, and in a sense then, ineffable – a point Dreyfus, far from shying away from, has been eager to insist upon. In sum, if Dreyfus's phenomenology of merging is faithful, then he has identified a form of activity that falls outside the reach of our power of rationality and its characteristic material, namely determinate objects fit to figure in reasons.[26]

## 9

While the argument from critical distance misfires, the argument from merging, if phenomenologically on key, challenges the truth of the venerable thesis that we are essentially rational animals (on its strong reading). The friend of the venerable thesis might rejoin by offering a short argument in favor of the strong version.[27] One natural way to approach the question "Are we essentially rational animals?" is to start with oneself: "Well, what am I?" Descartes's meditator poses this question to himself in the Second Meditation (*Meditations on First Philosophy*). His immediate answer is "rational animal." But the meditator quickly loses patience with this answer: time is short, even for a meditator, and such "subtleties" of encrusted Aristotelian tradition evidently are not worth pursuing.

But suppose we linger with the question rather than the meditator's immediate answer. That is, perhaps the very asking of the question – "what am I?" – contains the materials for an answer to it. In reply to the question, I can think the thought: I am a human being. After *this* reply to my first-personal question, I can entertain the more general question: What, then, is a human being? And *then* "rational animal" would presumably be available to me as an answer to the more general question, thanks to my original first-personal interrogation. After all, only a rational animal is capable of thinking about what it is.

This seems undeniable. But the argument, as it stands, does not favor the strong reading of the venerable thesis. For, the "rational" in rational animal that is available to me by the very posing of the question, "What am I?," and subsequently the question, "What is a human being?," could very well be the rationality that is one capacity among others, and not the very form or essence of my being. It hardly follows from the fact that my rational power is *called upon* in grappling with a question about what it is that I am that my essence *consists in* my rational power.

Consider Heidegger, for whom the question – what, or rather who, am I? – is central to his project in *Being and Time*. He introduces his very term for human beings, "Dasein," as picking out the ones for whom inquiring, particularly inquiring into its own way of being, is one of its essential possibilities.[28] Heidegger notes that asking the self-reflective ontological question is an exercise of one's power to *question*, which he considers distinctively human. He would also, as I read him, grant that the power to question has important links to our power of reason. However, on Heidegger's view, it is care, and ultimately temporality – not rationality – that most fundamentally captures the distinctively human, even if rationality belongs in the picture. How rationality is to be placed within this broader and more fundamental characterization of the distinctively human is a wide open and indeed pressing exegetical question.[29] The point here is that one can, like Heidegger, accept that rationality belongs in the picture, thanks in part to our power of self-interrogation, without granting it the status of *the* core element.[30]

## Notes

1 I take my title question from Dreyfus's essay "Detachment, Involvement, and Rationality: Are we Essentially Rational Animals?"
2 Robert Brandom draws the distinction as follows:

> This evaluative or comparative normative dimension of rationality rests on a conceptually prior constitutive one. The constitutive issue concerns whether one is a rational creature at all, rather than whether one is better or worse, more or less reliable, at doing what rational beings as such do. ... It is only creatures that are in the space of reason in this sense – ones for whom the question of what attitudes they have reason to adopt and what they have reason to do arises, or to whom demands for reasons are appropriately addressed – that are then further assessable as to how sensitive they are in

fact to their reasons, how good they are at actually doing what they have good reason to do.

(*Reason in Philosophy*, p. 3)

3 I owe this formulation to John McDowell, a version of which he offered in conversation in Berlin. This distinction between the two readings of the venerable thesis does not correspond to a related distinction drawn by Matthew Boyle between "additive theories" of rationality and "transformative theories" of rationality in his "Additive Theories of Rationality." For the weak reading, as I am presenting it, is not committed to rationality as something "tacked on" to an existing stock of other capacities (e.g. perception) to which it is at most externally related.
4 McDowell, *Mind and World*, p. 46.
5 Dreyfus, in conclusion to Chapter 1 of this volume, p. 36 (my emphasis).
6 What premise(s) might be added to make the original argument valid?
  One candidate premise: experience, or "sensibility," can bear one and only one kind of content. Another candidate premise: the role and significance of experience in human life is exhausted by its contribution to rational knowledge of objective reality. McDowell, however, puts forward neither of these premises, so far as I know.
7 McDowell, "Responses," p. 283.
8 McDowell, "What Myth?," p. 349.
9 McDowell, this volume, p. 54.
10 Dreyfus, this volume, p. 26.
11 Dreyfus, "Response to McDowell," p. 372.
12 *Pace* the tradition of philosophers, from Aristotle's metaphysical opponents the Megarics to David Hume, who deny the validity of the distinction.
13 Kenny, *Metaphysics of Mind*, p. 69.
14 Ryle, *Concept of Mind*, p. 18.
15 McDowell, *Mind and World*, p. 52.
16 Two small remarks about the argument are worth noting. One might think, as Dreyfus used to think (see his APA Presidential Address, "Overcoming the Myth of the Mental"), that this conclusion is a way of recognizing our kinship with nonhuman animals and how they comport themselves in their respective environments. Or one might think, as Dreyfus has come to think (see Chapter 1 of this volume), that skillful, absorbed coping is distinctively human, and that McDowell's stress on rationality as the distinctively human is a tired "Athenian" prejudice that we should learn to get beyond. While the conclusion of the argument here is, strictly speaking, consistent with either of these positions, I believe Dreyfus's later view of the status of absorbed coping is a positive development, or at least makes for a more interesting debate with McDowell. So I will treat the question about how we should understand the distinctively human as what is at stake in the presented argument in what follows. Second remark: "Determinate" can be read less robustly as "determinable" without changing the argument for our purposes. So McDowell's anti-Brandomian stress, in his exchange with Dreyfus, on the point that that we need not have labels or names for every aspect of our experience for that experience to be conceptual in nature ("nameable") is irrelevant to the argument.
17 Haugeland, "Truth and Rule-Following," p. 325.
18 Kant, at B72 of the *Critique of Pure Reason* (among other places), distinguishes finite sensible intuition from infinite originary intuition. Infinite intuition creates or produces its objects. Finite intuition, by contrast, is given its objects from without, and thereby must be affected by objects to know them. So whereas an

infinite intellect is wholly self-sufficient, a finite intellect is dependent on existing objects that are, for the intuiting subject, *other* than it and *already there*. For an account of Heidegger's conception of the finitude of understanding as an elaboration of this sense of Kantian finitude, see my essay "Historical Finitude."
19 See, for example, Lecture 2 of the McDowell's Woodbridge Lectures, "The Logical Form of an Intuition," at p. 41 of the reprinted version in *Having the World in View*.
20 Kant, *Critique of Pure Reason*, p. A104.
21 Ibid., p. 41.
22 McDowell, *Mind and World*, p. 27.
23 Hegel, *Phenomenology of Spirit*, §74, p. 47.
24 Heidegger makes several misleading remarks early on in *Being and Time* that suggest he is committed to a contemplative conception of judging. I relieve him of this in my "Judgment and Ontology in Heidegger's Phenomenology."
25 Merleau-Ponty, *Structure of Behavior*, pp. 168–69.
26 How exactly lines of force, or attractions and repulsions, can be themes of phenomenological description is a methodological question the argument from merging obviously invites.
27 Matthew Boyle offered a version of this argument in conversation at the Wissenschaftskolleg workshop in Berlin.
28 Heidegger, *Being and Time*, p. 27. I am grateful to Stephen Mulhall for reminding me of this passage.
29 *Pace* Dreyfus, Heidegger believes that the "Greek definition" of man as a rational animal is "not indeed false," but it covers over the ground which makes our rationality possible. See *Being and Time*, p. 165/208. I discuss Heidegger and the problem of reason in my book manuscript, *Horizons of Intentionality: From Husserl to Heidegger*.
30 I thank Hubert Dreyfus for helpful conversation in Berkeley and John McDowell for helpful conversation in Berlin. For their productive reactions, I thank audiences at Reading – especially Severin Schroeder and Noa Leibowitz – and at the London meeting of the American Society for Existential Philosophy – especially Wayne Martin and Mark Wrathall. The participants at the workshop on the exchange at the Wissenschaftskolleg zu Berlin, especially Robert Pippin, provided invaluable discussion, for which I am grateful.

## Bibliography

Boyle, M., "Additive Theories of Rationality: A Critique," *European Journal of Philosophy* (forthcoming).

Brandom, R., *Reason in Philosophy*, Cambridge, MA: Harvard University Press, 2009.

Descartes, R., *Meditations on First Philosophy*, trans. and ed. J. Cottingham, Cambridge: Cambridge University Press, 1996.

Dreyfus, H., "Detachment, Involvement, and Rationality: Are we Essentially Rational Animals?," *Human Affairs* 17, no. 2 (2007): 101–109.

——, "Overcoming the Myth of the Mental: How Philosophers Can Profit from the Phenomenology of Everyday Expertise," Presidential Address, *Proceedings and Addresses of the American Philosophical Association* 79, no. 2 (2005): 47–65.

——, "Response to McDowell," *Inquiry* 50, no. 4 (2007): 366–70.

Haugeland, J., "Truth and Rule-Following," in *Having Thought: Essays in the Metaphysics of Mind*, Cambridge, MA: Harvard University Press, 1998, pp. 305–61.

Hegel, G. W. F., *Phenomenology of Spirit*, trans. A. V. Miller, Oxford: Oxford University Press, 1977.
Heidegger, M., *Being and Time*, trans. J. Macquarrie and E. Robinson, New York: Harper & Row, 1962. (Page reference is to the Macquarrie and Robinson translation and the marginal, *Gesamtasusgabe* page.).
Kant, I., *Critique of Pure Reason*, trans. P. Guyer, Cambridge: Cambridge University Press, 1998.
Kenny, A., *The Metaphysics of Mind*, Oxford: Oxford University Press, 1992.
McDowell, J., *Having a World in View: Essays on Kant, Hegel and Sellars*, Cambridge, MA: Harvard University Press, 2008.
——, *Mind and World*, Cambridge, MA: Harvard University Press, 1994.
——, "Responses," in *Reading McDowell: On Mind and World*, London: Routledge, 2002, pp. 269–305.
——, "What Myth?," *Inquiry* 50, no. 4 (2007): 338–51.
Merleau-Ponty, M., *The Structure of Behavior*, 2nd edn, trans. A. L. Fisher, Boston, MA: Beacon Press, 1966.
Ryle, G., *The Concept of Mind*, London: Penguin Classics, 2000.
Schear, J., "Historical Finitude," in M. Wrathall (ed.), *The Cambridge Companion to Heidegger's Being and Time*, Cambridge: Cambridge University Press, forthcoming.
——, *Horizons of Intentionality: From Husserl to Heidegger* (in preparation).
——, "Judgment and Ontology in Heidegger's Phenomenology," *New Yearbook of Phenomenology and Phenomenological Philosophy* 7 (2008): 127–58.
Taylor, C., "Foundationalism and the Inner–Outer Distinction," in N. H. Smith (ed.), *Reading McDowell: On Mind and World*, London: Routledge, 2002, pp. 106–19.
Wrathall, M. (ed.), *The Cambridge Companion to Heidegger's Being and Time*, Cambridge: Cambridge University Press (forthcoming).

# 14

# A DANCER REFLECTS

### Barbara Montero

> The awareness of tension and relaxation within his own body, the sense of balance that distinguishes the proud stability of the vertical from the risky adventures of thrusting and falling – these are the tools of the dancer.
>
> Rudolph Arnheim[1]

I remember how difficult philosophy seemed when I was an undergraduate at Berkeley. I was taking epistemology with Barry Stroud at the time and feeling a bit disheartened, went to his office and asked, "Does it ever get easier?" No, it doesn't, he told me, since as you grow as a philosopher you work on increasingly more difficult problems. Although this was not the response I was hoping for, it made sense immediately, for I was entering college fresh from a career as a professional ballet dancer. Ballet, I knew, never gets easier; if anything, it gets harder because as you develop as a dancer you develop higher standards for what counts as good dancing as well as your ability to evaluate your own dancing, finding flaws that previously went unnoticed. Just as Socrates is wise because he knows that he is ignorant, it is, among other things, the ability to recognize where there is room for improvement that allows expert dancers to reach great heights.

The ability to see room for improvement, however, is not of much use unless one also has a strong and ongoing desire to improve. And it may be that, more so than talent, it is this desire to improve, an attitude the Japanese call "kaizen," that turns a novice into an expert. I certainly had kaizen in abundance, as did almost every professional dancer I knew. It was ingrained in my body and mind to the extent that every class, rehearsal, and performance was in part aimed at self-improvement. And improving, especially after you have acquired a high level of skill, typically requires an enormous amount of effort. Sometimes this effort is physical – and it certainly involves more physical effort than philosophy – yet it also involves concentration, thought, deliberation, and enormous amounts of will-power.

Be this as it may, the idea that performing a ballet typically involves tremendous effort is contrary to the widely touted view that great performances are natural and effortless. Although practice may be hard work, it is thought that during a performance an expert just lets the movement happen. Indeed, thinking about what you are doing during a performance is, if anything, thought to interfere with expert skill. Let me call the view that expert action is natural and effortless, "the principle of automaticity." Just as I would have liked to have heard Professor Stroud say that philosophy gets easier as your skills develop, you might like to hear me uphold the principle of automaticity, for how leisurely the performing life would then seem. Unfortunately, I cannot do this since, as I shall argue, it is not true.

My plan is as follows. I shall first explain how I understand the principle and provide some examples that illustrate its widespread appeal. I then critically examine some arguments for the principle, the first group of which is based on the idea that thinking about your actions while performing them interferes with action; the second group, on neurological data. After this, I present a number of reasons for why we should reject the principle, perhaps the strongest being that automatic actions are stagnant, yet expert performers are always trying out new approaches. Finally I suggest some reasons for why the principle has such widespread appeal despite its falsity.

## Doing what comes naturally

The principle of automaticity states that expert action is natural and easy. But what, exactly, does this mean? Clearly proponents of this principle do not think that it doesn't take Herculean strength and endurance to run a marathon or perform the leading female role in Swan Lake. No marathon runners cross the finish line feeling ready to go out for a night on the town, and no dancer comes off stage after completing a performance of the dual role of the Swan Queen Odette and her evil imposter Odille and says, "that was easy!" Of course, ballet is supposed to look easy. But looking easy and being easy are quite distant cousins.

I think that what is more often meant by the claim that expert action should be easy is that during a performance, an expert doesn't and shouldn't think much about what she is doing; rather, the expert acts intuitively and automatically. Such action might be physically exhausting, it might involve sweat and blood, but it shouldn't involve tears, and it shouldn't be mentally exhausting; it should just happen. As the great choreographer, George Balanchine, would say to his dancers, "Don't think, dear; just do."

Although various theorists, no doubt, mean different things when they champion automaticity, the following, I think, captures the general idea:

> *The principle of automaticity.* When all is going well, expert performance significantly involves neither self-reflective thinking, nor planning, nor predicting, nor deliberation, nor mental effort.

This, however, needs some further unfolding. First off, how should we understand these various cognitive processes? By "self-reflective thinking" I mean thinking about what you are doing, while you are doing it. I engage in self-reflective thinking, for example, when I think, *I'm straightening my posture*, while I am sitting more upright in my chair. By "planning," I mean making decisions about what you ought to do. For example, I may be walking down the street and decide to turn left at the next corner. You make a prediction about your movement when you, say, have the thought that you're about to step in a puddle and you deliberate over your actions when, for example, you think about whether it would be better to avoid the puddle with an extra long and invariably awkward stride or just step down and suffer the consequences. The idea of "mental effort" is a bit less straightforward, but at a minimum, mental effort involves the will. When the words just come to my fingers, writing seems easy. But sometimes, it's rather painful. I need to struggle to figure out what I want to say and how to say it. It is that type of struggle that I call "mental effort." The principle claims that when all is going well, experts do not in any significant way engage in these cognitive processes.

But what is an expert? Sometimes proponents of the principle take an expert to be anyone who engages in expert action, where expert action is defined as being natural, effortless, and automatic. Obviously, this is not how I am using the notion. Rather, I understand the term "expert," to apply to those that are generally recognized as experts in their fields and whose skills are usually thought to conform to the ten-year rule, which states that the journey from novice to professional typically takes ten years of intensive practice.[2] And intensive practice means close to daily, extended practice with the specific aim of improving. For example, I would call professional athletes, professional performing artists, grand master chess players, experienced doctors and nurses all experts in their various fields. Although, proponents of the principle often group together commonplace well-worn skills, such as everyday driving or (if you live in New York City) crossing the street, and the skills of professionals, I count only the latter as expert skills. You may be a good driver but most likely you are not recognized as an expert driver and, sad to say, after learning the basics you probably did not engage in strenuous efforts to improve. So as I understand the notion of expert, everyday skills do not count as expert skills. Indeed, I think that one of the reasons the principle of automaticity is so widely accepted is that theorists have overgeneralized a principle that may very well be correct for commonplace skills.

Experts may be amazingly good, but they are not perfect. And no one denies that if something goes seriously wrong, an expert's attention might be called to what he or she is doing in order to fix things up. When your partner jetés upstage rather than downstage, you need to figure out how to adjust your movement so that the two of you can meet up. Thus the principle aims to exclude the various cognitive processes only under "the best circumstances." This should be understood as circumstances that do not involve unusual problems or errors. These may not be ideal circumstances, if we understand "ideal circumstances" as those in which one's actions are perfect. But in ballet, at least, actions are never perfect and it is not at all clear what one could say about situations in which they were.

Moreover, the principle tells us that the expert does not in any *significant* way rely on these cognitive processes. This allows proponents to claim that some reflection or thinking (or other cognitive activity) may occur during the best performances, as long as it is fleeting. Thus, consistently with the principle, a professional dancer should be able to think for a moment about, say, the line of her *penché*. The principle denies that the expert engages in extended thoughts about what she is doing.

You probably also want to know whether these cognitive processes should be thought of as conscious processes. I think that typically, though not exclusively, proponents of the principle of automaticity think of them as conscious. And that is my focus as well, in arguing against it.

Finally, I should mention that although to refute the principle it would, of course, suffice to show that when an expert is performing well she employs (in a significant way) just one of these cognitive processes, I shall suggest, however, that depending on the circumstances, any one of them may come into play.

## The widespread acceptance of the principle of automaticity

Assertions of, and arguments for, the principle of automaticity (or for either somewhat weaker principles that exclude some but not all of these cognitive processes or somewhat stronger ones that exclude more) are found in a wide variety of contexts. For example, Fitts and Posner, in their 1967 *urtext* on the psychology of skilled performance, tell us that although during the first phase of skill acquisition, what they call "the cognitive phase," one aims at understanding and intellectualizing the task, this is not true of the expert. "In learning a dance step," they tell us, a dance student "attends to kinesthetic and visual information about the feet, information *which* is later ignored."[3] After the cognitive phase comes the "associative phase," where one acquires some mastery over the movement, yet still needs to think about various aspects of it. Finally, in the "autonomous" phase, one achieves, as they see it, autonomy from cognition and moves without focusing on the movement. At this level, they explain, "if the attention of a golfer is called to his muscle movements before an important putt, he may find it unusually difficult to attain his natural swing."[4] Expert dancers, they tell us, "ignore kinesthetic information and visual information about their movements," and if an expert golfer thinks about, say, stabilizing her torso muscles during a swing, things may go awry.[5]

The view that expert action is automatic is also a central tenet of Hubert Dreyfus's similarly highly influential work on expertise. Dreyfus, along with his brother Stuart Dreyfus, argues that expert action proceeds "without calculating and comparing alternatives"; rather, "what must be done, simply is done."[6] Beginners, according to Dreyfus and Dreyfus, "make judgments using strict rules and features, but with talent and a great deal of involved experience, the beginner develops into an expert who sees intuitively what to do without applying rules and making judgments at all."[7]

Dreyfus may accept a principle that is stronger than the one I have stated, for he claims that "mindedness is the enemy of expert coping" and "expert coping [is] ... direct and unreflective" which he takes to be "the same as nonconceptual and nonminded."[8] This might make it sound as if he sees an expert's actions as entirely nonminded. But I don't think that this is quite right. He does not deny, for example, that expert chess players deliberate over their moves.[9] But such deliberation arises only when expert intuition fails to provide the grand master with the right move. These are situations where something goes wrong, and thus they are not excluded by the principle. However, Dreyfus does accept a stronger principle in a different sense since he sees expert action, when all is going well, as *entirely* nonminded and thus he would include more mental processes – conscious ones as well as unconscious ones – than are stated in the principle. Of course, since his stronger principle implies the principle of automaticity, in arguing against the principle of automaticity I shall be arguing against his view as well.

In the world of sports, the principle of automaticity is ubiquitous. In baseball, for example, coaches may tell proficient batters to hum a tune while batting so as to not think about what they are doing. When a player is off you may hear sports commentators say, "she's focusing too much on what she's doing," "he needs to just let it happen," "she's overthinking," and so forth. The case of the New York Yankee's former second baseman, Chuck Knoblauch, is illustrative. When he developed throwing problems – sometimes being barely able to toss the ball, other times throwing it outrageously far out of bounds – it was often claimed, as Stephen Jay Gould put it in summing up the popular press's analysis of the situation, that "his conscious brain has intruded upon a bodily skill that must be honed by practice into a purely automatic and virtually infallible reflex."[10]

In addition to these contemporary affirmations of the principle of automaticity, there is a long and distinguished history of thinkers who have supported it. We find intimations of it, for example, in *The Principles of Psychology* where William James champions leaving as much of our daily life "to the effortless custody of automatism" as possible.[11] "We fail of accuracy and certainty in our attainment of the end," he tells us, "whenever we are preoccupied with ... consciousness of the bodily means."[12] Or as one of the founders of neuroscience, Charles Sherrington put it, "our minds are not concerned with the act but with the aim."[13]

There is also the Taoist tradition that advises "nonaction" or "effortless action." In the Zhuangzi, this idea is illustrated by the final stage of knowledge in the story of a butcher:

> When I first began cutting up oxen, I did not see anything but oxen. Three years later, I couldn't see the whole ox. And now, I encounter them with spirit and don't look with my eyes. Sensible knowledge stops and spiritual desires proceed.[14]

These three stages are analogous to Fitts and Posner's three stages of skill acquisition. In the first stage the butcher needs to think about where to draw his knife; three years later he develops a degree of mastery and the divisions become apparent to him; and in the final stage the oxen are encountered with spirit, where the notion of spirit is opposed to conscious visual perception and deliberate action. The butcher does not focus on the movements of his hand holding the knife nor does he try to move in any particular way; he just moves naturally and effortlessly. This understanding of expert action is in accord with both Fitts and Posner's and Dreyfus and Dreyfus's theory of expertise. An expert's movement is automatic; it is not movement that is directed by the self, but, as it's put in the Zhuangzi, "by what is inherently so."[15]

And I probably need not point out that the principle has long been part of popular culture, with, for example, James Barrie, the author of *Peter Pan*, explaining, "of course, when you have mastered the action [of wriggling up and down your hollow tree trunk] you are able to do these things without thinking of them, and nothing can be more graceful."[16]

## The argument from cognitive interference

One central line of reasoning that leads theorists to accept the principle of automaticity is based on the maxim that thinking about what you are doing while doing it interferes with performance, or as Dreyfus puts it, "monitoring what we are doing as we are doing it degrades performance to at best competence."[17] This maxim, Dreyfus claims, is supported by cases such as Chuck Knoblouch's inability to throw the ball. It also appears to be supported by various behavioral studies of expert action. If it is correct, experts, it would seem, must not be engaged in self-reflective thinking. But it is not at all clear that such cases and studies show what supporters of the principle of automaticity take them to show.

Although Dreyfus thinks that Knoblauch's throwing problems support the principle,[18] I question whether attention is the culprit here. From what I gather in reading the media coverage on this, neither Knoblauch nor any of the other players who have been struck with what is called "Steve Blass disease" claim that the cause of their throwing problems is related to their thinking about what they are doing.[19] Rather, they say that they don't know why they can't throw and, indeed, Knoblauch has criticized the media's claim to understand the cause of his condition.[20] Moreover, the fact that Knoblauch's problem did not respond to what I can only imagine were the best and most expensive psychological interventions suggests – doesn't imply, of course, but suggests – that the problem was not psychological. True enough, as Dreyfus points out, one could sometimes see Knoblauch looking in a puzzled way at his gloved hand, but that doesn't mean that his problem was caused by thinking about how he ought to throw since it might very well be that he is puzzling over his hand because (for neurological reasons, perhaps) he can't throw the ball properly.

It could be that these players are not able to identify the fact that their thinking about what they are doing is interfering with their actions. And, of course, it is difficult to know whether this is so. But even if players like Knoblauch are missing the cause of their troubles, these situations, it seems, are not what tests the expert's mettle. The difference between Knoblauch at his prime and a minor league player is not Knoblauch's abilities to perform the easy throws, but rather his ability to perform the difficult ones.

Perhaps more telling than the Knoblauch case, however, are the many behavioral studies that are thought to show that self-reflective thinking interferes with expert performance. Most of these studies, such as those by Robert Gray (*Consciousness*), Beilock and Carr ("From Novice to Expert Performance"), Beilock et al. ("When Paying Attention Becomes Counterproductive"), and Ford et al. ("Online Attentional-Focus Manipulations in a Soccer Dribbling Task") take expert athletes and have them perform a skill while either directing their attention to a specific aspect of their movement or while engaging in an extraneous task. And the result is that experts perform worse in the skill-focused condition than in the extraneous-task condition. Moreover, Beilock and Carr ("From Novice to Expert Performance") and R. Gray (*Consciousness*) found that the skill-focused condition produced worse results than having the experts perform as they usually would without an additional task (single-task condition). According to Wulf, "these findings clearly show that if experienced individuals direct their attention to the details of skill execution, the result is almost certainly a decrement in performance."[21]

It seems to me, however, that the findings are not as clear as Wulf indicates. During the skill-focused condition, experts were not simply told to think about their movements but were given instructions to focus on a particular aspect of their movement. For example, during the skill-focused condition Gray had expert baseball players indicate whether their bats were moving upward or downward by saying either "up" or "down."[22] But the fact that a request to focus on some particular aspect of action interferes with performance does not mean that thinking about what one is doing generally interferes with expert skill, since it may be that the skill-focused condition, more so than the extraneous-task condition (where the players were asked to identify whether the sound of a tone was either high or low), distracted the players from the aspects of their movements that they needed to be thinking about. Moreover, subjects performed best of all during the single-task condition, where they were just asked to swing the bat as they normally would. Where is the mind then? For all we know, it's on the action.

## The expert brain

Apart from the argument from cognitive interference, there are various neurological studies that might be seen as supporting the principle of automaticity. Such studies compare neural activity of individuals learning a task with neural activity in these same individuals after they have mastered the task. And they suggest that performing a skill you have mastered involves less mental effort than performing one you are just learning how to do. For example, both Tracy *et al.*, who observed differences in brain activation before and after two weeks of practice tying a complicated knot, and Puttemans *et al.*, who looked at differences before and after eight days of practice performing a bimanual coordinated wrist movement, conclude that one possible interpretation of the data is that practice leads to reduced cognitive demands.[23]

Of course, since there is much uncertainty as to what areas of the brain underlie cognition, the conclusions drawn are speculative. But I would not be at all surprised if the speculations turned out to be correct, since there is no need to think much when you are doing some rather dull, utterly predictable task which, once you can do it, you have no motivation to improve. Performing a ballet, in most cases, however, is unpredictable and far from dull. And the desire to improve, as I mentioned before, is ongoing.

It might also seem that the principle of automaticity receives support from the view that there are two anatomically distinct visual streams, vision for perception (which we use, for example, when we look at a coffee cup for the purpose of describing it and which may be conscious) and vision for action (which is what we use for the purpose of picking up the cup and which is thought to be unconscious). Some of the evidence that these two separate visual streams exist in humans comes from research on patients with neural damage, the most well known of which is a young woman, referred to as "D.F.," who, after suffering from carbon monoxide poisoning became unable to identify the form and dimensions of objects even though she could still properly position her hand when asked to reach out and grasp certain objects.[24] For example, although, if asked to describe what she was seeing, she could not tell whether she was looking at a vertical or horizontal rectangular object, she could accurately position her hand while reaching for it. Apparently, the carbon monoxide poisoning damaged her ventral (vision-for-perception) stream but not her dorsal (vision-for-action) stream, which, was still able to guide her actions without her having any conscious awareness of what she was seeing.

Should we conclude from this research that the vision we use to guide our action does not provide conscious information about what we are seeing? That, I think, would be an oversimplification. Though D.F. could accurately adjust her grasp to correspond to a few very basic spatial parameters, she was not able to do this when an object was even minimally complex, such as a cross. And the visual scene before the dancer is very complex, and it includes many features that guide actions besides shape, location, and dimension. For example, in dancing with a partner you are often trying to determine your partner's persona, and in doing so you might look at your partner's gestures and facial expressions in order to decide on how you want to color your own movements and expressions. Is your partner being sly right now? I'll respond teasingly. Or is this a bold move and I'll respond boldly in turn. Here, your action is being guided in part by conscious visual information. Moreover, it seems that even if all vision for action were not conscious, expert action uses the mind in a number of ways that have nothing to do with vision. When a dancer is deciding how to finish a turn, for example, she is not looking at her turn. When she is thinking about the lilting quality of her glissade as she's performing it on stage, she doesn't see her movements. And it seems to me that such decisions and thoughts are sometimes conscious.

Another line of reasoning that is loosely based on neurological data is that thought, or at least conscious thought, would arise too late for it to be relevant to performance. The expert, it is sometimes argued, is not conscious of her movements since she has to move before consciousness can kick in. Jeffrey Gray argues for this when he tells us that in grand-slam tennis the speed of the ball after a serve is so fast and the distance it needs to travel is so short that a player must strike it back before she even consciously sees the ball leave the server's racket.[25] According to Gray, "consciously [the receiver] neither sees nor feels his arm move before the stroke is completed."[26] The brain, of course, receives the information about the serve, says Gray, but given that it is commonly estimated to take about 250 milliseconds to become conscious of an event after it has happened, this awareness cannot be relevant to return. Gray concludes "that conscious awareness should guide immediate behavioral reaction to them is – on the experimental evidence – impossible."[27]

The results Gray cites, however, are more controversial than he makes them out to be since it is not clear how to determine when a person becomes conscious of an event.[28] Moreover, as Gray points out himself, top players anticipate the ball's trajectory well before it leaves the server's racket. According to Gray, this still does not allow time for consciousness to play a role in the game. For support he cites the science journalist John McCrone (*Going Inside*) who tells us that top players do not claim to get their clues about the ball's trajectory prior to the time the ball leaves the racket, but rather seem to be conscious of the shots as they happen.[29] But this would hardly seem to be rock-solid experimental evidence. And even if it were, not all aspects of expert bodily skill occur at high speeds. So even if returning a serve in grand-slam tennis does not involve thinking about what one is doing, performing the White Swan *pas de deux* very well might.[30]

## Effortful expertise

So it seems that the neurological data are not very telling and the argument from cognitive interference is not as strong as many assume. However, it cannot be denied that experts sometimes say such things as performance involves "being in the groove," where it is the groove and not your conscious mind that is directing your actions. The best performances, it is said by some, are where the mind is not present. "When you're thinking, you're stinking," is the oft-touted phrase in the world of Jazz. Or as thirteen-times PGA winner Dave Hill put it, "Golf is like sex. You can't be thinking about the mechanics of the act while you are performing." What are we to make of such assertions? Introspection may be unreliable and highly influenced by what you think you should find upon introspection, however, if upon introspection most experts claimed that they perform without thinking about what they are doing, this would be prima facie support that the principle of automaticity is correct.

But I wonder whether most expert ballet dancers would claim that they perform best when they are not thinking about what they are doing. Often I would be thinking about how to capture, accentuate, or play with the music in my movement, thinking, perhaps, "let me extend that note beyond the end" or some such loosely formulated idea such as that. And this at times involved deliberation (should I do this here, or wait), and it took mental effort, as it involved concerted concentration. Sometimes my thoughts would be self-reflective, being about, for example, various aspects of the performance quality, presenting a movement with more attack, or making some other movement flow. Such thoughts typically do not involve thinking about the mechanics of movement, if that means thinking more on the anatomical level, that is, thinking about what my feet, ankles, wrists, and other body parts should be doing. And I think that most dancers are not focusing primarily on such fine-grained details of their movements. Yet, since performance quality is created by bodily movements, such a focus occasionally occurs even in the best performances. For example, sometimes a very specific detail, such as "lift" directed at, say, my elbow, might be what is in mind. In addition to these sorts of thoughts, there were the willed commands (I *am* going to nail that coming balance!), which can be seen as a form of planning – as well as numerous thoughts about what the other dancers are doing on stage, making predictions about my partner's timing, for instance.

There is much more as well: there are thoughts about lighting, sets, the floor (which, as I recall, was often a major concern: Is it slippery? Is it sticky? Where is the bump in the tape?), and so on. Some of these thoughts might not be part of the best performances. In those rare best performances, the floor, for example, needn't require much thought. But some thoughts, such as reaching a mark on stage, are just part of the performance.

I recall sometimes even thinking about what I was doing aloud and also hearing others do this. Thinking aloud is certainly more common during the early rehearsals of a piece, but sometimes it continues on until and during performances. For example, to keep my mind and body on task, I might whisper something like "stretch-lift-whoosh" (the "whoosh" representing the sort of feeling that I am trying to capture in the movement), or even an occasional muted reprimand, such as "shoulders" (which is short for "shoulders down"), might be appropriate. Yet Fitts and Posner warn against thinking aloud during performance. They tell us that "there is a good deal of similarity between highly practiced skills and reflexes [since] both seem to run off without much verbalization or conscious content."[31] Indeed, they tell us that "overt verbalization may interfere with a highly developed skill."[32]

Dancers may also count the music, either silently to themselves or aloud, during a performance. Sometimes this is required because the music has no discernible rhythm or even landmark passages that typically guide a dancer. A vivid example of this is Laura Dean's *Night*, which she choreographed for the Joffrey Ballet (1980). Because the movements were very complex rhythmically and because the music had no recognizable structure, dancers counted continually for the entire eighteen minutes of the piece for the several years they performed it. Eric Dirk, a former Joffrey (New York) dancer (as well as a partner of mine at Oregon Ballet), told me that when he was not in the cast, he sat in the pit, next to the two pianists, counting in order to ensure that the music finished exactly when the dancing did.

I imagine that a proponent of the principle of automaticity might object to this example, claiming that the Joffrey dancers are evidently not experts at performing the piece. And it is true that usually the counts become something you can just feel. But I don't see why the need to count a difficult piece such as *Night* during performances shows that the dancers are not expertly performing the piece. It certainly appeared to the audience to be the work of experts, with the sometimes biting former *New York Times* chief dance critic, Anna Kisslegoff, calling it "a smashing success."[33] To be sure, it might not have felt so smashing to the performers, but little does for the professional.

Clearly one reason why the best dancers are thinking about what they are doing is that the best dancers – and presumably experts in all fields – are always striving to improve. To become a Barishnikov, for example, one has to be driven to achieve such heights, and once at the top, one's drive does not simply stop. Yet a performance on autopilot, as it were, leads to doing the same thing in the same way.

But can't the expert merely strive to improve during rehearsal and then just let it happen during performance? Well, certainly there are some things that one needs to work on and master solely during rehearsal, such as learning the steps and becoming proficient at performing them. You might start a rehearsal not being able to, say, perform a small jump sequence fast enough or there might be a lift that you have trouble with. These technical aspects of the performance ought to be tamed – not perfected, as, I repeat, nothing is ever perfect in ballet – before going on stage. Eric explains it like this:

> It is usually pretty difficult to work on improving my ballet technique much during an actual performance. I had better have already done that in the rehearsal period before. But I definitely would work to improve my performance quality. If I was doing a leading role, say Mercutio, then I would be constantly looking for more drama, playful, tragic, whatever that section needed. For a more generic role, say like [James Canfield's] Equinox, not so much personality to work on. My mind would be thinking of spacing, being together with my fellow dancers if I need to be in sync. Staying on the music, adjusting to injuries, if I had some pain going on. Watching out for someone who might be new to a part and needs help. This is not to say that if you were doing a run of 30+ Nutcrackers and were stuck in the corps without much variety, you could probably space out a bit and just go through the motions.

Working to improve performance quality is often what makes performing interesting for a dancer. Certainly, as Eric says, after performing the same piece over and over again, you could just let habit take over and "simply spontaneously [do] what has normally worked."[34] But this is not going to be much fun, even for dancers in the corps. Moreover, performing the same piece in the same way day in and day out can result in a performance without any spark; and you never get out of the corps without spark.

To be sure, many decisions about how to move are automatic and unconscious. One might be inspired on the spot to change dynamics of a certain step, for example. But it seems to me that the best performances also allow observers to witness deliberate, conscious thought in action, for a performance that proceeds entirely automatically would be flat. (Think of the difference between listening to someone lecture on her feet and listening to someone read a paper. Part of the interest of the lecture is that we see someone think in real time.) It would be, in certain respects, like watching a machine; although the output could be amazing, that most interesting of spectacles, the human mind, is lacking.

Beilock and Carr ("From Novice to Expert Performance"), Dreyfus and Dreyfus (*Mind over Machine*), and Fitts and Posner ("Learning and Skilled Performance,") all admit that when something goes wrong, a performer or athlete's attention may be directed to her actions. Yet they seem to think that, at least for the crème of the crème, things go wrong rarely. This, though, is not the case. Although from the audience's point of view the dancer's moves may be flawless, the dancer's view is otherwise, for professional dancers are their own worst critics. With extensive practice and a bit of luck, things won't go terribly wrong, but, again, they are never perfect.

## Coda

I have argued that even though the principle of automaticity has widespread appeal, there is little reason to think it describes expert dancers' performance (and my hunch is that if it is not correct about dancers it is probably not correct across the board). Why, then, do so many accept it? Why do we have the great choreographer, Balanchine, saying, "don't think; just do"?

Certainly, the arguments from cognitive interference and the neurological data play an important role in promoting the view. But it is likely that there are a number of other somewhat more indistinct ideas that motivate the acceptance of the principle as well. One may be that the principle does appear to be true in a restricted sense. Thinking about what we are doing as we do it does seem to interfere with our everyday skills such as tying knots, typing, and going downstairs. As you are carrying a glass of water, try to think about what you ought to do to prevent it from spilling. Or think about just how you are supposed to shift from second to third gear while driving. Movement in these situations will be awkward, at best.[35] And it is easy to see how an evolutionary advantage could accrue to those who could think about more important things during, say, grooming. But for the performer on stage there is nothing more important than the task at hand.

Another reason why people accept the principle may be that focusing on something other than your own movement is often useful when performing or competing, as it can help ease excessive nervousness. And trying to do well (rather than just letting things happen) can lead to excessive tension. However, it may be that the best performers can think about how they are moving while keeping nerves in check and not becoming excessively tense. Furthermore, the experience of trying is most pronounced when you are doing your best yet still fail. Of course, that's a bad thing. But doing your best and succeeding is not.

Moreover, the reason for why the principle is so widely accepted in popular culture may have less to do with the above considerations than with the fact that most people prefer ease to hard work. Books like *Zen in the Art of Archery* and all of its play-offs turn upon this tendency.[36] They reach the status of best-sellers, I believe, for the same reason as diet books that advocate the idea that you can eat as much as you want as long as you don't eat one somewhat arbitrary category of food are popular: not because they work, but because they are easy to follow.

So, people may be drawn to accept the principle for a number of reasons besides or in addition to the argument from cognitive interference and the neurological data. And once propounded the principle is perpetuated because introspection here is very susceptible to suggestion.

As for Balanchine's claim that his dancers shouldn't think, I asked Violette Verdy, one of the premier ballet dancers of the twentieth century, about this. Verdy was a principal dancer with New York City Ballet for eighteen years under Balanchine's direction, during which time he created many famous roles for her. But Verdy brushed off the question. "Oh that," she replied, "he only said that when a dancer was stuck; like an elevator between floors." And after thinking this over, I realized that it makes perfect sense. Unreflective, automatic action does play an important role in performing. But quite contrary to the principle of automaticity, it is when things go wrong, not when they go right, that we need it. And isn't this true of philosophy as well? When is it that you need to step back from thinking and just let your unconscious mind guide your writing? Precisely when you're stuck between floors. The principle, I conclude, ought to be rejected.

## Notes

1 Arnheim, *Toward a Psychology of Art*, p. 261.
2 The "ten-year rule" was first formulated by Bryan and Harter (see "Studies on the Telegraphic Language"). Chase and Simon apply it to chess ("The Mind's Eye in Chess"). Ericsson *et al.* show that it extends to music composition, sports, science, and the visual arts ("The Role of Deliberate Practice in the Acquisition of Expert Performance").
3 Fitts and Posner, "Learning and Skilled Performance," p. 12.
4 Ibid., p. 12.
5 Ibid., p. 16.
6 Dreyfus and Dreyfus, "Ethical Implications of the Five-Stage Skill-Acquisition Model," p. 253.
7 Ibid.
8 Dreyfus, "Return of Myth of the Mental," p. 355.

9 Dreyfus and Dreyfus, *Mind over Machine*.
10 Gould, "Brain of Brawn," *New York Times*, 25 June 2000.
11 James, *Principles of Psychology*, p. 126.
12 Ibid., p. 128.
13 Sherrington, *Integrative Action of the Nervous System*, 1947.
14 Ivanhoe and Van Norden, *Readings in Classical Chinese Philosophy*, p. 225.
15 Ibid.
16 Barrie, *Peter Pan*, p. 994.
17 Dreyfus "Return of Myth of the Mental," p. 352.
18 Ibid.
19 Steve Blass made his major league baseball debut in 1964, and upheld a very strong strikeout record until the 1972 season when his pitching suddenly and inexplicably deteriorated. His game never recovered, and he retired from baseball in 1975. The expression, "Steve Blass disease," has subsequently been used to refer to a major inexplicable change in a player's skill level.
20 "Knoblauch's Throwing Troubles May Force Him to Play Left Field," *Daily Texan* (Associated Press), 6 August 2004; updated Friday, 9 January 2009.
21 Wulf, *Attention and Motor Skill Learning*, p. 23.
22 R. Gray, "Attending to the Execution of a Complex Sensorimotor Skill."
23 Tracy et al., "Regional Brain Activation Associated with Different Performance Patterns during Learning of a Complex Motor Skill"; Puttemans et al., "Changes in Brain Activation during the Acquisition of a Multifrequency Bimanual Coordination Task."
24 Summarized in Goodale and Milner, *Sight Unseen*.
25 J. Gray, *Consciousness*, pp. 7–8.
26 Ibid., p. 8.
27 Ibid., p. 9.
28 See Block, "Consciousness, Accessibility, and the Mesh between Psychology and Neuroscience," for discussion.
29 J. Gray, *Consciousness*, p. 8.
30 Indeed, Morgan and Pollock (1977) report that world-class marathon runners almost invariably report that during a race they are acutely aware of their physiological condition.
31 Fitts and Posner, "Learning and Skilled Performance," p. 15.
32 Ibid.
33 Anna Kisselgoff, "Ballet: Joffrey Stages Laura Dean's 'Night,'" *New York Times*, 31 October 1981.
34 Dreyfus and Dreyfus, "Ethical Implications of the Five-Stage Skill-Acquisition Model," p. 253.
35 See Norman and Shallice, "Attention to Action," and Perner, "Dual Control and the Causal Theory of Action," for discussions of why this may be so.
36 Moreover, see Yamada, *Shots in the Dark*, for an argument that the idea of "it shoots" which is the central tenet of *Zen in the Art of Archery* and which the author claims to have learned from his Japanese teacher, Asa, was either a misinterpretation of the Japanese "that's it" or simply invented by the author himself.

# Bibliography

Arnheim, R., *Toward a Psychology of Art: Collected Essays*, Berkeley: University of California Press, 1966.

Barrie, J. M., *Peter Pan* (1911), in J. Griffith and C. Frey (eds), *Classics of Children's Literature*, Upper Saddle River, NJ: Prentice Hall, 1996, pp. 959–1042.

Beilock, S. L., "Understanding Skilled Performance: Memory, Attention, and 'Choking under Pressure,'" in T. Morris, P. Terry, and S. Gordon (eds), *Sport and Exercise Psychology: International Perspectives*, Morgantown, WV: Fitness Information Technology, 2007, pp. 153–66.

Beilock, S. L. and Carr, T. H., "From Novice to Expert Performance: Attention, Memory, and the Control of Complex Sensorimotor Skills," in A. M. Williams, N. J. Hodges, M. A. Scott, and M. L. J. Court (eds), *Skill Acquisition in Sport: Research, Theory and Practice*, London: Routledge, 2004, pp. 309–28.

Beilock, S. L., Carr, T. H., MacMahon, C., and Starkes, J. L., "When Paying Attention Becomes Counterproductive: Impact of Divided versus Skill-Focused Attention on Novice and Experienced Performance of Sensorimotor Skills," *Journal of Experimental Psychology: Applied* 8 (2002): 6–16.

Block, N., "Consciousness, Accessibility, and the Mesh between Psychology and Neuroscience," *Behavioral and Brain Sciences* 30 (2007): 481–99.

Bryan, W. L. and Harter, N., "Studies on the Telegraphic Language: The Acquisition of a Hierarchy of Habits," *Psychological Review* 6 (1899): 345–75.

Chase, W. G. and Simon, H. A., "The Mind's Eye in Chess," in W. G. Chase (ed.), *Visual Information Processing*, New York: Academic Press, 1973, pp. 215–81.

Dreyfus, H. L., "Response to McDowell," *Inquiry* 50, no. 4 (2007): 371–77.

——, "The Return of Myth of the Mental," *Inquiry* 50, no. 4 (2007): 352–65.

Dreyfus, H. L. and Dreyfus, S. E., "The Ethical Implications of the Five-Stage Skill-Acquisition Model," *Bulletin of Science, Technology & Society* 24 (2004): 251–64.

——, *Mind over Machine: The Power of Intuition and Expertise in the Era of the Computer*, New York: Free Press, 1986.

Ericsson, K. A., Drampe, R. T., and Tesch-Romer, C., "The Role of Deliberate Practice in the Acquisition of Expert Performance," *Psychological Review* 100 (1993): 363–606.

Fitts, P. M. and Posner, M. I., "Learning and Skilled Performance," in *Human Performance*, Belmont, CA: Brock-Cole, 1967.

Ford, P., Hodges, N. J., and Williams, A. M., "Online Attentional-Focus Manipulations in a Soccer Dribbling Task: Implications for the Proceduralization of Motor Skills," *Journal of Motor Behavior* 37 (2005): 386–94.

Goodale, M. and Milner, D., *Sight Unseen*, Oxford: Oxford University Press, 2003.

Gray, R., "Attending to the Execution of a Complex Sensorimotor Skill: Expertise Differences, Choking, and Slumps," *Journal of Experimental Psychology: Applied* 10 (2004): 42–54.

Gray, J., *Consciousness: Creeping Up on the Hard Problem*, Oxford: Oxford University Press, 2004.

Ivanhoe, P. J. and Van Norden, B., *Readings in Classical Chinese Philosophy*, Indianapolis: Hackett Publishing, 2005.

James, W., *The Principles of Psychology* (1890), Cambridge, MA: Harvard University Press, 1983.

McCrone, J., *Going Inside: A Tour Round a Single Moment of Consciousness*, London: Faber & Faber, 2000.

Morgan, W. P. and Pollock, M. L., "Psychologic Characterization of the Elite Distance Runner," *Annals of the New York Academy of Science* 301 (1977): 382–403.

Norman, D. A. and Shallice, T., "Attention to Action: Willed and Automatic Control of Behavior," in R. J. Davidson, G. E. Schwartz, and D. Shapiro (eds), *Consciousness and Self-Regulation*, New York: Plenum, 1986, vol. 4, pp. 1–18.

Perner, J., "Dual Control and the Causal Theory of Action: The Case of Nonintentional Action," in N. Elian and J. Roessler (eds), *Agency and Self Awareness*, Oxford: Oxford University Press, 2003, pp. 218–43.

Puttemans, V., Wenderoth N., and Swinnen, S. P., "Changes in Brain Activation during the Acquisition of a Multifrequency Bimanual Coordination Task: From the Cognitive Stage to Advanced Levels of Automaticity," *Journal of Neuroscience* 25, no. 17 (2005): 4270–78.

Schneider, W. and Shiffrin, R. M., "Controlled and Automatic Human Information-Processing: I. Detection, Search, and Attention," *Psychological Review* 84 (1977): 1–66.

Sherrington, C., *The Integrative Action of the Nervous System* (1906), Cambridge: Cambridge University Press, 1947.

Tracy, J., A. Flanders, S. Madi, J. Laskas, E. Stoddard, A. Pyrros, P. Natale, and N. Del Vecchio, "Regional Brain Activation Associated with Different Performance Patterns During Learning of a Complex Motor Skill," *Cerebral Cortex* 13 (2003): 904–10.

Wulf, G., *Attention and Motor Skill Learning*, Champaign, IL: Human Kinetics, 2007.

Yamada, S., *Shots in the Dark: Japan, Zen, and the West*, Chicago, IL: University of Chicago Press, 2009.

# 15

# MINDEDNESS, MINDLESSNESS, AND FIRST-PERSON AUTHORITY

*Dan Zahavi*

Whereas the recent exchange between Dreyfus and McDowell has largely highlighted differences in their respective accounts, my focus in the following will be on what I take to be some of their shared assumptions. More specifically, I wish to argue that Dreyfus's frequent reference to mindless coping is partly motivated by his endorsement of a conception of mindedness that is considerably closer to McDowell's view than one might initially have assumed. In a second step, I will discuss to what extent the notions of mindlessness and conceptual mindedness can do justice to the first-personal character of our experiential life. In pursuing this issue, I will at the same time challenge Dreyfus's claim that his position is one with a venerable phenomenological ancestry.

## Mindless coping

In his American Philosophical Association Presidential Address, Dreyfus rejects the claim that perception is conceptual all the way out, and argues that we have to make room for the nonconceptual embodied coping skills that we share with prelinguistic infants and higher animals.[1] In making this claim, Dreyfus specifically targets McDowell and argues that the latter's showdown with the Myth of the Given entails a endorsement of what Dreyfus labels the Myth of the Mental,[2] which for Dreyfus amounts to the view that all intelligibility is conceptual in nature. One question that immediately arises is why Dreyfus has chosen this specific label. Why not rather talk of the Myth of the Conceptual or – to acknowledge the Merleau-Pontyan background of the criticism – the Myth of Intellectualism? Contrary to what might perhaps be the initial assumption, the label Myth of the Mental isn't meant to suggest that McDowell's conception of the mental is mistaken or flawed. What Dreyfus objects to, isn't the conception per se, but rather the idea that the mind, thus defined, has as central and pervasive a role to play in our engagement with the world as McDowell thinks. As

Dreyfus writes, the idea that our embodied coping is permeated with mindedness is a mentalistic myth that is untrue to the phenomenon. In reality, the contents possessed by our embodied skills are not only non-conceptual, nonpropositional, nonlinguistic, and nonrational. They are also nonmental.[3] Dreyfus even goes so far as to declare mindedness the enemy of our pervasive mindless absorbed coping.[4] He also speaks of subjectivity as the lingering ghost of the mental, and denies that there is any immersed or implicit ego in absorbed coping. Indeed, in total absorption one ceases to be a subject altogether.[5] Thus, our immersed bodily life is so completely and totally world-engaged that it is entirely oblivious to itself. It is only when this bodily absorption is interrupted that something like self-consciousness emerges. Dreyfus doesn't deny the existence of self-consciousness, but he definitely wants to see it as a capacity that is only exercised or actualized on special occasions. When that happens, I retrospectively attach an "I think" to the coping. Moreover, although Dreyfus doesn't deny that we have the capacity to step back and reflect, we cannot on his view exercise this capacity without disrupting our coping and radically transform the kind of affordances that are given to it.[6]

So far, Dreyfus seems to be equating mindedness, mindfulness and the mental with a form of reflective or self-monitoring rationality,[7] and to distinguish this from a kind of mindless *experiencing*.[8] In other places, however, Dreyfus likens absorbed coping to an airport radio whose beacon doesn't give a warning signal unless the plane strays off course. And as he then writes, "when the pilot is on the beam there is no experience at all."[9] As long as everything goes smoothly there is only silent guidance. It is only deviation that occasions a warning signal, and it is this signal that is then registered experientially. As Dreyfus puts it, a coper must have the capacity to enter a monitoring stance if the brain sends an alarm signal that something is going wrong.[10] When reading statements like these, and when comparing them to places where Dreyfus writes that consciousness is only called into action once the brain has detected something gone wrong,[11] that features of the environment that are available to the perceptual system needn't be available to the mind,[12] and that adults, infants, and animals in their direct dealing with affordances can cope without thinking at all simply by taking "input energy" and processing it appropriately,[13] one gets the impression that the relevant processing takes place nonconsciously.

The question to ask is consequently whether or not absorbed coping for Dreyfus involves experience? In his contribution to the present volume, Dreyfus's reply is by and large negative. He claims that there is no place for experiential content in absorbed coping and speaks of the possibility of mind-free practical activity,[14] just as he also refers to the phenomenon of unconscious coping and likens Olympic swimmers, who are performing at their best, to sleepwalkers.[15] But this stance inevitable gives rise to the following question: How can one meaningfully speak of a *phenomenology* of mindless coping – as Dreyfus repeatedly does – if the coping is completely unconscious?

Of course, a possible retort could be that it all depends on the kind of phenomenology one has in mind. Consider Dennett's *heterophenomenology* for instance. According to Dennett, heterophenomenology is simply the standard third-person scientific method applied to consciousness. It is *the* scientific way to investigate consciousness, and thus "the way to *save* the rich phenomenology of consciousness for scientific study."[16] But as Dennett also says, zombies are not just possible; they are real, since all of us are zombies. If we think we are more than zombies, this is simply due to the fact that we have been misled or bewitched by the defective set of metaphors that we use to think about the mind.[17] It is important not to misunderstand Dennett at this point. He is not arguing that nobody is conscious. Rather he is claiming that consciousness does not have the first-person phenomenal properties it is commonly thought to have, which is why there is in fact no such thing as actual phenomenology.[18] To put it differently, Dennett does recognize that people believe they have experiences, and he considers these facts – the facts about what people believe and express – to be phenomena that any scientific study of the mind must account for,[19] but as he then continues, from the fact that people believe that they have experiences, it doesn't follow that they do in fact have experiences.[20] The moment that Dennett reaches the conclusion that our commonsense self-ascription of mental states is persistently mistaken, he starts sounding somewhat like Dreyfus. So when Dreyfus advocates a phenomenology of mindless coping, perhaps he is really thinking of a heterophenomenology of mindless coping?

In a recent paper, co-authored with Sean Kelly, Dreyfus has, in fact, engaged directly with Dennett's heterophenomenology. Dreyfus starts out by saying that Dennett's heterophenomenology might be an improvement and better alternative than the phenomenologies of Husserl and Sartre.[21] But eventually Dreyfus expresses two qualms about Dennett's proposal. On the one hand, heterophenomenology attributes beliefs to the subject, but this is unwarranted, since there are no beliefs (in our everyday coping), but merely motor intentionality.[22] On the other hand, Dreyfus also claims that heterophenomenology fails to do justice to a certain class of conscious experiences, namely those that aren't beliefs.[23] What kind of experiences does he have in mind? Somewhat surprisingly, Dreyfus writes that a subject must believe or think that he is having a qualitative experience in order to be having it – thus the possession of higher-order beliefs turns out to be a precondition for qualitative experiences – but as he then continues, there are some conscious intentional experiences that a subject can have without believing that he is having them. In fact, Dreyfus even claims that having these experiences depends on the subject not having a belief about them.[24] Presumably, the idea is that the moment we start having thoughts or beliefs about these experiences, the experiences in question are radically transformed. But given his previous claim, it must also mean that the experiences in question aren't qualitative experiences (since the latter, on his account, do require beliefs). What kind of nonqualitative experiences are we then dealing with? The only further detail that Dreyfus provides us with is that the experiences involve a certain felt or sensed solicitation to act, and that this is a datum of phenomenology.[25] It remains unclear to me why this felt solicitation should lack a qualitative character, but if we disregard this complication, we might conclude that Dreyfus, in some places at least, allows for an experiential dimension to some forms of mindless coping, although he still considers it to lack a first-person character as well as mindedness and subjectivity.

## Conceptual mindedness

In his reply to Dreyfus, McDowell has argued that embodied coping – in the case of mature human beings – is permeated by mindedness, and that the mind is everywhere in our lives.[26] More specifically he urges us to accept that mindedness is operative in our unreflective thinking and acting and consequently by no means foreign or alien to an immersed bodily life.[27] Indeed, McDowell argues that Dreyfus, by taking it for granted that mindedness is detached from bodily life, seems to embrace a form of dualism reminiscent of Descartes and to be vulnerable to the Myth of the Disembodied Intellect.[28] A crucial question though is what precisely McDowell has in mind when he talks of mindedness. He persistently emphasizes the role of rationality and language, and repeatedly speaks of our conceptual mindedness.[29] McDowell does accentuate the importance of respecting the essential first-person character of acting, but a decisive question is whether the tight link between mindedness, conceptuality, and language allows him to account for the first-personal character of consciousness. Let us take a closer look at McDowell's more elaborate account in *Mind and World*.

As is well known, McDowell is out to deny that there is a basic level of nonconceptual experience. In experience one takes in *"that things are thus and so."*[30] McDowell consequently claims that experience already has conceptual content and that conceptual capacities are at work in the experiences themselves (and not just in our judgments based on them).[31] He furthermore argues that it is because experience involves conceptual capacities belonging to spontaneity that experience can count as openness to the layout of reality.[32] Elsewhere he defines spontaneity as "a faculty that is exercised in actively self-critical control of what one thinks, in the light of the deliverances of experience."[33] This is obviously a reflective capacity. Indeed, for McDowell, only a self-conscious subject, a subject capable of self-ascribing experiences, can have awareness of an objective world. On

McDowell's understanding it is "the spontaneity of the understanding, the power of conceptual thinking, that brings both the world and the self into view."[34] Creatures without conceptual capacities consequently lack both self-consciousness and experience of objective reality.

A succinct presentation of McDowell's guiding idea is provided by Thomas in the following quote:

> McDowell's account of concept possession involves both self-consciousness and the capacity for critical reflection. Both of these ideas express the common intuition that the mind must be able to reflect on its own operations, by reflexively applying those operations to itself, if it is to enjoy the full normativity which for McDowell is the essence of mentality.[35]

Now, the most common way of discussing the merits of this proposal has been by looking at perception, but as McDowell points out, the Myth of the Given, the idea that there is a nonconceptual experiential intake that can constitute a reason or warrant for believing or judging that such and such, is also alive, and perhaps especially so, in the case of inner sense.[36] Is our inner experience, our experience of, say, our own sensations (of pain or nausea) and emotions (of fear and anger) also conceptually structured through and through, or is it rather the case that inner experience should fundamentally be understood as a form of nonconceptual acquaintance?

How should we in the first place think of inner experience, how should we understand the relation between the inner experience and that of which it is an experience? One option that McDowell rightfully rejects outright is the idea that inner experience has the same kind of objects as outer experience, except that the object of the inner experience is not very far out.[37] It is, in other words, quite misleading to construe the relation between a pain and an experience of pain in the same way as the relation between a chair and a perception of a chair, although "seeing a chair" and "feeling a pain" have the same grammatical structure. McDowell's own proposal is that the objects of "inner experience" are internal accusatives to the awareness that "inner experiences" constitute; they have no existence independently of that (conceptual) awareness.[38] But if so, can we at all speak of an awareness–object distinction, and if we cannot, aren't we forced to accept the idea that inner experience is a form of nonconceptual acquaintance? McDowell obviously wants to resist this conclusion, and as far as I understand his argument, this is what it boils down to: For a subject to have an experience of pain, for a subject to be presented with pain in a first-personal mode of presentation, a certain conceptual understanding of what it means to be in pain is required. The subject must understand her being in pain as a particular case of a more general type of state of affairs, "someone's being in pain." She must understand that the pain is not exclusively tied to a first-person and present-tense mode, but that being in pain is something that can also happen to someone else or to oneself at a different time.

Needless to say this conclusion has a number of striking implications. As McDowell admits, it is not just self-critical thinkers who can feel pain. Indeed, it would be outrageous to deny that creatures that lack conceptual capacities can feel pain.[39] But given his claim concerning the intimate link between conceptuality and experience, this forces McDowell to introduce a distinction between *experience*, on the one hand, and *sentience*, on the other. And although nonhuman animals and infants (and for McDowell infants are mere animals, distinctive only in their potential[40]) might feel pain and have sentience, they don't have any (inner or outer) experience.[41] Animals and infants can feel pain, but their pain and our pain are two different kinds of pain. By denying that animals and infants have experiences, McDowell is consequently not trying to reduce them to automatons; rather his main aim is to deny that there is a common substratum to nonconceptual sentience and to conceptual experience. Conceptuality is not to be seen as a layer added on top of an existing structure, but as something that radically transforms that preexisting structure. In a related move McDowell urges us to accept a distinction between protosubjectivity and full-fledged subjectivity. As he admits, the former notion is introduced precisely in order to permit the ascription of sentience to animals (and infants).[42] Whereas animals and infants might have protosubjectivity, they don't possess full-fledged subjectivity which involves a conceptually mediated orientation to the world, one that is essentially characterized by freedom and critical distance.[43]

On the face of it, there is a tension between McDowell's emphasis on the link between conceptual rationality and critical reflection, on the one hand, and his notion of conceptual capacities that are operative in our unreflective embodied coping, on the other, but regardless of how he intends to resolve that tension, it should be obvious that infants present a more pressing challenge to McDowell than nonhuman animals in general. The reason for this is that infants do not remain in a merely animal mode of living; at some point they are transformed into full-fledged subjectivities.[44] It is rather urgent to understand how this transformation occurs and how it is possible. We must avoid a two-tiered account that leaves us with an unbridgeable dualism between the nonconceptual sentience of the infant and the conceptualized mind of the adult. How does McDowell make the developmental connection between the two intelligible? The answer supplied by McDowell is revealing. He describes the initiation into conceptual capacities as a question of *Bildung*, and argues that the transformation occurs as a result of being initiated into a language.[45] Indeed, it is language that for McDowell constitutes the prior embodiment of mindedness.[46] As he puts it in the very conclusion of *Mind and World*:

> The feature of language that really matters is rather this: that a natural language, the sort of language into which human beings are first initiated, serves as a repository of tradition, a store of historically accumulated wisdom about what is a reason for what. The tradition is subject to reflective modification by each generation that inherits it. Indeed, a standing obligation to engage in critical reflection is itself part of the inheritance. ... But if an individual human being is to realize her potential of taking her place in that succession, *which is the same thing as acquiring a mind*, the capacity to think and act intentionally, at all, the first thing that needs to happen is for her to be initiated into a tradition as it stands.[47]

One obvious question to ask is how McDowell intends to explain the very process of language acquisition, given that he takes infants to be mindless.[48] But more importantly, it should be clear that McDowell defends a rather rarefied notion of what mindedness consists in. Would it be one that Dreyfus would oppose? I don't think so. To repeat the point made earlier, in his discussion with McDowell, Dreyfus doesn't propose or offer an alternative conception of the mind and the mental. Rather, his disagreement expresses itself in his defense of the notion of mindless coping. There would be no reason for this choice of term had Dreyfus not endorsed a conceptualist definition of mind, one that links it to concepts, thoughts, and reasons. This is not to say, of course, that there is no important difference between Dreyfus and McDowell, but the main difference is located elsewhere, namely in the question of whether or not mindedness is to be found at the level of absorbed coping.

## Detectivism and nonobjectifying self-acquaintance

### *First-person authority and first-personal givenness*

In contrast to both Dreyfus and McDowell, I think there is a perfectly legitimate and quite relevant sense in which copers, infants, and various nonhuman animals are subjects of experience. Moreover, I also think there is a sense in which their experiential lives possess a first-personal character. Even in their case, we need an account that does justice to what McDowell at one point has referred to as the "from within" character of consciousness.[49] To put it differently, in contrast to Dreyfus, I think the level of absorbed coping involves a dimension of self-experience – at least in so far as that level is supposed to be experiential rather than simply a matter of nonconscious automaticity – and in contrast to McDowell, I don't think the self-experience in question requires concepts and language acquisition.

One way to get at the type of self-experience I am interested in – we might also label it the first-personal character of consciousness or the for-me-ness of experience – is to raise the question regarding first-person authority. When I say "my arm hurts" or "I thought you had forgotten our appointment" or "I plan to work at home tomorrow" it is customary to say that I make such statements with first-person authority. This is not to say that I am infallible, but if people disbelieve me, it is generally because they think that I am insincere rather than mistaken.[50] On what is such first-person authority based? As Finkelstein has rightly stressed in a recent contribution, we only speak with first-person authority about our *conscious* mental states. We don't speak with such authority about our un- or non-conscious mental states, even though we might know about them through various indirect means, say, through long conversations with a psychoanalyst or cognitive psychologist. Of course, in so far as we come to know about the states, they are to some extent something of which we become conscious, but that doesn't make them conscious in the relevant intransitive sense of the term. No, in order for us to speak with first-person authority about a mental state, the mental state must be one we *consciously* live through.[51]

What is gained by adding the adverb "consciously"? What is the difference between those mental states that remain nonconscious and those that make us consciously aware of objects? A decisive difference is that there is something it is like to consciously perceive, imagine, or remember $x$. Now, on a standard definition of phenomenal consciousness, a mental state is phenomenally conscious if there is something it is like for the subject to be in it. But this necessarily requires the subject to have some awareness of the state in question, although this isn't supposed to mean that the subject must be aware of the state in the robust sense of noticing or attending to or thinking about the state. In a moment, I will discuss to what extent this proposal represents the orthodox view in phenomenology, but independently of the phenomenological tradition, similar views have recently been defended by Block, Burge, Kriegel, and Flanagan.[52] As the latter puts it, consciousness involves self-consciousness in the weak sense that there is something it is like for the subject to have the experience.[53] Picking up on a recent suggestion of Kriegel's, it might here be helpful to distinguish two types of self-consciousness, a transitive and an intransitive. We might say that a subject is in possession of transitive self-consciousness when "she is conscious of her thought that $p$ or conscious of her perception of $x$" and in possession of intransitive self-consciousness when "she is consciously thinking that $p$ or consciously perceiving $x$." What is the difference between the two types of self-consciousness? Kriegel lists four differences and claims that, whereas the first type is introspective, rare, voluntary, and effortful, the second is none of these.[54] According to Kriegel, the latter type of self-consciousness, intransitive self-consciousness, captures one of the important senses of consciousness. Indeed, intransitive self-consciousness can be seen as a necessary condition for, and constitutive feature of, phenomenal consciousness. Or to put it differently, a mental state that lacks intransitive self-consciousness is a nonconscious state.[55]

If one accepts this line of reasoning, one has a ready answer to the question regarding the basis of first-person authority. I can be first-person authoritative with respect to the mental states I consciously live through because these mental states are characterized by a first-personal, subjective, presence.

This proposal is obviously one that Dreyfus would oppose. In defending his own view of mindless coping, and when denying the first-personal character of our embodied coping, when denying that it is characterized by any form of self-experience or minimal self-awareness,[56] Dreyfus makes repeated appeals to what he terms the existential phenomenologists. But is he really right in presenting his position as one with a phenomenological ancestry? I have offered extensive analyses of Husserl's, Heidegger's, Sartre's, Merleau-Ponty's, and Henry's accounts of self-experience in previous books and articles,[57] so let me here restrict myself to a few references to Sartre and Heidegger.

Sartre famously argues that intentional consciousness is *for-itself* (*pour-soi*), that is, self-conscious. An experience does not simply exist, it exists for itself, i.e. it is given for itself, and this (prereflective) self-givenness is not simply a quality added to the experience, a mere varnish; rather it constitutes the very *mode of being* of the experience. As Sartre writes, "This self-consciousness we ought to consider not as a new consciousness, but as *the only mode of existence which is possible for a consciousness of something.*"[58] And as Sartre then adds a bit further in the text, "consciousness is self-consciousness. It is this same notion of *self* which must be studied, for it defines the very being of consciousness."[59] It is consequently important not to conflate the *self*, which Sartre claims is present in prereflective experience, with the *ego*, which he takes to be a product of reflection.[60] In that sense, Dreyfus's own narrow focus on Sartre's early work *La transcendance de l'ego* doesn't give the full picture. One also has to consider the far more elaborate analyses one finds in *L'Être et le néant* and in Sartre's 1948 lecture "Conscience de soi et connaissance de soi."

In his very first lecture course from 1919, Heidegger addresses the question as to whether every experience contains a reference to an I. Although Heidegger denies that my experiences do contain any explicit reference to an I, he nevertheless insists that the experiences are nevertheless rightly called *my* experiences, and are indeed part of *my* life.[61] The experiences do not simply pass by me, as if they were foreign entities; rather they are precisely *mine*.[62] Thus, whenever I experience something, my self (and Heidegger also prefers to speak of a self rather than of an I, ego, or subject) is present, it is so to speak implicated. Thus, the intentional directedness towards ... is not to be understood as an intentional experience that only gains a reference to the self afterwards, as if the self would have to turn its attention back upon the first experience with the help of a subsequent second (reflective) experience. Rather, as Heidegger emphasizes on many occasions, the co-disclosure of the self belongs to intentionality as such.[63] When we look at concrete experience, we always come across a co-givenness of self and world, and as Heidegger puts it, every worldly experiencing involves a certain component of self-acquaintance and self-familiarity, every experiencing is characterized by the fact that "I am always somehow acquainted with myself."[64,65]

One way to resist this conclusion – a way that Dreyfus might feel is appealing – is by embracing a strong version of the intentionalism. Back in 1903, G. E. Moore called attention to the so-called *diaphanous* quality of experience: when you try to focus your attention on the intrinsic features of experience, you always *seem* to end up attending to that *of* which it is an experience.[66] And as Tye has subsequently argued, the lesson of this transparency is that *"phenomenology ain't in the head."*[67] To discover what it is like to have a certain experience, you must look at what is being intentionally represented. Thus, as the argument goes, experiences do not have intrinsic and nonintentional qualities of their own; rather experienced qualities, the way things phenomenally seem to be, are – all of them – properties the experiences represent things as having.[68] Indeed, the reason an experience of a green cucumber is subjectively distinct from an experience of a yellow orange is precisely that different kinds of objects are represented. But if this is the case, one might deny that experiential states or episodes are in any way self-presenting, they do not present me with aspects or dimensions of my own consciousness; rather they are strictly and exclusively world-presenting. Or to rephrase the view with some of Dreyfus's terms: Initially, there are mindless forms of world engagement. We only become minded, we only attain mindedness, the moment we start to reflect.

I think there is something right about intentionalism – there is something right in the claim that phenomenal qualities, rather than amounting to some ineffable qualia, have to do with the way in which worldly objects are presented – but ultimately I think the strong transparency thesis operates with too impoverished a notion of phenomenality. Not only has there occasionally been a tendency to focus on the perceptual domain (the loudness of a sound, the smoothness of a surface, the sweetness of a taste, the pungency of a smell), and to forget that it also feels like something to be nervous, angry, fearful, distressed, hungry, tired, etc. But more importantly, even if we restrict ourselves to the former range of examples, the dimension of phenomenality is not exhausted by the qualities belonging to the objects of experience. Phenomenality *is* world-presenting but it is *also* self-involving. We need to distinguish as Husserl did between the intentional object in "the how of its determinations" (*im Wie seiner Bestimmtheiten*) and in "the how of its givenness" (*im Wie seiner Gegebenheitsweisen*).[69] In short, not only is what it is like to perceive a *green square* subjectively distinct from what it is like to perceive a *red circle*. What it is like to *perceive* a green square is also subjectively distinct from what it is like to *remember* or *imagine* a green square. Moreover, we shouldn't forget that when I consciously see, remember, know, think, hope, feel, or will something, the objects are there *for me* in different modes of givenness (as imagined, perceived, recollected, anticipated, etc.). It could of course be objected that it is patently implausible to claim that each and every experience is accompanied by a distinct feeling of for-me-ness, i.e. that it simply isn't true to phenomenology to claim that all my experiences possess the same quale, a common stamp or label that clearly identifies them as mine. But this objection misunderstands the claim being made. Rather than referring to a specific experiential content, say a quality like yellow, salty, or spongy, i.e. rather than referring to a specific *what*, the for-me-ness of experience refers to the distinct givenness or *how* of experience. It refers to the first-personal presence of experience. It refers to the fact that the experiences I am living through are given in a way to me that in principle is unavailable to others.

Does this view amount to a form of *detectivism*, to use the label coined by Finkelstein? No. The suggestion is not that first-person authority is to be explained by means of a kind of inward observation or introspection that allows us to detect or discover the content of our own mind.[70] The claim is not that experiences are things we perceive or observe and that the relation between an experience and its first-personal givenness (subjective presence) is to be cashed out in terms of an act–object structure. The point is rather that experiential processes are intrinsically self-revealing or self-intimating. This is also why it is better to say that we see, hear or feel *consciously*, instead of saying that there is a perception of an object, and in addition an awareness of the perception. The decisive advantage of the adverbial phrasing is that it avoids interpreting the secondary awareness as a form of object-consciousness. This temptation remains as long as we talk of experiential episodes as episodes *of* which we are conscious.

As we have seen, Sartre and Heidegger both consider a form of self-consciousness to be an integral part of intentional consciousness. They also deny that the self-consciousness in question comes about by means of some additional second-order mental state. To that extent they both reject a *higher-order account* of consciousness according to which the distinction between conscious and nonconscious mental states rests upon the presence or absence of a relevant meta-mental state. In contrast to some recently proposed same-order accounts of consciousness, which follow Brentano in interpreting intransitive self-consciousness as a form of marginal or secondary object-consciousness, Sartre and Heidegger (along with Husserl and Gurwitsch) would deny that the self-givenness of experience involves a subject–object structure.[71] They would not only reject the view that a mental state becomes conscious by being taken as an object by a higher-order state, they would also reject the view espoused by Brentano according to which a mental state becomes conscious by taking itself as an object. Brentano and the phenomenologists both share the view that self-consciousness (or, to use Brentano's terminology, "inner consciousness") differs from ordinary object-consciousness. The issue of controversy is over whether self-consciousness is (i) merely an extraordinary object-consciousness or (ii) not an object-consciousness at all. In contrast to Brentano, the phenomenologists would think the latter, more radical, move is required. In our everyday life, we are absorbed by and preoccupied with projects and objects in the world. Although this necessarily entails that we are (prereflectively) aware of our experiences – they are like something to us – we are not aware of them as a succession of internal objects. My prereflective access to my experiential life is nonobjectifying in the sense that I do not occupy the position or perspective of a spectator or in(tro)spector on it, which of course is yet another reason why we are not dealing with a form of detectivism.[72]

To exemplify, let us consider the early lecture course *Grundprobleme der Phänomenologie* of 1919/20, where we find Heidegger arguing that one of the tasks of phenomenology is to disclose the nonobjectifying and nontheoretical self-understanding that belongs to experience as such.[73] Thus, Heidegger clearly acknowledges the existence of a basic self-acquaintance that is part and parcel of experience. And as he repeatedly emphasizes, this self-familiarity does not take the form of a reflective self-perception or a thematic self-observation, nor does it involve any kind of self-objectification. On the contrary, we are confronted with a process of lived self-acquaintance whose distinctive feature is its nonreflective character, and which must be understood as an immediate expression of life itself.[74] In a lecture course given seven years later, Heidegger pursues the same line of thought, and writes:

> Dasein, as existing, is there for itself, even when the ego does not expressly direct itself to itself in the manner of its own peculiar turning around and turning back, which in phenomenology is called inner perception as contrasted with outer. The self is there for the Dasein itself without reflection and without inner perception, *before* all reflection. Reflection, in the sense of a turning back, is only a mode of self-*apprehension*, but not the mode of primary self-disclosure.[75]

Just like Sartre, Heidegger would deny that we only gain awareness of our own experiences through reflection. Prior to reflection, our experiential life is not a question of nonconscious automaticity, rather qua experiential life it is precisely self-disclosing. This first-personal self-disclosure is immediate, nonobservational, noninferential, and nonobjectifying.

## The power of reflection

Dreyfus consistently interprets self-consciousness as a form of self-monitoring. This is far removed from the idea of an immersed, non-objectifying self-acquaintance that we find in phenomenology. Indeed, it is tempting to criticize Dreyfus for remaining a detectivist, and for having fallen victim to a myth of his own, namely the Myth of the Spectatorial Subject. In addition, Dreyfus also claims that the fundamental structures of mindless coping are off-limits to any kind of reflective investigation, since he considers the latter a kind of falsifying mirror or telescope that utterly transforms whatever it makes appear. One question to consider is again to what extent this view is in line with those found in classical phenomenology. Another question concerns the methodological impasse it arguably results in.

There is a long tradition in phenomenology for discussing the issue regarding the disclosing versus producing character of reflection. Most phenomenologists recognized that, rather than merely copying or repeating the original experience, reflection actually transforms it, or as Husserl explicitly admitted, it *alters* it.[76] Husserl spoke of reflection as a process that – in the best of circumstances – discloses, disentangles, explicates, articulates, and accentuates those components and structures that were implicitly contained in prereflective experience.[77]

I think one should view the phenomenological position as being situated between two extremes. On one hand, we have the view that reflection merely copies or mirrors prereflective experience faithfully; on the other, the view that reflection distorts lived experience irredeemably. The middle course is to recognize that reflection involves both a gain and a loss. For most phenomenologists, reflection is constrained by what is prereflectively lived through; it is answerable to experiential facts and is not constitutively self-fulfilling. But at the same time, they recognized that reflection qua thematic self-experiences does not simply reproduce the lived experiences unaltered, and that this may be precisely what makes reflection cognitively valuable. Reacting against a direct attack on phenomenology that Natorp articulated in his 1912 book *Allgemeine Psychologie* – an attack that basically consisted in the claim that the phenomenological method is incapable of capturing experiential structures in their pretheoretical immediacy, since the reflective method employed is not only theoretical and objectifying, but also one making use of generalizing and subsuming concepts that merely estranges us from experience itself (this all sounds somewhat like Dreyfus) – Heidegger maintained that the phenomenological articulation and conceptualization of life experience is something that belongs to life itself; it is not something that is imposed on life arbitrarily from without, as if the conceptualization were driven merely by certain epistemological or foundational concerns. A true phenomenological description does not constitute a violation, is not an attempt to impose a foreign systematicity on life, rather it is something that is rooted in and motivated by factic life experience itself.[78] As Heidegger writes in the lecture course *Phänomenologische Interpretationen zu Aristoteles* of 1921/22:

> The categories are nothing invented, no "framework" or independent society of logical schemata; they are rather in an originary fashion *in life itself of life*; of life, in order to "cultivate" it. They have their own mode of access which, however, is not such as would be foreign to life itself, imposed upon it arbitrarily from without, rather it is just the eminent way in which *life comes to itself*.[79]

Life is comprehensible because it always spontaneously expresses itself, and because experiencing is itself a preliminary form of understanding, is itself what might be called a preunderstanding.[80] Thus, Heidegger basically argues that there is an intimate connection between *experience, expression,* and *understanding*.[81] It is also in this context that Heidegger speaks of philosophy as a continuation of the reflexivity found in (experiential) life.[82] In other words, for Heidegger phenomenology must build on the familiarity that life already has with itself; it must draw on the persistent care of self that is build into the very life stream.

Rather than simply distorting lived experience, our articulation of it might, at best, simply be accentuating structures already inherent in it. This is not to say that reflection does not contain the potential for error and distortion, but as long as reflection is imbued with a self-critical awareness of precisely such dangers, reflection retains its value. Moreover, the claim that reflection necessarily falsifies lived experience and that lived experiences elude it completely is one we should avoid. As Husserl already pointed out in his discussion with H. J. Watt in §79 of *Ideen I*, such a skeptical claim is ultimately self-refuting. The problem is obviously that in order to argue that reflection falsifies lived experience, you have to have some other access to the very same lived experiences, an access that allows you to compare them to what reflection presents us with. Otherwise your skeptical claim is utterly empty. But how are you to obtain such access, how are you to scrutinize the lived experience in order to allow for a comparison if not through some form of reflection?[83]

To put it differently, how does Dreyfus know that reflection falsifies lived experience? How does he know that it is a myth that reflection makes something implicit explicit?[84] Moreover, how do we on Dreyfus's account make the level of absorbed coping accessible to phenomenological investigation and description? Given his own restrictions, it can hardly be based on a reflection, nor for that matter can it be based on the verbal reports of interviewed subjects, since those verbal reports are considered retrospective rationalization, i.e. post-hoc fabrications. Is it then a question of inference to best explanation of behavioral data? If so, it is hard to see why Dreyfus's account should merit the label "phenomenological."[85]

## Phenomenality and conceptuality

So far, I have argued that Dreyfus's reference to mindless coping must be seen in the context of his endorsement of a conception of mindedness not unlike McDowell's. I have shown that Dreyfus's attempt to bolster his account of mindlessness by reference to existential phenomenology is quite problematic.[86] Not only do Sartre and Heidegger endorse a notion of an immersed, nonobjectifying self-acquaintance which falls outside the alternatives of unconscious coping and observational self-monitoring allowed for by Dreyfus, but it also remains quite unclear to what extent Dreyfus is able to offer a phenomenology of skilful coping given his categorical distrust of reflection. Dreyfus's relatively positive appraisal of Dennett's heterophenomenology is in this context revealing. The outcome of all of this is a decisive lacuna in Dreyfus's account. It is not doing justice to the first-personal character of experience. Paradoxically, I think one of the problems is that Dreyfus isn't sufficiently radical in his rejection of Cartesianism. The right way to counter Cartesianism is not to do what Dreyfus has done, namely to accept its definitions of subjectivity and experience and then to argue that we need to get rid of both. No, the right way to counter it is by proposing an alternative and better understanding of what experience and subjectivity amount to, which is precisely what the phenomenologists have been doing. In short, I am not persuaded by Dreyfus's appeal to mindlessness. But what then about McDowell's notion of mindedness?

McDowell's denial that one can have experiences as of an inner or outer world in the absence of concepts[87] is reminiscent of the Strawsonian idea that one cannot be said to have a subjective perspective unless one possesses a certain understanding of the objectivity condition, an understanding that environmental objects persist independently of the experiential perspective we bring to bear on them. The obvious question to ask, however, is whether the requirements that must be met in order to recognize an experience *as* subjective or categorize it *as* inner are identical to those that must be met in order to simply have experiences, experiences that are essentially and by necessity characterized by what Kriegel terms intransitive self-consciousness, and what other thinkers have called "prereflective self-consciousness," "first-personal givenness," "for-me-ness of experience," "subjective presence," "self-intimation," or "reflexiveness" (to use a term recently favored by Burge).

McDowell can of course decide to reserve the word "experience" for something that involves the actualization of conceptual capacities,[88] but this merely highlights the fact that the discussion can easily derail into a terminological dispute. And indeed, not only do different people employ different terms to designate one and the same phenomenon but one and the same term, be it "self-consciousness," "for-me-ness of experience," or "first-personal givenness," has definitely also been used to designate quite different phenomena.

Let me – in the face of some recent criticism[89] – try to be as clear as possible about what I mean when I talk of the first-personal givenness or for-me-ness of experience. I don't mean a self-reference by means of the first-person pronoun, in fact, I don't mean a linguistically conditioned self-reference at all. Nor do I have an explicit or thematic kind of self-knowledge in mind, one involving an awareness of oneself as a distinct individual, different from other individuals. No, I am simply referring to the self-presentational character of phenomenal consciousness. As I see it, we have three options. We can (1) endorse a radical version of the transparency thesis and argue that phenomenality is strictly and exclusively world-presenting, i.e. when consciously scrutinizing a lotto coupon or when consciously admiring a portrait, we are de facto self- and mind-blind. If we deny this and concede that experiential episodes (the perceiving, the admiring, the hoping, fearing etc.) are also given when consciously lived through, the obvious question is how, i.e. in what manner. We can then either claim (2a) that they are given in the same way as public objects (i.e. in a way that is equally accessible to a variety of subjects) or we can claim (2b) that they are given in a distinct way, with a distinct subjective presence to the subject whose experiential episodes they are, a way that in principle is unavailable to others. When saying distinct, the claim is not that the subject of the experience is explicitly aware of their distinct character; the point is not that the subject is necessarily attending to the distinctness in any way. But experiential givenness differs from objectual givenness even before, say, a child becomes explicitly aware of this difference. In my view, 2b is the only admissible option if one is serious about wanting to do justice to the "from within" character of consciousness. I obviously don't think that first-personal givenness in and by itself amounts to authoritative first-person knowledge (or critical self-deliberation), and I am not trying to obliterate the difference between the two, but I think the former is a necessary prerequisite for the latter. I consequently don't think we will be in position to explain the latter unless we acknowledge the former. And it is entirely unclear to me how this subjective presence, this self-presentational or reflexive feature – something that Husserl explored in great detail in his lectures on the phenomenology of inner time-consciousness – could be conditioned by and dependent upon concepts and language.[90]

There is, of course, one proposal on the market that purports to offer an explanation of why experience requires thoughts, concepts, and language. Indeed, this is precisely what one version of the higher-order thought theory in contemporary analytic philosophy of mind is all about. But since the defenders of this view typically bite the bullet and deny phenomenal consciousness to creatures that lack the capacity for higher-order thoughts,[91] I take it that this is not McDowell's view. In fact, McDowell doesn't seem particularly interested in the character of phenomenal consciousness in the first place, rather his main concern is with the question of how experience can rationally constrain and justify our beliefs and thoughts. His claim is that it can only do so, if it already has conceptual content, and even if it should turn out that our experiential life possesses a form of prereflective self-consciousness, for-me-ness, or first-personal givenness that doesn't depend on language and concepts, he might deem it irrelevant, since on his view, it would have no bearing on the issue he is concerned with.

Another slightly different way of presenting McDowell's take is as follows: If we for a moment set aside his preference for a different terminology, perhaps McDowell could concede that animals and other non-language-using creatures do have some kind of mind, and that their experiential life is characterized by some form of first-personal givenness, but he might then insist that it is a decisive mistake to equate and identify that first-personal givenness with the first-personal givenness characterizing the experiential life of competent language users.[92] Indeed, he might want to argue that the two have no common denominator, no shared core. Just like dye mixed with water, leaves no water uncoloured, concepts and language are not merely layers on top of a preexisting structure, rather they radically transform that structure. Given such a view, one might again reach the same conclusion: even if some form of prelinguistic first-personal givenness exists, it is of no significance if our aim is to do justice to human consciousness.[93]

Is this line of thought convincing? I think not, and here are two reasons.

(1) Let us grant that our rational capacities pervasively shape our experience, let us grant that we experience the world and ourselves differently because of the conceptual capacities we have. If we grant this, would it then be misguided to search for a common core, a commonality, between our experiential life and the sentient life of infants and nonhuman animals? We should not make the mistake of overlooking the difference between the *what* and the *how* of experience, between the *content* and the *mode* or *form* of presentation. What we experience might well be different, but that doesn't show that the basic structure of first-personal givenness is also different. Indeed, if, as Sartre and many other phenomenologists insist, prereflective self-consciousness is an integral and constitutive feature of phenomenal consciousness then it is

difficult to see why that shouldn't hold for experiences that are conceptually structured as well.

(2) Even if it could be argued that there is no commonality between the protosubjectivity of animals and infants and the full-fledged subjectivity of those humans who have been initiated into a language (neither when it comes to the content nor when it comes to the mode or form), even if it could be argued that there is no commonality between the nonconceptual self-disclosing character of consciousness and conceptualized self-experience, I don't see how one could deny that the former constitutes a necessary condition of possibility for the latter. The former might not be sufficient for the latter, it might not in and of itself justify our first-person beliefs, but without it nothing like the latter would ever be possible. But if this is so, I don't see how a satisfactory account of conceptualized mindedness can permit itself to ignore it. By the same token, however, one would also have to concede that an exploration of this basic but fundamental dimension of our experiential life doesn't capture that which is distinctive about human consciousness.

It is clear that McDowell is far more interested in the normative dimension of the mind than in its phenomenal character. But whereas I find it both justifiable and commendable to emphasize the importance of rationality and self-critical thinking when discussing the nature of mind, I also think we need to consider phenomenology and account for the dimension of lived subjectivity. It is precisely an exploration of this dimension that I find wanting in the accounts provided by Dreyfus and McDowell.[94]

## Notes

1 Dreyfus, "Overcoming the Myth of the Mental: How Philosophers Can Profit from the Phenomenology of Everyday Expertise," p. 47.
2 Ibid., p. 52.
3 Dreyfus "The Return of the Myth of the Mental," p. 352.
4 Ibid., p. 353.
5 Dreyfus "Response to McDowell," p. 373
6 Dreyfus, "Overcoming the Myth of the Mental," p. 61; "Return of the Myth of the Mental," p. 354. One can detect a certain tension in Dreyfus's account. On the one hand, he frequently refers to experts such as Israeli fighter aces, Olympic athletes or chess masters when exemplifying mindless coping, but he also argues that one of the virtues of his account is that it can accommodate the nonconceptual coping skills we share with prelinguistic infants and higher animals. The tension consequently has to do with the question of whether the mindless coping that Dreyfus wants to call attention to is one where concepts no longer play any role – although they did play a role when the skill was initially acquired – or whether he rather wants to make the more radical claim that skilful coping is more basic than – and ultimately constitutes the basis for – conceptual rationality. I take it that he wants to claim both, but it is problematic to use examples taken from chess play or aeronautics as support of the more radical claim.

7 Dreyfus, "Response to McDowell," p. 373.
8 Dreyfus, "Return of the Myth of the Mental," p. 364.
9 Ibid., p. 358.
10 Dreyfus, "Response to McDowell," p. 374.
11 Ibid., p. 377.
12 Dreyfus, "Overcoming the Myth of the Mental," p. 54.
13 Ibid., pp. 49, 56.
14 Dreyfus, "The Myth of the pervasiveness of the mental," this volume, p. 31.
15 Ibid., p. 38.
16 Dennett, "Caveat Emptor," p. 50.
17 Dennett, "Living on the Edge," p. 143; *Consciousness Explained*, p. 406.
18 Dennett, *Consciousness Explained*, p. 365.
19 Ibid., p. 98.
20 Ibid., p. 366.
21 Dreyfus and Kelly, "Heterophenomenology," p. 47.
22 Ibid., pp. 48–49.
23 Ibid., p. 51.
24 Ibid.
25 Ibid., pp. 52–53. Elsewhere, however, he writes that in skilful coping, we "experience the situation as drawing the movements out of *us*" (Dreyfus, "Intelligence without Representation," p. 380; my emphasis). If this is a correct phenomenological description, it reintroduces and includes a crucial element of self-reference.
26 McDowell, "What Myth?," p. 339.
27 McDowell, "Response to Dreyfus," p. 370.
28 McDowell, "What Myth?," p. 349; "Response to Dreyfus," p. 369.
29 McDowell, "What Myth?," p. 346.
30 McDowell, *Mind and World*, p. 9.
31 Ibid., p. 24.
32 Ibid., pp. 26, 47.
33 Ibid., p. 49.
34 Ibid., p. 114.
35 Thomas, "Kant, McDowell and the Theory of Consciousness," p. 285.
36 McDowell, *Mind and World*, pp. 18, 21.
37 Ibid., pp. 36–37.
38 Ibid., pp. 21, 36.
39 Ibid., p. 22.
40 Ibid., p. 123.
41 Ibid., p. 50.
42 Ibid., p. 119.
43 Ibid., pp. 116, 119.
44 Ibid., p. 125.
45 Ibid., pp. 84, 125.
46 Ibid., p. 125.
47 Ibid., p. 126; my emphasis.
48 For some recent accounts, which highlight the importance of joint attention, see Tomasello, *Cultural Origins of Human Cognition*, and Hobson, *Cradle of Thought*.
49 McDowell, *Mind, Value, Reality*, p. 377.
50 Finkelstein, *Expression and the Inner*, p. 9.
51 Ibid., p. 116.
52 Block, "Consciousness, Accessibility, and the Mesh between Psychology and Neuroscience," p. 485; Burge, "Reflections on Two Kinds of Consciousness,"

pp. 404–5; Kriegel, "Consciousness as Intransitive Self-Consciousness"; and Flanagan, *Consciousness Reconsidered*.
53 Ibid., p. 194.
54 Kriegel, "Consciousness as Intransitive Self-Consciousness," p. 104.
55 Ibid., pp. 103–6.
56 Dreyfus, "Response to McDowell," pp. 373–74.
57 See, for instance, "Fracture in Self-Awareness"; *Self-Awareness and Alterity*; "Michel Henry and the Phenomenology of the Invisible"; "Inner Time-Consciousness and Pre-reflective Self-Awareness"; "How to Investigate Subjectivity"; "Back to Brentano?"; *Subjectivity and Selfhood*; and "Thinking about (Self-) Consciousness."
58 Sartre, *Being and Nothingness*, p. 9.
59 Ibid., p. 100.
60 As Sartre writes, "Finally we succeeded in getting rid of the pure unreflective consciousness of the transcendental 'I' which obscured it and we showed that selfness [*ipséité*], the foundation of personal existence, was altogether different from an Ego or from a reference of the Ego to itself. There can be, therefore, no question of defining consciousness in terms of a transcendental egology. In short, consciousness is a concrete being *sui generis*, not an abstract, unjustifiable relation of identity. It is selfness and not the seat of an opaque, useless Ego" (Sartre, *Being and Nothingness*, p. 263).
61 Heidegger, *Zur Bestimmung der Philosophie*, p. 69.
62 Ibid., p. 75.
63 Heidegger, *Die Grundprobleme der Phänomenologie* (1989), p. 225; *Einleitung in die Philosophie*, p. 208. In a recent article, Okrent has argued that Heidegger is committed to the view that one cannot intend anything as ready-to-hand unless one also intends oneself as "that for the sake of which" one engages in the kind of activity in which one engages. He then claims that this self-directed form of intentionality plays the same structural role in Heidegger's thought as the "I think" does in Kant (Okrent 2007, "The 'I think' and the for-the-Sake-of-Which," p. 162).
64 Heidegger, *Grundprobleme der Phänomenologie* (1993), p. 251. In his contribution to the present volume, Dreyfus concedes that Heidegger has his own understanding of the self as pervasive and always operative, and that even absorbed coping, on Heidegger's account, is pervaded by "mineness." However, Dreyfus insists that this has nothing to do with the presence of some form of (even marginal) self-awareness. In fact, Dreyfus opts for what might be called a non-experiential reading of "mineness," and argues that it should be interpreted as the manner in which my individual style of life structures the way I am solicited by the world (this volume, p. 30). Dreyfus's focus is on *Sein und Zeit*, but as indicated above (and see also Zahavi "How to Investigate Subjectivity"), the claim that Heidegger's account of self and "mineness" has nothing to do with self-awareness is quite hard to reconcile with what Heidegger's is saying in the lecture courses preceding *Sein und Zeit*.
65 Due to limitations of space, I cannot pursue the question of Merleau-Ponty's view in detail, but here are a few quotes from *Phénomélogie de la perception* that are supposed to challenge Dreyfus's reading: "Consciousness is neither the positing of oneself, nor ignorance of oneself, it is *not concealed* from itself, which means that there is nothing in it which does not in some way announce itself to it, although it does not need to know this explicitly" (Merleau-Ponty, *Phenomenology of Perception*, p. 296). "Behind the spoken *cogito*, the one which is converted into discourse and into essential truth, there lies a tacit *cogito*, myself experienced by myself" (Ibid., p. 403). "The fact that even our purest reflection on the flux is

actually inserted into that flux, shows that the most precise consciousness of which we are capable is always, as it were, affected by itself or given to itself, and that the word consciousness has no meaning independently of this duality" (Ibid., p. 426).
66 Moore, "Refutation of Idealism."
67 Tye, *Ten Problems of Consciousness*, p. 151.
68 Dretske, *Naturalizing the Mind*, p. 1.
69 Husserl, *Ideen zu einer reinen Phänomenologie und phänomenologischen Philosophie I*, pp. 303–4.
70 Finkelstein, *Expression and the Inner*, p. 2.
71 Cf. Zahavi, *Self-Awareness and Alterity*; and *Subjectivity and Selfhood*.
72 In addition, it could be argued that I not only *do* not occupy an objectifying attitude vis-à-vis my experiences, but I *cannot* prereflectively occupy such a position, if the experiences in question are to be given as *my* experiences (cf. Zahavi, "Back to Brentano?").
73 Heidegger, *Grundprobleme der Phänomenologie* (1993), pp. 155–57.
74 Ibid., pp. 159, 165, 257–58.
75 Heidegger, *Die Grundprobleme der Phänomenologie* (1989), p. 226.
76 Husserl, *Cartesianische Meditationen und Pariser Vorträge*, p. 72; *Aufsätze und Vorträge*, p. 89.
77 Husserl, *Einleitung in die Logik und Erkenntnistheorie*, p. 244; *Zur Phänomenologie des inneren Zeitbewußtseins*, p. 129; *Analysen zur passiven Synthesis*, pp. 205, 236.
78 Heidegger, *Phänomenologische Interpretationen zu Aristoteles*, p. 87; and *Grundprobleme der Phänomenologie* (1993), p. 59.
79 Heidegger, *Phänomenologische Interpretationen zu Aristoteles*, p. 88.
80 Heidegger, *Phänomenologie der Anschauung und des Ausdrucks*, p. 166.
81 Ibid., p. 169.
82 Ibid., p.156.
83 Husserl, *Ideen zu einer reinen Phänomenologie und phänomenologischen Philosophie I*, §79.
84 Dreyfus, "Return of the Myth of the Mental," p. 360.
85 For some related worries, see Thompson, *Mind in Life*, pp. 315–17.
86 Let me add that I find Dreyfus's distinction between a (Husserlian) pure and transcendental phenomenology, on the one hand, and a (Heideggerian and Merleau-Pontyan) existential phenomenology, on the other, quite problematic (see Zahavi, "Husserl's Noema and the Internalism–Externalism Debate"; "Internalism, Externalism, and Transcendental Idealism"; and "Phenomenology").
87 McDowell, *Mind and World*, p. 50.
88 McDowell, "Reply to Commentators," p. 410.
89 Cf. Lyyra, "Two Senses for 'Givenness of Consciousness'"; Prætorius, "Phenomenological Underpinning of the Notion of a Minimal Core Self"; Schear, "Experience and Self-Consciousness."
90 For a related argument to the effect that experiential qualities are self-manifesting or self-presenting and that this entails that they given nonobjectifyingly and nonconceptually, see Poellner, "Nonconceptual Content, Experience and the Self."
91 Carruthers, for instance, holds that only creatures that are in possession of a *theory of mind* are capable of enjoying conscious experiences or of having mental states with phenomenal feels (Carruthers, *Language, Thoughts and Consciousness*, p. 158), and he consequently argues that animals (and children under the age of three) are blind to the existence of their own mental states; there is in fact nothing it is like for them to feel pain or pleasure (Carruthers, "Natural theories of consciousness," p. 216; *Phenomenal Consciousness*, p. 203). Carruthers' position is extreme, though by no means unique. For similar views, see Gallup, "Self-Awareness

and the Emergence of Mind in Primates" and "Do Minds Exist in Species Other Than Our Own?" and Prinz, "Emerging Selves." For a criticism of higher-order representational accounts, see Zahavi, *Self-Awareness and Alterity*, "Back to Brentano?," and *Subjectivity and Selfhood*.
92 Consider, for comparison, Baker's distinction between weak and strong first-person phenomena (Baker, *Persons and Bodies*, pp. 60, 67).
93 For the very same reason, McDowell might, of course, also object to the suggestion made earlier, namely that first-personal authority is somehow based or grounded on experiential first-personal givenness. I don't have time on this occasion to discuss McDowell's conceptualism in more detail. Let me just add, however, that there are intriguing similarities and differences between his account and the one found in Husserl. To give just one example, consider that Husserl in *Ideen II* writes that a consideration of the development of the personal ego calls for a distinction between two levels of subjectivity. There is a lower level of "pure" animality, and a higher spiritual level that is home to all proper acts of reason. Husserl then writes that this distinction is linked to the distinction between reason and sensibility. And as he then continues "the latter also has its rules, and indeed its intelligible rules of harmony and discord; it is a stratum of *hidden reason*" (Husserl, *Ideen zu einer reinen Phänomenologie und phänomenologischen Philosophie II*, p. 276).
94 Thanks to Thor Grünbaum, Erik Rietveld, Charles Siewert, and Morten Sørensen Thaning for detailed comments on an earlier version of this chapter.

# References

Baker, L. R., *Persons and Bodies*, Cambridge: Cambridge University Press, 2000.
Block, N., "Consciousness, Accessibility, and the Mesh Between Psychology and Neuroscience," *Behavioral and Brain Sciences* 30, nos 5–6 (2007): 481–99.
Burge, T., "Reflections on Two Kinds of Consciousness," in T. Burge (ed.), *Philosophical Essays*, vol. II: *Foundations of Mind*, New York: Oxford University Press, 2006, pp. 392–419.
Carruthers, P., *Language, Thoughts and Consciousness: An Essay in Philosophical Psychology*, Cambridge: Cambridge University Press, 1996.
——, "Natural Theories of Consciousness," *European Journal of Philosophy* 6, no. 2 (1998): 203–22.
——, *Phenomenal Consciousness: A Naturalistic Theory*, Cambridge: Cambridge University Press, 2000.
Chalmers, D. J., *The Conscious Mind: In Search of a Fundamental Theory*, New York: Oxford University Press, 1996.
Dennett, D. C., "Caveat Emptor," *Consciousness and Cognition* 2 (1993): 48–57.
——, *Consciousness Explained*, Boston: Little, Brown & Co., 1991.
——, "Living on the Edge," *Inquiry* 36 (1993b): 135–59.
Dretske, F., *Naturalizing the Mind*, Cambridge, MA: MIT Press, 1995.
Dreyfus, H. L., "Intelligence without Representation – Merleau-Ponty's Critique of Mental Representation," *Phenomenology and the Cognitive Sciences* 1, no. 4 (2002): 367–83.
——, "Overcoming the Myth of the Mental: How Philosophers Can Profit from the Phenomenology of Everyday Expertise," *Proceedings and Addresses of the American Philosophical Association* 79, no. 2 (2005): 47–65.

———, "Response to McDowell," *Inquiry* 50, no. 4 (2007b): 371–77.
———, "The Return of the Myth of the Mental," *Inquiry* 50, no. 4 (2007): 352–65.
Dreyfus, H. L., and Kelly, S. D., "Heterophenomenology: Heavy-Handed Sleight-of-Hand," *Phenomenology and the Cognitive Sciences* 6, nos 1–2 (2007): 45–55.
Finkelstein, D. H., *Expression and the Inner*, Cambridge, MA: Harvard University Press, 2003.
Flanagan, O., *Consciousness Reconsidered*, Cambridge, MA: MIT Press, 1992.
Gallup, G. G., "Do Minds Exist in Species Other Than Our Own?," *Neuroscience and Biobehavioral Reviews* 9, no. 4 (1985): 631–41.
———"Self-Awareness and the Emergence of Mind in Primates," *American Journal of Primatology* 2, no. 3 (1982): 237–48.
Heidegger, M., *Einleitung in die Philosophie*, Gesamtausgabe, vol. 27, Frankfurt am Main. Vittorio Klostermann, 2001.
———, *Die Grundprobleme der Phänomenologie*, Gesamtausgabe, vol. 24, Frankfurt am Main: Vittorio Klostermann, 1989.
———, *Grundprobleme der Phänomenologie (1919/1920)*, Gesamtausgabe, vol. 58, Frankfurt am Main: Vittorio Klostermann, 1993.
———, *Phänomenologie der Anschauung und des Ausdrucks*, Gesamtausgabe, vol. 59, Frankfurt am Main: Vittorio Klostermann, 1993.
———, *Phänomenologische Interpretationen zu Aristoteles: Einführung in die phänomenologische Forschung*, Gesamtausgabe, vol. 61, Frankfurt am Main: Vittorio Klostermann, 1994.
———, *Zur Bestimmung der Philosophie*, Gesamtausgabe, vol. 56–57. Frankfurt am Main: Vittorio Klostermann, 1999.
Hobson, R. P., *The Cradle of Thought*, London: Macmillan, 2002.
Husserl, E., *Analysen zur passiven Synthesis*, Husserliana XI, The Hague: Martinus Nijhoff, 1966.
———, *Aufsätze und Vorträge (1911–1921)*, Husserliana XXV, Dordrecht: Martinus Nijhoff, 1987.
———, *Ideen zu einer reinen Phänomenologie und phänomenologischen Philosophie I*, Husserliana III, nos 1–2, The Hague: Martinus Nijhoff, 1976.
———, *Cartesianische Meditationen und Pariser Vorträge*, Husserliana I, The Hague: Martinus Nijhoff, 1950.
———, *Einleitung in die Logik und Erkenntnistheorie*, Husserliana XXIV, The Hague: Martinus Nijhoff, 1984.
———, *Ideen zu einer reinen Phänomenologie und phänomenologischen Philosophie II*, Husserliana IV, The Hague: Martinus Nijhoff, 1952.
———, *Zur Phänomenologie des inneren Zeitbewußtseins (1893–1917)*, Husserliana X, Hague: Martinus Nijhoff, 1966.
Kriegel, U., "Consciousness as Intransitive Self-Consciousness: Two Views and an Argument," *Canadian Journal of Philosophy* 33, no. 1 (2003): 103–32.
Lyyra, P., "Two Senses for 'Givenness of Consciousness,'" *Phenomenology and the Cognitive Sciences* 8, no. 1 (2009): 67–87.
McDowell, J., *Mind, Value, Reality*, Cambridge, MA: Harvard University Press, 1998.
———, *Mind and World*, Cambridge, MA: Harvard University Press, 1996.
———, "Reply to Commentators," *Philosophy and Phenomenological Research* 58, no. 2(1998): 403–31.
———, "Response to Dreyfus," *Inquiry* 50, no. 4 (2007): 366–70.
———, "What Myth?," *Inquiry* 50, no. 4 (2007): 338–51.

Merleau-Ponty, M., *Phenomenology of Perception*, London: Routledge & Kegan Paul, 1962.
Moore, G. E., "The Refutation of Idealism," *Mind* 12 (1903): 433–53.
Natorp, P., *Allgemeine Psychologie*, Tübingen: J. C. B. Mohr, 1991.
Okrent, M., "The 'I think' and the for-the-Sake-of-Which," in S. Crowell and J. Malpas (eds), *Transcendental Heidegger*, Stanford, CA: Stanford University Press, 2007, pp. 151–68.
Poellner, P., "Nonconceptual Content, Experience and the Self," *Journal of Consciousness Studies* 10, no. 2 (2003): 32–57.
Prinz, W., "Emerging Selves: Representational Foundations of Subjectivity," *Consciousness and Cognition* 12, no. 4 (2003): 515–28.
Prætorius, N., "The Phenomenological Underpinning of the Notion of a Minimal Core Self: A Psychological Perspective," *Consciousness and Cognition* 18, no. 1 (2009): 325–38.
Sartre, J.-P., *Being and Nothingness*, London: Routledge, 2003.
Schear, J., "Experience and Self-Consciousness," *Philosophical Studies* 114, no. 1 (2009): 95–105.
Thomas, A., "Kant, McDowell and the Theory of Consciousness," *European Journal of Philosophy* 5, no. 3 (1997): 283–305.
Thompson, E., *Mind in Life: Biology, Phenomenology, and the Sciences of the Mind*, Cambridge, MA: Harvard University Press, 2007.
Tomasello, M., *The Cultural Origins of Human Cognition*, Cambridge, MA: Harvard University Press, 1999.
Tye, M., *Ten Problems of Consciousness*, Cambridge, MA: MIT Press, 1995.
Zahavi, D., "Back to Brentano?," *Journal of Consciousness Studies* 11, nos 10–11 (2004): 66–87.
——, "Inner Time-Consciousness and Pre-reflective Self-Awareness," in D. Welton (ed.), *The New Husserl: A Critical Reader*, Bloomington: Indiana University Press, 2003, pp.157–80.
——, "The Fracture in Self-Awareness," in D. Zahavi (ed.), *Self-Awareness, Temporality and Alterity*, Dordrecht: Kluwer Academic Publishers, 1998, pp.21–40.
——, "How to Investigate Subjectivity: Natorp and Heidegger on Reflection," *Continental Philosophy Review* 36, no. 2 (2003): 155–76.
——, "Husserl's Noema and the Internalism–Externalism Debate," *Inquiry* 47 no. 1 (2004): 42–66.
——, "Internalism, Externalism, and Transcendental Idealism," *Synthese* 160, no. 3 (2008): 355–74.
——, "Michel Henry and the Phenomenology of the Invisible," *Continental Philosophy Review* 32, no. 3 (1999b): 223–40.
——, "Phenomenology," in D. Moran (ed.), *Routledge Companion to Twentieth-Century Philosophy*, London: Routledge, 2008, pp. 661–92.
——, *Self-Awareness and Alterity: A Phenomenological Investigation*, Evanston, IL: Northwestern University Press, 1999.
——, *Subjectivity and Selfhood: Investigating the First-Person Perspective*, Cambridge, MA: MIT Press, 2005.
——, "Thinking about (Self-)Consciousness: Phenomenological Perspectives," in U. Kriegel and K. Williford (eds), *Consciousness and Self-Reference*, Cambridge, MA: MIT Press, 2006, pp. 273–95.

# INDEX

absorbed coping 18–23, 27–32, 53–56, 146, 182, 195–96, 290–24, 321, 326, 333
action: as a form of rational engagement with the world 22, 45, 93; as rule-governed 181; as self-knowledge 48, 105; in flow 35, 45, 54; intentional 50–52, 57, 182, 273, 285, 295; reasons for 34–36, 227; self-awareness, in 28–29, 55, 169, 204; virtuous 52–53, 105
actualization: of conceptual capacities 15, 41–44, 54, 98–104, 168, 230, 334
aesthetic experience 186–89
affordances 16–18, 22, 37–38, 92–95, 171, 182–85, 321
agency: disengaged 79; intentional 5, 53, 185, 321; rational 294–95; unreflective 45, 53, 170
Allison, H. 97, 116–17, 137, 140
analytic philosophy vs. post-Kantian continental philosophy 3, 6, 126
Anscombe, G. E. M., 4, 57
anxiety 146–47, 156, 192
appearances 65, 96, 185, 201–10
"appearing as … " 200–201; doxic 200; focal vs. non-focal appearance 204–9, 211, 222; practical 200
apperception 3, 93–97, 102–4 *see also* self-consciousness
as-structures 195, 199–201
Aristotle 2, 10, 69, 73, 93, 210; hylomorphism 102
artificial intelligence 2, 251
assertion 19–21, 43, 212, 231, 266
attitude ascriptions 237
Augustine 86

background 61, 74, 83–86, 139, 144, 182, 204, 286–89; familiarity 18; as holistic and non-propositional 20–21, 27; as normative and social 19, 24–26
Balanchine, G. 304, 315, 316
ballet 9, 303–6, 313–16
Barrie, J. 308–9, 315
Beilock, S. L. 318
being-with 25 *see also* social norms
being-in-the-world 3, 5, 22, 25, 31–32, 144, 289 *see also* Heidegger
Bennett, J. 264, 269
Benveniste, É. 76
Berkeley, G. 115
Berkeley, California 301, 303
Bernard, H. 246
*Bildung* 23–24, 133, 325
blindsight 201
bodily skills 54, 170, 263, 272, 276–78, 283
Bourdieu, P. 24–25, 166, 172
Boyle, M. 106, 300
Brandom, R. 257–62, 299–300
breakdown 31, 38, 145–47, 154
Brentano, F. 330–31
Brewer, B. 233
Burge, T. 107, 222, 327, 334
Byrne, A. 234

capacities: conceptual 15, 24, 33–36, 41–44, 50–54, 96, 102–4, 197–205, 230, 282, 323; discursive 262; inherently general 291; rational 28, 45, 56, 194, 272–78, 289, 336
Campbell, J. 7, 183–86

# INDEX

Carnap, R. 153
Carruthers, P. 238, 340
Cartesian dualism 62, 64, 70
categorical properties of objects 183; vs. dispositional properties of objects 185
certainty 64–66, 74, 108
Chalmers, D. 236, 242, 245
chess: blitz 35, 252–56; grandmaster 36, 95–96, 144, 251–56; lightning 45–49
circumspection 18, 32
cognitive psychology 183
cognitivism 101, 110, 148, 182
Conant, J. 2, 56, 103
conceptual capacities *see* capacities
conceptual readiness 203
conceptual understanding 198, 250–57, 287, 324; descriptive account vs. normative account of 250
contact theories 62,72
content 29, 42, 92, 106, 238, 273, 336; as conceptual 21, 29, 43, 111, 118, 272, 323; as intentional 28; as mental 28, 65, 110, 126; as motivational 92; as motor intentional 32, 131; as nonconceptual 92, 102, 106, 11, 135, 167; as phenomenological 239; as propositional 230, 235; of an experience 43, 55, 91–93, 102, 188, 232; of an intuition 230–31
content pluralism 238
Copernicus 79
coping *see* absorbed coping
Crane, T. 229
criticism 27, 35, 186–91; self-criticism 299
culture 19, 24–27, 61, 146, 167

Darwin, C. 79
Davidson, D. 257–59, 264, 295
Dennett, D. 129, 258, 322, 334
Descartes, R. 61, 154, 250, 298, 323
detached: observer 34; self 41–42; mindedness 323; reason 145, 152; style of being in the world 296; understanding 180 *see also* distance
detectivism 326
determinate identities 294–97
Dewey, J. 182
discursive: activity 42–44, 55, 96, 231; practice 260–67
distance: critical 17, 21–23, 32, 44–50, 53, 295–96; mind/world 17, 21

distance standing 24–27, 31, 38, 51, 55, 173
Dretske, F. 258, 340
Dreyfus, H. 15
dualism of reason vs. nature 167, 289

effort 303–5; effortless 175, 182, 305–8
ego 28–31, 152, 169, 195, 214, 321, 328–31
empirical psychology 111
empiricism 83, 126, 131, 179–80; antiempiricism 180
epistemology 63–65, 69, 74, 78–79, 118, 229; as encompassing a "metaphysics of cognition" 118; as juridical 118, 127–28, 137
equipment 18, 23, 125, 130, 147–48, 266
ethical character 24
Evans, G. 8, 193, 278, 287
expertise 26, 92, 110, 148, 251, 312; "ten year rule" 305

Feigl, H. 69
Fichte, J. G. 113–31, 169
Finkelstein, D. 327, 330
first-person authority 320, 326
first-personal givenness 330
first-personal mode of presentation 324
flow *see* action
Fodor, J. 250, 259
for-itself (*pour-soi*) 328 *see also* Sartre
for-the-sake-of-which *see* Heidegger
foundationalism 64, 78, 83
Freeman, W. 110
Frege, G. 153, 235, 239, 243
Freud, S. 79
fundamental ontology *see* Heidegger

Gadamer, H. G. 93
Galilean science 167
Galileo 67
Gibson, J. 37, 92, 171, 182–86 *see also* affordances
"the Given": as a purely sensory item 67; transcendental theories of 112 *see also* Myth of the Given
God 66, 153
gods 151
Gould, S. 307
Gray, J. 311
Gray, R. 309
Guyer, P. 117

345

# INDEX

Harrison, B. 261
Haugeland, J. 1–2, 8, 38, 72, 252–60, 294
Hegel, G. W. F. 6, 80–83, 105, 120–31, 263, 294–96; "mediated immediacy" 105
Heidegger, M. 15, 19–21, 80, 167; anxiety 192; as a Kantian 85–86, 111, 125, 153; *Dasein* 18, 124–25, 331; "for-the-sake-of-which" 266, 339; formal indication 128; fundamental ontology 124; "mineness" 30–32, 38, 328, 339; on the distinctively human 26, 95, 157, 264, 29; thinking 145–50
Henry, M. 328
heterophenomenology 322, 334
Hornsby, J. 88, 129
Hume, D. 64, 67, 82–84, 94, 113, 119, 300
Husserl, E. 25, 126, 165, 215, 234, 322; "real content" 240, 243

imagination 66, 100, 104, 130, 243
immersion theories 74
intellect 24, 73, 178; spontaneity of 172 *see also* Myth of the Disembodied Intellect
intellectualism 3, 94, 101, 126, 163, 194; about perceptual experience 98; and reflection 166–67; anti-intellectualism 171
intelligibility 3, 92, 117, 124, 156, 320; conditions of 84–86; kinds of 172
intentional content *see* content
intentionalism 234, 238–41, 329
intentionality 84, 130, 203–8, 234–35, 253–56, 329; intellectual vs. sensory 211–12; motor 3, 139–40, 175, 322; subject-object 32
introspection 62, 189, 312, 316, 330
intuition: empirical 15, 63, 96–100; expert 307; finitude of 295; Kant's concept of 122, 153, 230–34; non-discursive (Fichte) 120
image 62, 73, 239, 243
irrationality 285

Jablonka, E. 265
Jackson, F. 258, 264
Jacobi, F. H. 114, 121, 125
James, W. 307
judgment 15–19, 42, 65, 255, 286–88, 295, 307; as deliberative 180, 187; faculty of 91; perceptual 208; propositional content of 232, 241; spontaneity of 91; theories of 268
justification 22, 48, 74–76, 91–92, 111, 117, 121, 153, 187; of beliefs 229; of perceptual judgments 208, 232

kaizen 303
Kant, I. 45–46, 59, 63, 186–88, 295; categorical unity 91, 208, 231; idealism 115, 128; "Kantian" 15, 29, 45, 93, 120, 145; synthesis 113–21, 131; to Merleau-Ponty 112; transcendental deduction 83–84, 112–13, 119–20, 128, 136; transcendental turn 128 *see also* apperception
Kelly, S. 95, 106–7, 149, 175, 181, 190, 322
kindness *see* virtue
Knoblauch, C. 53, 57, 252, 307–9
Kriegel, U. 327
Kukla, R. 261, 266

Lance, M. 261, 266
language 111, 171, 180–81, 255, 260–66, 323, 326: "bits of" 21, 152; Heidegger on 149; private 86; second 87, 256, 262; theory of 86
Leibniz, G. W. 82, 119–20, 130
Lewis, C. I. 8, 229
Lewis, D. 8, 235–38, 242
life 3, 16, 52, 131, 259–61; animal 55–56, 191; forms of 37; leading a 107; way of 30, 87, 107, 266
Locke, J. 67–68, 71, 78, 84, 86, 250
logic 19, 49–50, 152–53, 159, 188, 245, 262; disposition to think logically (Athenian) 26; generic logical powers 100

Maimon, S. 119–20, 133, 137
Martin, W. 2, 225, 254–55, 268, 301
"maxim of cognitive interference" 208
Merleau-Ponty, M. 4, 15, 52, 73, 94, 143, 194; absorption 17, 22; anonymity/impersonality 195, 216–20; anti-intellectualism 171–72, 320; as Kantian 111–12, 213, 218, 251, 258; Dreyfus's 126–31; on oration 28; on perception 166, 196, 258; optimal grip 173, 259; soccer

# INDEX

player passage 17, 27, 37, 45, 296
*see also* motor intentionality
meaning 4, 20, 50, 70, 172, 179–80; of being 124–25; social 25; space of 24–27, 167
mediational theories 77
mental content *see* content
mentalism 64
mental states 233, 250, 259, 272–76, 322, 327–30
"merging": with our bodies 107, 215–19; of absorbed coping 285, 290, 293–98
Millikan, R. 259
mind-body problem 69
mindedness 32, 41, 44–45, 56, 143–46, 320; as enemy of expert coping 144, 307, 321; conceptual 93, 96, 104–5, 323; determinate forms of 92, 95; rational 41, 53–56
mindless coping *see* absorbed coping
mind-world distance *see* distance
"mineness" *see* Heidegger
Minksy, M. 71, 110
Montaigne, M. 64
Moore, A.W. 248
Moore, G. E. 193, 233, 246, 248, 329, 340
Mulhall, Stephen 301
Müller-Lyer illusion 189
"myth of the disembodied intellect" 194, 213, 323
"myth of the given" 17, 25, 42–43, 81, 91, 113, 124, 212, 229, 320, 324
"myth of the mental" 15–16, 91, 181, 195, 320
"myth of the mind as detached" 41–58
"myth of the pervasiveness of the mental" 15–40
"myth of the spectatorial subject" 332

Natorp. P. 332
naturalism 57, 88, 112, 129, 133
Nietzsche, F. 150, 158
nonconceptual content *see* content
normative forces 22–23, 26, 33
normativity 31, 93, 134, 170, 324; biological 259; conceptual 252–54, 265–67
norms 213, 220; conceptual 251–57; culturally instituted 51, 170; rational 167, 170, 196, 250; social 23

object: as "autonomous, authoritative, accessible" (Haugeland) 294
Okrent, M. 223–26, 264, 266, 269, 339
ontic vs. ontological, 27, 125, 149
over-intellectualizing 98, 100, 178–93

Peacocke, C. 245
phenomenological conception of content *see* content
phenomenology: "ain't in the head" 329; as difficult 165; as explanatory 126; as post-Kantian 111, 134; of conceptual understanding 253; of embodiment 16, 289; of mastery 35; of "merging" 297–98; of subject-object presence 294; nature of 189
Plato 69, 70, 72, 77, 144, 158, 188; Platonism 133, 136, 140
pre-objectivity 126, 131
principle of automaticity 304–16
propositions 18, 22, 153, 234–35, 243; Fregean view 235–36, 239; Lewis-Stalnaker view 237; Russellian view 235
Putman, H. 185
psychologism 181, 245

Qualia 69, 233, 239, 329
Quine, W. 62, 64, 264

rationality: additive theories of 106, 300; and second nature 51, 167; as distinguishing humans from other animals 54, 285–86; as pervasive 47–48, 54, 93, 140, 176, 196, 290–92; capacity vs. property 285; cultivated 5, 47, 52; of the *phronimos* 93, 101, 105; practical 49–52, 93, 196; self-critical 26, 194, 210–20, 290–92, 337; self-monitoring 101, 190, 321
rational subject 41–44, 55–56, 152, 168, 296
reasons 22, 33–35, 46–51, 93, 181, 197, 218, 286, 294; space of 24–26, 35, 42, 49, 56–57, 67, 111, 131–35, 167–68, 170, 172, 229
reflection 38, 79, 152, 255; analytical 131; as enemy of engaged expertise 3, 27, 166, 175, 292, 306; as rationalizing 166; critical 26,

347

33, 46, 293–97, 324–25; no need for 46–47; power of 332; self-conscious 22
Reinhold, K. L. 118–24, 127–28, 137–38
representation: vehicle vs. content of 242
representationalism: Dreyfus's critique of 94, 129, 182
Rorty, R. 1, 66, 88, 140
rule-following 92–94, 150, 210
Russell, B. 8, 235–36, 246

Sacks, M. 114–15, 136–40
Sartre, J. P. 28, 33–35, 46, 127, 144, 151, 165–76, 190, 195, 322, 328–31
Schear, J. K. 285, 302, 340, 343
Schlick, M. 233
scholastic fallacy 165–66
Schulze, G. E. 114, 120, 138
Searle, J. 25, 139, 156, 170, 176, 259
self-consciousness 251, 321; intellectual 194, 213; loss of 22; Merleau-Ponty on 213–19; pervasiveness of 195, 210, 213, pre-reflective 336; rational-pragmatic 199, 203; transitive vs. intransitive 327–31
self-awareness 169–70, 195, 328; in action 28, 45; marginal 30
Sellars, W. 23–26, 42, 51, 56, 98–107, 132, 229, 256, 262
sensation 66–70, 84, 99, 102, 114, 165, 185, 188, 203, 210, 237, 324
sensibility 16, 91, 96, 100–111, 119–20, 168, 231–32, 286–89, 341
sentience 94, 325
Sherrington, C. 308
Siegel, S. 233–34, 238, 243, 280
skepticism 64, 81, 113, 118–20, 149
skills *see* bodily skills
socialization 25
solicitations 18, 30–31, 37–38, 144, 150, 298; to act 22, 52; to respond 152, 182, 196, 209–10, 251–52

spontaneity 33–35, 50, 81–82, 91, 100, 167–68, 172, 219, 288, 323–24 *see also* apperception
Stalnaker, R. 235–38, 247
Strawson, P. F. 104, 112–13, 117–18, 128, 334
Stroud, B. 302, 304
subject-object presence 294–97

Taylor, C. 61, 288
teleology 68, 73, 217, 259, 266
theory of mind 340
Thomas, A. 324
Todes, S. 88, 106, 111, 257, 258–59, 268–69
transcendentalism 110–42
Travis, C. 230–33
Turing, A. 71
Tye, M. 234–38, 329

virtue, 4, 10, 55, 151; McDowell's writings on 52; of kindness 34, 46, 291–92
visual illusion 201
visual imagination 243
*Vorstellung*: in Kant's system 63; in Rheinhold's system 119–28

Watt, H. J. 333
Weber, M. 69
withdrawing (of affordances) 18–19, 31–32, 92, 144–48
Wittgenstein, L. 61, 72, 80, 104, 132, 143, 148, 260; as a Kantian 85, 187–88; *Philosophical Investigations* 86, 149, 180, 261; *On Certainty* 74; on linguistic breakdown 154; on understanding as akin to an ability 180–82
world: openness to 15, 22, 52; disclosure 93, 118, 197, 203, 208
Wulf, G. 309

Zhuangzi 308
zombies 322

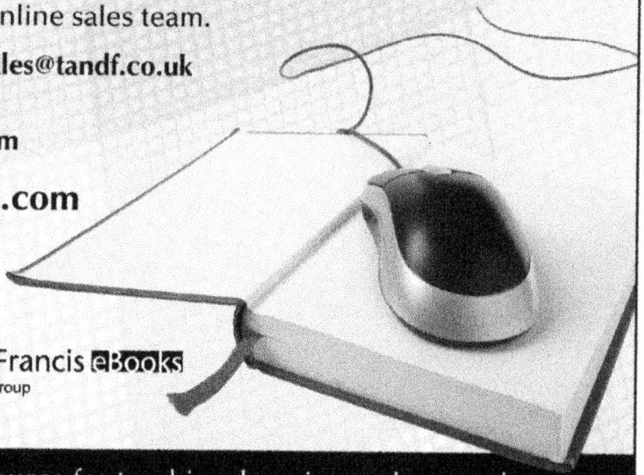

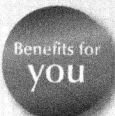

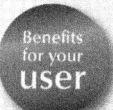

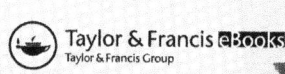

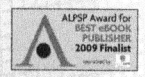

Lightning Source UK Ltd.
Milton Keynes UK

9 780415 485876